KALAMAZOO
The Place Behind the Products

To the inventors, entrepreneurs, and especially to the working people who made Kalamazoo what it is today.

Kalamazoo Paper Mill, Kalamazoo, Mich.

The Kalamazoo Paper Company mills were located east of the city on the Kalamazoo River, circa 1910. Courtesy, Western Michigan University Archives

KALAMAZOO
The Place Behind the Products

An Illustrated History by
Larry B. Massie and Peter J. Schmitt

The Verdon Cigar Company on
Willard Street manufactured La
Verdo cigars. This cigar box top
dates from about 1905. From the
author's collection.

SPONSORED BY THE KALAMAZOO COUNTY CHAMBER OF COMMERCE

Barefoot papermakers pause from
their work at the Kalamazoo
Paper Company circa 1910 to be
photographed. For almost 30
years the Kalamazoo Paper
Company was the major paper
producer in the Kalamazoo
Valley. Courtesy, Western
Michigan University Archives.

Library of Congress Cataloging in Publication Data

Massie, Larry B., 1947-
    Kalamazoo, the place behind the products.

    Bibliography: p. 296
    Includes index.
    1. Kalamazoo (Mich.) — History.   2. Kalamazoo
(Mich.) — Description. I. Schmitt, Peter J.
II. Title.
F574.K1M37   977.4'1804   81-52750
ISBN 0-89781-037-6   AACR2

The authors gratefully acknowledge permission to quote from
the following:
    "The Sins of Kalamazoo" by Carl Sandburg. From *Smoke and
Steel* by Carl Sandburg. Copyright 1920. Reprinted by permission
of Harcourt Brace Jovanovich, Inc.

TABLE OF CONTENTS

Kalamazoo's Globe Pattern
Works fitted out an automobile
for the Fourth of July Parade
circa 1912. From the author's
collection.

FOREWORD

Kalamazoo and Kalamazoo County have provided a broad base for several regional histories, all successful because all filled an existing need: the desire to know about our past. The recording of Kalamazoo history is not a local manifestation; it reflects a statewide urge. Nearly a decade before Michigan was admitted to the Union in 1837, it already had a historical society—the Michigan Historical Society, established in 1828. A later group, the Michigan Pioneer Society, placed in print the recollections of the first settlers. The Society's publication, the "Collections," first appeared in 1877 and was replaced by *Michigan History Magazine* in 1917.

One early publication dealing with the settlement of Kalamazoo and Kalamazoo County by permanent farmers, merchants, and businessmen appeared in 1869. James M. Thomas's *Kalamazoo County Directory with a History of the County...*, though short, presents the names and brief biographies of many of the families who came to develop the area in the 1850s. It was the basis for the county history that followed.

By 1880 the time had arrived to record not only the names and biographical facts, but also the accomplishments, of the men and women who had subdued the forest and the prairies. They created peaceful and productive farms, bustling villages, hamlets, and even crossroads. The settlements were interconnected by roads that linked them to the world of the eastern seaboard. For a while Kalamazoo was also the staging area and gateway for those who continued in the surge to push civilization towards the setting sun. Everts and Abbott's *History of Kalamazoo County*, (Philadelphia, 1880), was a part of the larger national effort to capitalize on the need of the first settlers to see their lives and accomplishments in print. They were proud of their personal histories and anxious that their descendants and others know of their sacrifices and successes. The promoter's profits, if any, were dissipated a long time ago. The publication, however, remains as the invaluable source of details on the history of Kalamazoo and Kalamazoo County. Woodcuts of the people themselves and the views of their ever-so-tidy farms bring to the eye and mind a part of American history that has passed, never to return.

Publications on local historical events and personalities were published from time to time from 1880 to 1959. In the later years, Dr. Willis F. Dunbar authored the 20th century's last extensive city and county history. *Kalamazoo and How it Grew* was well received and extensively read because it brought local historical data up to date. The late Dr. Dunbar, as Professor of History at Western Michigan University, lecturer, and author of many books and articles, was eminently qualified to extend Kalamazoo's historical horizons.

Now, in 1981, we have the latest publication delineating the personalities and events that form the background of our historical heritage from the early 1830s to the present. The reader will discover that the approach to the subject is somewhat different from previous publications. The authors, Larry B. Massie and Peter J. Schmitt, are both on the staff of Western Michigan University. The two authors have extensive experience in lecturing, research, and writing relative to state and local history.

Dr. Peter J. Schmitt's impact upon Kalamazoo's recognition and appreciation of its architectural past is well known and appreciated. His more than successful book, *Kalamazoo: Nineteenth Century Homes in a Midwestern Village,* (Kalamazoo, 1976), is recognized as of state and national significance.

Larry B. Massie, archivist and historian, is well known statewide as a lecturer and author on historic subjects and the intricacies in the preservation of historical documents, photographs, maps, and related topics.

While Dr. Schmitt recounts Kalamazoo's early years, Larry B. Massie delves into forgotten, or almost forgotten, Kalamazoo industries and some of the personalities behind them. The reasons for Kalamazoo's success as a viable community are evident in the energy, imagination, and daring of the men and women behind the community's economic development.

Reading *Kalamazoo: The Place Behind the Products* is a rewarding, informative, and pleasant experience.

Alexis A. Praus
Kalamazoo, Michigan
1981

The Western State Normal School, which topped Prospect Hill, is pictured here about 1918. During a visit in the 1920s, Will Rogers reportedly called it the "Acropolis of Kalamazoo." Courtesy, Western Michigan University Archives.

INTRODUCTION

Kalamazoo, the place behind its products, has a story worth telling. As a brawling frontier town in the 1830s, it did the greatest land office business America had ever known. The next half-century saw increasing interest in "manufactures" as local businessmen capitalized on natural resources, skilled labor, and yankee ingenuity. After the Civil War, when "Industrialization" and "Urbanization" were dominant themes in American life, the "Age of Industry" found Kalamazoo proudly claiming to be the world's largest producer of vehicles, windmills, and spring-tooth harrows. In the early 20th century, 272 factories poured out an extraordinary range of products for the national market. If people could imagine a product, someone tried to market it, from mandolins, paper products, stoves, and sleds to photo shutters, pants, and peppermint. Some industries mushroomed overnight and faded as quickly. Others prospered for decades, only to fail when the need for their products disappeared. Still others, able to respond to changing times with innovation, are active today.

Trolley cars and telephones, electric lights, sewers, and sidewalks came in the 1880s, and more and more people crowded into Kalamazoo from surrounding farms as well as from abroad. Tall buildings rose at the turn of the century. Life seemed thoroughly urban and increasingly complex. People moved to the suburbs, bought land on the lake shores and generally responded to the same urban pressures generated in great metropolitan centers. In the 20th century, the great issues of American life—the "Progressive Era," the Roaring Twenties, the Depression, the World Wars, and the technological revolution—all were reflected locally.

Though deserving attention for many reasons, nothing brought as much fame to Kalamazoo as its products of industry. America once crunched celery grown almost exclusively in the "Celery City"—and enjoyed celery mustard, celery tonic, celery cereal, and drops of "celeryade." Men smoked millions of cigars labeled "Miss Kazoo" and "Lazoo" and "Little Beauty." They drove its cars—the Michigan, the Cannon Flyer, the Barley, and the Roamer. Women popped bread into ovens stamped "Kalamazoo" and shaped their figures with American Beauty, Puritan, or Madam Grace corsets. Children wore "Hip-Zip" knickers in summer and coasted on Kalamazoo sleds in winter. Sears catalogs offered Kazoo Suspenders to "Hold Up the Pants and the Stockings, Too"; and everyone played the card game Flinch, the rage of the 1920s.

Much of Kalamazoo's history is the story of talented inventors and businessmen who recognized a need, developed a solution, and marketed a product. Follow the fascinating adventures and little-known episodes in the lives of people like Jacob Kindleberger, paternalistic founder of Parchment, who was "stung" one day by Yellow Kid Weil. Frank Henderson made fraternal regalia and built a castle that still stands on West Main Hill. Fred Root's first product was a basket to catch pedestrians before the trolley ran them over. The Upjohn family developed "friable" pills in the 1880s and sent out salesmen to demonstrate by crushing them under a thumb while hammering competitor's products into pine boards like nails. Charles and Maurice Blood designed the revolutionary racer that Louis Chevrolet drove at Indianapolis in 1915. William Shakespeare's fishing tackle added new excitement to bait-casting, and Caroline Bartlett Crane swept the nation with her crusade for clean streets.

Immigrants toiling in the celery muck, women in the corset factories, and children in the cigar-factory stripping rooms have a story to tell as well. The changing world of work in the 19th and early 20th centuries altered their lives, working conditions, and rates of pay. This book explores their ways of doing things, even follows them home "after hours."

If the workplace was important to local residents, it was also part of a larger picture. "I hear America," Carl Sandburg wrote in his poem about Kalamazoo, and from pioneer settlement to "All-American City," Kalamazoo's history is the story of America itself. Urbanization was hardly confined to metropolitan centers any more than factories were found only in big cities. Kalamazoo, like the majority of American small towns, rejected the rural trading center image and tried mightily to bring manufacturing to Main Street. As Michigan's Commissioner of Labor wrote in 1902, "every city, village and hamlet has some industry giving employment to labor, the remuneration of which contributes to the growth and prosperity of the municipality."

A great city like Detroit might lead in every Michigan population census, but smaller towns were just as important to any understanding of American life. Twenty-three of the state's 27 cities claimed fewer than 5,000 residents in 1860. While the number of cities steadily increased through the next half-century, roughly half remained under 5,000 people. Only three of Michigan's 90 cities boasted more than 30,000 in 1904. Communities under 4,000 and rural districts supported nearly half of all manufacturing establishments then, and the Bureau of Labor reported that 55 smaller towns and villages averaged 30 factories each.

Detroit outdistanced the rest of the state in most manufacturing categories, but grew more slowly between 1900 and 1904, showing an increase of eight percent while Kalamazoo grew 21 percent, Jackson 26 percent, and Lansing 32 percent. Capital investment soared 35 percent in Detroit, but 72 percent and 191 percent in Kalamazoo and Lansing, where the work force doubled. Local wages leapt 79 percent, averaging $1.50 to $3 a day in 1904. No wonder one contemporary noted that Kalamazoo produced "almost everything from a pin to a piano." David Fisher, the local historian, wrote in 1906:

> Kalamazoo is now a progressive city of thousands of progressive people full of business and bustle and toiling tirelessly. Her citizens are pleased with her past, proud of her present and confident of her future. The fleeting years have made much of her and she stands today a queen amid queens and destined for great ends. Men come and go; clouds form and burst; stars rise and fade; but fair Kalamazoo came to stay. Her pulse beats with enduring vigor and the chill of decrepitude can never reach her heart.

Smaller communities such as Kalamazoo may also permit us to more readily gauge the impact of individuals. Small-town industry is far more complex than the old radio dramas about Ma Perkins's lumberyard or Lorenzo Jones's backyard inventions. Yet individual ingenuity or "mechanical genius" played a significant role again and again. Patent Office records suggest that "invention" remained a major part of the American dream, and the same records show what small-town inventors could produce. Such individuals might be lost in the laboratories of giant corporations. In their home towns they made visible and lasting changes. Melville Bissell put the broom on wheels to give Grand Rapids and America the "carpet sweeper" after the Civil War. Philo Beckwith patented the "Oak Stove" and brought 600 workers to Dowagiac by 1904. E.K. Warren of tiny Three Oaks saw turkey feathers as a substitute for whalebone corset stays in 1883, and his success drained the labor pool in Three Oaks and all surrounding towns. Kalamazoo's entrepreneurs showed similar ingenuity, whether Albert Todd, the "Peppermint King," S.J. Dunkley and the cherry pitter, or Jay Rhodes with his self-ventilating funnels.

We have been researching local industries since

1976, giving talks and workshops on forgotten ways of making a living. In a community the size of Kalamazoo we could see workers and managers as people and collect their experiences firsthand. We could ask questions about social needs in the factory—about wages and purchasing power, about working conditions and the roles of women and children—and find the answers in readily accessible records. We found ourselves reading old newspapers and government documents, such as census abstracts and patent records, to piece together the story of local manufacturing. The Michigan Bureau of Labor's annual "Factory Inspector's Reports" gave us information on hundreds of companies and their employees. Old photographs and business letterheads let us see the hopes people placed in one product after another, from the time when the town claimed Michigan's largest iron mine in the 1840s to the wide range of products made locally today.

We soon discovered that, for all the past attention to pioneer life and politics, earlier writers largely ignored the world of work. Historians began telling Kalamazoo's story in the 1850s and 1860s, when the village was scarcely a quarter-century old. The Centennial ignited new interest in the 1870s. Then the annual picnics of the county "Pioneer Societies" attracted thousands as aging orators retold the tales of early days. In 1880 Thomas Durant published the first formal "County history"—a fat volume that would be succeeded nearly every generation thereafter as later historians brought the narrative down to their own time and paid their respects to community leaders. Durant "searched *to the bottom* records, both public and private, and determined many matters about which the best citizens differed materially." He claimed to resolve "a thousand and one matters about which there has been much disagreement," but had he told the whole story? Hardly.

Early days and Indian tales fascinated Durant and other writers. Pioneer Society speakers preferred a pastoral age where simple entertainment sufficed and barter prevailed. Local historians following these first accounts stressed land-clearing, social institutions, politics, and military service. They remembered the first and most prominent residents. They chose to forget the hard work and ingenious accommodations to the real world that early settlers called "getting ahead." In every case, these historians gave only a few pages to their own times, trusting that their readers knew those times full well.

But pioneering meant more than breaking new trails, "making land," or running for office. Early settlers worked hard to make a living, as did every generation coming after. Many farmed, but others kept store, ran gristmills, or manufactured the variety of products their neighbors needed. To some, these tasks seemed so commonplace as to lack even local color. But anyone who has ever enjoyed a piece of hand-made furniture, an old tool, or an aging building can appreciate the significance of just such everyday activities.

Enthusiastic community support made the search for Kalamazoo's industrial heritage both pleasant and rewarding. When the Kalamazoo County Chamber of Commerce chose to sponsor a new history, we were pleased to have a chance to tell the story we had uncovered. The Chamber agreed that the community had already been well served by general accounts, such as Willis Dunbar's *Kalamazoo and How It Grew* in 1959, and the city-sponsored *Kalamazoo: Nineteenth-Century Homes in a Midwestern Village* in 1976. Now we hoped to add our new findings to the "Kalamazoo story."

We divided our presentation into three parts. I have tried to tell the adventures of pioneer mechanics and manufacturers in Part I, which covers the period from 1830 to 1890. Larry Massie has written Part II, chronicling events from 1890 to the present. Each of us researched our own part as thoroughly as possible, and each of us is responsible for any errors that remain. We have worked together in the Partners in Progress section to provide histories of individual businesses. The Chamber of Commerce selected the firms to be included in this section, and the firms provided us with information about their development. The resulting "business biographies" let us test the theories of commercial enterprise we explored in the basic narrative.

Peter Schmitt
Western Michigan University

KALAMAZOO

The Place Behind the Products

PART ONE

1830–1890
by

Peter J. Schmitt

Yes, Kalamazoo is a spot on the map
And the passenger trains stop there
And the factory smokestacks smoke. . . .
Listen with your ears on a Saturday night in Kalamazoo
And say to yourself: I hear America, I hear,
                    what do I hear?

from "Smoke and Steel"
Carl Sandburg (1920)

SIGNIFICANT DATES

1805 An acorn sprouts. Michigan Territory is established. Potawatomie Indians are in possession of the land.

1812–1815 Legend indicates that the British operated a forge in the vicinity of Kleinstuck Preserve to repair Indian weapons used against Americans during the war.

1823 Rix Robinson builds fur trading post near present-day Riverside Cemetery on the Kalamazoo.

1825 The Erie Canal opens, making travel to the West easier for emigrants from New York and New England.

1827 The Potawatomies deed the site of Kalamazoo to the United States. The township is surveyed by John Mullett.

1828 The Baltimore & Ohio Railroad, first passenger line in America, is begun on July 4. Bazel Harrison and his family become the first white settlers in the county, locating on the north side of "Prairie Ronde" near Schoolcraft on November 3.

1829 Titus Bronson camps near the future site of City Hall and resolves to live here. Ten counties of southwestern Michigan, including Kalamazoo, are formally organized October 29.

1831 Titus Bronson constructs a log cabin, buys 160 acres now comprising downtown Kalamazoo, and plats a town which he calls "Bronson." After a spirited contest with the village of Comstock, Bronson is named the county seat. Hosea Huston opens the first village store. Justus Burdick purchases a half-interest in Bronson's village for $800. Thirty-one voters qualify for first county election.

1832 The village is granted a post office with the town's first doctor, Jonathan Abbott, as Postmaster. Smith Wood, the first carpenter, arrives. The county militia departs to take part in the "Black Hawk War," but the conflict ends before they become involved.

1833 Town population reaches 100. The Michigan and Huron Institute (later Kalamazoo College) is granted a charter under the influence of the Reverend Thomas Merrill and Caleb Eldred. Miss Eliza Coleman teaches the first public school. "Judge" Bazel Harrison presides at the first county court session. First township elections are held. The Kalamazoo House, the town's first hotel, is opened by Justus and Cyren Burdick. Joseph Wood, at 72, is the

A pioneer artist who remembered Rix Robinson's American Fur Company post near the Gull Road bridge made this drawing many years later. Courtesy, Western Michigan University Archives.

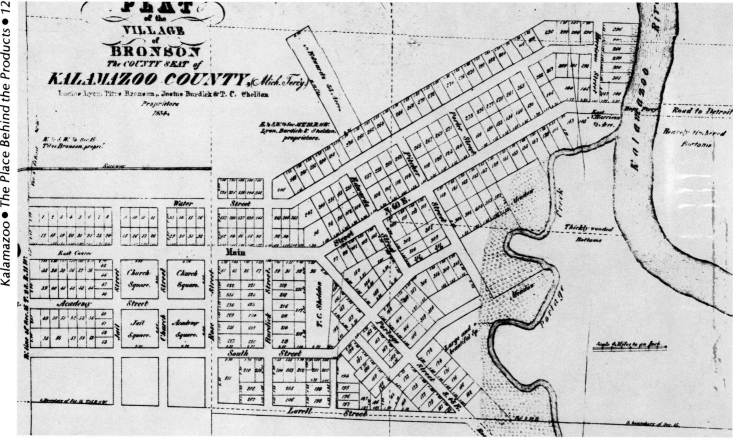

The second plat of "Bronson" was drawn up in 1834 when Titus Bronson was joined by Lucius Lyon, Justus Burdick, and T.C. Sheldon, who added the right-hand portion of the village. Note that settlers had only a rope ferry to help them across the river at this time. Courtesy, Western Michigan University Archives.

town's first death. Lucius Lyon is elected delegate to Congress from Michigan Territory.

1834 After the Federal Land Office is moved from White Pigeon, Bronson becomes a frontier boom town. Three thousand one hundred twenty-four people live in the county. Mary Heydenburk and Robert Burdick are the first white children born in the village. Robert Knight, from Ireland, is first to apply for citizenship.

1835 Lucius Lyon and Hezekiah Wells are delegates to convention that draws up state constitution. A branch of the Bank of Michigan opens on March 2. Henry Gilbert moves his newspaper, the *Michigan Statesman,* to the village from White Pigeon. First established in 1833, this paper later

becomes the *Kalamazoo Gazette.* First bridge across the Kalamazoo River.

1836 The village of Bronson and Arcadia Township are renamed Kalamazoo and Kalamazoo County, respectively. Titus Bronson moves to Davenport, Iowa. Sales at the Land Office reach all-time high. Erie & Kalamazoo Railroad, the 11th railroad line constructed in the United States, is built from Toledo to Adrian, Michigan Territory. Independent Republic of Texas is established. Local enthusiasm is shown in naming of "Texas" and "Alamo" townships. President Andrew Jackson issues "Specie Circular," requiring gold or silver as payment for land, which contributes to a severe depression in the Western states.

1837 Michigan is admitted to the Union on January 26. Epaphroditus Ransom is the first Circuit Court Justice named under the state constitution. Lucius Lyon goes to Senate. *Gazette* estimates village population at 1,000 to 1,200. County has 6,377.

1838 Branch of the University of Michigan is established in a building located in Bronson Park. The state authorizes incorporation of Kalamazoo as a village but no local action is taken. First hardware store in western Michigan is opened by Milford Joy.

1840 Army troops transport Michigan Indians to reservations west of the Mississippi. Some return to form settlements nearby, particularly in Calhoun County. "Log Cabin and Hard Cider" campaign helps military hero William Henry Harrison of Ohio defeat Martin Van Buren for the Presidency.

1842 Board of County Commissioners is replaced by new Board of County Supervisors, which holds first meeting on July 4.

1843 Kalamazoo is officially incorporated as a village and Hosea Huston is elected first village president. Fire protection ordinance requires that all homes and businesses have two buckets and a ladder.

1844 *Kalamazoo Telegraph* newspaper is founded. Theodore P. Sheldon opens a private bank to replace the branch bank of Michigan which had closed. Population of village: 1,800.

1845 First agricultural society in Michigan is organized January 10 in Schoolcraft. Three hundred sixty-eight children in school.

1846 The Michigan Central Railroad connects Kalamazoo with Detroit and boom times return. Kalamazoo gets a volunteer fire company headed by Alex T. Sheldon. Population of the village reaches 2,000.

1847 Colonel Frederick Curtenius and other Kalamazoo County men leave for the Mexican War. Epaphroditus Ransom is elected governor of Michigan as a Democrat.

1848 Discovery of gold at Sutter's Mill in California. More than a hundred Kalamazoo men will leave for the gold fields over the next few years. Telegraph communication to Kalamazoo begins.

1849 Mountain Home Cemetery is established.

1850 Paulus den Bleyker arrives with party of immigrants from Holland. First Dutch Reformed Church organized. First serious fire strikes "Main Street," destroying five stores, three carpentry shops, and the *Telegraph* office. In August the first "Burdick Hotel" is built on the site. Town Marshal begins improving the "wasteland" that is now Bronson Park, laying out crossings and wooden sidewalks, planting trees, etc. "Quick to Rescue" fire company under Benjamin Orcutt is organized. First business building west of Burdick on land of Justus Burdick's home. (Burdick

The earliest drawing of a local scene in the *Kalamazoo Gazette* showed the newspaper office, built in the mid-1830s. It appeared in an advertisement in 1842. Courtesy, Kalamazoo Public Library.

This stylized drawing depicts the interior of Parsons Business College in the early 1880s. The students in the back of the room seem to be practicing their newly acquired banking skills. Courtesy, Western Michigan University Archives.

had died in 1849, and the administrators of his estate quickly sold such choice lots for business blocks.) Census shows 2,507 population, including 34 black people. Six hundred seventy-five children in school.

1851 Corporation limits are extended south of Lovell Street. First parochial school is begun in connection with Catholic Church. Woodbury and Potter's blast furnace burns.

1852 Ladies' Library Association is organized—the oldest women's club in Michigan and the third oldest in the United States. Michigan Central Railroad now extends west to Chicago.

1853 Fireman's Hall is built on South Burdick. The "Cataract," the first town fire engine, is placed in service. William DeYoe is named Postmaster.

1854 The village population reaches 5,000. Kalamazoo has 150 stores, shops, offices, and factories, as well as one plank road, one railroad, two banking houses, and two weekly newspapers. Nine hundred sixty-two children in school.

1856 Abraham Lincoln, a little-known Illinois lawyer, speaks at a Republican rally in Bronson Park.

1857 Kalamazoo Union School building is constructed. Dr. Edwin VanDeusen arrives to organize the Kalamazoo State Hospital. Illuminating gas plant begins operation.

1858 Public High School is established. National

Horse Association is organized to operate National Driving Park near Washington Square.

1859 Kalamazoo State Hospital opens as the Michigan Asylum for the Insane, the first such institution in Michigan. Flora Temple sets a world's record for harness horses at the Driving Park with a 2:19 three-quarter mile. Government land office closes. Kalamazoo Light Guard Company is organized as forerunner to Company C in the Michigan National Guard.

1861–1865 The Civil War. Three thousand two hundred twenty-one men serve from Kalamazoo County. The 6th, 13th, and 25th Michigan Infantry, the 11th Michigan Cavalry, and the 14th Battery of the 1st Michigan Light Artillery are organized locally. The First National Bank in the state of Michigan opens here in 1863.

1866 The YMCA opens local branch. Grand Army Post is organized with 10 members. Kalamazoo Paper Company is organized.

1868 The Kalamazoo, Allegan & Grand Rapids Railroad opens from Kalamazoo to Allegan. County Medical Association is formed.

1869 Engineer William Coats crusades for pure drinking water and Kalamazoo is one of the first Michigan communities to have a municipal well and waterworks. William Parsons's Business College opens. Grand Trunk Railroad crosses the southern part of the county. Last stagecoach to Grand Rap-

	ids leaves on October 22. Population is 9,607.
1870	Grand Rapids & Indiana Railroad opens to Kalamazoo in September. Narrowgauge Kalamazoo & South Haven Railroad opens January 3.
1871	County Pioneer Society is formed to collect local history.
1872	Benjamin Lyon and Hale Page organize a paper mill at Plainwell. *Kalamazoo Gazette* becomes a daily on March 26.
1874	The "Kalamazoo School Case" establishes the right of a school board to levy taxes for support of a high school, setting a precedent for free high schools in Michigan and elsewhere. Population of the county is 32,284. Dr. Foster Pratt plays instrumental role in organizing Michigan's first state board of health.
1875	First Dutch Reform parochial school is organized on John Street.
1877	William Dewing organizes "Children's Home" on South Westnedge near Vine. Frederick Curtenius is elected village president. First paid fire department of six men is formed under Captain Byron J. Healy.
1878	First telephone line in Kalamazoo between Merrill and McCourtie mill and downtown offices begins March 1. Bronson Park is given its name at the suggestion of Foster Pratt.
1879	Ladies' Library Building, the first structure in America specifically con-

	structed for a women's group, is completed. Population tops 12,000.
1881	First local telephone exchange opens. First sanitary sewers are begun. Four hundred homes are now served by village waterworks, but only six bathtubs reported.
1882	Police department is organized on April 10. City mail delivery begins October 10. Academy of Music Building opens May 8.
1884	The country's biggest village, with 16,500 people, adopts a City Charter. Allen Potter is elected first mayor. Streetcars pulled by horses go into operation. New brick courthouse replaces earlier building.
1886	Upjohn Pill and Granule Company is founded. First electric light and power plant opens February 11. Elks lodge is established September 17. St. Luke's Episcopal Church holds dedication ceremony January 10. Main Street is ordered paved from Portage to Rose.
1888	The Chicago, Kalamazoo & Saginaw Railroad, locally organized, begins operation. Former U.S. Senator, Charles Stuart, one of the town's earliest pioneers, dies here. The "Kalamazoo House," first local hotel, burns on March 27.
1889	Through the stimulus of Father Francis O'Brien, Borgess Hospital, the city's first, opens on Portage Street. Miss Caroline Bartlett accepts call as pastor of the "People's Church."

Pioneer merchant Allen Potter came to Kalamazoo in 1845. He was elected the city's first mayor in 1884. Courtesy, Western Michigan University Archives.

CHAPTER I
A SPOT ON THE MAP:
1830–1845

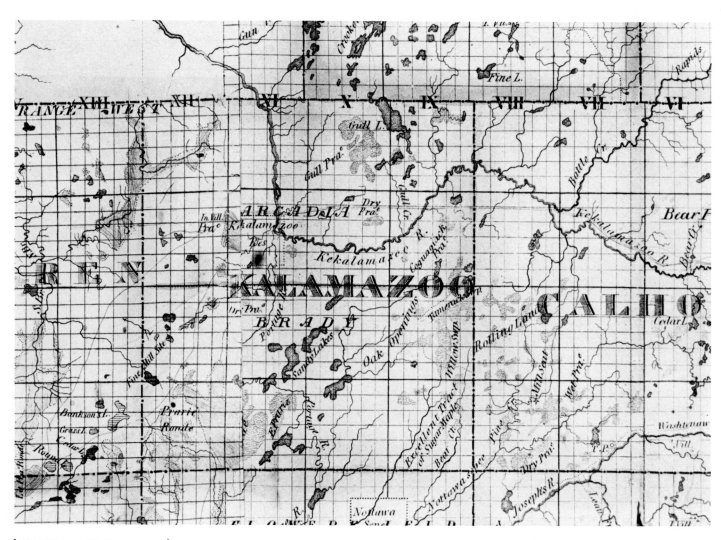

This 1831 map of Kalamazoo County showing prairies, timberland, mill sites, and settlements may have been used by a land-looker of the time. Courtesy, Western Michigan University Archives.

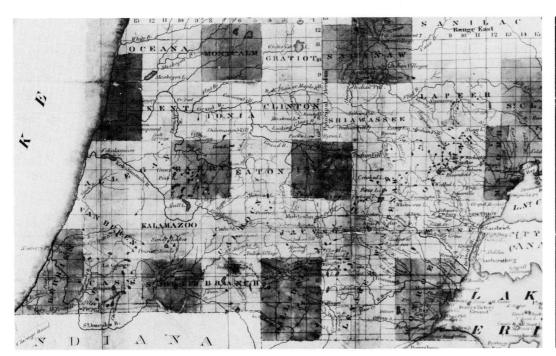

The records say the old man thanked God he was home again where people had known his family for six generations. He died the sixth of January, 1853, at the age of 64, on his brother's bed in Connecticut. They carved on his tombstone: "A Western Pioneer, Returned to Sleep With His Fathers"—a "pioneer" who paid a price for leading the way.

He had been an awkward young man, always seeming to miss the main chance, heading west in his middle thirties, wandering alone to western Ohio, then back briefly to marry Sarah Richardson. He moved among the first settlers wherever he went, planting potatoes and selling them to newcomers thankful for food that didn't have to be ground at distant mills. In each neighborhood he soon found people "too thick, too thick, too thick," and traveled on through Michigan, Illinois, and finally to Iowa. Trouble followed everywhere. One of his three children died; he was cheated out of his land in Davenport and lost his wife in 1842. Too poor to live alone, he stayed 10 years with his daughter's family in Illinois.

His name was Titus Bronson, and people in Michigan remembered him. Some called him a drunkard; others said he never drank. Some thought he was tall and others short. But however vague their recollection, most found Kalamazoo's first settler a comic figure. In the language of the time he "was slovenly in the general adjustment of his dress." He looked thin and nervous, walked "by fits and starts," talked entirely too rapidly, and repeated himself over and over. He argued every question and had no time for shrewd dealing. His face, said one pioneer, looked "like stubble land at harvest time" when he shaved. Another said that "he ran with his lame leg as no other man could run; he laughed as no other man could laugh; he te-heed, and showed his long teeth, stretching his mouth from ear to ear, as no other man could." The best that could be said with certainty about him was that he was eccentric, read a great deal, shared what he had with his neighbors, and hoped for better times.

For a while he lived in Ann Arbor, and on a spring day in 1829 he joined a surveying party heading west along the "Washtenaw Trail." Railroads preceded settlers on later frontiers, but Michigan's pioneers moved far beyond wilderness roadways. Bronson may have been the first to take a wagon over the Washtenaw Trail. He wound around marshes soggy with runoff from melting snow. He searched for shallows where streams were high, and several days passed before he reached the borders of Kalamazoo County. According to Cyrus Lovell, who came to Ann Arbor just after Titus Bronson left, the party crossed Toland's Prairie on the eastern edge of the county and pushed on to the trader's post at the great oxbow of the Kalamazoo River.

Potawatomies knew of the shallows at the oxbow long before Bronson. For years they had maintained a village on the flat land just west of the river and other encampments nearby. Potawatomie trails

Bazel Harrison (1771-1874), often credited as the first white settler in the county, arrived with his family on Prairie Ronde in 1828. He led a party of 21 people in five wagons with three cows and 50 sheep to Harrison's Lake on the north side of the prairie. Courtesy, Western Michigan University Archives.

branched in many directions from the only reasonable river crossing. During the War of 1812 the Indians rallied there to help the British at the battle of the River Raisin. Rix Robinson located his American Fur Company post at the ford in 1824. Eighteen-year-old Gurdon Hubbard served as resident trader in those first years. Later a Frenchman named Recollet, "Old Reckley," dispensed cloth, trinkets, and salt to Indians and pioneers alike. Though no records of the local post survive, Robinson described an elaborate picture language which his French-speaking agent used to keep accounts. In neighboring Kent County one trader went to court to recover damages for stolen pelts. His faded, handwritten "Bill of Particulars" suggests that the most common furs were muskrat and raccoon skins, along with deer hides. Steel traps were scarce in the 1820s and gunpowder expensive. Indian hunters probed muskrat houses with short spears, and set snares and deadfalls for raccoon and other small game. Few beaver, otter, mink, marten, or fisher ventured so far south, and the local post lasted only until 1837. Falsely accused of urging the Indians to harass squatters on unsurveyed land, Rix Robinson retired soon after, and the "trapper's frontier" moved on.

The Treaty of Chicago opened southwest Michigan to white settlement in 1821. Government surveyors dragged their chains almost 600 miles up and down the section lines of what would become Kalamazoo County, marking corner posts throughout the 16 townships. They noted the kind and size of their "bearing" trees, meandered lakes, marked Indian trails, and made occasional comments about the terrain in handwritten journals. Historians have used surviving surveyor's notes to reconstruct the appearance of the land before the first pioneers arrived. A broad plateau, dotted with "oak openings," covered most of the county. Larger prairies ran to several thousand acres, like "Gull Prairie" to the north and the 14,000-acre "Prairie Ronde" at the southern boundary. Later soil surveys labeled the fertile prairie land "Warsaw silt loam," but when Eastern visitor Charles Hoffman wrote his *Winter in the West* in 1833, one settler told him the land in the county was simply "so fat it would grease your fingers." "Grand Prairie," "Genesee Prairie," and "Dry Prairie" lay in the center of the county west of the river. "Dry Prairie" promised welcome relief from annoying wetlands where marsh hay grew along with scattered tamarack trees and poison sumac. Heavily timbered land, particularly in the rugged southeastern portion of the county, held mixed hardwoods—beech, maple, sycamore, basswood, and "tulip" trees or "whitewood," which could be worked into great wide boards at the early sawmills.

Early settlers liked to think they built Kalamazoo, like Rome, on "seven hills" because the river flat was surrounded by a number of steep and ragged bluffs. Several streams wound through the bluffs to join the river. They would provide water power for local mills, as would the slow-moving Kalamazoo itself. Eventually communities such as Comstock, Galesburg, and Augusta developed at these mill sites.

The surveyors simply numbered townships. Later settlers named them as current events or favorite people came to mind. "Texas" and "Alamo" townships recalled the excitement of Texan efforts at independence in 1836. Lucius Lyon named "Schoolcraft" after Indian Agent Henry Rowe Schoolcraft; and "Comstock" recognized the flamboyant but unsuccess-

ful town founder Horace Comstock, who married the celebrated novelist James Fenimore Cooper's niece. Other township names described local conditions or borrowed Indian words. Known as "Arcadia" until the mid-1830s, "Kalamazoo" derived from a Potawatomie expression applied to the rapids at the river crossing—"place where water boils in a pot."

In the months before Bronson's arrival, 50 or 60 families followed Bazel Harrison into the southern part of the county. They pushed up from neighboring St. Joseph County and laid claim to prairie lands wherever they could. Most sought prairie edges because they needed wood for shelter, fuel, and fencing. They built log cabins that seemed primitive and small to one witness. The first course of logs rested on the ground and often measured no more than 16 by 20 feet. Yet the first comers always managed to find room and food for weary travelers. Occasionally these early settlers might have a treasured rocking chair from the East, but generally they hewed their benches and tables from logs and squared off puncheons for their floors. Needless to say they looked forward to the first sawmills, and early cabinetmakers found a ready market for their products.

Many pioneer farmers used axes to open holes for planting their corn in the heavy prairie sod. They found underground root systems or "grubs" so extensive that they had to hire giant "breaking plows" pulled by long lines of oxen to turn over the virgin land. Sometimes they plowed extra strips of garden land in an effort to win the friendship of neighboring Indians. Corn and wheat grew well, but markets were far away. To have their wheat made into flour, settlers traveled as much as a week in 1830, perhaps as far as Tecumseh or Ann Arbor, to get to the nearest mill. Until John Vickers and Horace Comstock began milling the next year, some ground corn in coffee mills to make johnnycakes at the fireside.

The first settlers shot game or butchered hogs for meat, grew "garden truck" for vegetables, and planted slips of fruit trees they had brought from home. They generally helped their neighbors, came from miles around to barn raisings or husking bees, and insisted somewhat truculently that there were no social differences on the frontier. They heard the booming of prairie chickens and the howl of brush wolves. They told wonderful tales of prowling panthers and shot down the occasional wandering bear. In summer they built smudge fires in their homes to keep mosquitoes at bay. In winter they complained of the cold and wondered how the Indians managed. Hezekiah Wells once asked a Potawatomie friend how he stood the cold with so little clothing. His companion asked Wells whether his face felt cold without covering, and added, "Indian all face!" But however uncomfortable the weather, and however annoying the "Michigan Itch" and "fever 'n' ague," they somehow managed to "make land." Many years later they would tell each other at pioneer picnics of the pleasant times they remembered, looking back with pride and nostalgia on the early days. Henry Little put it this way—each year they cleared a little more land, fed

routes came together. He petitioned the commissioners named by Territorial Governor Lewis Cass to have his site declared the "County Seat." Bronson knew that professional men would settle near the courthouse and that bankers would follow to handle public funds. A newspaper would be certain of business publishing official notices. Storekeepers and tradesmen would cluster nearby.

But Bronson also needed industry to succeed. He chose the best power source the slow-moving Kalamazoo River could offer. In other parts of the county, men dug millraces for a mile or more to harness the river's current. George Gale of nearby Galesburg went bankrupt trying to provide his water power, but local entrepreneurs at Kalamazoo needed only to dig a ditch a few yards across the neck of the great ox-

Pioneer resident Anthony Cooley painted this somewhat glamorized picture of Bronson's first cabin. Courtesy, Western Michigan University Archives.

themselves, paid their taxes, and laid by a little extra for hospitality.

Yet they were hardly self-sufficient. They needed contact with the outside world as much as they needed each other. They needed capital for improvements and for taxes; they needed markets for their crops and sources for their supplies; they needed someone to make and repair the things they could not do for themselves. In short, they needed towns where they could transact business and gather for political and religious affairs. They needed men like Titus Bronson.

Bronson left Ann Arbor with a plan. He moved to territory so new that no local government had yet been organized. There he chose centrally located land at a transportation hub where land and water

bow bend to gain enough drop for one of the new-fangled "horizontal" water wheels that made the most of lazy midwestern currents. Over the years, more and more of the river was diverted across this neck until the city fathers closed off the oxbow in the 1880s. Today the Michigan Avenue Bridge crosses the river at the millrace and Red Arrow Golf Course stretches over the old bend. "Arcadia Creek" crossed Bronson's land from west to east and Portage Creek entered the Kalamazoo at almost the same point. Even as late as the 1870s, these streams provided power for half the local industry.

All of this lay in the future in the summer of 1829. Bronson had much to do to establish his claim to the new land. He cut tamarack poles from the marshy edges of the Arcadia and built an open-faced shanty which he roofed with grass. His structure was as much a symbol as a settler's home. He fenced in a portion of his claim with the low split-rail fence so popular in the days before barbed wire. When winter brought chilly mornings and shorter days, Bronson moved to Prairie Ronde to spend the season in the settlement Bazel Harrison had established a year earlier. Other land-lookers honored Bronson's claim. Cyrus Lovell remembered visiting the empty shanty in the spring of 1830. He turned south and spent the night with Bronson and his family on Prairie Ronde.

Bronson improved his land in 1830, but left again for Prairie Ronde in the fall. In the spring of 1831, he made his final move to a two-story log house on what is now Church Street. The commissioners had promised to locate the county seat on his claim, and he agreed to plat his village, offering free lots for a courthouse, school, and jail, as well as for the first four church organizations to inquire. Bronson named the village after himself and engaged one "Phinias Hunt, mathematician" to lay out the village lots. Hunt's problems as a surveyor can still be noted where Westnedge jogs at Lovell Street. There Hunt located the corner of the original plat several feet west of the proper section line. The boundaries of this original village were to be North Street, West Street, and South Street. The plat duly appeared on Liber A, page eight of the new county's land records. Bronson controlled one half of the village, and Stephen Richardson, his brother-in-law, the other half west of Rose Street. In 1833 Richardson would sign his interest over to Sally Bronson. At first the village existed chiefly on paper, but Bronson chose his site wisely, and he would soon attract the major elements that every town proprietor hoped for: capital, commerce, and manufacturing.

Bronson tried hard to interest other settlers; yet virtually all who came in 1830 and 1831 crossed the river and passed on to the west—to Grand Prairie, where Benjamin Drake settled, or to Genesee Prairie in Oshtemo Township. There they found Enoch Harris, the county's earliest black settler who had already plowed land and set out young fruit trees. With apples selling at a penny each, the man with a barrel of apples found many new friends. Bronson hoped to sell his lots to raise badly

This painting of Titus Bronson on his front porch was done by pioneer artist Benjamin Cooley in 1879. Note that Bronson is reading the *New York Herald.* Courtesy, Western Michigan University Archives.

Benjamin Drake and his wife settled on Grand Prairie west of Kalamazoo in 1830. They built this fine home before the Civil War. The avenue of trees and the remodeled house still stand on Drake Road. Courtesy, Western Michigan University Archives.

needed funds, but he found no buyers. Henry Little thought that anyone selling the land must feel it had no value. Even when Bronson offered him his pick of lots for free, he still preferred to go north to Gull Prairie. Horace Comstock and George Gale had capital, but both went bankrupt trying to finance improvements that would make their nearby villages attractive. Bronson, failing to find buyers, turned instead to partners. He was surprisingly successful.

Michigan's frontier caught the attention of Eastern speculators in the early 1830s, and it was clear that a land boom was beginning. Word of Bronson's county seat reached influential people in Detroit. Lucius Lyon, first U.S. Senator from

KALAMAZOO HOUSE

Michigan, had interests in both Schoolcraft and Grand Rapids. He urged a friend, "General" Justus Burdick, to tie his fortunes to Bronson and later joined him.

Kalamazoo's future looked promising on paper when Justus Burdick visited in the summer of 1831. The new county was two years old and growing. Bronson's site not only served local government, but also, for judicial purposes, Calhoun, Barry, and Eaton counties, as well as everything north. When Burdick arrived, however, he found only Bronson's home and three or four log cabins scattered outside the village. David Dillie, a cooper, had chosen land southwest of Bronson. Rodney Seymour was burning bricks west of present-day Douglas Avenue. Hosea Huston's unfinished store stood on the northeast corner of Rose and Michigan Avenue. It was the only frame building in town and bravely copied the "Greek Revival" style. Dr. Jonathan Abbott and his family hoped to live on the second floor above the store. Most of the streets existed only on Bronson's map, and few other improvements were under way. Still Burdick found reason to hope. He bought a half-interest in the village in October for $850. Then he sent his brother Cyren to manage his affairs and to begin work on the "Kalamazoo House" hotel that fall. Cyren engaged the only three carpenters in town for the 30'-by-40' two-story building, built partly of logs and partly of lumber hauled from the new mill at Comstock. Burdick opened the Kalamazoo House in September 1832. It served as a central gathering place for years under several owners.

Marcus Hounsom constructed a sawmill for Bronson on Portage Creek the same winter, but his machinery proved bulky and inefficient. Smith Wood brought carpenter's tools with him when he came in the spring of 1832. He redesigned the sawmill equipment and soon had it running, but Bronson lost interest and sold the mill to Cyren Burdick.

The government established a post office at Bronson in 1832, naming Dr. Abbott as Postmaster in July. Lucius Barnes of Gull Prairie took the contract to deliver the mail from Jackson once each week by covered wagon. Smith Wood put up the first frame house in 1832, and the log-cabin era came to an end. Nevertheless the town grew slowly, numbering only about 40 in 1834. That year the land office moved from White Pigeon to Bronson and Justus Burdick's administrative skills began to bring results. The *Michigan Statesman* followed the land office. Soon to be renamed the *Gazette,* the *Statesman* was a four-side weekly newspaper that published official notices, advertisements, and reports on national events (everyone knew what was happening close to home). The land officer, Thomas C. Sheldon, would join forces with Burdick, Lucius Lyon, and Bronson to draw up a new plat extending the village to the east and assuring the intersection of Portage and East Michigan at just the point where Sheldon now owned the Kalamazoo House. The territorial legislature then authorized a branch of the

State Bank of Michigan for Bronson, a fortunate decision that saved the community from the disastrous "wildcat bank" fever spreading in other parts of the country. Merchants, lawyers, and land speculators followed. Some prospered, others failed. Many moved on, but several remained for years. A few lived on the periphery of society, others at the center.

Epaphroditus Ransom came in 1834 to be the town's first distinguished citizen. He left Vermont in October on the month-long journey west. At Troy he put his family and goods on a canalboat for a 10-day trip to Buffalo. There he transferred everything to the lake steamer *Henry Clay*. Five days later he stood in Detroit—a frontier hamlet of less than 2,000. It took his party more than three days to cross the marshy land between Detroit and Ypsilanti. He followed the Territorial Road westward chiefly by tracing "H" blazes left on trees by previous travelers. Eleven days out of Detroit, Ransom reached the trader's post. The new bridge over the Kalamazoo was still unfinished, so Ransom hired Nathan Harrison to ferry his family across the river. They took lodgings first at the Kalamazoo House and surveyed their new home. The village showed prominent scars from a tornado that had swept along Arcadia Creek less than two weeks earlier. According to early historian

George Torrey, there was not much to be damaged. The town could boast no more than three frame houses and a dozen log cabins connected by footpaths that led through the brush from door to door. "The population," said Torrey, "were a motley crew of Yankees, Hoosiers, Canucks, speculators, dogs and Indians—the latter greatly predominating." Ransom came "full-handed," as the frontiersmen put it, and played the part of prominent citizen from the start. He stayed for a short time on Grand Prairie, then, when Titus and Sally Bronson moved to a new home on Water

Above
The first court session was a "County Court" held in Titus Bronson's home in 1833. Bazel Harrison is seated as acting judge. Titus Bronson (on the left) and Stephen Hoyt were associate judges. Stephen Vickery keeps the court record with a quill pen in this painting done by Anthony Cooley in 1879. The first case involved Robert Frackes and Isaac Brown. Courtesy, Western Michigan University Archives.

Left
One of the earliest houses in the county, Lucius Barnes' stagecoach stop, was located north of Richland. This 1880 drawing shows the house when it served as the residence of H.M. Peck. Courtesy, Western Michigan University Archives.

Epaphroditus Ransom was elected governor of Michigan in 1848. He had served previously as Michigan Circuit Court judge and both associate and chief justice of the State Supreme Court. Courtesy, Western Michigan University Archives.

Street, he headquartered in their two-story log cabin. The next year he bought most of the north side of Michigan Avenue between Rose and Burdick for $600 and built the most imposing home in western Michigan Territory. Ransom was 37 when he came. He had graduated from a Massachusetts law school with distinction 10 years earlier, returning to Vermont to practice law and serve several terms in the state legislature. Now he set up an office with another influential newcomer, Charles Stuart.

Ransom was the first circuit court judge appointed under the new constitution, even before Michigan was admitted to the Union on January 26, 1837. He served as associate justice of the State Supreme Court until 1843, when he was named chief justice. Ransom's district extended through the 10 new counties of southwestern Michigan, from Allegan and Kent to Branch County on the southeast. Twice each year he traveled the "circuit." Wherever he went, local communities held "court week" as litigants, witnesses, and observers flocked to the sessions.

Michigan's voters elected Ransom gov-

ernor in 1848. He returned after one term and settled down to farming on an estate that bounded the village south of Lovell Street. He sold his land to Paulus den Bleyker, who accompanied the first party of Dutch immigrants to Kalamazoo, in 1851 and retired from active life. Unfortunately his investments failed in the 1850s. He accepted President Buchanan's offer of a position as receiver for the Osage Land Office in Kansas and died there two years later.

Others coming in 1834 were less prominent, but they contributed to a growing number of services the little community could offer local settlers. The sawmill and brickyard provided materials for several carpenters and at least three masons. Andrew Gray served as village blacksmith. John Everard, harnessmaker, moved from Schoolcraft. Lot North opened a bakery, and two men kept shops as tailors. The next year Johnson Patrick built the second hotel. Local entrepreneurs opened at least two restaurants, a tannery, a grocery store, two new dry-goods establishments, and a wagon shop.

Early settlers brought little furniture and relied chiefly on their axes to furnish frontier cabins. When Epaphroditus Ransom came in 1834, the proprietor of the Kalamazoo House ushered him into a parlor lined only with homemade wooden benches. Cabinetmakers provided very necessary services and a touch of elegance to otherwise spartan surroundings. Three men offered their wares that year. All three put their roots deep into the community. Isaac Vickery advertised in the *Kalamazoo Gazette,* offering to trade furniture for cherry, walnut, or whitewood boards. Amariah Prouty moved from New England to Glen's Falls, New York, with his 20-year-old bride in 1826. He earned a considerable reputation as a furniture craftsman before coming on to Michigan. His family spent a week on the road from Detroit to Bronson, fording the river with considerable difficulty and spending the night with Sophia Prouty's brother, Epaphroditus Ransom. As it proved with so many of these early settlers, this would be the Prouty's last fling at pioneering. He and his family remained in Kalamazoo more than half a century. Prouty worked at cabinetmaking for many years, advertising in 1836 that he would build all kinds of furniture and offering "House Painting, Paper Hanging and Glazing Done on Short No-

tice." In 1852 Prouty and his large family moved to farm land on Elm Street, where he raised corn and apples and opened the town's first nursery. Still later, when a long court case ended in his favor, Prouty moved back to Park Street in comfortable circumstances. He died in 1887 at 85. Successful businessmen served the community in many ways. Prouty played an active role in Whig politics, held several local offices, took a prominent part in Congregational Church affairs, and found time to write on scientific agriculture.

More and more people poured into Bronson in 1835. Land-lookers pitched their tents on any available space and lined up at the land office, which sometimes fell weeks behind in processing applications for land patents. The rush peaked in 1836 when George Torrey found "one great mass convention of men almost raving with the land mania." Some came to settle, others to speculate. Some hunted everywhere for just the property they wanted, then rushed to the land office to claim it. Others chose their entry from the map and never bothered to visit it at all. Men stood in line for hours only to return the next day. Some spent days trying to reach the clerk's window to

submit their land descriptions. But many who came never intended to enter government land. They besieged luckier landholders with offers to buy at inflated prices. Some hoped for town sites, some for water power, others for paper wealth as everything changed hands. They crowded into both hotels and every home. Some land-lookers gave up getting shelter for themselves and begged for some place to store their moneybags instead. Food was at a premium as land-hunting pressure increased month by month. The land office did $281,437 worth of business in January and February of 1836. Receipts doubled that in May. George Torrey said "everybody was crazy for land, and felt rich, and wanted to be crazier and richer!"

Land bought from the government at $1.25 an acre doubled overnight. Town lots sold at incredible prices to men who would sell them again at a profit. Kalamazoo did the greatest "land office business" the country had ever known, receiving $2 million in 1836. Eventually the excitement had to end, and the end was triggered in the summer of 1836. Andrew Jackson insisted in his "Specie Circular" that the government would accept only silver and gold

An early drawing of the *Kalamazoo Gazette* office as it looked in 1835 captures the spirit of the bustling pioneer community. Courtesy, Western Michigan University Archives.

in payment for land. Speculators' notes and the shaky paper issued by unregulated or "wildcat" banks had supported much of the land fever. Now the time for taking stock arrived. Speculators turned homeward as did some early settlers unable to pay their taxes. Those land-lookers who remained swelled the Territory's population beyond the magical 60,000 required for statehood, and gave the country a significant population boost that would be reflected for years to come.

A split developed in 1836 between Titus Bronson and his partners. The newcomers charged that Bronson's eccentricities hurt the town's image, and they found him a difficult man to work with. They prevailed on the legislature to change the name of the town from "Bronson" to "Kalamazoo." Bronson resented the indignity and soon left for Illinois. He had chosen the site, gained the county seat, and done what he could to make his town a success. Now it was up to his partners to carry on. They took control at an awkward moment. Jackson's "Specie Circular" and the collapse of wildcat banks plunged the whole frontier into a depression that lasted for years. Cash flowed out of the region. Pioneer settlers carried on their business with "store tickets," promissory notes, and barter. A.D.P. Van Buren recalled that "everybody borrowed and everybody lent, and by it business was kept prosperous and

suffering often avoided." Labor became "capital" on the frontier. If a necessary item could not be borrowed or paid for in "dicker," then necessity proved a good teacher.

The *Gazette* editor complained that several of his subscribers were years behind. He offered to trade papers for firewood. Another storekeeper took "Live and Let Live" as his motto, urging his customers to pay anything at all on their accounts. Many of the merchants took wheat in trade, but wheat so far from markets fell to 37½ cents a bushel and scarcely repaid the planting. Still the local storekeepers did a surprising amount of business.

They offered an array of goods on their shelves. In January 1837, the *Gazette* carried advertisements for Snow & Fisk's bookstore, three cabinet shops, and no less than nine local stores carrying general goods. H.B. Huston offered "a 'bunkum' stock of GOODS, comprising a general assortment of all things in the line necessary to the comfort and convenience of the public generally," at prices "which will suit and do the people good." He called special attention to 20 barrels of pork, more than half a ton of butter, and 20 bushels of dried apples. He also offered 100 plows ready for spring delivery. He hoped for cash from his customers, but claimed to be happy with "Cattle, Pork, Furs and Skins, all kinds of Produce, Lumber, Pine Shingles, and Prompt Pay Prom-

This famous cartoon suggests the disruption of the national economy after Andrew Jackson issued his "Specie Circular" in 1836. Kalamazoo entered a period of depression that lasted several years. Courtesy, Western Michigan University Archives.

ises at three and six months."

Horace Comstock praised his "old friends and customers" for their abundant harvest and published a plea for payment on long-standing debts. He promised to accept anything, even going so far as to say that he would "when the quantity is large, pay one half CASH." Winslow & Brownson carried everything from "a bead needle to a CROW BAR (except ardent spirits)." They also reflected the hard times by calling attention to "a heavy amount of Notes, and accounts on hand which are due." Thomas Clark offered "CASH for grain" at his new distillery.

Several firms sought business from every quarter. The bookstore carried garden seeds, "a good cow," penknives, and a rifle. John Powers, an early black settler, offered "*Razor shaving*, clothes cleaning, hair dressing and boot blacking," and claimed that his styling "becomes both man and woman." He added an engaging plea to his customers: "Do not withdraw your heads and faces, / These hard times from Powers' graces." David Vosburgh's cabinet company promised to "furnish steamboats, vessels, public houses, etc., etc., in the most approved style," as well as furniture of all kinds. Most of those who advertised bought stock type describing their goods. Everyone claimed "New Goods," "Dry Goods," "Hardware," "Groceries," etc. None listed their prices. Three of the advertisements declared new management as merchants struggled in the hard times. Not all survived.

Storekeepers and their representatives traveled to Boston, Philadelphia, or New York for goods they hoped would sell. They arranged for transportation along the canal routes and through the lakes. Goods bound for Kent County could easily be sent up the Grand River; those destined for Kalamazoo had to be reloaded on keelboats for the slow trip upstream to forwarding warehouses at Three Rivers. Teamsters then hauled everything in great freight wagons through the woods and across the prairies. Prices for many items were understandably high. Local merchants generally paid for part of their purchases and gave a note for the remainder. They hoped to sell for cash to pay off their notes, and they offered strong inducements to their customers; but they often found themselves discounting bank notes or sight drafts on third parties to make a sale. On other occasions they would trade for almost anything. One pioneer

remembered that "he took leather of the shoemaker in exchange for potatoes; he paid the merchant in wheat, the blacksmith in marsh hay, the carpenter in beef, the tailor in wood, the parson with a pig, and split rails for the postmaster to pay the twenty-five cents for his letter." Bartered goods might be sold again locally, or sometimes used by the storekeeper. Otherwise they in turn had to be freighted out to market. Some pioneers with neither cash nor barter asked to be carried "on account" through the growing season in hopes of good harvests. Such merchants provided vital supplies and sometimes touching reminders of the fashionable "East."

We will probably never know exactly what Kalamazoo's pioneers saw on their storekeepers' shelves, but we can make some judgments from the experience of early settlers in Kent County. Judge Epaphroditus Ransom traveled north to the wilds of Kent County one July day in 1837. There in the hamlet of Grand Rapids he presided over 10 cases involving James Anderson, Alfred Williams, and their creditors. Anderson and Williams stocked their shelves with goods from a Boston company and two New York firms, including that of the famous Lewis Tappan. They failed to meet their promissory notes, and creditors presented detailed lists of goods purchased. Court-appointed appraisers inventoried hundreds of items on Anderson & Williams' shelves. These inventories suggest the wide range of Eastern goods available to frontier shoppers.

Men might choose from a supply of hoes and spades, hay and manure forks, scythes, axes, and two-man crosscut saws, as well as a generous selection of

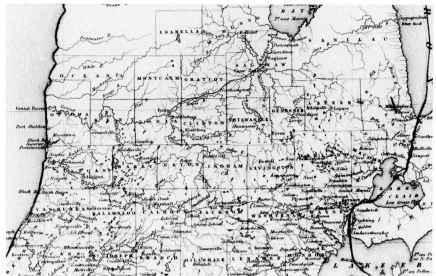

The spread of new settlements west and north of Kalamazoo can be seen in this 1838 map of Michigan. Courtesy, Western Michigan University Archives.

carpenter's tools. Contrary to legends which told of settlers burning cabins to save the nails, Anderson and Williams carried 31,000 cut brads and tacks, and 1,200 pounds of cut nails in various sizes. At $7.12 a hundred pounds, nails cost much less than a bushel of seed corn. The frontiersman shopping for clothing might choose one of 96 hats, including 15 made of palm leaves. He might have a silk vest if he chose to part with a day's pay. The store carried frock coats, monkey jackets, "P Coats," pantaloons, and "wading pants," as well as half a dozen money belts for those who had money.

Women on this particular frontier found a bewildering selection of goods of all kinds. They might examine 162 bolts of cloth totaling well over 5,000 yards and ranging from "mourning prints" to Irish linens. The average yard of cloth cost less than 50 cents, but still represented two or three hours' work for a laboring man. Anderson & Williams stocked pins, thread, buttons (including 2,562 suspender buttons), and 560 yards of ribbon. They also offered a choice of 144 steel and 48 silver thimbles, as well as 87 scissors and shears. Women with a flair for fashion might choose from 83 bonnets or 366 combs. The combs included ivory, horn, "wrought," and wood. They were classified as "pocket," "straight," "coarse," "curved," "side," and "round." In a village where stumps still stood in the middle of the main street, smart shoppers found parasols, silk and whalebone umbrellas, opera capes, and lace caps, as well as damask, crepe, cotton, and cashmere shawls at one to three dollars. For winter weather Anderson & Williams included four dozen fur robes and a dozen pair of "ladies' overshoes," as well as brass andirons, fire tongs, and bellows.

For household use the store carried everything from a dozen coffee mills to candlesticks and "polished snuffers," 98 reams of paper, and patent inkstands—even "2 cases, 4 dozen artificial flowers." Young buyers would find 74 pocketknives with one to four blades, and a dozen fearsome "dirks." They would choose from eight dozen fishlines and a thousand hooks. Davy Crockett carried his trusty flintlock when he went off to the Alamo in 1836, but Anderson & Williams stocked four of the new percussion rifles and 10,000 percussion caps.

In the general line the store included

13,000 cigars at a penny and a half apiece and more than 1,100 pounds of bulk tobacco. People on the edge of settlement could select from 903 gallons of wines and liquors. They would see casks and kegs and "pipes" of brandy, gin, whiskey, Jamaican and St. Croix rum, old port, Malaga, Lisbon, Muscat, and light and dark sherry. As so often was the case in the 19th century, the store carried four times as much tea as coffee, more than a quarter of a ton in several varieties at an average of a half-dollar a pound. Anderson & Williams carried no flour, but they did offer one box—278 pounds—of loaf sugar at 14 pennies and a half a pound. Chocolate sold for the same price, and the store stocked molasses, lemon syrup, nutmegs, ginger, allspice, pepper, cloves, and other spices—even 144 pounds of walnuts and a quarter of a ton of raisins.

Not all business stood still in the hard times. Many of the land-lookers had come to stay. They needed homes and services. Justus Burdick set builders to work on a courthouse in 1837. Then he began his own home across the street from Judge Ransom's. He chose the half-block between Rose and Burdick for his house lot and raised the largest house in all of southwestern Michigan—a great square Greek Revival mansion some said cost as much as $6,000 when carpenters worked for a dollar a day.

The *Gazette* reported, in 1838, that 40 carpenters and joiners kept busy meeting the settlers' need for housing. In five years' time the village grew from three or four log homes to 250 "neat and commodious" houses and a variety of businesses. The

Right
A variety of tools was available to early Michigan pioneers. This "tradesman's cut" appeared in an early newspaper advertisement. Courtesy, Western Michigan University Archives.

Facing page
Top
Hunting and fishing were as important as "sports" as they were as businesses on the Michigan frontier. Local gun shops catered to sportsmen as this "tradesman's cut" suggests. Courtesy, Western Michigan University Archives.

Bottom
Even on the edge of settlement, 19th-century pioneers relied on store-bought staples. Courtesy, Western Michigan University Archives.

912   $1.50

Mortised

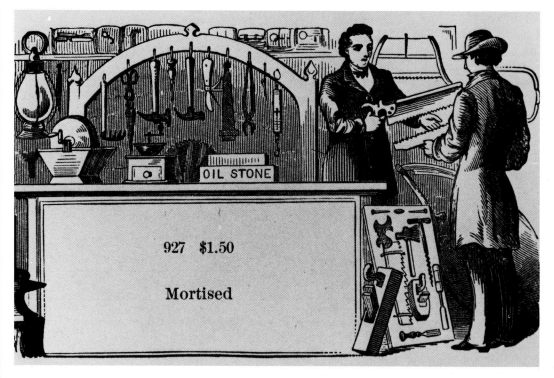

OIL STONE

927   $1.50

Mortised

Gazette found:

ten drygoods, three druggist, one book, one provision and two grocery stores. There are four blacksmiths, two carriage, one cooper, and two cabinet shops, and one chair factory; there are three tailor's, one jeweler's, two harness and saddler's shops, two shoe shops and stores, one tannery, three saw and two flouring mills; two yards for making brick, three taverns, two churches, a courthouse, one bank and a land office.

The *Gazette* editor clearly hoped other papers would reprint his glowing description. He spoke of two free schools and two literary academies, including the Kalamazoo Literary Institute (now Kalamazoo College), which was open to young men and women and "conducted on the manual labor system." The professions were thriving, and the town boasted six lawyers and six physicians, though the county seemed so healthy there was little for doctors to do. The *Gazette* proudly reported only two dozen graves in the new cemetery and discovered that "youthful bloom and manhood's vigor are every where seen." The editor furiously concluded: "Neither Andalusian plains, or enamelled islands in tropic seas would so gratify the scientific and curious visitor as the prospect of our wood-shaded and wood-begirt village."

One of those youthful faces belonged to Luke Whitcomb. He left Genesee County in western New York in the spring of 1838 bound for Kalamazoo with ro-

mantic hopes and a flair for description. He boarded his first steamboat in Buffalo for a 40-hour trip to Detroit. As he wrote at once to a friend back home:

nothing could be more smooth and beautiful than Lake Erie during the first part of our passage. Scarcely a ripple was seen for a moment upon any part of its surface, which, however, was undulating. We had a severe blow the night before we entered Detroit river which made us all sea sick for a short time.

He docked in Detroit with 70 other passengers, mostly emigrants from New York and New England. Not all were happy with the move. Whitcomb described one couple at length. The man was 50, "tall and gaunt, and bony, with a long neck, sharp visage, quick movements, long arms, and broad hands." His wife was "half his years" and shepherding three young children, who alternately clung to her skirts and raced around the open deck. Whitcomb went on to say:

... The *father* partook of the pleasures of these little ones, but the *mother* was pensive! I noticed that her eyes were often filled with tears; I did not see her smile once during the passage—but noticed that she often sighed. This never failed to affect her husband, who would sit by her and take her hand, and show more feeling and sympathy than his rough leather-stocking exterior authorised the belief that he possessed—but it was of no avail! The wife remained the same pensive, sorrowful sufferer. . . .

This family, too, was going to Michigan. Whitcomb kept his spirits up, however. He thought it "hardly possible for anything to excell in beauty the river Detroit and its shores and islands." Here was history, too. He saw a schooner "full of British Soldiers" at Malden and a sentry at Amherstburg. He noted that "the shores on the British side are bolder than those on the American, but look as they must have looked half a century ago." Detroit showed "a new face" on everything, stretching, he thought, for two miles at least, though buildings were interspersed with parcels of open land. Whitcomb said goodbye to his fellow travelers who were headed for Pontiac. Epaphroditus Ransom had struggled over difficult roadways west of Detroit, but Whitcomb could now "take the cars" as far as Ypsilanti. He filled up the last of his stationery, turned it sideways to add a few more lines, and promised, "I shall write again at Kalamazoo."

A full eight months went by before Whitcomb did find time to write. One Sunday in January 1838, he began with great apologies—blaming his delay on the press of business. He hurried his lines down the page, making errors without bothering to correct them, and complained that "ever since I commenced business in this place," he was "as unfit to write a letter of humour as to write a commentary on the Revelations of St. John the *Divine.*" Whitcomb, his brother, and two helpers were paying $20 a week for room and board while they set about "making pork." They were feeding hogs and had already packed 50 barrels of pork and cured "lots of bacon." Yet he complained that he could find "no one to cook a piece for me."

Whitcomb's enthusiasm had not been dampened entirely by his new job. "Imagine you see me," he wrote, "with a striped woolen frock on, with a swill pail in one hand, a large club in the other, and two hundred hungry hogs close to your heels. Such musick no one can describe." Perhaps his correspondent would be kind enough to tell him whether there were any "acquaintances" back home "that are now living, that are not *married* or engaged to be." If so, he must know at once "if there is any chance for me!"

The "Old Branch" of the University of Michigan once stood in Bronson Park. This drawing shows the building as it looked after 1838. Courtesy, Western Michigan University Archives.

However hard he worked at feeding hogs, Whitcomb found time for recreation. At one point he noted:

> I attended a party on the first day of this month in the evening four miles from this village, moved just to see how things were done in *Michigan,* and to show them how they could be done. There is a Dancing School, and a Cotillion party at our house every week. I have not as yet attended.

Perhaps the lessons were too expensive. Young men and ladies paid $4 a quarter for sessions on Wednesday and Saturday afternoons at Mrs. Clark's home on Water Street.

Young people and their elders found relief from work in many ways. Most village entertainment had to be organized by the residents themselves. The new bookstore took a full column in every issue of the *Gazette.* The weekly Lyceum meeting debated such topics as "Has dancing a tendency to corrupt morals" to a standstill and promised to discuss, "Should Capital Punishment be Abolished?" at the next gathering. Amariah Prouty and several other "leading citizens" boosted the local temperance society, but the *Gazette* gave most impressive coverage to the University of Michigan's local branch as the center of intellectual life. Opened on May 1, 1838, it attracted young people from most of the prominent families in the county. Pioneer settlers attached so much importance to education that they had already provided a building on Walnut Street in 1836 for the first college in Michigan. Caleb Eldred, Horace Comstock, Thomas Merrill, and others secured a charter from the legislature in 1833 for the "Michigan and Huron Institute," suggesting by that name that students from across the Territory from shore to shore would be welcome in Kalamazoo. Later the legislature changed the name to "Kalamazoo Literary Institute," and later still authorized it to absorb the "Old Branch."

The federal census taker made his rounds on the hot summer days in 1840. He counted 7,380 settlers in Kalamazoo County, almost half in Kalamazoo and neighboring Comstock townships. The new county gained a thousand people since the "statehood" census in 1837 and ranked ninth in Michigan, a position it would retain through several more censuses. Kalamazoo village had no corporate identity, but numbered a thousand people within its borders. That population swelled suddenly in September as Potawatomi families assembled on the open land at the corner of Burdick and Ransom—waiting. They waited only briefly. A local man, Colonel Thomas A.H. Edwards had the responsibility for assembling them. He soon satisfied himself that all who came willingly had arrived and others who had hidden in the forest and the swamps had been brought to the rendezvous. On October 10, 1840, the Potawatomie people began the trek west of the Mississippi that came to be called "the Indian Removal." An era was ending and townspeople watched with mixed emotions.

Early settlers had always been divided over the Potawatomies, who numbered perhaps 1,100 in southern Michigan. On the one hand, they held some romantic notions about "nature's noblemen." On the other, many remembered all their lives the stern face at the cabin window, and attitudes toward food and gifts so different from settlers' customs. Almost every family had its "Indian story," and most conveyed deep-seated uneasiness. Titus Bronson liked the Potawatomies, though he showed no concern in laying out his village on the best land in the "Matchebenashewish Indian Reserve." His wife remembered the day the Potawatomies rode away with their daughter, bringing her back at nightfall dressed in buckskin.

Pressure came from all sides to resolve "the Indian question." Governor Lewis Cass felt the Potawatomies were "sojourners" on the land who should not stand in the way of permanent settlers. He professed no animosity himself, but urged the government to consider "removal" as a military policy, since any concentration of former allies in Michigan might prove awkward if hostilities with the British should resume. Missionaries Isaac McCoy and Leonard Slater urged removal for other reasons. McCoy had established the Carey Mission at Niles in 1821, and Slater headed a similar effort at Grand Rapids. Sometimes called the "father" of the "Indian Territory" idea, McCoy made a dozen trips to Washington trying to protect the Potawatomies from white whiskey, disease, and greed. In 1830 he left for Missouri and Kansas to further his idea. The government recognized that settlers were "pre-empting" fertile Michigan lands in the 1830s and negotiated 17 treaties with various Potawatomie groups between

The Reverend Leonard Slater, an early Baptist missionary in the Grand Rapids area, urged the removal of the Potawatomies to protect them from the "evils" of the white man. Later Slater moved to Kalamazoo. Courtesy, Western Michigan University Archives.

1832 and 1837. The treaties offered gifts in exchange for land and pushed the signers to accept removal.

Local Potawatomies lost the Matchebenashewish Reserve with the Treaty of Tippecanoe River, Indiana, in September 1832. The Treaty of Chicago the next year required them to leave Michigan by 1836. From that time on, scattered bands traveled west under guard.

The *Gazette* gave a florid and romantic eulogy for the Potawatomies in 1838. The editor commented on the name "Kalamazoo":

> The deep-felt associations which it brings, of those daring, native, matchless men, who once so fearlessly and proudly outrode its moving tide, and roamed through the lofty forests that shade its banks, led our citizens to adopt it as their own; that they and all subsequent generations might be reminded, that the site of their beautiful village had, long ere the footsteps of civilized life disturbed its repose, been the theatre of many a wild and savage, though tragic scene.

"But," said the *Gazette,* "the red man's drama has closed; the council fire has gone out." The Potawatomie that "seven years since, lorded it over all our borders, now treads timidly through our streets."

As the government moved more and more Potawatomies westward, others fled north to the Ottawa or to Canada. Some remained defiant. Isaac Ketchum called a council at "Notawassippi" in St. Joseph County for August 20, 1839. "Your Great Father," he announced, "now wants these lands for his white children." He described the western country where "you will be on your own lands and not be trespassers." No further treaty payments would be made "east of the Mississippi."

Muckmote answered for the Potawatomies:

> We say again, we will not go. We wish to die where our forefathers died. . . . We are very poor, and one of our nation came back from there and told us that there was no bark to build lodges with, and our women and children would be obliged to live in tents, and it is well known that we are not able to build houses like your white children. Now, there are a great many whites that want us to stay here. They hunt with us and we divide the game, and when we hunt together and get tired we can go to the white men's houses and stay. We wish to stay among the whites, and we wish to be connected with them, and therefore we will not go.

Ketchum responded by asking a group of whites at the council to show "the uplifted hand" if they wanted the Potawatomies to leave. All raised their hands. "You say you are poor," said Ketchum, and warned, "the longer you stay here, the poorer you will get." Red Bird spoke then:

Father, you have heard our decision: we shall never go. The reason the whites lifted their hands is they are afraid of you. We will never meet in council again.

Red Bird's charge ended the council. Annuities went unpaid and the Michigan Potawatomies spent a difficult winter. When the government sent troops to begin a final removal in 1840, many accepted defeat or disappeared into the back country. George Torrey was a young man in October 1840. Many years later he wrote, "whatever may be said as to the justice of the act, there is no doubt but their removal was devoutly wished for by the whites." Others were less certain. They were embarrassed by their own sentiment as many Potawatomies openly wept and all uncovered their heads as a gesture of respect when they passed Judge Ransom's house. The settlers missed the mococks of maple sugar, and beadwork, and venison traded for a dollar a deer. They missed Potawatomie muscle at barn raising and Potawatomie skill in woodcraft. One pioneer remembered that "within six months we all wished them back." Later census takers noted a few who did return, particularly near Athens in Calhoun County. But the settlers could no longer think of themselves as making a home in "Indian country."

The *Gazette* was far too busy arguing national politics to notice the "Indian Removal." The paper backed Martin Van Buren and denounced William Henry Harrison's "log cabin and hard cider campaign." The editor even printed an elaborate cartoon showing a massive log cabin rigged like a "deadfall" trap, about to crush the unwary public nibbling at the hard-cider bait. Harrison won in spite of the editor's opposition.

The political excitement underscored the interest local people had in national affairs and their dependence on the East. They were sure their prosperity depended on finding a way to get their goods to Eastern markets. The first settlers found a ready sale for their crops as newcomers poured into the county. They offered their marsh hay and potatoes locally to those who still had money left. The first entrepreneurs envisioned industries to serve the same local market. Gristmills ground corn and flour for home consumption. The local handle factory and the chair factory supplied immediate needs. But eventually the local market could absorb no more. Farmers struggled to get surplus crops to warehouses on the St. Joseph River. Often they found prices low because buyers had to pay high freight charges to reach their own markets. Local people had known since 1837 that the state planned to bring a "Central Railroad" from Detroit through Ypsilanti, Jackson, Marshall, and Kalamazoo. Eventually the line would reach Lake Michigan and ultimately Chicago. But dreams of future convenience moved no goods to market.

David Walbridge arrived in 1841, hoping to solve the marketing problem as a middleman. He brought a new supply of hard cash that invigorated the sagging local economy as it passed from hand to hand. Walbridge bought wheat that first season to be shipped down the St. Joseph River and on to Buffalo. But he saw at once that shipping flour would bring higher profits than shipping bulky wheat. He rented Elkinah Walters's new mill on Portage Creek for the next season. Then he built a "fleet" of freight scows suitable to the narrow, twisting Kalamazoo. Lewis Cass's commissioners had originally chosen Kalamazoo as the county seat because the river was navigable by keelboats "of several tons burthen." But local businessmen did not finance the first boat-building effort until 1836. Then Albert Saxon spent several days taking on wheat at the mouth of the Portage. He made his first trip that summer, but lost his boat when he tried to take a second cargo onto Lake Michigan. Walbridge proved more successful and soon his boats began carrying flour and other cargo on a regular basis. For several years he provided Kalamazoo with its coveted outlet to the East.

The great issues facing Kalamazoo in the 1840s no longer revolved around pioneering or "making land." Now local people worried about attracting industry and expanding markets. The legislature officially incorporated the village in 1843, and Louisa McOmber found no frontier community when she came in 1845.

Louisa and her husband traveled from

New York in 20 days. She sat down to write her friends on her first morning in Kalamazoo. Her gravest concern on the trip had been the loss of her best handkerchief in the canal. She and her husband boarded the *Nile* for the trip across Lake Erie along with 300 passengers. She reached Detroit at two in the morning and left on the train at eight. By two in the afternoon she had come 80 miles and "was tired riding" so she stopped a day in Sandstone before coming on to the end of the line at Marshall. There she had tea and then took the stage, arriving in Kalamazoo seven hours later, having "found it not as easy as a boat or car." The McOmbers stayed overnight "at a public house" and surveyed the village next morning. They soon found a place to stay which Louisa described in detail:

It is in the south part of the village—a very pleasant place and comfortable house. It is not large but enough for us. . . . one large front room and a large bedroom and pantry below besides a place for the stove and to do work in. I have not been in the chambers, but I guess they are comfortable. There is a fine yard around it with fruit trees and flowers and a garden spot and a good barn. We pay about $40 a year for the use of it including the stove. I think I shall enjoy myself well there.

As to my liking the place—I do not like many places on the railroad for it is laid out of the poorest part of the state generally. But on leaving that I find many beautiful places. If you could see some of the great pieces of grain (a great many acres in a piece) & the beautiful farm houses & orchards, etc. close by, I think you would like the look of them. I like K better than any other place I have been in the state. It is more healthy than many places with very good water here, and a pretty village. They seem to be building a good deal.

Sixteen years had passed since Titus Bronson drove the first wagon west from Ann Arbor. He himself had left Kalamazoo almost a decade before. The McOmbers, like other newcomers, might have lived in town a long time before they heard his name. Some of the old-timers remembered the prophecy he left behind. When his village was new, a scoffer came who found transportation poor, capital lacking, and industry feeble. He was sure that "in twenty years from that time they would not be able to find a solitary hut in Bronson." Bronson answered that the boy was now living who would "see a large city here, and be able to go to and from Detroit in one day by the railroad cars." That prophecy was not fulfilled in 1845, but townspeople knew that it soon would be.

This Indian mound in Bronson Park reminded early settlers of the heritage of the area. Courtesy, Western Michigan University Archives.

CHAPTER II
PASSENGER TRAINS STOP
THERE: 1846–1865

The Erie & Kalamazoo Railroad was completed from Toledo to Adrian in 1836. The "rails" were four-inch-square oak beams with strap-rails of iron five-eighths inches thick by two-and-one-half inches wide. The first steam locomotive arrived in June 1837 and the "pleasure car" (shown here) came the same year. The latter held eight passengers in each compartment with baggage below. Courtesy, Western Michigan University Archives.

The rapid, widespread settlement of Michigan actually preceded the development of modern transportation routes, instead of following it, as was so often the case in other parts of the American frontier. In the middle 1800s, Michigan settlers moved in ahead of roads and railways, choosing land and founding towns with little consideration even to future ties to Eastern markets. But the large number of settlers, especially in western Michigan, soon brought intense demands for "internal improvements." The pioneers were not satisfied with the newly constructed territorial roadways, although these helped a little. They dreamed of river improvements, canal routes, and even railroads to carry their goods to market, and supply them with the things they could not produce for themselves.

But when Titus Bronson had come to Kalamazoo in 1829, few Americans had ever seen the one or two railroads then in existence, and many had never heard of them. Within 10 years, however, some 3,300 miles of track would be in place and town proprietors would be calculating future prosperity in relationship to a growing network of rail lines. Many towns (Kalamazoo would be no exception) dated the end of the frontier—and the beginning of industrialization—to the coming of the railroad.

Peter Cooper built Tom Thumb, America's first steam locomotive, for the Baltimore & Ohio Railroad in 1830. That same year Nathan Thomas came to Kalamazoo when "there was not a shingled roofed house in the country, and no government land had been sold." At 27 and just out of Cincinnati Medical College, Thomas was the county's first doctor. He settled in Schoolcraft, but served so many patients that he lived on his pony for the next seven or eight years. Finally he decided, in February 1838, that he would go "off to see the elephant," as people were saying in those days.

Thomas had never seen a train, but he had heard increasing talk of railroads and all they might do for Michigan. The Michigan Legislature chartered the Detroit & St. Joseph Company in 1832, and Epaphroditus Ransom, Charles Stuart, Horace Comstock, and their associates received a charter to build a railroad from Kalamazoo to Lake Michigan in 1836, but nothing came of these efforts. The next year, however, the old "Erie & Kalamazoo Railroad" completed 33 miles of track be-

Nathan Thomas, a pioneer physician in Schoolcraft, was active in the "Underground Railroad." He lived the rest of his life in Schoolcraft. Courtesy, Western Michigan University Archives.

tween Toledo and Adrian. The *Gazette* announced the new road as "the great thoroughfare to the West." At first the Erie & Kalamazoo used horses to pull their daily trains, but they tested their first locomotive in June 1837; it might travel at 20 miles an hour, "carrying with her the whole train of passage and lumber cars."

Now Nathan Thomas set off on horseback, in midwinter, for a 300-mile round trip because he "had never seen the moving of cars on rail roads." Imagine his chagrin when he arrived in Toledo to find the tracks covered with snow. The engine made repeated attempts, but "the wheels played round without any forward movement," and the engineer abandoned the effort. There was nothing for Thomas to do but return home. He remarked somewhat caustically that a year later he saw "the cars moving at a slow pace, propelled by horsepower."

Many people had mixed feelings about these early railroads. The Massachusetts Legislature, for instance, had issued a report in 1827 saying that steam locomotives would never prove practical. Others worried about the effect of great speed on the human body. Still others argued that birds and vegetation would die—that hens would refuse to lay and livestock starve. Early locomotives ran slowly and only in daylight, and more than one pioneer remembered winning a race against one. It was possible to outstrip the early trains even with a heavy freight wagon, particularly if the engine had to take on water at some roadside ditch or stopped—as the president of the Erie & Kalamazoo insisted it do—to pick up anyone who walked out to the tracks.

The early locomotives ran on wooden rails overlaid with strap iron, which curled up on occasion and pushed through the cars. Life-insurance companies generally sold no policies to trainmen. The *Maumee Times* said of the troubled Erie & Kalamazoo in 1842: "If all the bones that have been broken by accidents which have befallen people travelling, and those employed on this road, could be collected, there would be well near enough to build a rail-way half way from Toledo to Adrian." Sometimes local settlers took direct action against the lines. In 1843 disgruntled Erie & Kalamazoo creditors pulled up track, threw up log barricades, and stood ready to collect their debts with loaded rifles.

Nevertheless Michigan lawmakers committed themselves heavily to railroad construction, promising the "Michigan Northern" from Port Huron to Grand Rapids, the "Michigan Central" from Detroit westward, and the "Michigan Southern" near the Indiana border. Kalamazoo residents discovered that the Michigan Central was headed their way in 1837. They waited with increasing excitement as the road opened to Ann Arbor in 1839, Jackson in 1841, Marshall in 1844, and finally Battle Creek on November 25, 1845.

Towns along the rail lines prospered. New immigrants and heavy freight followed the railroads and bulky goods returned. At first Michigan pioneers hoped to profit by developing natural resources. They would turn logs into lumber, wheat into flour, iron ore into pig iron, and so on. The resources had been known to exist for years, but local markets were quickly saturated. Now the iron "veins" stood ready to speed the "blood" of commerce throughout the national "body," according to the *Kalamazoo Telegraph*. Local entrepreneurs were no longer limited by local needs. They could use their skills and ingenuity to create hundreds of products marketable on a national scale.

George Torrey, the *Telegraph* editor, assured his readers on the day the Michigan Central arrived in Battle Creek that Kalamazoo would "receive the cars from Detroit in three to four weeks." He praised the town's new station as "the best in the state," and hinted that Kalamazoo, "the Eden of the West," was about to become "the Eldorado." The great announcement in the *Telegraph* came on January 30, 1846:

Last Sunday, as the good people of our village were returning from afternoon service, they were somewhat surprised at the appearance of a Loco-Motive belching forth volumes of smoke, as it came up to the Depot. It being its first appearance, a large number of the natives (Wolverines) hurried to the spot, to see this *land leviathan* for the first time. Great curiosity was manifest to discover the *modus operandi* of this "thing of life," and to pry into the mystery of its motive powers.

On Wednesday we had another visit, the *"iron horse"* brought in the balance of the iron to complete the road. On Monday next the passenger cars are expected.

Torrey described the great celebration at the Kalamazoo House organized by the town's business leaders. It was, he said, "a proud epoch in the history of their beautiful and rapidly growing town, destined to become the *literary, commercial* and *industrial* emporium of western Michigan." The celebrants even sang the anthem Torrey wrote in praise of "Steam's Triumphant Car," harmonizing as best they could on:

The East and West in one are join'd,
  Detroit and Kalamazoo.
We've laid our rails to Kalamazoo,
  Uniting town to town.
We meet to bless the science new,
  That breaks all barriers down!

Everyone anticipated great changes in the months following. Torrey noted that "the rush of travel increases daily by the cars to this place and westward." He announced in May: 'Verily, we are beginning to *live* in this western region; hitherto we have only *stayed* here." The first settlers in Kalamazoo, as anywhere on the frontier, had "been beating the bush." But now that the trains arrived each day, "those who are coming will catch the bird."

Even politics were set aside. George Torrey and his *Telegraph* supported the Whig party. Volney Haskall, his arch-rival at the *Gazette,* supported the Democrats.

Good Intent Line
OF COACHES.

Tri - Weekly

Line Between

KALAMAZOO, BATTLE CREEK & GRAND RAPIDS,

The **PROPRIETOR** has recently Stocked this Route with **GOOD** Horses; new Coaches and careful and experienced drivers. No pains will be spared to make this a Comfortable and Agreeable route to travelers.

This is the nearest and best route, and over the best roads to

Hastings, Flat River, Saranac, and Ionia.

Leaves Battle Creek and Kalamazoo, Tuesday, Thursday and Saturday mornings, on the arrival of the M. C. R. R. Cars from the East and West. From Battle Creek, this line passes through Ross Centre, Yorkville, Gull Prairie, and there connects with the Stages from Kalamazoo for Prairieville, Orangeville, Yankee Springs and Middleville, connecting there with Stages for Grand Rapids, which pass through Caledonia, Whitneyville and Cascade.

LEAVES GRAND RAPIDS

for Middleville, there connecting with Battle Creek and Kalamazoo Line, passing through the above named places, on Monday, Wednesday and Friday mornings, arriving at Battle Creek and Kalamazoo in time to take the Cars for the East or West, and also in time for Humphrey & Co.'s line of stages for the Southern Railroad.

Stages Leave & Take Passengers at all Public Houses!

Conveyances may be had at all of the principle places on

the Route, to any part of the country.

C. W. LEWIS, Proprietor.

Yankee Springs, Nov. 1854.

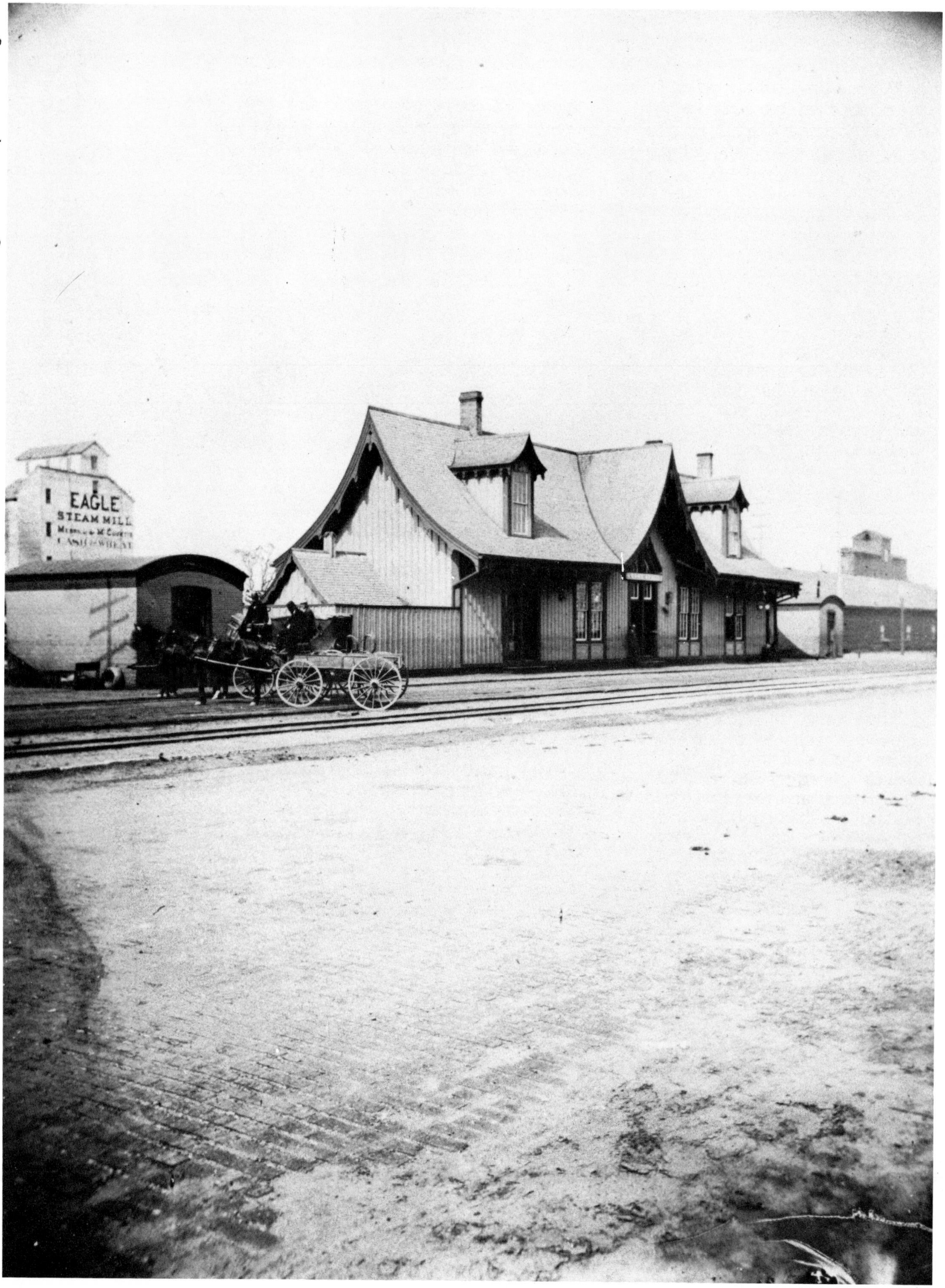
EAGLE
STEAM MILL

But both eschewed partisanship to praise the railroad. A week after the railroad's arrival, Haskall crowed, "Who shall anticipate the destiny of this wonderful country!" He launched into a reverie:

> . . . As we were strolling a few evenings since, in the vicinity of the Rail Road depot, at the moment of the arrival of the cars, and as we witnessed the scene of animation that ensued— the bustle of discharging large quantities of merchandize from the heavily freighted train—the clamor of the various runners of the hotels, each striving to rival the others, in praises and recommendations of their respective houses—in short, as we viewed the busy, excited multitude gathered around that spot, where but a few years since, stood only the rude wigwam of the Indian, our mind involuntarily wandered back, through the past, to the time when, fifteen years ago, we rambled over the same spot, where then no sign of civilization presented itself.

Writing as village historian a quarter-century later, Torrey placed the opening of the railroad as the major date in Kalamazoo's history:

> From that day the "forward movement" in the prosperity of our village is dated. Mills, warehouses, manufactories, stores, associated capital and enterprise, churches, colleges, seminaries, schools, asylums, halls, marble blocks of stores, palatial residences, paved streets, railroads, a well ordered and well governed city (without a public debt) and a happy prosperous people, are among the results that have followed that event and filled the intervening years with busy scenes. Each year has outdone its predecessor in progress. . . .

Time justified these elaborate claims. Both editors expected an immediate surge in immigration. In this they were mistaken. It was definitely easier to get to Kalamazoo, but the census taker counted no greater increase in the five years after the railroad than in the five years before. Nevertheless the village population did grow later on, doubling in the first half of the 1850s so that Kalamazoo held its place for decades as the fourth or fifth largest town in Michigan.

Other changes came more quickly. The telegraph line followed the railroad to Kalamazoo, establishing immediate contact with the outside world and effecting a revolution in business and political communication. David Munger and Chauncey Kellogg provided visible signs of Kalamazoo's new role as railhead with their big forwarding warehouse by the station. For years local merchants had been dealing with freight agents in Three Rivers and more favored towns. Now others had to come to them. People in Allegan, Grand Rapids, and Schoolcraft wondered how to get their goods to Kalamazoo. Within two years Epaphroditus Ransom organized a "Plank Road" company to build a toll road to Grand Rapids. Others planned feeder rail lines from north and south that led eventually to five railroads sending 100 trains a day through Kalamazoo by the end of the century.

The state of Michigan sold the Michigan Central to a private company for $2 million in 1846. The new owners agreed to use iron "T" rails in all new construction and to replace all wooden track over the next decade. They also promised to charge passengers no more than three cents a mile to travel in the drafty stage-bodied coaches. The Michigan Central reached Niles in 1848 and Chicago four years later.

Kalamazoo's cultural life improved rapidly after the railroad opened. Many residents continued to organize home-grown entertainment at the Lyceum, the temperance meetings, or the singing school. Kalamazoo had its own orchestra of indifferent quality, as well as a resident artist, Benjamin Cooley, who had studied with the National Academy. Luther Trask began to make daguerreotype portraits for $1.50 each in 1847. Early *Gazette*s carried a variety of literary efforts by local contributors, and George Torrey wasn't above printing a few lines of his own poetry in the *Telegraph*. Kalamazoo College grew under J.H. and Lucinda Stone to be one of the largest in the state and a focal point for lecturers and other entertainers.

The new railroad brought touring entertainers right from the start. Both newspapers urged readers to patronize Raymond and Waring's traveling menagerie, featuring lions, tigers, leopards, camels, and a pair of "tremendous elephants." Like the Duke and Dauphin in Mark Twain's *Huckleberry Finn,* Raymond and Waring failed to live up to elaborate notices of their "Grand Zoological Exhibition." Volney Haskall took a certain delight in setting the story before the public:

> The exhibition was a miserable hoax; but a small part of the animals

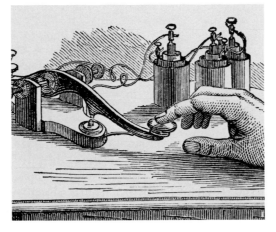

The telegraph, which reached Kalamazoo in 1846, brought the frontier into closer touch with the rest of the nation. Courtesy, Western Michigan University Archives.

advertised for exhibition were to be seen, and they of an inferior order, with the exception of the Elephants. It must have been highly gratifying to the citizens of this county to pay their money to see two or three red foxes, a raccoon, and a young black bear. In one of the cages the most prominent object was a dead, stuffed, common duck: the whole cage being offensive to the nostrils of any person. But setting aside the gross and shameful imposition practised upon us in regard to the animals, the wanton insolence and outrageous impertinence of the attendants richly merited a tarring and feathering from the citizens of this place.

By contrast, the Swiss Bell Ringers came to town the same week. They offered "a very rare treat" to an appreciative crowd, many of whom were hearing this kind of music for the first time. When the rail lines opened to Chicago, Kalamazoo became a regular stopover for traveling entertainers. The Stones brought to the college many of the most distinguished lecturers of the day, such as Bayard Taylor, Lucy Stone, Horace Greeley, and Ralph Waldo Emerson.

The real impact of the railroad would only be felt over the next several decades.

Kalamazoo gained a new identity separate from the rural county around it. Residents increasingly defined it as a commercial and industrial center. Local businessmen now looked forward to shipping their products to distant markets. The pastoral rhetoric of frontier times gave way to business metaphors, just as cottage industries gave way to factories. The *Gazette* broadcast an earnest appeal for capital investment to exchange subscribers in other towns. Arcadia and Portage creeks became "some of the most excellent water privileges in the world." The Portage offered at least four or five "of the best locations for machinery that can be found in any country." Among Kalamazoo's rare opportunities, Volney Haskall listed three:

> . . . With an abundance of the richest iron ore within a half a mile of this village, we have yet no proper means established to turn it into a source of profit. With a great surplus of wool in our county and vicinity, we have yet no adequate machinery to convert it into fabric.

> With a wide country around us, having an unprecedented number of printing establishments, we are dependent on Eastern Mills for our supply of paper—perhaps, this branch of business would afford a larger profit, for the capital invested, than any other that could be immediately put into operation.

Existing industries felt the first rush of prosperity after the railroad came. For years men had looked for ways to process local surplus. Even before the railroad, Lucius and Elisha Clarke built up a local market for hogs. They countered imported sperm-whale oil from the East Coast at half the cost "without color, smell, or smoke" by making "lard oil" for lamps, lubrication, and cooking. The *Gazette*

Trains brought freight and passengers to fortunate towns along the tracks where forwarding warehouses held goods until merchants in outlying areas could arrange overland or river transportation. Courtesy, Western Michigan University Archives.

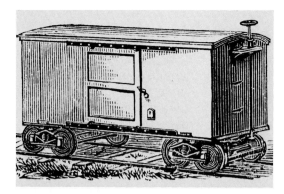

noted in 1842 that the Clarkes' new lard mill would also "keep in the county a vast amount of money" and, more importantly, "create for the farmer a market for his pork —any quantity of which article they are prepared to purchase."

When James Fenimore Cooper visited Kalamazoo in 1847, he found "the whole country was a wheatfield" between Marshall and Kalamazoo. Cooper thought "America could feed the world" if only this wheat could be transported to market. Ever since David Walbridge arrived in 1841 to serve as a marketing middleman, flour-milling had been a major local industry. By 1848 the *Telegraph* reported five large mills, including two new steam mills built next to the rail line.

With the railroad in operation, the Beals and Johnson woolen factory renovated machinery and stepped up their output. The *Telegraph* described the "clock-work precision and perfect harmony" at the plant on Portage Creek, which produced 80 to 100 yards of cloth a day. "There are many curious operations," the editor said, "by which the dirty looking fleeces sheared from the flocks which graze on our openings, are converted into a fabric fit to be worn in the Presidential chair." Volney Haskall reported that Beals and Johnson were ready to supply "cassimeres, sattinets, plain cloth, flannels, plain and twilled" produced by "experienced workmen, mostly from eastern factories." He ended on a lighter note:

> I couldn't help casting sly glances at the tidy lassies, seated at the work, who, to my thinking, were decidedly the *cunningest workmanship* there. It's astonishing how much a piece of cloth improves by looking at it over the shoulder of a pretty girl, or immediately in front of her.

Ezra Wilder began the first major effort to capitalize on the railroad in 1847. Wilder, from New York state, began buying land on the riverbank just north of the village. Townspeople knew what he was after. As early as 1837 they had identified a large deposit of "bog iron"—a sedimentary deposit from iron-rich water—along the riverbank. Until the railroad there seemed no way to use this resource. Now Wilder, an experienced ironmaster, spent more than $10,000 readying his land and building a blast furnace at the corner of present-day Riverview Drive and Mount Olivet. Then he tapped a nearby stream for water, cut surrounding oaks for charcoal, and set his men to digging and hauling ore from the riverbank. By January 1, 1848, he was ready to begin. Indeed he successfully produced 120 tons of pig iron his first year. Starting costs proved higher than Wilder could handle. He defaulted on promissory notes in New York and shut down the furnace.

Two young local men, Allen Potter and Jeremiah Woodbury, bought the idle furnace and ore deposits for $2,500 in November of 1849. They expanded the operation, adding a stove factory and rebuilding after a disastrous fire in 1852. Theirs was the largest blast furnace in Michigan. In 1853 the *Gazette* indicated that Woodbury and Potter hauled 15,000 tons of ore to the furnace where they produced 700 tons of pig iron valued at $40 a ton. In 1854 another Eastern ironmaster, William Burtt, came to Kalamazoo with $20,000 in hard cash. He bought out Woodbury and Potter and added a steam foundry and machine shop near the railroad tracks. The next year the *Gazette* described the whole "iron business." The remaining ore bed covered 160 acres, varying in depth from six inches to about

Though early freight cars were very small, they carried many a merchant's dreams of success. Courtesy, Western Michigan University Archives.

Oysters shipped in on the railroad were a local favorite even before this advertisement appeared in 1860. Courtesy, Western Michigan University Archives.

four feet. Twenty men were employed digging ore and another 10 as teamsters. In the previous nine months, they had raised 20,000 tons. Another 30 men furnished 120,000 bushels of charcoal. Twenty men were engaged "in attending on the blast." William Burtt produced 900 tons of pig iron in a single blast. This constituted a year's output at the furnace. Burtt used 500 tons at his stove factory, where 25 workers cast 4,500 parlor, box, and cooking stoves. In stove form Burtt's pig iron returned $90 a ton—at the furnace, $40. The *Gazette* reckoned his work force at 105 men and his gross income at $61,000 a year.

With a plentiful supply of pig iron, the foundry business flourished. The Burtt steam foundry and machine shop used 200 tons and kept 25 men busy in mill work, screw and bolt cutting, and assembling "some of the finest steam engines we have ever seen." Local water-power sites were limited and went to first comers. Now, with industry expanding and rail lines rather than streamsides dictating choice locations, Burtt found a ready market for his engines. Farmers needed machinery to take advantage of increasing markets for their crops. The Glover and Reese Foundry employed 16 machinists and used 80 tons of pig iron in custom work and agricultural implement-making. Arnold Arms, who had come to Kalamazoo with the railroad, opened another farm implement shop. He offered threshing machines, plows, stoves, sleigh shoes, and wagon boxes, and specialized by the 1850s in a new "wheel cultivator," which had drawn orders "far beyond his capacity to meet." Kalamazoo's bog-iron industry flourished through the 1850s, but could not compete with discoveries elsewhere in the state. Burtt sold the blast furnace in 1867 to Leverett Whitcomb, who established a flour mill on the site.

In 1850 Nathaniel Gibbs went through the town asking everyone's name, age, and occupation, and where they were from and whether they were deaf, dumb, idiotic, or insane. For the most part they answered because it was the year of the Federal Census. Gibbs found 2,500 people in the village and 13,000 in the county. As might be expected, with a thriving village on the railroad, the county ranked 10th in population, though 14th in number of farms among 43 counties then organized.

Dramatic changes in agriculture and industry swept the country in the middle of the 19th century. Government officials, showing an increasing interest in statistics, thoroughly revamped the census forms to monitor these developments. They now required for the first time the names of all household members, their ages, places of birth, occupations, and many other details. Each census taker also carried a number of "special schedules." One such "special schedule" recorded detailed information about anyone who died the previous year. A "Productions of Agriculture" schedule made room for 46 questions about farmland, crops, and livestock to be asked of every farmer. In cities, towns, and villages all across the country, census takers used a "Products of Industry" form to question anyone who manufactured a product with a yearly value of $500 or more. Census takers noted company names; products; raw materials, including fuel; power sources; employees and wages; and quantities, kinds, and value of annual product.

Gibbs walked the dusty lanes from house to house, but he also worked his way through downtown, filling out his special forms for "Products of Industry."

We can almost hear the clang of hammers and smell the oak charcoal at the foundry where blacksmiths and molders turned out plows and stoves and wagon parts. Up the street the odor of John Marsh's tannery mingled with the smell of sour mash from the town's two distilleries. Through these smells came the unmistakable odor of hundreds of hogs squealing over the spent mash that constituted their main diet. Steam whistles blew as the shops began their daily routine. Here and there in the distance was the grating sound of the old up-and-down gang saws, turning logs into lumber and great piles of sawdust, or the quieter sounds of millstones grinding wheat into unbolted flour.

Some of the sights and smells were milder as men and women stitched on harness leather and woolen clothes. Shoemakers worked at their lasts and coopers beveled their staves. Now, in 1850, the government wished to know a great deal about the "Products of Industry" in every village. "How do you call your firm and what do you make?" Gibbs would ask, as he moved through the hustle and bustle. He talked with everyone about capital and

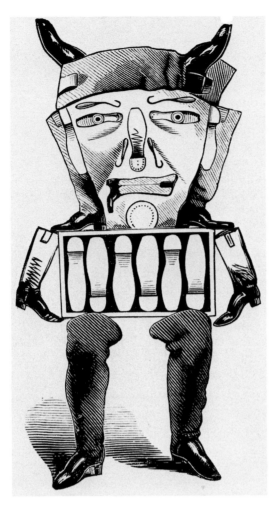

In the days before photography, newspaper readers depended on engravings for their ideas of what things ought to look like. Occasionally an advertiser might try a whimsical abstraction like this "shoeman" to attract attention. Courtesy, Western Michigan University Archives.

raw material and counted workers. He asked about wages and production and market values. From his handwritten schedule we can sense the world of work in Kalamazoo that year. The railroad was beginning to have its impact, but many of those who answered his questions bought their materials from neighbors and turned them into products their neighbors needed. Here was the hatter with his 500 fur caps, and Thomas Kenyon, the mitten-maker of Augusta who turned his 3,000 deer hides into 12,000 pairs of leather gloves. Three shoemakers produced 5,200 pairs of boots that year. Harvey Bush built 50 wagons, and the machine shops turned out 250 plows, as well as stoves, wagon tires, and "custom work." Turner and White even built two steam engines worth as much as a man could earn in a year.

Gibbs may not always have recorded exact information, but his record does give us some idea of manufacturing and its importance. With 456 families in the village, 142 men and 25 women worked in 34 firms representing 17 different industries. Isaac Moffatt's flour mill produced 8,000 barrels of flour valued at $30,000. The blast furnace was second with 650 tons of pig iron at $16,000. Flour mills, blacksmiths, and machine shops appeared most frequently, along with sawmills and leatherworkers. As convincing evidence that local markets could not entirely absorb local production, the two distillers made 120,000 gallons of liquor and two brewers added 76,000 gallons of beer. John Marsh's tannery processed 2,000 sides of leather and 400 skins, much of which went to four shoemakers and three saddle-and-harness shops. William Clark burned 50 tons of "Saleratus," as baking powder used to be called, at his ashery, and local sawmills produced more than a half-million feet of lumber.

Some men spread their interests widely. Andrew Taylor, 32-year-old bachelor from Scotland, gave his occupation as "merchant tailor," but Gibbs reported that he owned a blacksmith shop where three men did custom molding. He also operated a woolen factory with four looms and 180 spindles; 10 workers there made 24,000 yards of cloth. At his tailoring establishment, eight men and 10 women sewed up 40 coats, 1,500 pants, and 1,000 vests.

Luke and Le Grande Whitcomb held

one of the best water-power sites on the Kalamazoo, next to the railroad bridge. They used this power to operate a sawmill and a gristmill. The gristmill provided mash for their distillery where they made 60,000 gallons of "high wines." They fed the mash to a herd of pigs and packed 30,000 pounds of more or less edible pork. Isaac Moffatt also tried to integrate his efforts. He ran a flour mill, a distillery, a sawmill, and a cooper shop with steam power. His mill produced 8,000 barrels of flour a year. He also turned 14,000 bushels of corn, barley, and rye into 60,000 gallons of liquor at his distillery. His cooper shop made 8,000 barrels and 1,200 liquor casks from lumber provided by the sawmill. Like the Whitcombs, he kept hogs, 400 of them, which yielded 100,000 pounds of pork.

When the census taker counted residents that summer, he missed the young men and many not so young who were in California to prospect for gold. Local newspapers kept up a steady accounting of "News from California" through 1848, and each spring for the next five years they described "a regular stampede for California." Gold excited people, but local residents and many who made the trip were not entirely happy with the dream of getting rich without working. The *Gazette* editor announced the leave-taking of the first "Kalamazoo Boys" in March 1849: "it was a melancholy scene to see these young men bid farewell to parents and associates." On the other hand, he thought that "wealth and independence, adventure, an enlarged view of mankind and the world are tempting prizes." The *Telegraph* editor commented a month later: "we fear that in seeking to dig for gold they will only dig their graves. It is a mournful question whether any will ever return." The *Gazette* later offered a sure cure for California fever:

> sleep 3 nights in your woodshed with the door open and swinging in the wind, at which time let your diet be pork cooked by yourself at a smoking fire in your garden. . . . Improve all the rainy nights in sleeping between your currant bushes and garden fence. . . . Thereafter dispense with all kinds of food save dog-meat.

Yet the search for riches on distant riverbanks did become a kind of community epic—an experience vicariously shared through letters home that passed from family to family. The Kalamazoo Boys, whenever they started out, kept in close touch with each other and with their home town. Both papers printed letters almost from the start. Every writer commented on prospects and prices and made special mention of friends along the way.

Some men traveled by ship to Panama, crossing the isthmus by log canoes and muleback, and writing home of tigers and alligators and tropical forests. They waited interminably, it seemed, for steamers to San Francisco. Others, such as Henry Gregory, went across the plains. Writing home from "Summit of South Pass, Rocky Mountains" on July 21, 1849, he said his party averaged about 20 miles a day in spite of chasing their runaway cattle 40 miles at one point. West of Fort Laramie food and water were hard to come by, and the party sometimes wandered 10 miles from the trail looking for grass. Earlier travelers struggled on ahead. Gregory noted that "the road is lined with shovels, picks, crowbars, wagons, dead oxen, etc., and in fact, everything that is not necessary to sustain life has been left by the wayside, in order to get along a little faster. We have passed fifty dead oxen in one day."

However arduous the trip, most of those who wrote home bragged a little about their own endurance. Gregory concluded:

> I should like well to have some of the wise ones of Kalamazoo, who thought I was not made of the right kind of material to stand this journey, work with me a few days. I think I could satisfy them that I am tough enough for almost any journey. I never have been healthier in my life, not withstanding I have been exposed in every possible way.

Most of the Kalamazoo Boys finished the journey in time, though Amos Brownson spent several harrowing days with nothing but horsemeat for food. William Glover's party "left nearly all our clothing and things we could spair," as well as wagons and weapons, behind in the last sprint over the "Nevada Mountains" to the gold fields. Most tried their hand at mining, and some sent samples of gold dust pasted between sheets of paper to family and friends. Few were as fortunate as Amos Dunn, who wrote in October 1849 that "there is an abundance of gold, though it requires hard labor in digging and washing to procure it. We have got in twelve days, four of us, one thousand dollars." Three weeks later he added a postscript: "Since I commenced writing we have done well. We have got $5,000—the digging continues good."

Clement McNair said in September that "comfort is unknown in these diggings. But the gold is here . . . I have now been at work 10 days, and it is my opinion that any man with the least disposition to work, and an ordinary run of luck, can make from $16 to $20 per day." Young men working for a dollar a day in Kalamazoo must have envied McNair. Still, he concluded, "gold digging is a pretty fair imitation of hard work."

Increasingly, in 1850 and after, the Kalamazoo Boys found other work—freighting like the Drake boys, or ranching like the Walbridges and Curtis McLin. Others, like Milo Goss, went into storekeeping. Goss ran a store in Kalamazoo before he left for California in April 1850. His wife saved his letters along with copies of many of her own. He, too, told of loneliness and hopes for better prospects. "It is the best place for a man to get rich probably in the world," he wrote in September, "but it cannot be done in one year." His wife once urged, half-jokingly, "Husband, do make haste and make a large pile, and leave the rest for someone else." Later she told him what she had kept secret before

he left: "We have another daughter born September third." Goss found opportunities supplying other miners with goods. He turned his back on mining, noting, "I have aged nine years in the last nine months." Time passed quickly as months turned into years, and still Goss hoped to make his "pile." In 1852 he observed in one of his weekly letters: "I can now see that the facilities are gradually diminishing, and few are making much except those who have been established in business as long as myself." Two weeks later he concluded: "My own judgment says stay a while longer, but my heart says go! go! g - o !!!" Goss stayed on, but others turned back. The lucky ones came home with capital to invest in Kalamazoo.

William Gibbs had that luck. He reached Sacramento in August 1850, and moved on 75 miles to the Yuba River, where he and his partners struck pay dirt in a gravel bar "fairly rotten with gold," that yielded $800 in one glorious bucket. Four men panned out $1,700 that week, but expenses ran high and Gibbs stayed three years before starting back by sea. He took 182 ounces of gold to the mint in New Orleans where it was made up into 164 $20 gold pieces. These Gibbs carried home in a specially made cotton vest, which the Kalamazoo Museum keeps as a reminder of the gold field days. Forty

Millinery shops offered employment to women and brought the latest fashions to the frontier. Courtesy, Western Michigan University Archives.

years later Gibbs took his wife on a pleasure trip to the very same claim and panned out a sample of gold particles still in the gravel.

But not everyone who rushed to the gold fields was as lucky as William Gibbs. According to Clement McNair: "Many who started with good prospects for getting through lie buried by the roadside. Others who had invested largely in teams, wagons, etc., have been obliged to leave them, and walk hundreds of miles with provisions on their backs." The expedition from Marshall, Michigan, lost its stock in heavy mountain snows and walked nearly 300 miles with barely enough food to survive. The *Gazette* carried George Hogle's letter in 1850. He wrote: "I would advise all men to stay at home, who are comfortably situated. No man can realize the fatigues of an overland journey who has not tried it." He went on to say "there have been some men very lucky, who came over the plains last summer. I know of a number that have made four or five thousand dollars and gone home. But there is not one in a thousand that has done it." Sherman Hawley added: "I have not seen a man that crossed the plains, that is willing to go over the same again, for all there is in California."

Another account a few weeks later concluded that "there are many in the mines; some have died of scurvy, some have drowned and some have been murdered by the Indians. All is peace and harmony; each man's claim is respected; the Sabbath is observed and kept. I hope to be home next spring."

Neither the *Gazette* nor the *Telegraph* could maintain an extended interest in California gold. Volney Haskall announced the first trickle of returning miners in January 1851 by remarking that "a very uncertain business is gold-seeking, and in the long run, don't pay so well as steady honest perseverance in some useful occupation." He carried a poignant note in 1853 from one miner who wrote: "I have not been homesick a moment since I left Kalamazoo for all my sickness and slow luck, but keep looking forward for better times as I cannot have much worse." He noted, in November 1853, that some men brought "the yellow boys" home with them, but "it must be confessed that others have returned with little else than a rough experience accompanied with a loss of time and health, while not a few yet remain in the modern Ophir, un-

able to come back for want of means. Fortune hunting in California is, after all, a precarious business."

The experience proved too much for some men. Monroe Salisbury, a returned Californian, hung himself by his horse's reins one day in 1855. Amos Brownson, one of the earliest merchants in Kalamazoo, lost his store to fire and joined the Kalamazoo Boys in 1850. Several letter-writers showed special concern for the old pioneer. They said Brownson wandered into the mountains alone and they feared for his health. Milo Goss wrote that Brownson hadn't "accumulated any thing but a great quantity of fat—I never saw one fat up so quickly—he does not look natural." Goss hoped to talk Brownson into steadier habits but failed. When he returned in 1854, the *Gazette* found Brownson "broken in spirit and feeble in body." He died in Niles a year later.

Besides the lure of the Far West, other frontiers beckoned to wanderers from Kalamazoo. In the 1850s local papers carried notes of the new mining districts of northern Michigan and the prospects of the Minnesota Territory. Edmund Rice, for example, left as a forty-niner, but chose to make his fortune in Minnesota. He "read law" in Kalamazoo and served with distinction as a lawyer for several years. Then he decided to move west at 30. He helped bring Minnesota into statehood, served six terms in the legislature, and two more as mayor of St. Paul. Known as "the father of the railway system in Minnesota," he realized an estate of $400,000 by the 1880s.

More than remarking on distant opportunities, however, the papers preferred to talk of prosperity and prospects at home. As the *Gazette* editor wrote in 1854, one wheat harvest on Prairie Ronde was an "exhibition of wealth far more gratifying than would be the shining placers of California." Business boomed in the 1850s, and by 1855 the *Gazette* could claim a genuine housing shortage as factory workers crowded into town:

"Where can I find a House?" is a question asked fifty times a day in our streets. The fact is, there are no houses to be had except as they are built. The demand for residences is absolutely overwhelming. Every shanty, every dark room over stores and in basements, is seized upon and occupied until something better shall turn up. All over the village are heard the sounds of the builders, and

MRS WM. S. DELANO.

WM. S. DELANO.

houses are rising upon vacant lots as if by magic, and still the insatiate demand is unsupplied—strange faces throng our streets, and new business combinations are daily taking place. We once knew every resident of our village—now, scarcely one in ten.

Much of the new industry served local farmers whose prosperity still provided the foundation for Kalamazoo's expansion. Area farmers steadily increased their wheat acreage. In 1860 the county ranked 10th in population in Michigan but fifth in wheat production. Village millers tripled their output of flour in the decade, and the county stood third in flour milling with 157,250 barrels. Isaiah Pursel's distillery in Schoolcraft led the state in the 1854 census and again 10 years later, when Pursel produced 105,000 gallons of whiskey at a quarter a gallon. In 1855 the *Gazette* described seven leatherworking firms turning local hides into harnesses, saddles, boots, and shoes. The annual premium lists for the County Agricultural Fair show the importance of livestock breeding, particularly in sheep production, and the spread of orchard stock along the temperate hills to the west.

Local farmers showed increasing interest in machinery during the 1850s, invest-

ing nearly twice as much in implements at the end of the decade as they had at the beginning. Merchants quickly capitalized on this interest. In 1851 Volney Haskall summed up the bond between local farmers and businessmen by noting, "whatever shall tend to increase the market facilities of the farmer and open a wider demand for his products, especially that of the great western staple—corn—should be hailed with general rejoicing and satisfaction by the community." Corn could be fed to livestock, distilled, or ground into meal, but its moisture content contributed to spoilage. Flour also turned "musty and sour" and could not "be held with safety, like dry goods and hardware." H.G. Bulkley responded by patenting a steam grain dryer that took flour direct from the grinding stones and dried it so efficiently "that the meal will retain its natural taste and remain unspoiled for years in the hottest climate."

Lovett Eames thought about the timber that meant profit for local farmers if it was sawed into lumber. He perfected a portable steam sawmill in 1852 that could be taken directly to farm woodlots or along the route of the new plank roads. The mill would cost less than $2,000 complete, and the *Gazette* editor watched it cut a

This fine Greek Revival farmhouse replaced an earlier homestead in 1858. The Delano family held this land until the 1960s. The Kalamazoo Nature Center is presently restoring it as a 19th-century working farm on E Avenue. Courtesy, Western Michigan University Archives.

single oak log into 400 feet of plank in 38 minutes. Eames estimated that the mill could be taken down, carted five to 15 miles on four wagons, and reassembled in less than a week.

Pioneer carpenters tediously worked rough lumber into smooth boards for flooring, millwork, and cabinetry, using a variety of wooden planes and draw knives. Benjamin Brown hoped to save both money and time with the planing mill he designed in 1849. Other machine shops followed with similar planers and molding machines for sash-and-door-makers. The *Gazette* noted that William Burtt's planing machine in 1853 was "the finest piece of mechanism of the kind we ever saw. It is a self-acting or self-adjusting machine when set in motion, and does its work as if possessed of mental endowments. It is 28 inches wide and about 8 feet long but can be gauged to any smaller size."

Ingenious tinkerers worked for years around the country to mechanize the process of farming itself. They began in the 1830s to develop machinery to better prepare the soil, as John Deere did with his steel plow that cut like a knife through heavy sod. Others thought of sowing, cultivating, and harvesting with machinery. Eastern farmers had long determined field sizes by the amount of hand labor available. On the open Western prairies, the opportunities for mechanization seemed limitless.

Harvesting created a major bottleneck in the farm operation. The scythe and cradle replaced the ancient sickle, but still hand labor controlled the harvest. So it was that Cyrus McCormick patented his mechanical "reaper" in 1834, but small fields made even the reaper seem unwieldy. McCormick managed no sales at all until 1840 and only a handful each year afterward.

James Hascall brought the dream of a much more elaborate harvester to local prairies in 1830. He soon joined with Hiram Moore on Climax Prairie to develop a giant machine that would cut, thresh, clean, and bag grain at the unheard-of rate of 20 acres per day. By 1837 they had a patented, operating thresher that one New York paper called "the greatest thing of this kind ever known." Still they experimented under Moore's direction. Ten years later the *Gazette* claimed no invention ranked "higher in the prospect of future usefulness than the Harvester," which was then successfully at work on Prairie Ronde. Yet Moore continued to simplify the machinery and cut the cost. In 1849 the paper paused in its praise of California gold to comment on the thresher again. A joint stock company was projected to take the Harvester to the prairies of Illinois, Wisconsin, and Iowa. Such mechanization would be the future of farming, said the editor, adding:

> . . . The time will come, and that soon, when the laborious and expensive operations as now carried on in the production of the finer grains, will be to a great extent superseded by the omnipotent power of steam; and through the agency of labor-saving machinery, of which the present machine will constitute an important and leading feature. Steam ploughs, steam sowing machines, steam harrows, and steam harvesters, are necessary to keep pace with the progressive spirit of the age, and will soon be seen presiding over fields whose extent will be measured by square miles instead of acres.

At its best the big machine cut a 14-foot swath, drawn by 16 horses with four drivers. Three men worked on the platform; one kept busy simply tying bags of threshed and cleaned grain. Several farmers tried Moore's Harvester, and most found that it lived up to all the claims. Yet the costs continued high, the original patent expired, and Moore moved to Wisconsin, his dream deferred. Andrew Moore of Schoolcraft bought one Harvester that had been running several years at Prairie Ronde. He exhibited what the *Gazette* called "this magnificent invention—by far the greatest in the field of agriculture" at the "Crystal Palace" World's Fair in New York in 1853, then sent it on to California. Pioneer historians claimed that Moore had "really invented and used on Prairie Ronde the sickle-edged and saw-tooth cutting bar," but his Harvester proved too large and costly to compete with McCormick's less expensive reaper and a variety of stationary threshing machines.

Local farmers did turn to Kalamazoo firms for other equipment, however. Local blacksmiths sharpened and repaired tools and plows. Foundries provided iron castings, and some men even specialized in implement-making. The *Gazette* noted in the summer of 1855 that George Dodge of Batavia, New York, was moving his plow works to take advantage of Kalamazoo's iron supply. He built a two-story brick factory on the corner of Rose and Eleanor, measuring 40 by 100 feet, and started making a plow of his own design in several sizes. He would prosper almost from the start. By 1860 he could turn out 1,200 plows a year at an average of $10 each.

With farm business booming during the decade, the local paper concluded that when harvests were good, "everybody breathes easier—plenty to eat—plenty to drink and wear—and all getting rich as fast as desirable." Kalamazoo did rank sixth or seventh in taxable property of all the 57 counties then organized. Changes in the downtown area signaled this prosperity. New businesses along Main Street crowded out private homes. When Justus Burdick died in 1849, his front yard was sold for business blocks. Over the decade new brick buildings rose on both sides of the street. Behind them on Water and Eleanor and Edwards, stood the foundries and factories of heavy industry. When the Ladies' Library Association held its "Quarter-Centennial Celebration" in 1854, guests toasted industry as enthusiastically as the ladies, and Frederick Curtenius praised local businessmen with prospects "of one day becoming princes and closing their career on these western heights, amid splendor and honor and usefulness. . . ."

T.S. Atlee contributed this summary: . . . We have now reached an epoch in our history, of great moment to us, and to those who shall come after us. Printing Offices, School Houses, Churches, Theological Institutions, and Colleges; Courts of Law, Banks, and Shaving Shops; Medical Dispensaries and Drug Stores; busy marts of Commerce and Merchandise; Factories and places for all mechanical and industrial pursuits; Literary, Benevolent, and Sewing Societies;— in short, a little of everything in general, and too much of some things in particular, are crowding upon each other, in rapid succession, to the manifest horror of lazy people, and the total extinction of men and women of "one idea"!

In 1856 the *Gazette* listed 63 business categories and 167 firms in the village. The next year the Kalamazoo Gas Company laid the gas mains and lit up the town. "When will Kalamazoo cease to be the 'fastest' town in the state," Haskall once asked, noting that commercial profits "are multiplying, constantly, in these days of

steam and lightning!" When the census taker came around in 1860, local growth and prosperity seemed as consistent as ever.

The census taker counted 1,100 homes in the village and 6,075 people. He didn't complete his "Products of Industry" schedule, but did include 39 firms employing 204 men and nine women. S.E. Walbridge reported the highest valued product from his flour mill with 20,000 barrels of flour at $5 each and 13 tons of cornmeal at $1,000 a ton. Luke Whitcomb made 25,000 gallons of rectified whiskey valued at 58 cents a gallon. William Whitney owned the "ashery" now. He turned tallow, grease, and wood

George Dodge came in 1855 and offered local people a wide range of implements for farming, lumbering, and manufacturing as indicated in this 1869 advertisement. Courtesy, Western Michigan University Archives.

ash into 60,000 pounds of candles, seven tons of hard soap, and 480 barrels of soft soap. The wood ash yielded 30 tons of potash. One cooper shop made 30,000 flour barrels, one chairmaker 1,200 chairs. Two carriagemakers built 140 carriages and 70 sleighs. Three shoemakers made 7,200 pairs of boots and shoes; and two bakeries provided 135,000 loaves of bread and 3,400 pounds of crackers. Kalamazoo had indeed become "a fast town," the visiting editor of the *Niles Republican* said enviously, adding "its citizens are enterprising and 'go ahead' is their motto."

Yet the newspapers were greatly troubled by distant rumbles of secession in 1860. Politics meant a lot to local people, and now they regularly read of disagreement in Washington.

The news of Fort Sumter on April 12, 1861, brought meetings, speeches, and calls for volunteers. Seventeen-year-old William Shakespeare led the list of 45 who stepped forward the first day. The 1850s began with accounts of men leaving for California; now the Kalamazoo Boys were off to the battlefields. According to the *Telegraph,* "the town was a complete flutter of excitement" on April 30 as the first two companies marched to the depot and boarded three cars on the siding. H.G. Wells, Frederick Curtenius, and Charles

Stuart spoke to well-wishers. The 10:45 train from the west cut speeches short when, "amid the noise of artillery, the shouts of the people, the swinging of hats, and the waving of handkerchiefs, the first Kalamazoo volunteers departed."

These were the first of many from the county. Michigan's governor asked Frederick Curtenius to raise a full regiment. In August, the 6th Michigan Infantry, one thousand men and officers strong, sat down to a grand farewell dinner, where 10,000 people "gave them greeting."

Charles Stuart recruited the 13th Michigan Infantry, which finished its preparations and left for Kentucky on February 11, 1862. As the *Telegraph* described the scene:

. . . Twenty-one passenger, ten baggage, and eight freight-cars were required to transport the troops, with their arms, horses, and equipments. Two powerful engines drew the long and heavy train.

Shortly after eleven o'clock all were aboard, and the regiment slowly glided from the depot, amid the mingled cheers and tears of the assembled thousands.

One early historian, Samuel Durant, said so many men enlisted that the labor shortage "was seriously felt in all business circles and in the industrial development

Right
In the mid-19th century, newspaper readers saw what restaurant dining could offer thanks to illustrated advertisements like this one. Courtesy, Western Michigan University Archives.

Facing page
Top
Long before the time of the Civil War billiard parlors provided popular entertainment for men. Courtesy, Western Michigan University Archives.

Bottom left
Modern Italianate stores contrasted sharply with earlier Greek Revival buildings during the Civil War. Pictured here is Michigan Avenue at Rose before paving and the installation of curbs. Courtesy, Kalamazoo Public Museum.

Bottom right
William Blakeman began making pianos and melodeons in Kalamazoo in 1854. In 1866 he took on Delos Phillips as his partner. Phillips later made the "Star Organ," locally popular for many years. This advertisement ran in 1869. Courtesy, Western Michigan University Archives.

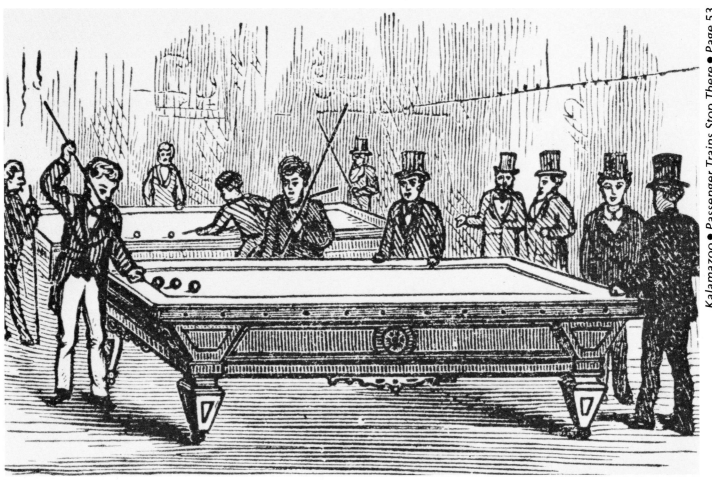

William H. Allcott built this large flour mill on Portage Creek near Lovell and Portage streets in 1859. This drawing dates from 1864. Courtesy, Kalamazoo Public Museum.

This 1861 view of Main Street (Michigan Avenue) looking west from Portage is the earliest photograph of the street. The Greek Revival buildings on the left were replaced in 1869. The tall building on the right is the Burdick Hotel. Courtesy, Kalamazoo Public Library.

of the county." He believed that as many as 1,000 men left from the village—about half the labor force. Official records show 3,221 enlistments from the county, but Willis Dunbar in *Kalamazoo and How It Grew* suggests that many of these were reassignments and that perhaps 1,400 different men actually went to war, including 60 who enlisted in the 102nd U.S. Colored Troops.

The Civil War might have been the last "romantic" war and the first modern one. In any event, it brought appalling casualties. Dunbar says that 365 county men died in service, but only 58 on the battlefield. Two hundred and seven died of disease and 48 of wounds. Another 307 men were discharged for disability, and the total casualty list neared 700.

Volunteers joined 10 regiments or parts of regiments that gathered in Kalamazoo, but as time passed and casualties mounted, the government considered conscription. On October 27, 1863, nervous spectators crowded into the courthouse for the first official call. As one witness put it: "it is one thing to swing the hat and cheer on the brave volunteers to the front of battle, but quite another to hear your name called by Uncle Sam's appointed officers as a

drafted man." Ninety-one draftees went into service and another 53 men hired substitutes or paid the required $300 avoidance fee.

Public officials tried a variety of ways to finance the war. In the beginning, the federal government budgeted no money for war. The state of Michigan had little to spare, and the call went out for private contributions. Forty-four local people gave $3,206—an average of three months' wages each. In 1862 the government established an elaborate system of special taxes, license fees, revenue stamps, and an income tax for Kalamazoo residents who reported earnings over $600. They were encouraged to be accurate by penalties of as much as $4,000 for understatements by local men. In addition the newspapers published annual tax lists for all to see. Surviving records indicate more about the ebb and flow of cash in local communities than they do about financing the war.

Successful men like Allen Potter or William Wood showed incomes of $4,000 to $6,000, which rose rapidly during the war years. Wealthy farmers might report from $200 to $1,000. Private banker Theodore Sheldon led the Kalamazoo list in 1864

Above left
The Pennsylvania oil boom after 1859 brought good times to Michigan coopers who made many of the barrels used to ship the oil. Courtesy, Western Michigan University Archives.

Top
In 1860 merchants' villas such as this one belonging to W.B. Clark lined streets that were barely trails 25 years earlier. Courtesy, Western Michigan University Archives.

Above
Cabinetmakers provided a touch of elegance to pioneer homes from the beginning of settlement. This advertisement for furniture manufacturers Goodale & Henika appeared in 1860. The firm installed the first steam whistle in town to call their workers. John Goodale, who came to Kalamazoo as a young man in 1853, later became a successful undertaker and remained in the city. Courtesy, Western Michigan University Archives.

U.S. Senator Charles Stuart had a distinguished career as a lawyer and officeholder. Stuart Avenue is named for him. Courtesy, Western Michigan University Archives.

with $8,850, including $1,000 interest on U.S. government bonds. Wagonmaker William Tomlinson had the second highest income at $8,414. Many people with high standing in the community recorded little or no taxable income. No doctor in the county, it seemed, ever earned more than $600, nor did many lawyers. Wages were up during the war, when labor was scarce, but working people still made much less than $600.

Congress provided for a system of national banks in 1863 to aid the sale of government bonds and the establishment of a national currency. Theodore Sheldon had begun his private bank in Kalamazoo in 1844. Jeremiah Woodbury, Allen Potter, and William Wood organized their own establishment in 1856. In 1863 the First National Bank opened with Latham Hull as president and a capital stock of $50,000. It was the first of the national banks in Michigan. At the end of the war Woodbury, Potter, and Wood reorganized as the Michigan National Bank with $100,000 capital. Both wages and profits rose during the war, but so did prices when the government began issuing "greenbacks." Nevertheless, as one his-

Drawing of early Kalamazoo, looking toward the southwest, circa 1864. Detail from bird's-eye view on front cover. Courtesy, Kalamazoo Public Museum.

torian wrote a few years later, "all kinds of businesses flourished and times were good."

People on the home front did what they could for the "boys in blue." The women of the village organized a Ladies' Aid Society in 1863 with Mrs. Sheldon as president. Lucinda Stone served as secretary and Ruth Webster of the Ladies' Library Association as treasurer. The Society raised more than $5,000 for woolen blankets, hospital stores, and relief to wounded soldiers and their families. The women organized a State Sanitary Fair at Kalamazoo in 1864 and raised an additional $9,300 for relief. The 13th Michigan came home at last in 1864 on "veteran furlough," and the town turned out in a grand reception to welcome them. Gradually other units were mustered out and large numbers of young men appeared on the streets again as the village began to return to normal.

A traveling artist visited Kalamazoo in 1864 and stayed to draw one of the "bird's-eye views" just coming into fashion. Today the Public Museum preserves his colored lithograph, which shows the village basking in the morning sun. The fourth largest community in Michigan

The First Baptist Church with its tall steeple and town clock was a prominent landmark in 1860 when this drawing was made. Courtesy, Western Michigan University Archives.

The sturdy Italianate Courthouse, seen in this stereoscopic view, served the county in the 1870s. Courtesy, Western Michigan University Archives.

with 6,797 people, it was bounded on the north by North Street and on the south by Vine. To the west, only two or three houses stood beyond Elm. The commercial heart of the town ran along Michigan Avenue from Portage to Rose. A few of the old free-standing wooden "temples of commerce" from the pioneer era stood looking forlorn and dwarfed by imposing brick storefronts in the new Italianate style that dominated both sides of the street. Industries lined Water Street, some still taking their power from Arcadia Creek, which ran openly through the town. Many other firms clustered near the depot along North Burdick and North Rose. The artist drew plumes of smoke to suggest the steam engines that made the factories independent. Luke Whitcomb's distillery stood on the riverbank and up the Portage the sun shone brightly on Merrill and McCourtie's big new flour mill.

The courthouse stood just west of Rose, and alongside were four churches as Titus Bronson had originally intended, including the imposing First Baptist Church completed in 1854. Kalamazoo College had a new president, John Gilbert. Its buildings ranked with the most notable in town on the western edge. Far on the horizon stood the new buildings of Michigan's first State Hospital for the insane, opened in 1858.

Houses clustered close around the

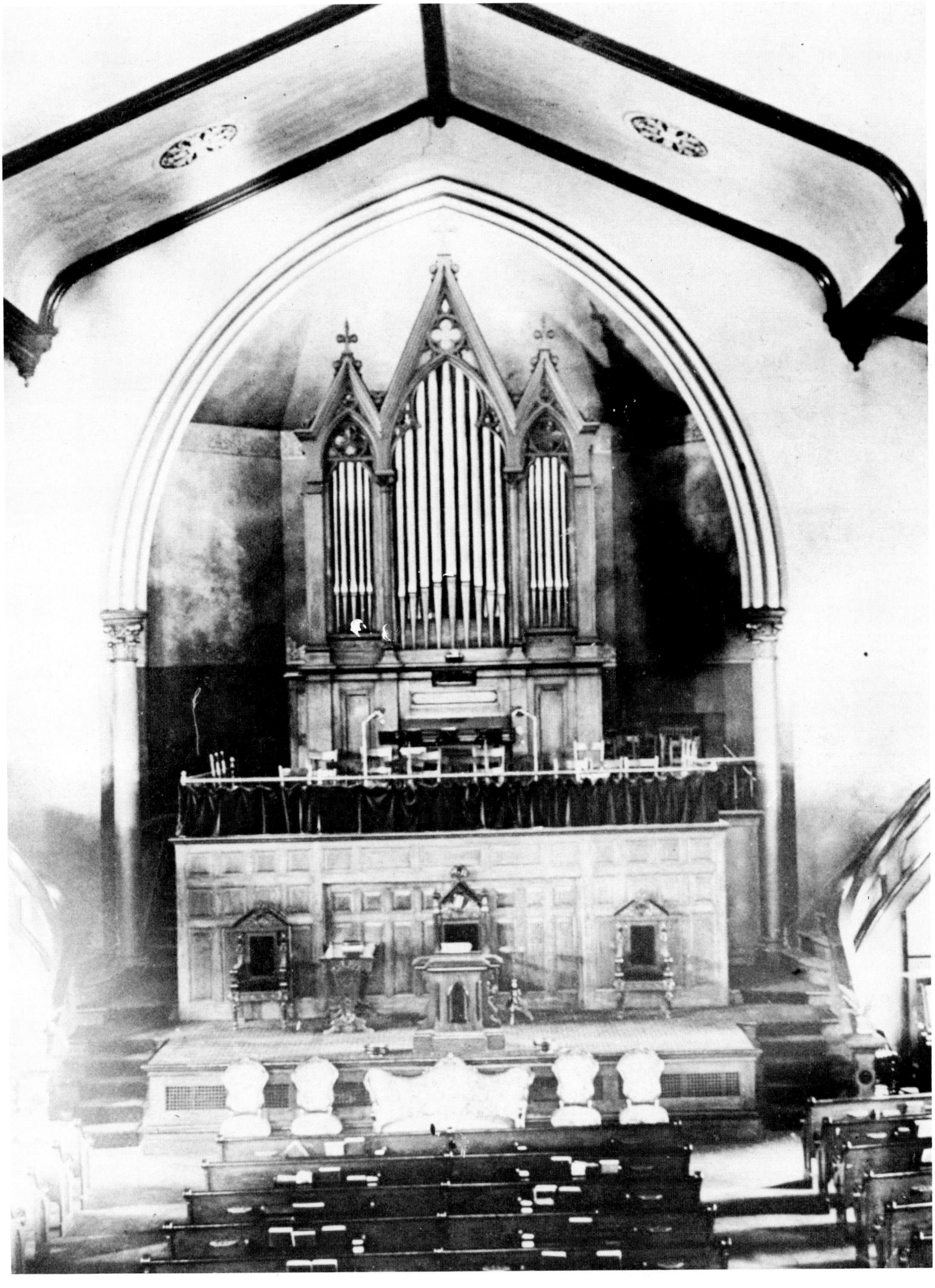

Hezekiah Wells, pioneer Schoolcraft settler, rose to prominence as a commissioner judging the famous "Alabama Claims" after the Civil War. He lived on the corner of South Street and Park in 1880 when this drawing was made. Courtesy, Western Michigan University Archives.

downtown area—a dozen on land where Gilmore's department store now stands and many more on Edwards Street. Private homes surrounded the park on three sides and lined Michigan Avenue west of Park. Villagers grazed their milk cows on the open land north and west of the railroad tracks.

This was a "walking village" typical of the times when zoning was unknown. People lived very close to where they worked, shopped, or entertained themselves. Few paid the government's special tax on carriages when they could walk wherever they were likely to go.

Kalamazoo in 1864—the Burr Oak Village—could hardly imagine the doubling and tripling of its population in the next 20 years, or the expansion of its industries to national prominence, or the development of national and international markets for its products. Instead the artist showed a complacent community, basking in the summer sunshine, its factory smokestacks trailing only wisps of smoke, its people walking calmly down the middle of its dusty streets, or rowing on the clean and placid river. Church steeples still towered over everything else in the village.

WOODWARD AVE. SCHOOL BUILDING.

MICHIGAN FEMALE SEMINARY.

Above
To Kalamazoo residents education was of prime importance. The Woodward Avenue elementary school, the Michigan Female Seminary, and Kalamazoo College are seen in this drawing that appeared in the 1880 county history. Courtesy, Western Michigan University Archives.

Left
Fashionable homes, like this one built on Rose Street by Frederick Curtenius in 1860, lined three sides of Bronson Park. Courtesy, Western Michigan University Archives.

CHAPTER III
FACTORY SMOKESTACKS:
1865–1880

Early paper mills were located outside of town to be near the purer water that was needed to produce clear white paper. This mill was built on Cork Street. Courtesy, Kalamazoo Public Library.

Many shopkeepers crowded the first and second floors of the few downtown business "blocks" in the 1860s. Pictured here is the corner of Michigan and North Burdick, circa 1867. Courtesy, Kalamazoo Public Museum.

Shock of assassination, surrender at last, mustering out, and the war was over. Young men, already old veterans, returned to find their towns the same, but somehow different. Not everything had changed, of course. Two fingers held up in a "V" still meant "let's go swimming," and white picket fences kept the neighbor's cow and stray pigs out of the flower bed. A thousand people might still turn out on New Year's Day for impromptu horse races on South Burdick. But the pace of life seemed quicker, and newspaper editorials expressed a certain urgency. Once political issues had moved people, now the talk was all of growth and commerce and factory work.

Returning veterans met some changes head on. Others they had to accept. The 1864 Census showed 237 more single women than single men in Kalamazoo—a balance the "boys in blue" quickly redressed after the war. On the other hand, people had to learn new ways to make a living as Kalamazoo grew into a commercial and industrial center far outstripping its local markets. The Grand Rapids & Indiana Railroad and the Lake Shore & Michigan Southern came to compete with the Michigan Central and to tap the northern

pinelands. Smokestacks jostled church steeples for supremacy on the skyline, and the *Telegraph* launched a daily edition.

Some of the Kalamazoo Boys, such as Orlando Moore and William Shafter, had enjoyed campaigning enough to stay in the regular army and see the West. Others, such as William Shakespeare, had come home earlier than planned. Shakespeare rose to sergeant and then to second lieutenant. On July 11, 1863, when his regiment charged at Jackson, Mississippi, he absorbed seven wounds and broke both legs. He waited 33 days before receiving adequate medical attention in Cincinnati. There he spent seven months on his back. Discharged for disability in 1864, he had made his way home crippled but "one of the heroes of this war," said Michigan's lieutenant governor, who wrote to the *Telegraph* that Shakespeare should "enjoy, in the respect and sympathy of this whole community, some compensation for his great suffering in the cause of the country." But Shakespeare rapidly picked up the threads of civilian life. He soon clerked in the provost marshal's office, overseeing the work of local draft commissioners. When the war ended, he was 21 and tried editing the

THE KALAMAZOO
TELEGRAPH.

Brightly Del.

Daily, Tri-Weekly and Weekly.

HERMAN E. HASCALL, Editor & Prop'r.

THE DAILY is made up of the latest Telegraphic, Foreign and Local Intelligence, and has taken a high stand in public favor. By the plan of distributing the reading matter over its pages, the advertisements become more conspicuous. For a daily, a large share of the space is occupied with reading matter, thus making the advertising portion more valuable. $4.50 per year.

THE TRI-WEEKLY is twice the size of the Daily, and contains the matter of two Dailies. $3.00 per year.

THE WEEKLY is an old and firmly established paper, and the largest and most popular one in Southern Michigan. It is printed on a sheet 29 by 44 inches, contains 36 columns of reading matter, and aims to give the latest news, particularly that news relating to home and affecting home interests. It is earnestly Republican in politics. $1.50 per year.

The Rates of Advertising are, considering the advantages offered, exceedingly low. Terms for the Daily and Weekly, or either, are matter of special contract.

THE TELEGRAPH JOB PRINTING OFFICE contains three Presses, over 175 Fonts of Type, and all the material necessary to the prompt and creditable execution of all kinds of Printing. Prices low. All contracts faithfully performed.

As this 1860 advertisement suggests, women often worked as compositors on village weeklies such as the *Telegraph*. Courtesy, Western Michigan University Archives.

Gazette for a year. In 1867, he married and turned to storekeeping, studying law in his spare time. Finally, in 1878, he joined Nathaniel Balch's prestigious law firm. Shakespeare spent the rest of his life in Kalamazoo, eventually building the "Shakespeare Block" on North Rose and becoming the owner and president of the Central Bank of Kalamazoo in 1896.

The 25th Michigan Infantry had left Kalamazoo in September 1862, under Colonel Orlando Moore and Lieutenant-Colonel Benjamin Orcutt. The regiment compiled a fine record and earned the nickname "Lucky." When it was mustered out in June 1865, Orcutt returned to Kalamazoo. He had first come there as a young man in 1836. Later he had served under Frederick Curtenius in the Mexican War, and then as deputy sheriff for several years. Local voters had made him sheriff from 1854 to 1858, and he ran for that office again in 1866. He had survived two wars without a wound, but one night in 1867 he heard a disturbance outside the jail. As he chased two men across Rose Street, one turned and fired three shots. A bullet entered high in Orcutt's chest and exited near the left shoulder blade. He roused the town and satisfied himself that the jail was secure, then told his wife, "I think he has killed me." He died nine days later at 52.

Many of the older veterans had served their apprenticeship in business before the war. Some were officers during the conflict and moved into responsible positions when they returned. At 39, Dwight May joined the first volunteers with William Shakespeare. His companions elected him captain when they left Kalamazoo. Later he served as lieutenant colonel in the 12th Michigan and was mustered out as a brevetted brigadier general. He turned immediately to politics and the voters sent him to Lansing as lieutenant governor. He went on to serve several terms as attorney general and died in 1880.

Frederick Curtenius carried the honorary title of "Colonel" for his service in the Mexican War. Early in the Civil War he had resigned his commission and come home rather than return escaping slaves in Louisiana. The Michigan Legislature expressed sympathy with his position. He went on to become president of the Kalamazoo City Savings Bank in 1866 and won a State Senate seat in 1867.

In the volatile postwar years thousands of men returned to new opportunities in

After the Civil War, the new "mansard" architectural style ushered in boom times for businessmen. Courtesy, Kalamazoo Public Library.

Kalamazoo ● Factory Smokestacks ● Page 65

their home towns, or moved freely about the country wherever employment or adventure might take them. Industry, bolstered by wartime profits, expanded everywhere. Incomes rose and the townspeople, wondering where the next new factory would appear, looked for new products on storekeeper's shelves. Although agriculture was still important, newspapers measured growth and prosperity in town size and factory employment. Young people thought as often of going to the city for work as they did of going west to homestead.

New times called for new skills. The Fourteenth Amendment strengthened business corporations by affording them due process protection and limited liability. Banking and finance seemed more complex. Industrial processes grew more intricate every year. Local communities tried to make themselves attractive to "visiting capitalists from the East" looking for new locations. Raw materials meant more than markets now, and rail transportation often proved a deciding factor in which areas would benefit from outside capital. But business skills contributed as well. Many young people from farm or village envied the local telegra-

pher, accountant, or bank clerk. The old apprentice system began to break down with postwar changes, because new skills had to be mastered more quickly and efficiently.

Captain William F. Parsons had been studying law at the University of Michigan when the war began. After it was over he went back to Ann Arbor and planned with his brothers to open a "business college" to prepare young people for the rapid industrialization he felt certain would follow the war. When it came time to expand, the family took a hard look at the industrial future of the state. They decided the need for business training was greatest not in Detroit or Chicago, but in the middle-sized communities along the rail lines, which were bursting with energy and enthusiasm and trying to leapfrog their neighbors into prominence. They opened a "Parsons Chain" of business schools in Adrian, Jackson, Marshall, Grand Rapids, and even as far away as frontier Duluth. Not all the schools succeeded, but the Parsons kept trying.

Kalamazoo already supported more institutions of higher learning than anywhere else in Michigan when William Parsons came to town. Undaunted he

Above
Parsons' Business College at the southeast corner of Michigan and Burdick was opened in 1869 by William Parsons. Note the men peering out each of the school's third-story windows. Courtesy, Kalamazoo Public Library.

Right
Parsons' Business College pioneered in equal education for men and women. Upon opening, the school had 45 men and five women enrolled. Courtesy, Kalamazoo Public Library.

Above
Fires often devastated areas of the village in the early days. The destruction seen here was caused by a fire in 1869 in the Pelick Stevens house at right that spread to several other homes on what is now Michigan Avenue at Park Street. Courtesy, Western Michigan University Archives.

Left
By the 1880s the business district was expanding out to Portage and East Michigan, and Parsons' Business College took larger quarters at the corner of Portage and Michigan. Courtesy, Kalamazoo Public Library.

took rooms on the third floor of the "House Block" on the corner of Burdick and Michigan Avenue. He arranged for furnishings and announced that he would open his Business College and Telegraph Institute on December 22, 1869. He offered daily sessions, as well as evening courses for those who were already at work. Full course tuition ran to $40. The shorter "penmanship" program cost $15. Parsons, who learned the elaborate "Spencerian" penmanship from P.R. Spencer himself, would teach all subjects —there were no other instructors. The school opened with 10 students who ignored any thought of Christmas vacation. Word spread quickly and, in a week, the *Telegraph* reported 33 people attending classes. Six months later, the census recorded 314 students in six commercial colleges throughout the state. Parsons's school ranked second with 45 men and five women. He continued to teach all classes himself and reported $1,800 income. In 1873, however, the *Gazette* claimed he had 375 students and a "competent corps of instructors." Parsons believed in "learning by doing" long before Charles Dewey made the expression popular. Students sent telegrams on his private lines, learned branch banking by dealing with Parsons schools in other towns, and generally experienced as much of the real world as possible. By 1880 nearly 1000 had studied under Parsons at one time or another. Parsons might well have taken as his motto Ralph Waldo Emerson's dictum, "Nothing astonishes men so much as common sense and plain dealing."

William K. Kellogg came to Kalamazoo to work in his uncle's broom factory in 1878. He saw no future in the job and enrolled in Parsons's college in 1880. Later he recalled:

> . . . He told the big, red-headed Irishman who ran the college that he wanted a business education but he did not propose to spend years in acquiring it. He was willing to work long and hard hours if there was some way to speed up the educational process. Thereupon the Irishman said, "You take this seat right next to my desk, work like hell, and any time you want to know something or to have more lessons piled upon you, just say the word."

Three months later Kellogg went back to Battle Creek as a qualified accountant.

His certificate indicated he was trained in "Single and Double Entry, Wholesale and Retail, Manufacturing, Banking, Commercial Calculations, Business Correspondence, Deeds and Mortgages."

Parsons carried on his business college for the rest of his life. In 1882 he published a standard textbook of business forms that sold more than 50,000 copies. His son continued the tradition when Captain Parsons died in 1913.

Another Civil War veteran, William J. Handy, wrote down Parsons's census return in 1870 and a great deal of additional information about the town. Kalamazoo's population grew 54 percent in six years and stood at 10,450. Handy found 704 men, 96 women, and 22 "children and youths" working at 109 manufacturing firms.

Census reports showed that several major changes had taken place since 1860. Sawmilling continued first among state industries. It had been important to local farmers and manufacturers for years. In 1870, 25 county mills cut nearly 8 million board feet, but this paled into a mere one-third of one percent of Michigan's output now that vast quantities of northern white pine reached the market. Flour-milling placed third after lumber-milling and blacksmithing. Kalamazoo County, ranking 11th in population, stood third in wheat production, and first in flour with more than a quarter of a million barrels.

The Hunter Woolen Mill in Kalamazoo looked like a Currier and Ives print of village industry, its 16-foot "overshot" waterwheel creaking slowly as the waters of the Portage tumbled over it. Yet two men and a woman, with three children to help, used that power and their own energy to make 20,000 pounds of yarn from the fleece of local sheep. Their output, valued at a dollar a pound, would be second in Michigan only to the great woolen industry of Clinton County.

The Kalamazoo Gas Company produced more illuminating gas from coal than any company outside of Detroit and Grand Rapids. Five men worked at its retorts and the company listed 75,000 bushels of coke and 30 tons of coal tar as by-products.

Most Kalamazoo firms employed one or two people who did their work by hand or with help from horses plodding on the endless tracks of "horsepower" machines. Waterwheels and expensive steam engines appeared about equally

Small buildings on the first block of North Burdick were known collectively as "Asbestos Row" because they escaped frequent downtown fires. This picture was taken in 1879. Courtesy, Western Michigan University Archives.

in Handy's record. Only a handful of companies needed more than a dozen workers.

The Kalamazoo Paper Company kept 20 men, 15 women, and three children busy making 500 tons of printing paper worth $240 a ton. Jeremiah Woodbury, Allen Potter, and a number of prominent businessmen organized the firm in 1866. They located on the Portage south of town where Cork Street crosses the creek. There they invested $80,000 in mill and equipment. Samuel Gibson came in 1868 to provide the technical knowledge. He found the Portage location quite suitable. Two high-speed "turbine" wheels provided 100 horsepower from the creek. The

pure water so far from the village meant the paper would be clean and white. Gibson needed wheat straw as a major ingredient and found ample supplies nearby. Handy recorded that the company used 500 tons of straw, 350 tons of rags, and 85 tons of wastepaper as raw materials. This firm reorganized after a major fire in 1872 and became one of Michigan's leading makers of fine book paper. By 1880 the Kalamazoo Paper Company had 100 people at work. A regular community of several hundred people developed around the plant, which could now produce as much as six to eight tons of fine paper a day. Early members of this pioneer company, such as Benjamin Lyon, George Bar-

Cigar making was an important local industry for many years. Lilie's Cigar Factory was located on East Michigan near Portage. Courtesy, Kalamazoo Public Library.

firm, too, had grown rapidly, and George Dodge was about to sell his share in the business to William Tomlinson. Handy reported that "Dodge, Kimball & Austin" made $50,000 worth of farm tools and four steam engines worth $1,000 each. In the process they melted and poured nearly 600 tons of iron.

Among the newer and more specialized firms that characterized Kalamazoo's postwar manufacturing, Handy listed two cigarmakers. Lilienfeld Brothers and Kepler & Company hired 31 men to produce over a million handmade cigars at four cents each. The Kalamazoo Morocco Factory tanned 30,000 skins of special shoe and book leathers from local sheepskins.

As important as industry seemed to many people, the Telegraph editor could not help remarking that the new Morocco Factory left something to be desired. He noted that "a tannery is not a delightfully odorous establishment, that's true, but morocco boots and shoes are quite refreshing, as well as shiny, and beautiful book bindings we all like to look at." Six women sewed up wet sheepskins ready for the tanning vats. It seemed to the Telegraph editor that their working conditions were not appealing and their piece-work rate discouraging. "If, therefore, a woman works steadily from morning till night, and is pretty skillful with her needle," he wrote, "she will earn $4 a week, almost enough to pay for her board, without taking into consideration her lights, fuel, and lodging." The editor added ominously, "these she must provide for by other means." He went on to note that Susan B. Anthony would speak on "Work and Wages" a few days later and asked whether she could find "some promise of a better time coming" to offer women who worked six days to board for seven.

Local wages did compare favorably with those in other counties. Unskilled laborers worked for $1.50 a day. Women domestics took home $5 a week if they boarded themselves. Farmhands received $18 a month and board. Construction wages reflected the business boom. Carpenters worked for $3 a day, the second highest wage in Michigan. Masons earned as much as $4. Prices kept pace with wages. Apples sold for 50 cents a bushel and potatoes for 65 cents. Ham cost 18 cents a pound and chicken 13 cents.

Kalamazoo papers began 1870 by declaring that "the streets were never fuller—

deen, and even Gibson himself, went on, in later years, to head paper companies of their own.

Kalamazoo's two largest employers— the Lawrence & Chapin iron works and the Dodge plow factory—located downtown. Sights and sounds and smells from their foundries were part of downtown life for years. The Lawrence & Chapin iron works stood on the corner of Rose and Water streets. William S. Lawrence and Dr. L.C. Chapin, "two of our most wide awake and enterprising citizens," as the Telegraph put it, came to Kalamazoo in 1867, quite by chance on the same train. Lawrence, an experienced iron manufacturer from Plattsburg, New York, bought out a struggling local firm in 1868 and Dr. Chapin joined him in 1870. The new company engaged architect L.D. Grosvenor to design new shops along Water from Rose to Church. Handy reported that the foundry was one of the largest in Michigan with 40 workers running six lathes and assorted drills, cutters, planers, and bandsaws. Lawrence & Chapin turned 265 tons of iron into steam engines and agricultural implements worth $40,000.

Even more men worked at the old Dodge plow factory a block up Rose. This

more busy," and "the business of Kalamazoo was never more prosperous." But by fall local residents began to wonder. Word of census returns from other towns suggested the village slept while others grew. Kalamazoo and Grand Rapids were comparable in 1860; Kalamazoo grew much more rapidly during the Civil War. Local "boomers" trembled six years later. Kalamazoo had increased 54 percent, but Grand Rapids nearly doubled and Jackson did double its population to more than 11,000. Any hopes that Kalamazoo might continue as the "inland metropolis" of western Michigan quickly faded. For reasons local residents never fully understood, Grand Rapids claimed the title by an unbelievable margin. At the state census in 1874, Kalamazoo showed a 12 percent increase, but Jackson marked 21 percent, and Grand Rapids 57 percent. In the 20 years following the Civil War, Kalamazoo doubled its population and called itself America's largest village, but Grand Rapids increased nearly fivefold to 42,000 by 1884, far outstripping any rival. Perhaps the new north-south rail lines and the rail link with Jackson had helped, or the

proximity to the pinelands might have proved critical in a "wooden age." But more likely, Grand Rapids's location at the finest waterpower site in Michigan contributed most.

The *Gazette* and the *Telegraph* editors blamed local businessmen. Both papers launched a long-running denunciation of capitalists squeezing their three percent from rentals and taking their profits from local workers. Investors ignored the community's need to outbid rivals for new factories. Local people, said the editors, must offer land and buildings and stock subscriptions. Who would improve Kalamazoo's waterpower with a long millrace from Comstock to downtown? Who would develop a "Trans-Portage" industrial park? The *Telegraph* editor said that "if we would make this a good business point, we *must encourage* MANUFACTORIES. This will bring in men and enhance the value of our property." Yet the Michigan Central repair shops went to Jackson with 1,000 workmen, and the Singer Company located in South Bend with hundreds more. Grand Rapids won a railroad-car factory and the Studebaker

Successful businessmen like Charles Barrett and planing-mill owner Rufus Tyler built Italianate villas at the edge of town. These two homes on the corner of Douglas and West Main were completed in 1871. Courtesy, Kalamazoo Public Library.

Wagon Works failed to move to Kalamazoo, even after a $100,000 stock offer. The *Telegraph* took to calling the village "Sleepy Hollow," and complained that local people coldshouldered visiting businessmen. In one series of articles praising local industry the editor wrote openly that "we may as well meet the fact squarely. We *must* take interest in our manufactures, build them up and increase or be content to have Kalamazoo a sleepy country village, without life or importance."

When townspeople proposed a new railroad, the "Kalamazoo, Lowell & Northern," to tap the pinelands, sash-and-doormaker William Dewing said the real issue was "whether we shall be a great manufacturing city—as great as any in the nation, or dwindle into a small, insignificant town like Paw Paw." Indeed, if Kalamazoo failed to attract more factories, if the village didn't wake up, "mercantile death" would make a booming market for William Clark's new casket factory. David Fisher later wrote a detailed history of the county. Now he described Kalamazoo as "a beautiful town, with plenty of pretty women, splendid bur-oaks, and elegant houses with well

kept lawns,—a religious town, a literary town and all that." But this wasn't enough for the new age. He went on to say that "our women wear beautiful white dresses, and our men always have clean shirts on." As the *Telegraph* put it, Kalamazoo's problem was, "Too Much Clean Linen and Too Little Factory Smoke!" Fervently echoing popular feelings, Fisher said that "he wished to God that the smoke from the soft coal burned in factories would so fill the air as to make it impossible to keep those dresses and shirts in such a painful state of cleanliness."

Yet perhaps the papers painted too bleak a picture. Not every town could be Grand Rapids. Throughout the 19th century, the majority of Michigan's factories located in smaller towns than Kalamazoo. In an age of rapid industrialization, everyone might find work easily enough. The *Telegraph* finally admitted that fault-finding proved not only inaccurate but bad for business. During the national economic crisis in 1873, the editor wrote that Kalamazooans should "beware of the croaker. He is a walking, talking embodiment of the green and yellow melancholy." Far better to report on young la-

This board sidewalk and wooden fence surrounded Bronson Park in the 1870s. Courtesy, Kalamazoo Public Library.

dies hosting "Panic Parties" than on firms going bankrupt. The *Gazette* agreed to look on the bright side, and both papers began to take note of local prosperity. They found many firms developing successful products and continuing to expand. New companies still came to town in surprising numbers.

Perhaps the Lawrence & Chapin iron works showed the local optimism most forcefully. Initial success after 1870 led to major expansion two years later. Twenty-five-year-old Calvin Forbes built the three-story front addition measuring 67 feet along Rose and 80 feet on Water. It towered 100 feet to the colorful slate roof and cupola. The *Telegraph* called it, "by far the most imposing and handsome front in Kalamazoo," counting a million and a half bricks in the walls and more than 50,-000 feet of floor space. Three steam elevators carried men and machines from floor to floor. The cupola, making the building much taller than any other in the downtown area, let observers stand for the first time on a level with the church spires and offered "a magnificent and far-reaching view."

Workmen enclosed the last of the new

addition November 11, 1872, just in time for Lawrence & Chapin to open the building to 300 guests at a great ball. The *Telegraph* reported that "no pleasanter party, certainly none on so grand a scale, has ever been given in Kalamazoo." The front office, gleaming in black and white walnut and plate glass, seemed more fit for a "metropolitan bank" than for "the soot and grime which one expects to find around a foundry and machine shop." On this night borrowed rugs, furniture, and wall hangings turned it into a reception room for the ladies. The rest of the first floor was given to banquet tables for a late supper hosted by the Burdick Hotel. The second floor served as "an elegant parlor." Delos Phillips sent a grand piano from his music store, the Ladies' Library loaned oil paintings, and the Knights Templar hung banners. The whole of the third story became a dance floor spacious enough for 200 to 300 people at a time. Guests came from Marshall, Battle Creek, Paw Paw, Dowagiac, and surrounding villages. The newspaper noted "the pretty faces, the happy moods, and the general enjoyment" of everyone concerned.

But parties gave way to production. By

Trees still grew along East Michigan in the 1870s. Courtesy, Kalamazoo Public Library.

1874 the company kept 60 to 100 men making steam engines, circle and "mullay" sawmills, plows, cultivators, scrapers, horsepower machines, wood-sawing machinery, iron fences, and ornamental ironwork. Thomas Clarage headed the main shop filled with "the latest mechanical inventions," including six big lathes and a variety of planing mills and power drills. The blacksmith shop reflected modern and labor-saving changes as well. Henry Wadsworth Longfellow's "Village Blacksmith" had swung his sledge,

"With measured beat and slow
Like a sexton rings the village bell,
When the evening sun is low."

Lawrence & Chapin's steam hammer delivered 3,000-pound blows 200 times a minute and did the work of 10 blacksmiths. The molding shop poured 3,000 pounds of iron a day in 1874 and could easily handle three-ton castings. The firm specialized in particularly hard "chilled iron" plows, adding a piece of cold scrap iron to the mold just before they poured to achieve the special strength. In 1874 they bought rights to a crystallizing process that allowed them to cast a very tough "diamond iron" plow, which took a special medal at the State Fair that year.

Kimball & Austin's buildings covered the square block west of Rose from Eleanor to Kalamazoo. One hundred and twenty men worked for the company in 1874 and the *Telegraph* reported a "red-hot business" of more than $150,000 a year. The firm seemed bigger every year, adding working space and building most of its own machinery. One home-built lathe, largest in outstate Michigan, could turn 15-ton flywheels 30 feet in diameter to perfect dimensions. The casting for this giant weighed 20 tons, largest in Kalamazoo's history when poured in 1872.

Pride of the shop was "The Flower of the West," the company's 80-horsepower steam engine. It sat in a separate whitewashed room "clean as a parlor." Engineer Charles Gady kept its brightwork polished and decorated it with fresh flowers. Built by Superintendent W.H. Gibson, it ran 500 feet of line shafting at a cost of 30 cents an hour. Gibson designed a half-stroke cutoff system that let the company increase or decrease power as necessary. With this power the firm produced steam engines, sawmills, and farming implements. Its plows were used to grade the Union Pacific roadbed from Omaha to Promontory Point in Utah. Brigham Young sent repeated orders and seemed to the local reporter "as extensive a farmer and merchant as he is a husband." A rush of orders kept the company running day and night and allowed President William Tomlinson to declare a 10 percent dividend in 1874.

The state census taker asked everyone what they did for a living that year. More than 8,500 people in Kalamazoo County answered with 268 separate occupations. The census taker recorded what he heard without analysis so the job descriptions have little statistical value, but they do suggest the increasing job specialization as seen by workers themselves. Half of the respondents said they were farmers or farm laborers. Another 1,200 admitted to day labor. Others ranged from 14 bakers, 12 bankers, and 27 barbers, through 49 clergymen, 40 gardeners, 87 grocers, and 57 millers, as well as weavers, well-diggers, whitewashers, and woodcarvers. Nearly 300 men worked as carpenters. Thirty-seven kept saloons and 17 claimed to be telegraphers.

One man, Henry Stockton, said he was "Superintendent of a Clothespin Factory." None of the concerns that Kalamazoo's boosters tried to entice caused such excitement and stirred such praise of automation as Stockton's Rockford Clothespin Company. The story had all the elements of romance and lost nothing in the telling. There was the lucky inventor, Chicago money, early successes, towns competing for the new factory, night watchmen guarding wonderful machines, piles of logs in the yard, whirling blades, tumbling pins, neat packages tied with wire. Something of Kalamazoo's enthusiasm over the very idea of industrialization emerges from the "clothespin story."

Published accounts described Rockford businessman H.P. Stockton's visit to the clothespin exhibit at a New England county fair. He came home with a sample and thought of promising improvements. With $10,000 he began a factory and found more demand for his pins than he had imagined possible. But the wood he needed cost $28 per thousand feet in Illinois. Chicago backers suggested he locate closer to timberland. Jackson promised a great deal of money, but Kalamazoo offered land with east-west and north-south rail ties and $3,000 in stock subscriptions, as well as wood at $8 a thousand. In May 1873, the new plant was ready to open. The Rockford Company, located on the block between Frank and North streets, had easy access to all three railroads. The *Gazette* quickly pointed out that 70 men could work at 50 different machines in the new brick building. Lawrence & Chapin built a 125-horsepower steam engine for power, and by August the firm was producing a varied line:

. . . hoe handles, broom handles, paint, lather, and tumbler brush handles, and long handles for brushes varying from 4½ to 12 feet in length, fork handles of various lengths, besides the clothespins, of which three kinds are manufactured—the ordinary round pin, the "Rockford" pin and the "Kalamazoo pin," which latter is square, and made on a patent belonging to the company.

Local people marveled at the ease with which the company's machinery turned green logs fresh from the country into finished products. Basswood, maple, cherry, beech, elm, and ash logs went to the handle lathes, one of which could turn 10,000 handles every day. Beechwood blocks were shunted off to the clothespin works where a variety of saws and shapers formed and headed the pins, and prepared the slots, almost automatically. Each pin-maker expected to turn 17,000 per day. Dried in steam-heated kilns for half a day, the pins went to huge tumbling machines that whirled so rapidly the pins came out glass-smooth by friction alone. Waste sawdust and scrap fueled the engine, and Kimball & Austin bought any surplus for their own boilers. By 1874 the company could ship four carloads of pins and handles every week. If the clothespin market slowed in the next years, the handle business flourished and the company reported one order in 1875 for 2 million hoe handles.

While the newspapers boasted that Kalamazoo had won the Rockford Company in 1873, another new firm announced its general line of "plain turned work." Unlike Henry Stockton, young Calvin Forbes grew up in the village. He studied at Parsons Business College and joined his father as a building contractor. But this was an age when every young man hoped to become a "Captain of Industry," or, as one humorist put it, at least a "corporal." Just after Forbes finished the new Lawrence & Chapin Block, he announced that he was putting up a factory for himself. He talked two of his neighbors, Darius Beebe and Oscar Cornell, into backing him and organized the Kalamazoo Handle Manufacturing Company. He chose a site across the Portage on Third Street where he would have access to the Grand Rapids & Indiana Railroad track, bought a 60-horsepower engine from Kimball & Austin, and prepared to hire 20 hands. *Gazette* editor A.J.

Shakespeare, who liked "goaheaditiveness" in any form, said Forbes's company was "just what Kalamazoo needs to make her prosperous." Forbes found handlemaking as profitable as the Rockford Company did. His double circular sawmill cut 15,000 feet of walnut and ash per day for "ball-bats, mallet handles, gymnastic-clubs, and ax, hammer, pick, sledge, and adz-handles, neck-yokes, buggy-yokes, wagon and buggy single-trees, etc." Still Forbes looked for a product that would set his firm apart from competitors. He found that product in "Croquet," the new game just introduced from France after the Civil War. He installed a special lathe, which the *Telegraph* insisted could be found in but one other factory in the country. Then he set about to put "Kalamazoo Croquet" sets in every home in the country. In 1874 the company operated night and day but found itself four months behind in deliveries. By 1876 the *Telegraph* reported the "heavy demand for Kalamazoo Croquet" was such that the company had become "the wildest shipper in this place," sending its goods at the rate of a carload a day even as far as Germany.

The *Telegraph* editor reported that the ball-turning lathes were "the very poetry of machine-work and a sight worth going a long way to see." Each worker could turn 11 perfectly round balls from a single block of wood in just two minutes. The finished balls rolled off to the painting rooms where they were striped in eight different colors by other marvelous machines. The rage for croquet increased every season until it seemed, in 1876, "the most popular of all outdoor amusements." As often happened, success brought reorganization and outside money. Early in 1876 Boston manufacturer Hale Page moved to Kalamazoo with "ample capital." He reorganized the company with himself as president. Battle Creek banker R.P. Kingman joined him as vice-president. A.C. Wortley, a merchant with 20 years' experience, served as treasurer. Calvin Forbes remained as secretary and superintendent.

In the spring of 1876, the *Telegraph* looked not just at the "poetry" of machines or the technicalities of reorganization. The editor thought even more of the effect of prosperous factories on the town itself. "Employment," "markets," "new wealth," and "resources" swirled through his accounts. He was sure that such investors were "the real benefactors of a town, for they foster its best interest and make its best and healthiest growth."

Americans found time for taking stock in 1876. The economy showed signs of recovery from the Panic of 1873, but President Grant's administration was rocked with scandal. Local papers carried con-

Calvin Forbes' Kalamazoo Handle Manufacturing Company did much to popularize the game of "croquet." As this lithograph illustrates, croquet courts appeared in the country as quickly as in the towns. Courtesy, Western Michigan University Archives.

stant reminders that this was the nation's Centennial year. Nostalgia gripped the country, "The Mania for 'Antiques' still Rules the Fashionable World," said the *Telegraph* as people dusted off attic relics. Pioneer societies formed to probe their own beginnings. "It is hardly possible to overestimate the importance and value of this suggestion if faithfully carried out," said the *Telegraph,* adding that it would provide "a fund of local history not possessed by any people on earth." Indeed, the editor said again, in an article titled "For the Year 1976," that every householder should "collect articles for relics, and preserve them for those who will represent their families when 1976 comes around." Family records, photographs, and descriptions of places, events, and ways of doing things, "would possess a fascinating interest at the next Centennial."

Governor John Bagley underscored the Centennial's meaning for Michigan with a special proclamation in which he said:

The lapse of time, the demands of business, the new life we are living, all tend to forgetfulness of the old time, and of the history our fathers made. . . . Have we not forgotten, in the hurry and strife of our money-getting, in the rapidity with which events have crowded upon one another in these latter days, the blessings that have come to us from the past, and the debt we owe it? Have we not taken the good that has come to us as rewards of our own merit, rather than the hard earnings of the early builders? Are we not growing thoughtless of our country, its institutions and government, and careless of its perpetuity?

Bagley went on to note that five out of six Michigan schools failed to teach American history, and the Centennial celebration might be an occasion to remember the past so that "we need not fear for the future." Local communities formed committees and drew up plans all across the state. Calvin Forbes and A.C. Wortley joined William Lawrence, L.C. Chapin, Delos Phillips, W.H. Gibson, William Shakespeare, and other prominent businessmen on a special executive board to prepare for the Centennial Fourth of July.

But the Centennial for most Americans meant just one thing—the great exposition in Fairmount Park outside Philadelphia. President Grant officially opened the Exposition on May 10, speaking so softly that

A. C. WORTLEY,

Dealer in

WALTHAM & ELGIN

American Watches,

RICH JEWELRY,

STERLING SILVER-WARE,

Coin Spoons and Forks,

Wedding Presents,	Birthday Presents,
French Clocks,	Bronzes, Vases,
Fancy Goods,	Fine Table Cutlery,
Castors,	Tea Sets,
OPERA GLASSES,	SPECTACLES,

few of the 50,000 on the grounds paid attention. Then he led a grand procession through the Main Exhibit Building and Machinery Hall, the two largest buildings in the world. Between May and November, the exhibition managers recorded eight million paid admissions at 50 cents each and another two million free passes. Kalamazoo papers published regular accounts by local visitors, explaining the intricacies of transportation, food, and lodging, and providing a running commentary on the various exhibits. Local people could board special Pullman Palace Cars on Saturday evening and travel direct to the Centennial Station by Monday morning ready for at least a week of sightseeing. Early visitors like A.C. Wortley quickly sensed that this was more than entertainment, it was a school of America's "mechanic's arts." Machinery Hall drew crowds every day. A quarter-mile long, with 14 acres of floor space, it seemed just like a factory with its whirring machines driven by the giant 1,400-horsepower Cor-

Prominent merchant A.C. Wortley advertised his fine jewelry and other wares in 1869. Wortley's Jewelry Store was located at the corner of Main and Burdick Streets. Courtesy, Western Michigan University Archives.

In the 1870s it took an occasion like the Fourth of July to bring this many buggies to Main Street. Courtesy, Kalamazoo Public Library.

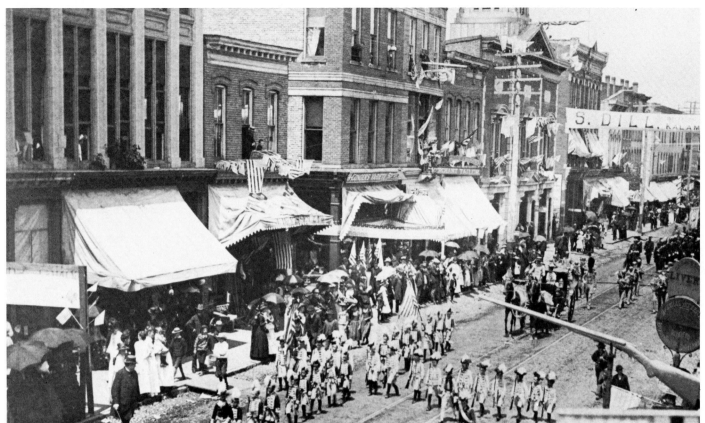

liss Engine. One correspondent wrote that he would rather have the "mechanical skill" of Mr. Corliss than be governor of Michigan. Surely this engine alone would make the designer's name immortal. Spectators viewed 1,851 exhibits in this building, most of which were operating with power from two miles of line shaft connected to the Corliss Engine.

Perhaps no one saw all 31,489 displays, and many people found transportation difficult (though one awed observer noted that trains and trolleys brought twice the population of Detroit into the grounds on "Pennsylvania Day"). Some complained that nearby hotels charged $5 a day and food was priced high. Michigan's own building, finished with 14 native hardwoods, did not open until July 16, and firstcomers found nowhere to rest or register. Many visitors overlooked three of the most significant exhibits: the telephone, the electric carbon arc light, and the portable electric motor in Machinery Hall. Nevertheless most felt, as S.B. McCracken said in *Michigan at the Centennial,* that they had been "pilgrims at the shrine of the Centennial."

Kalamazoo planned its own celebration for the Fourth of July. The committee did its work well. Bands were readied, parade routes drawn, houses and business blocks decorated, and speeches writ-

ten. A 100-voice choir was formed and young ladies wore new dresses, and flowers in their hair. One observer reported:

The morning opened with the booming of cannon, the firing of musketry, and of small guns and firecrackers, the ringing of bells, sounding of whistles, etc. Young America was too exuberant with patriotism and love of noise to sleep himself, or let others enjoy the luxury of rest. At an early hour people began to arrive in teams, and by trains, from all directions, and the busy note of preparation for the big procession went forward, and the town presented not only a gala appearance, but a very stirring and busy one.

Promptly at 11 a.m., Delos Phillips led the parade up Michigan Avenue from Pitcher—a quarter-mile-long procession that wound its way for two hours from street to street accompanied by local bands, flower-decked wagons with young ladies representing states and territories, and even the old stagecoach from pioneer days. Speeches occupied the middle of the day, and people gathered again at four in the afternoon for band concerts, an "historical address" by Dr. Foster Pratt, and a grand chorus of "Auld Lang Syne."

The Fourth of July brought many parades like this one on South Burdick. Courtesy, Kalamazoo Public Museum.

Kalamazoo windmills like Phelps & Bigelow's "IXL" once dotted the landscape nationwide. Courtesy, Kalamazoo Public Library.

Not everyone went to town that day. In Schoolcraft Mary Barney's husband promised to take her, but went by himself instead. She wrote in her diary that night: "The 100th Anniversary of Independence has come and gone. It has been very quiet here—a great many have gone to Kalamazoo." Mary went about her chores, visited in the evening, and ended her entry for the day, by observing:

I hope we as a people will begin our next century with the sure purpose of overcoming our faults and living more plainly and rationally than we have ever done. If wrong and injustice could only be put down that are now rampant in high places, if merit could be rewarded and the wrong doers be punished, we might hope for better days and brighter prospects. God grant his blessing on this nation now and in the coming centuries.

Back in Kalamazoo, people gathered again for fireworks at dusk. They watched Rockets, Stars, Serpents, Gold Rain, exploding mines, and bursting bombshells. "Letters of Fire" spelled out "Peace, Pros-

perity, Freedom: the Result of 100 Years." The 33 displays ended at ten o'clock and an hour later all special trains had left and the streets were emptying. By midnight, according to the committee's final report:

the town, so full of noise and bustle and enthusiasm during the day, sank at last to rest.

Thus, without an accident to mar the pleasure, or a delay in the execution of the programme to vex patience, the day passed, delightfully, from sunrise to midnight; and thus, auspiciously, did the people of Kalamazoo celebrate the first and welcome the second century of our National Existence.

Some of the Centennial excitement carried over into business affairs. Local papers reported great demand for farming tools. Nathaniel Chase now made more fanning mills than any other firm in the country, sending 11 carloads in one 10-day period to Ohio alone. Prairie farming brought new interest in windmills, and the *Telegraph* soon claimed Kalamazoo outstripped all competitors with their new "Wind Engines." Merrill & McCourtie's flour mills averaged eight carloads of flour, feed, and grain per day. Dudgeon & Cobb planned to buy one million pounds of wool. L.G. Bragg's Union Nursery on Oakland Drive was now the largest in the state with one million apple trees in stock. The three railroads handled 6,000 carloads of freight in the first third of 1876 and sold 10,631 tickets to passengers. Railroad sidings served 21 firms, and no town did more business for its size. The Michigan Central said two million pounds of freight entered or left Kalamazoo each month on their track alone. More than 60 trains a day passed through town, clanging bells and whistling at every crossing. The "music of the engines" sounded a wild, erratic chorus. Some companies mounted whistles and others chimes, but each "blew its own horn" several times a day, led by Kimball & Austin's whistle, which echoed 12 to 14 miles around the countryside. One proud resident declared that "our manufacturers are enterprising businessmen, who understand what the world wants and the best way to make it."

Perhaps nothing in Kalamazoo's business picture signaled the rush to new products as lustily as the Eagle Portland Cement Factory. All through 1876 both papers published one story after another about this fledgling company. Beginning

in February with the announcement of the building and machinery contracts, the *Telegraph* kept watch as Bush & Paterson built the buildings well out on Kalamazoo's "north side" and Kimball & Austin installed equipment. Local people believed with some justification that this would be America's first commercially profitable Portland cement works. Some years later Michigan developed a very promising cement industry. Now, in the summer of 1876, the Eagle plant went into operation, mining raw material near Spring Lake Park and trundling it across the river on a specially built tramway. In the plant a huge mixer ground the cement and forced it into cakes, which were baked in super-heated kilns by steam and burning coal tar. By year's end the company was sending four to five carloads a week to Chicago.

The *Telegraph* reported with great excitement that this new product might be adapted to uses beyond the traditional mortar. Banker William Wood poured a cement floor in the basement of his new house on South Street in 1877. He also experimented with cast concrete panels in his porch and even tried cement sidewalks. Wool merchant Stephen Cobb soon had 1,300 feet of the new walks on his extensive property at the corner of Michigan Avenue and Westnedge. Local enthusiasm proved prophetic, though the Eagle factory failed in the 1880s. By 1896 American plants produced one million barrels of Portland cement. Ten years later annual production reached 50 million barrels and the "Age of Cement" arrived at last.

The *Telegraph* conducted a housing survey in 1876, finding rental property at a premium. Residential building boomed, particularly in the Vine Street neighborhood. Many new families came to town who were not simply transients looking for work. They looked for a quality of life that went beyond factory whistles and freight rates. Where else would such families find a permanent croquet field on the courthouse lawn, or 1,000 swimmers on the

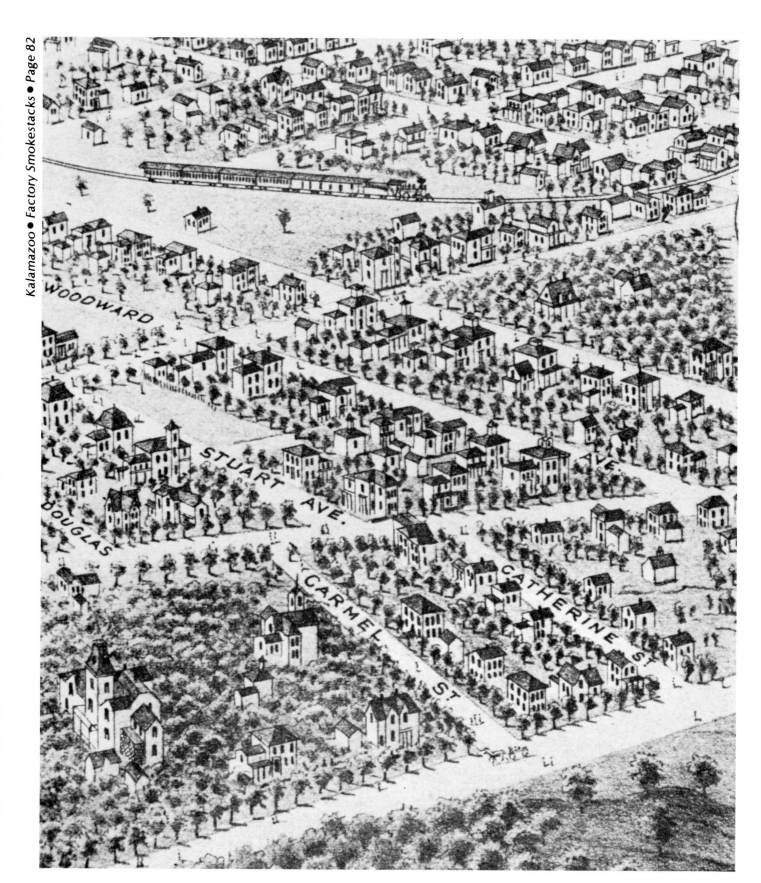

This 1874 drawing of the
suburban west side of Kalamazoo
shows Italian "villas" on Carmel,
Elm, and Woodward. Courtesy,
Western Michigan University
Archives.

banks of the Kalamazoo? The foundries might be noisy, but didn't Channing Underwood keep a hundred canaries, mocking birds, bobolinks, goldfinches and orioles singing in his shirt factory? Hadn't the Fish Commission stocked Spring Brook with 40,000 salmon? Since 1869 a deep well and steam pumps provided perhaps the purest running water in Michigan. The Village installed more than 100 gas lamps and wood block "Nicholson" paving on downtown streets. The gas company maintained 15 miles of gas line for residential customers. Where else in Michigan could newcomers find so many academies, colleges, and seminaries? The famous "Kalamazoo Case" established the right of local communities to have "public" high schools and professional school administrations.

Kalamazoo offered cultural opportunities few outstate towns could match. In addition to home-town bands and home-made theatricals by a local civic theater club, the "Argonauts," Kalamazoo hosted many traveling groups as well. The famous Theodore Thomas brought his 50-piece symphony orchestra several times. The Boston Philharmonic Club, the Mendelssohn Quintette, and the Jubilee Singers all performed in the 1870s. An Italian opera company gave *Il Trovatore,* and an English company presented *H.M.S. Pinafore.* Mark Twain spoke on *Roughing It.* Frederick Douglass came, and the violinist Ole Bull. When Anton Rubinstein treated villagers to a special concert in 1873, the

Telegraph said "such playing never was before heard or ever will be again."

The Ladies' Library Association sponsored many events. This group met informally in the 1840s. When Lucinda Stone, Ruth Webster, Mrs. Milo Goss, and a number of other women officially organized with a board of directors in 1852, they constituted the first such group in Michigan and the third in the United States. Members held meetings in various places around the village for the next 25 years. They accumulated a circulating library of several thousand books long before the village opened a public library in 1872. They also brought together a number of sculptures, paintings, and natural-history displays. In the 1860s and 1870s the group sponsored several public lecture series on history, literature, and travel. In 1878 they offered a benefit "Phonograph Concert" to introduce townspeople to Thomas Edison's "Talking Machine." The Association held an elaborate reunion reported by the *Telegraph* in 1877. Lucinda Stone and Ruth Webster were the two charter members still in Kalamazoo. Mrs. Stone gave the history of the group and described "the school of culture it had proved to many." She commented on the artwork, the casts of the Venus de Milo and Apollo Belvedere, the popular "Rogers Groups," the careful copies of European masters, all of which made the clubroom a "hall of the arts."

Later the *Detroit Post and Tribune*

Below left
The fashionable interior of merchant Stephen Cobb's home is pictured here about 1880. Courtesy, Western Michigan University Archives.

Below
Kalamazoo's Union School building made city residents proud. The "Kalamazoo school case" authorized the use of tax money for the establishment of high schools in 1872. Courtesy, Western Michigan University Archives.

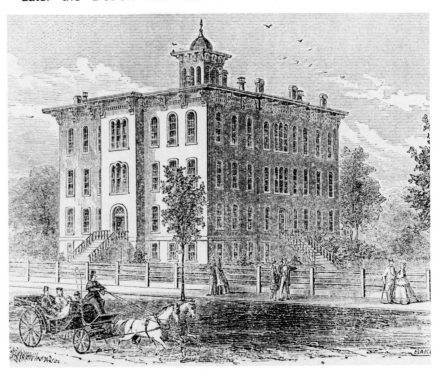

The 1880 county history contained this drawing of the new Ladies' Library Association building. Chicago architect Henry Gay designed the Venetian Gothic structure which was formally opened on May 20, 1879. Courtesy, Western Michigan University Archives.

reported:

> The library parlors in Kalamazoo are in themselves a means of culture both of the taste and intelligence of the ladies who weekly assemble there. The walls are covered with maps, drawings, engravings, and beautiful paintings. . . . There is a real culture in the very atmosphere of these rooms as well as in the literary entertainments of the club meetings, or in the results of study every week presented there.

Mrs. Bayard Clark, a fashionable visitor from North Carolina, found the Association remarkable. She wrote that "all the young girls attend these meetings, or classes, and grow up in an atmosphere of progressive thought, in which they seem to imbibe literary and scientific information, and become insensibly well-read and well-informed women." She went on to describe her visit to the town, adding breezily:

> I often wonder where the poor people live, for I have seen none but comfortable and few but pretty residences, and there are no people from whom a supply of domestic ser-

vice can be drawn; the consequence is, that many, even wealthy, ladies keep no servants, but do their own work, and prepare all the meals of the family in the nicest and cosiest of kitchens, many of which are really elegant in their appointments. How they can do this and yet find time not only to visit and receive company, but also to read and prepare papers on history, science, and art, to be read at their club, is mysterious to me.

In 1878 the Ladies' Library Association began its own building on South Park Street, the first time in the country that a woman's organization had done so. They paid Chicago architect Henry Gay $75 to draw up plans in the new "Venetian Gothic" style. Frederick Bush agreed to build the new meeting rooms for $8,000. On May 20, 1879, villagers turned out for the formal opening. The governor sent congratulations, and Frederick Curtenius gave the major address. He had been the main speaker when the Association sponsored Kalamazoo's Quarter-Centennial Celebration in 1854. Now he talked about the leavening effect the group had on the community as a whole. The new building of-

Above
The Ladies' Library Association building on South Park Street was lavishly decorated as indicated by this 1879 photograph. Many of the books, paintings, and sculpture remain today. Courtesy, Western Michigan University Archives.

Left
A pioneer who became a distinguished community leader, Colonel Frederick Curtenius served in both the Mexican War and the Civil War. Courtesy, Western Michigan University Archives.

Above
The sun shines on a quiet late afternoon on Main Street in the 1870s. Courtesy, Kalamazoo Public Library.

Right
Until the Academy of Music was completed in 1882, the auditorium of the Ladies' Library Association provided the town with its best meeting place. Courtesy, Western Michigan University Archives.

Facing page
The New York *Daily Graphic* published these drawings of Kalamazoo buildings to accompany an 1878 article praising the city as "one of the most attractive towns in Michigan, and, indeed, in the country." Courtesy, Kalamazoo Public Museum.

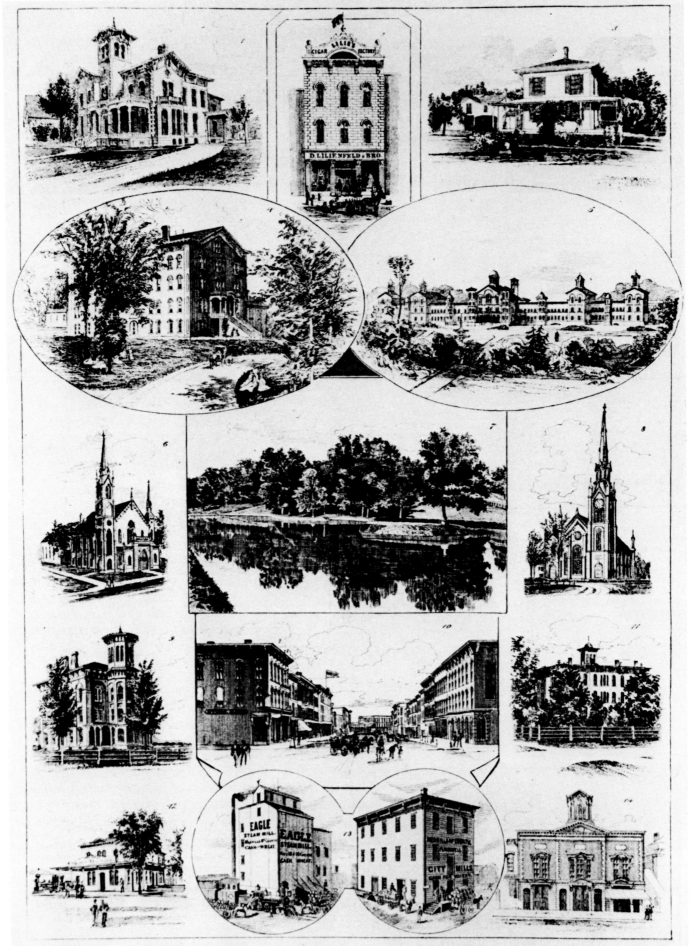

This early photographic view of Kalamazoo's south side was taken when the town was called the "Burr Oak Village." Courtesy, Western Michigan University Archives.

fered a library of 3,000 volumes, an art gallery, and a 30-by-60-foot auditorium with stage—the best such formal meeting place in town.

"The Big Village" bustled in 1879. A wave of prosperity swept the country, carrying Kalamazoo with it. European markets seemed eager for local products. The Centennial gave Americans a chance to look backward but also toward a brighter future. Even the local pioneer society praised both the past and progress. In December 1879, the whole county basked in self-congratulation when the Everts & Abbott publishing house of Philadelphia sent Samuel Durant to Kalamazoo to prepare the first great history of the county. He received such enthusiastic support from local residents that the projected 400-page "royal octavo volume" ballooned to more than 550 pages. A corps of writers, "viewers," and artists traveled from town to town soliciting subscribers. For a fee any family might find a place in history, and for a larger fee secure engravings of neat farmsteads and gracious village homes. Later historians treated these lavish histories lightly, but people at the time responded to them with pride. Here, as Durant would say, was the one great chance to search out events of the last half-century —"a thousand and one matters" he could "put into permanent shape for preservation." Durant relied heavily on local people whom he acknowledged profusely, including Anson Van Buren, William Shakespeare, Frederick Curtenius, George Torrey, and many others, as well as "officers of the Ladies' Association, bankers, merchants, and manufacturers generally. . . ." In addition to an exhaustive retelling of pioneer experiences, Durant was careful to pay tribute to Kalamazoo's present circumstances in the most reassuring fashion. He commented that the village location was "among the finest in the State or country," adding that "its surroundings are worthy of a great city, which it promises someday to become." In a self-evident catalog of "Progress," he listed its other attributes:

its telephonic communications; its water-works; its brilliant gas-lights; its public buildings; its opera-house; its police and fire departments; its great libraries; its smoking manufactories; its extensive wholesale houses; its

HARDWARE

IRON, STEEL & NAILS

HOME INSURANCE CO. N.Y.
CAPITAL TWO MILLION DOLLARS

Parsons, Wood & Phelps.

L.L. CLARK & Co. M. COHN.

L.A. Carder & Sons.

BOOTS

ample caravanseries; its paved streets; its beautiful rural cemeteries; its palatial private dwellings; its famous fair-grounds and trotting-parks; its fountains and statuary; its score of churches; its crowded schools; and its flourishing weekly and daily newspapers.

Who could disagree when he found that "its fine business blocks of stone, brick and marble; its broad streets, and general air of thrift and cultivation, make an exceedingly favorable impression upon the stranger and traveler"? Local residents could easily applaud this outsider when he judged that "its desirableness as a place of residence, with all its accompaniment of civilization and luxury, is hardly surpassed by any place of a similar population in the Union." A "county history" was, indeed, a marvelous work, particularly when the historian reached such gratifying conclusions. Local readers might even accept Durant's

occasional criticism, particularly when he couched it so carefully in his concluding line: "With the addition of street railways, solid sidewalks in place of wood, and a new courthouse worthy of its surroundings, Kalamazoo would be as near perfection as any provincial town in the West."

Durant's history might have brought order and respectability to the past. It might even have projected the future of Kalamazoo. But, however much they appreciated his interest, local readers could scarcely fathom the changes the next decade would bring. His history reflected a community in transition. Many of the first pioneers still held powerful positions in the village, and many things were done as they always had been done. Yet the *Telegraph* expressed the feeling of change with one graphic illustration. It was time, the paper said in May 1879, to take down the fences around the courthouse lawn: livestock no longer wandered on the streets of Kalamazoo.

Shopkeepers displayed their goods on wooden sidewalks in the 1870s. This view shows Michigan Avenue between Burdick and Rose. Courtesy, Kalamazoo Public Museum.

CHAPTER IV
MAIN STREET RUNS THROUGH THE MIDDLE OF THE TOWN: 1880–1890

Cutters and bobsleds brought farmers downtown on sunny winter days in the 1880s. Courtesy, Western Michigan University Archives.

Only a few farmers came to town on January 26, 1880, a cloudy, balmy day, the boardwalks damp with melting snow, the roads muddy, and sleighing poor. Samuel Durant hurried to the train; in his luggage was the bulging "county history" manuscript bound for printers in Philadelphia. He left behind a village 50 years old and about to become a city. Signs of change were everywhere. Local people were already taking for granted running water and a new park fountain. Ten years later they would be equally comfortable with telephones, electric lights, trolley cars, sewers, and suburbs.

As Durant boarded the train, the papers reported that "industrious little birds have taken possession of Main Street." A flock of English sparrows dodged the wagon traffic, feeding on fallen grain and scratching at horse manure in the gutters. Several Eastern cities introduced this immigrant to replace fleeing native birds in the 1860s. A "bird of the streets," the English sparrow moved along the rail lines, making its home only in urban areas. Now, for the first time, it came to Kalamazoo. In April a young Kalamazoo College student rode "the new-fashioned bicycle on our streets." He paid two month's wages, $85, for the 50-pound monster with its five-foot front wheel. Rubber tires helped him over the ruts "gracefully, swiftly, and with apparent ease," but few people were adventurous enough to imitate him until the "safety bicycle" arrived some time later.

Yet the same villagers who smiled at sparrows and bicyclists also sent the marshal to arrest one young lady who walked with her father down Main Street wearing pants and parting her hair "boy fashion." They might have been equally shocked when Jacob Ferber opened a "Ladies' Underwear" shop on Main Street. For nearly 10 years Kalamazoo tried to live with Jacob and Julia Ferber and their big-city ways. According to their daughter, novelist Edna Ferber, "the young Chicago bride, with her flashing black eyes, her fine figure and her city trousseau" made sure local people saw what "city life" could be. The Ferbers boarded at the International House, and before long the *Telegraph* announced the birth of their first daughter Fanny: "A new and very young boarder has taken rooms at the International. . . . Her name is Ferber, first name not given yet, and she will remain the guest of Mr. and Mrs. Ferber, they hope for many years

Above
By the 1880s, Bronson Park and its fountain had become a favorite meeting place downtown. Courtesy, Western Michigan University Archives.

Left
Jacob Ferber, father of novelist Edna Ferber, opened a ladies' "fancy goods" shop in 1881. Courtesy, Western Michigan University Archives.

Top left
Novelist Edna Ferber's birthplace stood for many years on Park Street opposite Ranney. Jacob Ferber had it built in the mid-1880s. Courtesy, Western Michigan University Archives.

Top right
John Gilmore opened his Fancy Dry Goods shop on South Burdick in 1881. Courtesy, Gilmore Brothers.

Above
Julia Ferber brought "Chicago ways" to Kalamazoo in the 1880s. She was the mother of novelist Edna Ferber. Courtesy, Western Michigan University Archives.

to come." In 1885 the papers reported on the birth of Fanny's sister Edna, "a nice little girl born Sunday morning."

Jacob Ferber tried his best to bring city fashions to Main Street all through the 1880s. Sometimes he advertised "Fancy Goods," sometimes underwear, sometimes children's clothing. Finally he sold his stock and took his family back to Chicago, hoping to make his fortune during the Columbian Exposition. John and Mary Gilmore started their own ladies' furnishings and fancy-goods shop on Burdick in 1881, with considerably more success. They put down deep and lasting roots, and townspeople soon made "Gilmore's" a local institution.

The Gilmores' business would endure for a century, but few firms lasted more than a decade in the yeasty economic climate of the 1870s and 1880s. Townspeople accepted the loss of one company, sure that another would take its place. The Rockford Clothespin Factory closed not long after the Centennial, but Paulus den Bleyker's son, Dimmin, bought the plant to manufacture furniture in 1879. Kimball & Austin failed, and the *Telegraph* reported that in 1881 William Hill would move his sawmill factory from Big Rapids to the old foundry buildings, where he would "establish a large industry which will grow very rapidly." Hill had invented

a steam log-turner and looked to the Kalamazoo rail connections to broaden his market. In six months he was shipping as far away as Minnesota, Texas, Florida, Arizona, and Georgia. Whenever cutting the "Big Trees" in the Northwest required heavier equipment, Hill would build it, until the end of the golden age of logging at the turn of the century.

The *Telegraph* printed 12,000 copies of a special "Trade Edition" praising local commerce in May 1881. Although the paper devoted nearly a page to Kalamazoo's "mining interests," the times had changed. In the 1850s, the papers shared letters from the Kalamazoo Boys recounting their adventures on the plains and in the diggings. In 1876 Thomas Roach came back from a summer in the Black Hills with his arm in a sling, shot by an angry Sioux. One of his party gave out the headline, "There's Plenty of Gold There Boys, But It Costs Hair!" In the 1880s the Kalamazoo Boys prudently stayed at home to study mining at William Parsons's Business College. Armchair investors spent $250,000 on property in the Black Hills, Utah, Arizona, Colorado, and Mexico. Frederick Curtenius liked Colorado mines, as did Colorado's Governor Robinson, a one-time Plainwell resident. Curtenius bought a major share in the $100,000 claim near Silverton owned by the "Kalamazoo

Bonanza Mining Company." Now the newspapers talked of pumps and hoists, stampmills, and rail connections. Francis Stockbridge, Benjamin Austin, William Tomlinson, and other senior businessmen hired engineers to develop their mines "on economical and correct business principles."

Just as the press had found prosperity at home in the 1850s, so this 1881 chronicle of local improvements called Kalamazoo "one of the finest residence towns on the continent." In 1870 the two largest firms in town had employed only 50 and 40 workers, respectively. In 1881, 60 Kalamazoo companies averaged nearly 40 workers each. Dewing & Kent's sash-and-door works employed 120 men; the Kalamazoo Paper Company, 125. One hundred worked for Lawrence & Chapin and another 100 for the construction firm of Bush and Paterson. Merrill & McCourtie's 40 millers ground 500 barrels of flour a day and needed 25 men as barrel makers. The mills ran night and day to keep up with orders from American and European buyers.

Lorenzo Egleston's Spring Works showed remarkable growth. Formed by Kimball & Austin in 1870, the plant posted modest gains until Lorenzo Egleston, an Illinois investor, arrived to take control. Within a year he hired 80 men and shipped two million pounds of carriage springs. By 1881, 100 men finished two million pounds a month, shipping carload lots all over the country. Egleston sold the works to Francis Stockbridge, who reorganized as Kalamazoo Spring and Axle in the mid-1880s.

Kalamazoo continued to specialize in the manufacture of agricultural implements. When D.L. Garver of tiny Hart, Michigan, developed a "spring-tooth harrow" in 1867, D.C. Reed felt that the new invention had enough promise to buy out the patent. Sales languished for several years as farmers got used to the idea and Reed made improvements. Then, in the 1880s, several local firms fought for growing markets. The Reed firm sold 500 harrows in 1878, 1,000 the next year, 6,000 in 1879, and 20,000 in 1881. Chase, Taylor & Company built 15,000 in 1879 and 1880 and hoped to treble production in 1881. Lawrence & Chapin entered their own model, and another competitor boosted sales from 90 in 1877 to 5,000 in 1880. Kalamazoo residents watched whole trainloads of the new harrows leave for distant farms.

New and larger factories turned pastures south, east, and north of downtown into bustling communities as workers moved to be closer to their jobs. Kalamazoo's "Northside" first developed in the heyday of the 1880s. Francis Stockbridge and Lorenzo Egleston bought the "National Driving Park" near Portage and Stockbridge. Soon it, too, was platted into streets and boulevards named for local factory owners.

Working together since 1855, Frederick Bush and Thomas Paterson had built many of the new plants as well as most of the commercial buildings downtown. In the 1870s the firm had made thousands of piano and billiard table legs in the off-season. As the years went by, Bush & Paterson came to control what villagers called "Factory Square." Their imposing row of Italianate storefronts stretched north along Burdick and east on Water. Underneath ran a block-long line-shaft, allowing Bush & Paterson to rent power to the Lakey Paint Company, two implement-makers, a tubular well company, a knitting works, and assorted smaller businesses. All told, 350 men worked in this "Hive of Industry."

When local firms fell on hard times, Bush & Paterson intervened. After the cement factory closed in 1881, Frederick Bush bought the plant at a sheriff's sale and

Above
Kalamazoo was the manufacturing center for spring-toothed harrows in the 1880s. D.C. Reed, who bought the patent from inventor D.L. Garver, sold 20,000 of these harrows by 1881. Courtesy, Western Michigan University Archives.

Left
The Doyle Building served as the early home of the Kalamazoo Pant & Overall Company on East Michigan. Courtesy, Kalamazoo Public Museum.

reopened the next year. The Kalamazoo Knitting Works employed 50 young women making 160 dozen stockings daily in 1880. Two years later Bush & Paterson forestalled a move to Milwaukee and reorganized the company under their own control. In 1882 windmill orders outran production, so Bush & Paterson retooled to build nearly 1,100 for local firms. The *Telegraph* called the company "the oldest and most extensive" building firm in the state, attributing its success to capital, skilled workers, owners who "study their business as a science," and, of course, "the thousand labor-saving machines which have revolutionized the order of things."

Signs of industrialization and city life went beyond factory smoke and English sparrows. Villagers touted the cultural advantages of a town used as a halfway stopover for entertainers and lecturers traveling between Detroit and Chicago. For years speakers, orchestras, actors, and singers had performed in a variety of public rooms, including Corporation Hall over the fire department's stables. Civic pride now demanded something better. "We are disgraced by the poorest halls for public amusements in the west," said the *Telegraph* in 1881. The paper reasoned that if Kalamazoo businessmen were willing to put up hard cash to lure manufacturers, they should do the same to bring an opera house to the village. So Frederick Bush, Francis Stockbridge, Lorenzo Egleston, and several others formed the Kalamazoo Opera House Company and pledged to buy a lot and build an auditorium costing no less than $30,000, provided townspeople would

contribute the first $10,000. A.C. Wortley led the "citizen's fund" committee. Frederick Bush broke ground July 5, 1881. By February the papers announced "walls up and roof on."

In May 1882, the opera house, dubbed "The Academy of Music," opened on Rose Street opposite the courthouse. Although villagers just managed to come up with the $10,000 in subscriptions, the company went far beyond its promise. The new building, with furniture, lighting, stage, and scenery, cost more than $65,000. In unprecedented multipage tributes, local papers used every adjective their typecases would allow: "magnificent," "impressive," "utmost," "marvelous." Chicago architect Dankmar Adler,

with chief draftsman, Louis Sullivan, had designed the opera house and this firm, already known for acoustic engineering, had promised the best auditorium of its size in the country. Local people agreed. Finished in polished cherry, the 1,200-seat auditorium featured private boxes draped with plush silk and antique lace. Even folding chairs in the upper balcony came with plush maroon cushions. Automatic steam boilers provided fresh air at constant temperatures to ventilators under every seat. Far overhead a glass chandelier, 11 feet high and nine feet across, held 100 gas jets. The chandelier and 300 other jets around the hall could be lighted simultaneously from the stage by electricity.

Lawyer Dallas Boudeman spoke for the community on opening night. He called

Right
This drawing of the Academy of Music building appeared in the *Kalamazoo Telegraph* "Trade Edition" in 1887. The building, which housed the Kalamazoo Opera House Company, was located on Rose Street. It cost more than $65,000 to build and decorate. Courtesy, Western Michigan University Archives.

Below
Frederick Bush, whose home (shown here) stood on South Street opposite Bronson Park, built three-quarters of the buildings in downtown Kalamazoo in the last half of the 19th century. Courtesy, Western Michigan University Archives.

Townspeople were proud of their
Academy of Music auditorium in
the 1880s. Courtesy, Kalamazoo
Public Museum.

the opera house "one of the greatest events" and "most progressive steps" in Kalamazoo's history. "This Academy of Music will do more for the development, the substantial growth and the future prosperity of Kalamazoo than any other one work," he said. Colonel Francis Stockbridge represented the company whose decision to have the best architect and the finest "seating, heating, lighting, and decorating" doubled the cost of the facility. He said the company planned only to offer "a bright, pleasant, comfortable, and safe house, where after the work and business of the day is over, we can gather and be entertained." But he recognized full well that the Academy of Music was a symbol of Kalamazoo's urban aspirations and a major selling point to prospective investors. He gave special thanks to Frederick Bush for his "untiring interest" in constructing the building (which, by agreement, Bush now owned). The *Telegraph* concluded, "It only remains for the people of this region to show themselves worthy of the institution."

Other civic developments inspired less sentiment but brought more enduring changes to the city. In 1880 one irate citizen called for a halt to the setting of "big-tree poles" at the curbsides. He admitted the need for gas lines and telegraph poles, but saw no "public necessity" for the new-fangled telephone. Thirty subscribers disagreed, and telephone service, first introduced privately in 1878, soon opened to everyone. Not all Kalamazooans were interested, but 100 subscribers could phone each other in 1881 and shout across the lines to Comstock and Galesburg. A new language was born. "Giving someone a ring" meant turning the old hand crank and asking the operator for a connection. "Hang up" now meant putting the receiver back on the "hook." Each phone was assigned a number in the order of subscription, but numbers were hardly needed. The operator knew everyone anyway.

Sells Brothers railroad circus came to town by special train in May 1880. Local papers showed proper respect for a menagerie, warlike Utes, and bareback riders, but people particularly turned out to see the well-advertised electric generator and lighting system, that bathed the big-top with "Sun Eclipsing, Heaven-Born Splendor." Two years later another entrepreneur brought crowds to Bronson Park to see "the brilliant meteor transfixed above the scene." In 1886 the Kalamazoo Electric Company first sent power to two dozen

Left
These men are laying wooden-block paving on Edwards Street. The city installed 59 "wood and stone" crossings in 1885. Courtesy, Kalamazoo Public Library.

Above
Hezekiah Wells came early to the county and became one of Kalamazoo's most distinguished citizens. Courtesy, Western Michigan University Archives.

downtown buildings. The city bought 90 electric streetlights that year, and the company debated whether to provide power all night long.

Electric lights and telephones seemed like toys in the 1880s. A patent-office spokesman even predicted that people might one day call from Boston to New York and see each other at the same time. Farfetched as this idea seemed at the time, townspeople did agree on the significance of one practical change that would mar the local streets for years to come—municipal sewers.

Allen Potter, Hezekiah Wells, Stephen Cobb, Frederick Bush, and other leading citizens jostled for seats on the prestigious Sewer Commission, and town fathers tore into the streets with a will in 1881. The commission's first report hammered home one message: "pure air, pure water, and a pure soil" never existed in a city without sewers. It graphically described the "nasty mass of corruption" in home cesspools and argued for sanitary ordinances. For the next several years the best-drawn map of the community was the "Sewerage Map," and "red no-passing lanterns" glowed over ditches from one end of town to the other. In the summer of 1881 one pundit wrote a poem called "The Ballad of the

Sewer," telling the whole story in romantic terms, including even a ghostly maiden:

And now by night a phantom white

Doth follow up the sewer,

To show that true love's constancy

Forever doth endure.

In September engineers called the flushing of the first mile of pipe "a perfect success," as a broad stain spread onto the Kalamazoo River.

At the general meeting of the village trustees in 1882, President Peyton Ranney announced "the village of today is not that of even a few years ago." He cited the waterworks and sewer systems as prudent future planning, and, considering the impact on visitors of wagon ruts and mudholes, he urged the board to improve street paving. He asked for better care of the village's 80 miles of roadways and recommended "that not another plank or timber crossing be laid in Kalamazoo." Only "first-class curbstone" would endure. He reported the telephone pole controversy resolved and added: "Our general business was never more flourishing than today. Our crowded streets and the clatter of the freight wagon are city-like; surely indicating the great increase in our commercial interests. Never have our business activities been so prosperous as at this moment."

The same summer brought exciting news. "Get your letter boxes ready and hang out your numbers," said the *Telegraph* in September. For 50 years townspeople trudged to the post office to pick up their mail. Now "The Big Village" was "a carrier town," offering delivery four times a day in the downtown area. Street addresses changed as the town adopted the new "Philadelphia System" giving each block preassigned numbers so people could estimate distances by street address.

Also in 1882 critics charged that the village was 25 years behind other modern cities because it had no streetcar line. That challenge was accepted and acted upon by September: "The Yankee" and "The Irish" trundled back and forth on Lovell Street pulled by patient horses in the town's first experiment with streetcars. The Kalamazoo Street Railway Company went into business in 1884, opening five miles of track in September with a free 22-car parade through the town, brass band and all. Three years later the company claimed a dozen miles of track and 30 cars. Historian Sam Bass Warner showed in *Streetcar Suburbs* how street railways converted communities

The streetcar line opened with a 22-car parade in 1884. Courtesy, Western Michigan University Archives.

from "walking villages" to sprawling cities. Edges of towns, once belonging to truck farmers and "the carriage trade," opened to working people who could choose between living in the shadow of the mills or "taking the cars" to work. Perhaps nothing indicated so dramatically that Kalamazoo had "outgrown the clothes which fitted her so beautifully in years gone by," as one village president put it. The town now needed "a new suit."

Indeed, said President Edwin DeYoe in 1883, "to be or not to be a city, that is the question." Some enjoyed living in

"America's largest village," agreeing with the *Telegraph* editor who claimed a city charter would only double taxes and add "a few more fat offices" to the public account. The paper argued that "there is no need for change" in 1880, but by 1883 many felt otherwise. During the next year the town and its charter commission labored over the shape the new government should take. Ultimately the charter created a system of five wards, and in April voters elected Allen Potter the first mayor.

Local businessmen continued to play a strong role in the new government. C.H. Bird, Hale Page, Otto Ihling, Albert Lakey, George Fuller, and marble-manufacturer George Winslow stood among the aldermen when the first city council was sworn in. The outgoing village treasurer reported no public debts other than a single $5,000 water bond. He asked for prudent management to attract investors and added hopefully, "Kalamazoo as a city should certainly be entitled to some of the floating capital, and will have it soon."

Outgoing President Edwin DeYoe recounted village history from the "prehistoric" days of 1836 to the time when "the goods, wares and merchandise of Kalamazoo manufacture are to be found in the markets of every clime and country." He also cautioned the new city council to preserve Kalamazoo's record as "best, least, and most economically governed." He added that the work of village government was at an end: "Nothing remains to be done but pulling the throttle and starting out from the station heretofore known as the "Big Village" which engineer Potter will do in approved style, and, we trust, run on the same line of prosperity that has characterized our Village for the past several years." The new city council continued to conduct its business in Corporation Hall, but the county gave final sanction to Kalamazoo's new status with a great brick and stone courthouse finished in 1885.

In the 1880s Kalamazoo meant people as well as products and politics. The well-to-do lived along South Street and west on Main. Increasingly they built great Queen Anne homes on Stuart and Woodward. The newspapers gossiped about their parties, their guests, and their travels. During the "season" they met at any of 30 lodges and societies. They performed with the Argonauts or the choral society, or attended winter lecture series

Above left
Workmen labored installing gas pipe and streetcar tracks in 1884, along Main Street from Rose to Portage. Courtesy, Western Michigan University Archives.

Above
By the mid-1880s Kalamazoo streets were generally crowded. Courtesy, Western Michigan University Archives.

Left
Nineteenth-century house movers used winches and short lengths of track to move large buildings like the old courthouse in the 1880s. Courtesy, Kalamazoo Public Library.

Bottom
Union soldiers marched once again in this 1886 parade that passed the new courthouse. Courtesy, Western Michigan University Archives.

and temperance meetings. They ran for public office, held important positions in the fashionable churches, and generally argued for sound management. In the fall, the men went north by special trains to hunt deer. In the summer they sent their wives and children to the resort settlements at Torch Lake, Elk Lake, or Traverse City.

Public Library, Kalamazoo, Mich.

The first superintendent of the state hospital, Dr. Edwin Van Deusen, donated this massive Romanesque Public Library building to the city in the 1880s. Courtesy, Western Michigan University Archives.

William Parsons helped organize "Wequetonsing," the Presbyterian Resort in Emmet County, and a number of Kalamazoo residents built impressive cottages at Charlevoix, where Peyton Ranney headed the Resort Association. By 1882 the papers were calling Charlevoix "Kalamazoo's annex," and the *Telegraph*'s editor sent copies of the paper to all the major hotels each day. Francis Stockbridge, Hezekiah Wells, W.H. McCourtie, and other local men spent considerable time looking after developments on Mackinac Island that same year. They were joined by Chicago businessman Gurdon Hubbard, once a youthful local fur trader. Stockbridge persuaded railroad and steamship companies to finance the Grand Hotel on land that he owned.

Local papers watched the comings and goings of "society" in daily "Jottings" columns. They only rarely mentioned what the superintendent of the poor said about less-fortunate residents. Generally they announced the marshal's report on drunk-and-disorderly arrests and prostitution. Working people left few other traces in the news. Yet we can draw some composite pictures. Government officials on all levels loved statistics in the 1880s. In 1884 they published a mountain of figures. Workers became numbers and their

words disappeared in percentage points. Nevertheless they did answer a variety of questions. Michigan's Bureau of Labor issued its first *Report* in 1884, followed for the next 35 years by book-length studies of working conditions throughout the state. The bureau began with an exhaustive survey of 10,000 workers in Detroit. Later came similar studies in other cities, including Kalamazoo. The commissioner of labor presented the reports as unbiased, though many workers first suspected the bureau might use information to lower wages or thwart union activity.

Polk's Michigan *Gazeteer* and the Kalamazoo city directory for 1883, along with village annual reports, provide some general background. Workers might read three daily papers, attend any of 18 churches, stop by 23 saloons, or pick up groceries at 46 shops. They could stop at nine shops for ice cream and six for candy. Eight dentists handled toothaches. Thirty-one men and five women practiced medicine. Sixty men advertised as celery growers. Thirty-eight women said they were dressmakers, and Mrs. Harvey Sullings sold a line of "Dress Reform Goods" just down the street from Jacob Ferber. The public library claimed 10,000 volumes and the Ladies' Library 3,000. Children could look forward to public or private school, three colleges and a private art school—or to the Children's Home if they were "friendless."

The 1884 census taker asked people their age and origin, their occupation and family size, and many other questions. State clerks tabulated all the answers for every township and community. Michigan claimed nearly two million people. Men, many of whom were in the mines and lumber camps of northern Michigan, outnumbered women by nearly 100,000. Thirty-five thousand people lived in Kalamazoo County—14,000 in the new city.

People in Kalamazoo County behaved much as they did in other parts of the state. More and more left the farm for factory work. One hundred fifty Michigan townships lost population statewide in the 1880 census, but Michigan grew by 500,000. Kalamazoo reported rural losses in 1884, though the city increased by 2,000. Girls came to town in significant numbers. Nine hundred more men lived in rural areas, but 435 more women lived in Kalamazoo, outnumbering men in nearly every age group.

Kalamazoo's hardware stores were packed with a wide variety of goods in the late 19th century. Courtesy, Western Michigan University Archives.

Local saloons such as Nicholas Baumann's were frequently known as the workingman's "club." The spittoon in the foreground testifies to the popularity of chewing tobacco. Courtesy, Western Michigan University Archives.

Unlike many newer counties, Kalamazoo aged significantly from census to census. The "average" man and woman, at 29, were older in Kalamazoo than in all but three of the state's 79 counties.

Three out of five adults were married. Two hundred fifty weddings during the census year reflected a statewide pattern: most couples favored fall and winter, frequently October, but wedding bells rang only ten times in June. Fifty-eight women and three men said they were under 20 when they married. Another 100 women said they were between 20 and 25. Most men married about five years later. The 420 divorced and widowed women outnumbered men by three to one. Men remarried more readily. Seventy percent of the children between five and 20 went to school, and nearly 99 percent of the "native-born" residents could read. But both public and parochial schools served less than half the immigrant children.

Most Kalamazoo residents were white, Protestant, and native-born; nevertheless 300 black people lived in town, nearly as many as in Grand Rapids. Fifty-four percent of all Michigan residents were immigrants or children of immigrants, while Keweenaw County ran 95 percent and Houghton 96. Again showing its age, Kalamazoo recorded two out of three people as children of native-born parents who could call themselves "old-stock." Most newcomers came from Holland, Germany, and Ireland.

Many families put great value on church activities. Methodists operated 18 of 45 county churches, with Baptists, Congregationalists, and Presbyterians far behind. Catholics attended St. Augustine's, the county's largest church with seating for 750. Jewish families, such as the Rosenbaums, Salomans, Israels, Sterns, Seligmans, and Ferbers, figured prominently in local commerce and supported one of only four synagogues in Michigan. Three of the 26 churches in the state listed as Dutch Reform served Kalamazoo and helped many newcomers find friends and jobs.

The 1884 census taker counted books as well as people. Statisticians felt that books and libraries measured culture and opportunities available to people in different parts of the state. Kalamazoo County, though 17th in population, ranked sixth with 163,499 books. The city stood fourth in size of private collections and second to Detroit in circulating libraries.

Despite the fact that Kalamazoo was the seventh largest town in Michigan at 14,000, half the county residents still lived in the country and worked at farming. In 1884 farms occupied 93 percent of available land in Kalamazoo County, compared to three percent in Keweenaw and one percent in Baraga. Between 1870 and 1880 the county added 288 more farms, but in the next four years the tide turned, and the census taker reported 50 fewer farms in 1884 and 1340 fewer acres in crops. At $2 a day, farm wages ranked among the highest in the state for a month of haying and harvest time, but farmworkers were lucky to earn their board and $18 per month year-round. Farmhands chored and worked in the fields long before the distant factory whistles reminded them of 10-hour days and Sundays free in Kalamazoo.

The Bureau of Labor canvassed more than 1,000 Kalamazoo men working in 75 different occupations in 1883. Half were under 30, and 30 percent were immigrants, chiefly from Holland and Germany. By far the greatest number worked in the building trades or called themselves "day laborers"—a statewide pattern. Youngsters between 15 and 20 entered the work force as clerks or laborers, and old-timers ended their working life chiefly as laborers, masons, or carpenters. Immigrants generally worked as laborers or carpenters, but all nationalities performed a variety of jobs. Clear dispari-

ty existed only in "clerking," where 64 of 68 called themselves "Americans."

Workers once tallied their pay with the weary expression, "another day, another dollar," but this was long outmoded by 1883. Men averaged $1.82 a day, with unskilled labor bringing $1.33. Local wages and occupations matched those in Detroit very closely. Women made up 10 percent of Michigan's work force, equally divided between business and manufacturing. Only three in 10 could hope for a dollar at the end of a 10-hour day. Women generally received half the wages paid to men and averaged only 78 cents a day in Wayne County.

While ages, hours, and job descriptions remained quite uniform in much of Michigan, the quality of life varied widely. Ninety percent of Kalamazoo families lived in detached dwellings. They kept 264 milk cows, but, with only 574 horses in town, most families walked everywhere. The Bureau of Labor used "huddling" to describe the housing problems workers faced around the state. Two of

three Michigan workers rented, and many found all too little space for their families. Seven hundred people crowded into fewer than 200 rooms in Wayne County; statewide, two out of three families lived in one to four rooms. Kalamazoo offered a pleasant contrast. In the 1883 report, of 250 families questioned, 70 percent lived in five or more rooms, and one out of four in seven to eight.

Rich people owned big houses and most of local property in practically every city. The Bureau of Labor investigated 12 out-state cities and found that three percent of the property holders controlled 27 percent of real-estate values. One percent (or 20 people) held 20 percent of all the property value in Battle Creek. But much of this value lay in commercial buildings. Most private homes were worth about two-and-a-half times a worker's annual wage or less. Two of three owned property valued under $3,000, and assessors credited $500 or less to 40 percent of all property owners in Battle Creek. Most workers in Kalamazoo, whether they owned or rented, came to live in homes much like those of their neighbors.

The census taker reported 2,690 dwellings in 1884. Those available to workers were often older and less attractive than the distinguished homes that lined Bronson Park or South Street. Local officials praised the city's waterworks and sewer systems, but only one home in four had running water and fewer still had sewer connections. Water rates discriminated against "luxuries." People paid four dollars for water and three dollars more for each toilet or bathtub. As a result the water department served 384 households in 1880, but reported only 17 toilets and two bathtubs. Health officer Foster Pratt pointed out that there were perhaps 3,000 outhouses and cesspools in backyards all over town and these stood dangerously close to 2,000 private wells, most less than 15 feet deep. Sewer lines reached new neighborhoods each year. In 1884 the city reported 662 water users, 208 toilets, and 18 bathtubs. Some households collected rainwater in attic tanks and piped it to their own private tubs. Still most families turned to "sponge baths" and Saturday night rituals next to the kitchen stove.

The proximity of outhouses to wells disturbed most of the early physicians. Rush McNair, Foster Pratt, H.B. Hemenway, and others wrote of typhoid and "cholera infantum" as water-related diseases, and everyone feared the diphtheria outbreaks that seemed so frequent among "the poor population." One in five diphtheria patients died, and death from typhoid was common among workers who stayed on the job too long before sending for the doctor. McNair complained about the number of celery growers who sank barrels in the muck next to their fields and drank whatever settled there. Clearly city officials had reason to praise their waterworks and to encourage sewers for health reasons, but it would be a long time before significant numbers of working people would have these advantages.

Laborers paid no income taxes. They worked only about a week to pay property taxes on a home valued at $1,000. On the other hand, they spent a good share of their income on food. Market basket prices were much the same over all of Michigan and varied little from year to year. Kalamazoo prices for 1884 included:

Flour, barrel (196 lbs.) . . $5.18
Cornmeal . . . . .02 lb.
Codfish . . . . .07 lb.
Rice . . . . .09 lb.
Tea, Black . . . . .52 lb.
Coffee, Roasted . . . . .23½ lb.
Butter . . . . .19 lb.
Milk . . . . .05½ qt.
Eggs . . . . .12½ doz.
Potatoes . . . . .37 bu.
Sugar, granulated . . . . . . .08 lb.
Beef, steak . . . . .13 lb.
Ham . . . . .14½ lb.
Coal, ton, soft 5.50
Wood, stove-size, cord . . 1.82
Calico, prints . . . . .06½ yd.
Sheeting, unbleached . . . .08 yd.
Shirting, unbleached . . . . .09½ yd.

Facing page
Though grocer A.B. Scheid's prices seem extremely low by our standards, in 1887, 50 cents represented more than two hours work for a laborer. Courtesy, Western Michigan University Archives.

Attractive as these prices seem today, the average laborer spent nearly three days earning a barrel of flour or a ton of coal. He worked an entire day for a cord of stove wood. Meat required a half-hour for a pound of beef and nearly an hour for ham. Milk, butter, and eggs cost more: 20 minutes for a quart of milk, 40 for a dozen eggs, and one hour for a pound of butter. A half-hour purchased a pound of sugar and 40 minutes a pound of cheese, but a man had to work three hours and more for a pound of tea.

In 1889 the Bureau of Labor profiled 600 men in the city's major iron foundries and implement factories. Again 70 percent were "Americans," and two of three immigrants came from Holland or Germany. No one person matched the bureau's "average" figures, but they are still instructive.

Two hundred fifty-eight supported themselves on $7.55 a week. Half the men in the survey were married and took home $9.79 weekly. Four in 10 owned their own homes, but three out of four of the homes were mortgaged for nearly half their value. Renters paid about $7.68 a month, or 20 percent of their pay. Seventy-five families reported no children; the rest averaged two, nearly half under five. Seven out of 10 children went to school. Half of all workers subscribed to magazines and newspapers; one in five owned a musical instrument, including 49 organs, 11 pianos, 20 violins, and 22 guitars. Two out of three families owned sewing machines.

Most men earned just under $400 a year, except newcomers from Holland who took home $337. Nevertheless four in 10 managed to save 13 percent of what they earned. "Americans," with somewhat smaller families, reported per capita expenses of $121 a year. Frugal Hollanders spent $85.50. As a result Dutch workers reported a net worth of $708 to the American's $646.

However reported, statistics give only antiseptic and impersonal images of working people. These images may be accurate in general, but working people lived real lives rarely touched by bureaucratic studies or completely explained by statistics. Consider Maggie Mallon, who came to town looking for work in 1869.

Maggie's parents were already middle-aged when they left Ireland some years before the great "potato famine" of 1848. They lived in Canada where Phillip was born, then moved to New York. They came to Kalamazoo from Buffalo when Maggie was 21, a middle child in a big family. Her mother Ellen, widowed by that time, ran a boarding house she didn't own on North Rose. Maggie's brother Phillip worked as a painter, and Maggie took a job clerking in a hat store. The boarding house was a small home left over from pioneer days, one of a few surviving residences surrounded by factories. Maggie would have laughed when historian David Fisher said Kalamazoo had "too much clean linen and not enough factory smoke!" She and her mother had trouble enough hanging their own wash on the line. The 1874 "bird's-eye" drawing of Kalamazoo showed her home sandwiched between Lawrence & Chapin on one side and Kimball & Austin on the other—the two biggest and smokiest foundries in town. There in the middle of the clatter and smoke and smell of heavy industry, Ellen kept her boarding house. One young man fresh from Grand Rapids came to visit frequently after 1872. Thomas Gleason had a good job as foreman with a local printing firm; the wedding vows were read at St. Augustine Church in 1876 . . . and Gleason married Maggie's younger sister, Agnes.

Maggie saved her money until she could open a stand selling candy and tobacco in the old post office building. With all of Horatio Alger's pluck and luck, she made "Maggie Mallon's" the most talked about candy shop in town, judging by newspaper notices. Subsequent city directories listed her in bold type as Miss Maggie Mallon, "dealer in fresh candies, confectionery, fruits in season, cigars and tobacco."

The boarding house stood on prime business property. Maggie and her mother soon had to move. She bought a modest lot on Woodward Avenue next to Agnes and Tom. There the census taker found them in 1880. Next door lived an itinerant Irish blacksmith whose four children had been born in three other states over the previous decade. But there were few working class neighborhoods in towns the size of Kalamazoo. Three doors down lived Julius Caesar Burrows, U.S. Congressman and soon to be Senator. William McCourtie, the wealthy flour mill owner, lived even closer, and William Parsons of the Business College only a block away.

The State Fair came to Kalamazoo in 1884 and captured all the headlines. When Ellen Mallon died on the last day of

READ WHAT IT COSTS TO LIVE IN KALAMAZOO!

I take the liberty of enlightening the world that you can buy groceries for less money in Kalamazoo than in almost any city in the world.

SUGARS.

20 pounds extra C sugar............$1.00
15 pounds standard A sugar............ 1.00
14 pounds standard granulated sugar... 1.00

TEAS.

The very best Japan teas (Samples free) 50c
A first-class Japan tea (equal to any in the city. Try it.)...................... 40c
A good tea, (This is just as good as any 50 cent tea sold with chromos or crockery. Try it.)...................... 30c
Finest Formosa Oolong, (Beats any 75 cent Oolong in Kalamazoo. A trial will convince.) 60c

Best Young Hyson....................... 60c
Best Gunpowder....................... 60c

COFFEES.
(Roasted Daily.)

Best O. G. Java, roasted, (When I say best I mean it....................... 35c
Gautemala 30c
My combination Java, Maracaibo and Rio, (This is a better coffee than you can buy elsewhere for 35 cents. Don't forget this.)...................... 30c
Maracaibo, choice...................... 30c
Fancy Golden Rio...................... 30c

FLOUR.

50 pounds full patent, very best........$1.30
50 pounds good flour...................... 1.00
50 pounds one-half patent............... 1.10

SOAP.

6 bars Bogue's soap........ .... 25c
5 pounds best laundry starch............ 25c
5 bars Kirk's soap...................... 25c

FRUIT JARS.

Mason pints, per dozen................$1.00
Mason quarts, per dozen............ 1.15
Mason two-quarts, per dozen........... 1.40
Lightnig pints, per dozen............ 1.10
Lightnig quarts, per dozen 1.25
Lightnig two-quarts, per dozen......... 1.60

CANNED GOODS

Salmon, per can...................... 15c
Sardines, 4 cans, domestic.............. 25c
Sardines, per can, imported.............. 15c
Sardines, in mustard...................... 10c
Lobsters, per can...................... 18c
Cove oysters, per can, small.............. 10c
Cove oysters, per can, large.............. 18c
Olives, per bottle...................... 25c
Two pounds cooked corn beef, (Cheaper and better than beefsteak at 8c a lb.... 20c
Boston baked beans...................... 20c
Bottled pickles, all kinds, cheap.

SUNDRIES.

4 pounds best Carolina rice.............. 25c
7 pounds Akron oat meal................ 25c
4½ pounds best crackers................ 25c
Choice white clover comb honey....... 15c
3 pounds cloverleaf codfish.............. 25c
Choice table nuts..................... 12½c
Full cream cheese..................... 10c
5 pounds bird seed..................... 25c
Raisins, choice Valencias.............. 10c
Currants, 3 pounds..................... 25c
Citron, per pound..................... 30c
Orange and lemon peel, per pound...... 20c

Fifteen cents buys a baking powder guaranteed equal to any you have used at double the price. Fresh vegetables and fruits at lower prices than any other house in Kalamazoo.

CASH TELLS THE STORY! REMEMBER THE PLACE, 208 WEST MAIN ST.

A. B. SCHEID, Opposite New Court House.

the fair, the county clerk recorded it as the law required, but the *Gazette* simply said, "the mother of Miss Maggie Mallon died." The pastor of her church wrote the date in Latin, but misjudged her age by several years. No one wrote an obituary for Ellen Mallon. Working people made news only when they died violently.

The directories listed other Mallons as teamsters, janitors, carriage painters, and domestics. Maggie gave up the candy business about the time her mother died and went to work at Mahony & Lynch's "Boston Store." Eventually she spent 14 years with Gilmore's department store. She boarded now with the Gleasons in a sturdy middle-sized Queen Anne house on Woodward. Gleason joined the business community in 1887 when he bought a controlling interest in the Kalamazoo Publishing Company. His neighbors soon elected him alderman for two terms.

Miss Maggie married Patrick Redmond, a widowed paper worker with nine children, in 1902. He was 55 and she nearly as old, though she gave her age as 50. They attended a private ceremony at 5:30 in the morning and left for Redmond's home after a wedding breakfast at the Gleasons. Few working people took time for honeymoons. The papers did notice the wedding, mentioning the Gleasons and indicating that bride and groom were "well-known and highly respected." City directories now listed Maggie as "Margaret C." in parentheses after Patrick Redmond's name. Only Agnes and a brother in San Diego remained of the Mallons when Maggie died in 1914. She had lived in Kalamazoo for 45 years, just as long as William Parsons. Both died within days of each other. Parsons's death was front-page news. Maggie's notice came several pages later. In brief announcements the papers remembered her only as "one of the pioneers."

At the beginning of the decade, the *Telegraph* covered the village's virtues in just four pages of its "Trade Edition." The next special run of the paper in 1887 took a whopping 20 pages to tell the story and still left much unsaid. A section entitled "A Busy Thriving City" began this new Trade Edition, adding a catalog of "all the privileges, comforts and conveniences" offered by the metropolitan center. At 16,000, Kalamazoo might seem like a small town, but in the 1880s, the govern-

ment called any community with 2,500 people an "urban center." Kalamazoo boosters boasted of:

Broad shaded streets; residences not extravagant but built and furnished in good taste; an admirable system of electric lighting; a uniform supply of pure water, drawn direct from a deep stratum underlying the city; a well-managed street-car system; the telephone, with connections to the surrounding towns; a paid fire department and complete protection; a well handled police force; forty-two daily trains for passengers leaving and entering for all directions; a sewer system covering the principal residence streets; one of the handsomest and most complete theatres in America; the American District telegraph system; a variety of pretty lakes and pleasure resorts distant from 15 minutes to an hour's drive, for a passing diversion during the heated spell; and many other advantages that count for a great deal in the current comfort and satisfaction of living.

"Kalamazoo Leads the World" one headline read, expressing the city's pride in producing more spring-tooth harrows than any competitor. But the city claimed a lead for two other products as well—windmills and buggies.

Five firms monopolized the windmill business. The two oldest, B.S. Williams & Company and Phelps & Bigelow, made "wind engines" under other patents in the 1870s. They made various improvements and soon put out the Manvel and the I.X.L. models on their own. Other firms joined them with the Bird, the Eureka, and several smaller brands. By 1882 Kalamazoo claimed to be the "windmill center of the world." Travelers could find reminders of home whirling away in Europe, South America, Africa, Australia, or in virtually any county in the United States. B.S. Williams sent three carloads of windmills to Africa in 1880, and one week in 1882 shipped to Alabama, Tennessee, Ohio, Australia, and New Zealand. By 1886 local production reached 4,000 per year, as well as 10,000 tanks, pumps, and pipes. A year later, overseas shipments reached 1,500.

The buggy industry grew even more rapidly. Pioneer wagonmakers located in Kalamazoo to serve the immediate neighborhood, but proximity to hardwoods and good rail lines attracted outside investors

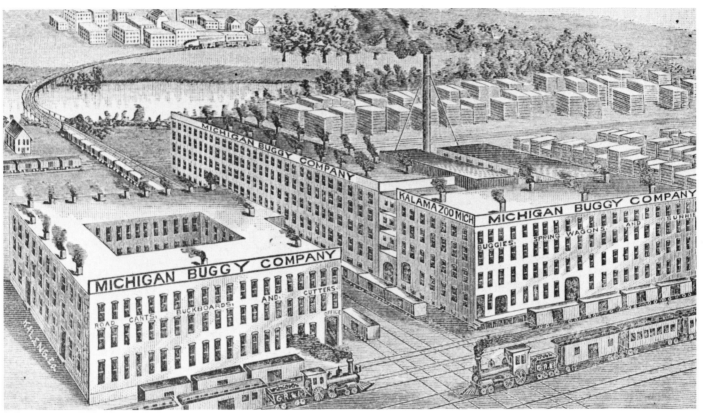

in the 1880s. Village businessmen outbid several Michigan towns when Hicks & Lane decided to move from Cortland, New York. The town's offer of free land and buildings helped Moses Lane and I.V. Hicks establish the Kalamazoo Wagon Company. The company employed 200 men and put out 12,000 vehicles in 1887, including 5,000 of the two-wheeled "road carts" that were a local specialty. Moses Lane set up his own firm with his brother-in-law Frank Lay in 1883. Called the Michigan Buggy Company, it acquired spacious new quarters on Factory Street in 1886 and produced 19,000 vehicles in 30 patterns. Though these were the largest firms, 16 other factories made buggies, carts, cutters, wagons, springs, tops, and accessories. Kalamazoo's combined output reached 47,000 for 1887.

The *Telegraph's* Trade Edition also listed "Minor Industries" and "Peculiar Manufactures." W.E. Hill's sawmill firm appeared under this heading, as did Dewing & Kent's sash-and-door mill, now the largest in Michigan. The Globe Casket Company was one of the "peculiar manufactures" destined for success and long life. Oscar Allen, William Clarke, and Jeremiah Woodbury organized the casket factory in 1870. Allen assumed sole control from 1874 to 1887, then remained as president until he retired in 1899. The casket company located in the "Allen Block"

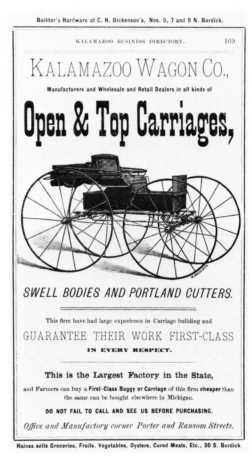

Builder's Hardware at C. H. Dickenson's, Nos. 5, 7 and 9 N. Burdick.

KALAMAZOO BUSINESS DIRECTORY.   169

KALAMAZOO WAGON CO.,

Manufacturers and Wholesale and Retail Dealers in all kinds of

Open & Top Carriages,

SWELL BODIES AND PORTLAND CUTTERS.

This firm have had large experience in Carriage building and

GUARANTEE THEIR WORK FIRST-CLASS

IN EVERY RESPECT.

This is the Largest Factory in the State,

and Farmers can buy a **First-Class Buggy or Carriage** of this firm **cheaper** than the same can be bought elsewhere in Michigan.

DO NOT FAIL TO CALL AND SEE US BEFORE PURCHASING.

Office and Manufactory corner Porter and Ransom Streets.

Haines sells Groceries, Fruits, Vegetables, Oysters, Cured Meats, Etc., 30 S. Burdick.

Above
This huge Michigan Buggy Company plant was built in 1886 on Factory Street. It brought many workers to the immediate neighborhood. Lay and Lane boulevards were named after the company's vice-president and president. Courtesy, Western Michigan University Archives.

Left
Though Kalamazoo became a center for wagon manufacturing early in its history, the industry boomed in the 1880s. Moses Lane and I.V. Hicks established the Kalamazoo Wagon Company after relocating from Cortland, New York. Courtesy, Western Michigan University Archives.

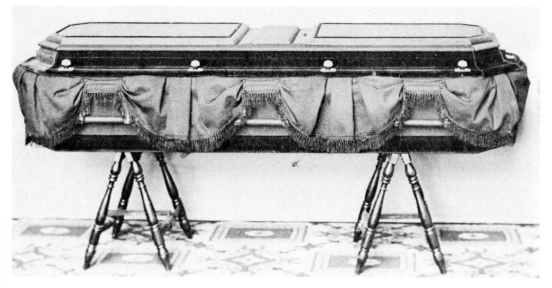

at the northwest corner of Burdick and Water Street. There the firm did "a mammoth business" in "funeral furniture" and cloth-covered caskets, so efficiently designed that many competitors fell by the wayside.

Two companies kept busy making heavy leather- and canvas-bound "Blank Books." The Kalamazoo Publishing Company and Ihling, Everard & Company bound local paper into volumes suited to the many public recorders and private accountants who needed plain ruled paper in permanent volumes for deeds, books, court calendars, tax rolls, and other items.

Starting with a dozen sewing machines above his store in 1880, Samuel Rosenbaum built an overall "empire" six years later. Seventy-five hands sewed up 65 dozen pairs a day in his three-story factory on East Michigan. Nearby, Saloman & Company rented power from Bush & Paterson to make overalls, jackets, shirts, and woolen pants, and kept four salesmen on the road drumming up orders.

"Kalamazoo celery" appeared on hotel menus from Delmonico's to San Francisco. Lowland celery grew large and tender under the care of local gardeners, who worked nearly 1,500 acres of rich black muck on the edges of the city. S.J. Dunkley, the "celery king," claimed the world's largest celery plantation in 1887 —40 acres. The leading shipper, C.G. Bullard, kept his crews on night and day in season and sent out "225,000 dozens of celery" worth $60,000 in 1886. Perhaps as many as 1,800 people took part in the celery industry.

"Celeryville" was Kalamazoo's nickname to some people, but long after celery was forgotten another "peculiar manufacture" would still be growing. The Upjohn Pill and Granule Company came to town in 1885. The *Telegraph* noted that it expanded "in a quiet way" over the ensuing months. The Upjohns were hometown folks; Uriah came to Richland as a young doctor in 1835. He married a local girl and raised 11 children who grew up with the country. When they reached high school and college age, Uriah rented a house in Ann Arbor and packed them all off under the care of a daughter. In 1871 eight of the children attended the university at the same time. Historian David Fisher wrote that Mary and Amelia Upjohn were "the first lady graduates of the University" in pharmacy. Helen, Henry, and William E. Upjohn studied medicine there, and James T. Upjohn graduated from Michigan State.

Henry and W.E. Upjohn loved to tinker. Henry patented several improvements to farm implements, including a self-tying knot device, which he sold to Cyrus McCormick for $1,500. W.E. developed an electric "slave clock" mechanism in 1880. He also experimented with a new pill-rolling process, which he patented in 1885. This looked so promising that he gave up his practice, moved to Kalamazoo, and went into business with Henry. Henry died of typhoid in 1887, and the company continued under W.E. and his younger brothers, Frederick and James.

The Upjohn pill was "friable," that is, it could be easily crushed to a powder and assimilated. The company kept its trademark, a pill under W.E. Upjohn's thumb, for 60 years, long after the process was outmoded. Rush McNair, who opened his own practice in 1887, told the story of the

Above
Employees of the W.E. Hill
Company pose with products
manufactured by the sawmill
firm. Courtesy, Kalamazoo Public
Library.

Left
Manufacturer William Hill built
this imposing home on
Kalamazoo Avenue about 1890.
Courtesy, Western Michigan
University Archives.

Above
This artist's rendering of the town's new railroad station appeared in *Railroad Review*, November 12, 1887. Courtesy, Western Michigan University Archives.

Below right
By the 1890s townspeople played at pioneering. Carl Kleinstuck build this log cabin in his side yard on Oakland Drive. He also kept a tame bear for a time. Courtesy, Western Michigan University Archives.

Facing page
Small children gather to watch the village band on Michigan Avenue about 1880. Courtesy, Kalamazoo Public Library.

Upjohn sales demonstrations in his memoirs. He said competitor's pills proved so hard and durable that they often passed entirely through the patient untouched. Upjohn agents collected these "used" pills and compared them to their own product by driving them into pine boards like nails! The Upjohn Company's first catalog in 1886 advertised 186 formulas, including quinine, iron, and, one of the most popular, anticonstipation pills. Signs on the factory walls warned employees: "Keep the Quality Up—W.E. Upjohn." The *Telegraph* hinted that the Upjohn Pill and Granule Company was "sure to be well known."

Praising the factories and shops, streets and homes, schools, churches, and modern improvements, the *Telegraph* summed up Kalamazoo's history in one slogan: "THE HARD WORKERS WIN!" Like Horatio Alger, the editor felt "it is the people who can do things who are most honored and most in demand." Where did Kalamazoo stand at the end of the 1880s? The town had weathered the crises of pioneer life, developed its resources and its products, and reached increasingly wider and larger markets. In the process it passed from village to city and claimed its place in Michigan commerce. Whether or not the city had accomplished all the *Telegraph* editor claimed, he still wrote with some justification, "when the multiplication of modern advantages for business, social, moral, or material purposes furnishes anything of real value, the people of Kalamazoo are bound to have it."

Every fall the pioneers came together for a picnic at Gull, Austin, or Long Lake. They listened to old stories of the times before the railroad. They bowed their heads during the reading of the list of those who had died since the last gathering. As the ranks of pioneers thinned, younger people came to the picnics instead. They looked on white-haired "old-timers" now in their seventies and eighties with affection and a little awe, but little real empathy. These young people looked forward instead to growth and markets. They talked of opera houses and waterworks, of trolley cars and telephones, of arc lights and cement walks, of sewers and suburbs. Now that Kalamazoo had all the attributes of city life, they wanted recognition from other towns and other countries. They knew where they stood; and the *Telegraph* concluded:

A city is the men who make it. Are they pushers, hardworkers, industrious, ever at it? The city shows it at once. They put the "go" into their enterprises. They reach out and get customers and trade. Their wits are tireless in inventing ways to excel their rivals in the service of their patrons. They compel patronage by the superiority of their goods and their success in accommodating their customers. This is the secret of the greatest successes in Kalamazoo.

In the century to come they and their children would gain that recognition in ways they could hardly imagine.

Masonic Hall.
CLOTHING
MILLINERY.
J.R.Jones.
SCOTT & SABIN
H.Bishop&Son.
C.C.CAPEN
MILLINERY
& STRAW GOODS.
BOO

KALAMAZOO

THE PLACE BEHIND THE PRODUCTS

PART TWO
1890-1981

by

Larry B. Massie

Kalamazoo has 35,000 people . . . most of whom manufacture for a living and the rest of whom sell celery. . . . If it were not for Kalamazoo, the banqueters of the land would have to go hungry until the first course were served.

Kalamazoo has an insane asylum inhabited chiefly by actors who have tried to get up new jokes on it and also a large variety of colleges drawn hither by the exceptional facilities for a college yell which the city's name affords. . . .

Quiet and unnoticed towns should consider Kalamazoo and get a little ragtime into their names. It is the cheapest form of advertising.

George Fitch, "A Glimpse of Kalamazoo the Beautiful" (ca. 1914)

SIGNIFICANT DATES

1893   Electric streetcars replace the horse-drawn cars.

1894   The first brick paving is laid in the city. U.S. Senator Francis B. Stockbridge of Kalamazoo dies; the following year Julius Caesar Burrows is appointed to take his place.

1896   The first rural free delivery mail service in Michigan begins at Climax on December 1.

1897   The "Celery City" receives a Catholic school for girls, Nazareth Academy. Kalamazoo County Bar Association is organized.

1898   Two hundred fifty men from Kalamazoo County serve in the Spanish-American War. General William Rufus Shafter, from Galesburg, is Commander of the American Army in Cuba.

1899   President William McKinley visits the city for the opening of the local Street Fair. The area's first golf course, the Wanikin Golf Club, is established west of Monroe Street. The Kalamazoo Public School System becomes the first in the state to include manual training in its curriculum.

1900   George W. Taylor takes delivery on the first automobile in the city—a Locomobile. Electric interurban service to Battle Creek is inaugurated. Theodore Roosevelt speaks in Bronson Park.

1903   After a spirited battle with other cities, Kalamazoo is designated the site of Western State Normal School, which opens the following year under the leadership of President Dwight B. Waldo.

1904   Cornerstone of "Kalamazoo Hospital" (later renamed Bronson Hospital) is laid. First automobile-related fatality in Kalamazoo.

1905   The *Kalamazoo Gazette* is the first local employer to put the eight-hour day into effect.

1906   The "Bijou," Kalamazoo's first motion-picture theater, opens on South Burdick Street.

1911   President William Howard Taft dedicates the new Burdick Hotel and lays the cornerstone of the YMCA building.

1914   Sheriff Ralph Chapman introduces fingerprint-identification procedures at his office.

1915   The fire department purchases first two motorized firetrucks. Kalamazoo

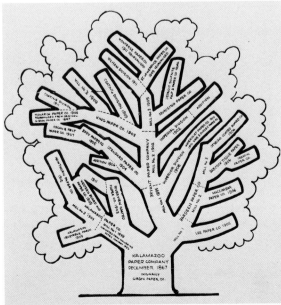

The Kalamazoo Valley's many paper mills grew out of the original Kalamazoo Paper Company. Courtesy, Georgia Pacific Paper Company.

Above
On July 17, 1928, local officials gathered for ceremonies at the inauguration of airmail service to Kalamazoo. Courtesy, Kalamazoo Chamber of Commerce.

Below
The Checker Cab Manufacturing Corporation sponsored this splendid float at the 1929 Kalamazoo Centennial parade. Courtesy, Kalamazoo Public Museum.

votes in Prohibition under the local option law.

1917 America enters World War I. By June 4, 4,140 Kalamazoo men register for the draft. Nearly 2,200 Kalamazoo men will serve in uniform, including two companies of the 126th Infantry of the 32nd Division commanded by Colonel Joseph B. Westnedge.

1918 Kalamazoo is among the first cities in the nation to adopt the City Manager-Commission form of government.

1920 The Douglass Community

Association is incorporated. It serves initially as a recreational center for black servicemen stationed at Camp Custer.

1921 Kalamazoo Symphony Orchestra is organized.

1923 Kalamazoo Institute of Fine Arts is created.

1925 Cornerstone of St. Augustine High School is laid. Kalamazoo Foundation is organized.

1928 Airmail service is inaugurated at the first municipal airport in Michigan, located south of the city and called "Lindbergh Field."

1929 Kalamazoo celebrates the "Centennial" of the arrival of the city's founder, Titus Bronson.

1931 The new City Hall is dedicated. Last of the Grand Circuit horse races held in Kalamazoo. The Civic Auditorium, a gift of the Dr. William E. Upjohn family, opens. WKZO, the city's first radio station, begins broad-

casting.

1933 All Michigan banks close for an eight-day holiday on February 14, and Kalamazoo city workers are paid in scrip.

1934 City buses replace the last trolley cars.

1936 Cornerstone is laid for the new W.P.A.-financed County Building.

1937 In the midst of the Great Depression, the last remaining bonds against the municipal government are burned, and Kalamazoo becomes the only city of 50,000 or more in the nation to be free of debt.

1941–1945 World War II. Many local industries produce defense goods, and more than 12,000 people from Kalamazoo County serve in the Armed Forces.

1949 First parking meters installed on the city's streets.

1950 WKZO-TV, the city's first television station, begins broadcasting.

1951 The National Municipal League designates Kalamazoo as an "All-American City."

1957 Kalamazoo is chosen by U.S. Information Service as a typical medium-sized American city for display in Europe.

1959 First two blocks of Kalamazoo Mall, the first permanent pedestrian mall in the U.S., are completed.

1963 Amidst mounting racial tension, the city is visited by the Reverend Martin Luther King, who proclaims that Americans must "live as brothers or perish as fools."

1964 The city of Portage is incorporated as a separate entity.

1968 Kalamazoo Valley Community College opens under the leadership of Dr. Dale B. Lake.

1975 The Kalamazoo Center, a unique joint venture by the Inland Steel Development Corporation and the city government, provides new life for the downtown district.

1980 The May 13 tornado strikes the heart of Kalamazoo, killing five and causing $50 million in property damage.

During an auto show in the fall of 1958 Burdick Street was a busy place. Courtesy, Kalamazoo Chamber of Commerce.

CHAPTER V
THE CELERY CITY:
1890–1900

Large families were essential in the labor-intensive celery industry. Here a grower's child poses next to some prime stalks. Courtesy, Portage Public Library.

In 1890 William E. Hill, successful manufacturer of heavy sawmill machinery accepted the gavel of office from outgoing Mayor Otto Ihling, manufacturer of blank books, forms, and stationery. Mayors who were manufacturers not only augured well for the ensuing decade's industrial expansion, but also symbolized Kalamazoo's characteristic interaction of business, community, and government.

Mayor Hill set the tone for the coming years in his inaugural address, when he proclaimed: "Our manufacturers are getting to be numerous, many new ones are coming every year. They should be encouraged." During the last decade of the 19th century, partly as a result of this encouragement, Kalamazoo enjoyed a dramatic increase in both number and type of factories. Out of 93 manufacturing concerns visited by the state factory inspector in 1901, 43 were established in the 1890s. Though Kalamazoo had already gained a reputation for its diverse industrial output, these new establishments further broadened the spectrum to include skirts and petticoats, fishing reels, bicycles, corsets, preserves, rugs, uniforms and swords, bedding, folding canvas boats, peppermint oils, camera shutters, silos, playing cards, gasoline engines, sleds, cattle guards, railway velocipedes, mandolins, and many other items.

As these developing industries attracted more workers, the city grew in population as well. In 1890 the population stood at 17,853. Ten years later the federal census taker counted 24,404 inhabitants, an increase of 37 percent. The U.S. census director in his report for 1890 announced that "there can hardly be said to be a frontier line." Yet a host of entrepreneurs demonstrated, through their ingenuity in adapting a product to society's changing needs, that manufacturing and marketing frontiers still awaited conquest and the "frontier spirit" was alive and well in Kalamazoo.

At the beginning of the decade, Kalamazoo still exhibited many of the primitive characteristics associated with the frontier. But the city was undergoing a technological revolution that would soon make it almost unrecognizable to its early settlers. Each year saw more homes connected to city water lines and public sewers as the city government expanded its services to accommodate the increasing industrial and population pressures. This

was still the age of wood, however. The steam engine at the waterworks consumed 1,180½ cords of wood in 1890, and hollowed logs bound by iron bands served as water mains.

Many more sewer hookups would be necessary before the job of City Scavenger—whose unenviable task it was to empty by hand the contents of privy vaults—no longer appeared in the city's *Annual Report*.

In 1890 the Committee on City Lighting proudly reported installing 10 new electric street lights, bringing the total in Kalamazoo to 128. But the committee also remarked, "There are still a few places more where a light would be great accommodation to our people." The streets themselves, often in miserable condition, either clogged traveler's lungs with dust or turned into rutted sloughs. The first brick paving did not appear until 1894. The Committee on Streets and Bridges in 1890 called attention to the new four-horse road scraper, which helped relieve the perennial springtime suffering brought on by "the Winter's avalanche of mud." The next year 700 newly placed street signs enhanced civic pride, as well as the ability to locate addresses.

Two hose carriages, a hook-and-ladder truck, and a chemical engine—all horse-drawn—guarded the city against confla-

Ihling Bros. & Everard's turn-of-the-century advertising was quite sentimental in design. Former mayor Otto Ihling's company manufactured blank books and printed business forms and stationery. Courtesy, Western Michigan University Archives.

grations. The city Fire Department responded to 59 alarms in 1890 and Chief Byron J. Healy reported that in "not a single instance have the firemen allowed any building to burn down within reach of the water mains." Throughout the decade, however, several spectacular blazes tested the firefighters' heroism. The Dewing Lumber Company fire destroyed 13 buildings and a large stock of lumber in 1895, and the Hall Brothers Chemical Company explosion in 1898 killed 10 persons, including four firemen.

Kalamazoo retained an aura of small-town innocence and, despite the scarcity of street lighting, few people locked their doors at night. But serious crime occasionally jolted the city, such as in 1893 when Louis Schilling was found dead in his Portage Street meat market. The police were never able to solve his murder. The city's police force then consisted of a marshal, his assistant, and eight patrolmen. Marshal Thomas F. Owens noted in 1890: "for the first time in the history of the city, the Kalamazoo police force impresses one as representing something. The men are completely and appropriately uniformed." During that same year, 498 miscreants of various sorts took a ride in the newly acquired paddy wagon. Drunkenness was the major offense.

It was an age when typhoid fever, diphtheria and scarlet fever still killed Kalamazooans. Father Francis O'Brien and the Sisters of St. Joseph had opened the city's

first hospital, Borgess, in a converted Italianate mansion on Portage Street in 1889, but those in need of a physician usually received a house call. Normally these rounds were made in a light buggy. A doctor looking for a new model could choose from a wide variety that were produced locally. In fact, with 11 factories employing more than 800 workers in 1895, carriage-manufacturing comprised one of Kalamazoo's most important industries.

Spoke drivers, iron banders, scrollers, woodworkers, blacksmiths, painters, fitters, springmakers, and wheelmakers plied their specialized skills to produce thousands of wheeled vehicles, sleighs, and component parts. D. Burrell & Son, from their factory at the corner of Main and Park streets, fashioned carriages, wagons, buckboards, and "bob sleighs in their season." Cornell & Company at the corner of Rose and Eleanor produced carriages, buggies and sleighs. Lull & Skinner (later the Lull Carriage Company) had a plant that covered three and a half acres at Grace and Pitcher streets with an annual capacity of 10,000 vehicles and 5,000 sleighs and cutters. The largest single employer in the 1890s, the Newton Carriage Company on Willard Street, made "ten styles of vehicles all provided with Newton's patent springs." Other manufacturers included: Thomas R. Bevans at his Kalamazoo Carriage Works on North Burdick Street, which produced "all kinds of carriages, cutters, and

Kalamazoo belles rode in a flower-covered buggy during the 1898 street fair. Among the Kalamazoo companies producing buggies in the 1890s were Cornell & Company, the Hicks Carriage Company, and the Michigan Buggy Company. Courtesy, Kalamazoo Public Museum.

sleighs"; the Kalamazoo Wagon Company, "fine surreys and cutters a specialty"; the Hicks Carriage Company, "A-grade buggies"; the American Cart Company, phaeton carts and road wagons; and the Michigan Buggy Company which produced "a full line of buggies, cabriolets, phaetons, surreys, spring wagons, etc."

In good weather some doctors relinquished their horse-and-buggies for that craze of the 1890s, the bicycle. After the safety bicycle replaced the dangerous high-wheeled velocipede, this period witnessed the golden age of bicycling for sport and business alike. Badly rutted roads offered hazards even for safety "wheels," so certain well-maintained routes received most of the traffic. A favorite Sunday recreational drive ran from Kalamazoo through Augusta to LaBelle Resort at Gull Lake for lunch, on to Richland, and then back over a special bicycle path at the edge of Gull Road.

Several ingenious Kalamazoo mechanics manufactured bicycles to meet the new demand. The Big Four Cycle Company widely advertised its product, and the Blood brothers, Maurice and Charles, successfully marketed their "Fortune" bicycles. The Kalamazoo Cycle Company, with Maurice Blood as general manager and a local physician Rush McNair as president, manufactured an early bicycle basket patented in 1891. The device appeared to be practical, especially for doctors with their medical bags, but the disappointed promoters failed to develop a successful market. Dr. Rush McNair stated in his *Medical Memoirs* (1939): "A stock company was formed to make and sell this carrier. I put a year's salary into it and it is there yet."

By the 1890s Kalamazoo relinquished its old sobriquet, "Burr Oak City," for "Celery City." This reflected the importance of the major product of the period. Celery, indigenous to Europe, was used there primarily as a seasoning herb. During the 1850s two Scotch brothers, James and George Taylor, imported celery seeds and introduced the vegetable to Kalamazoo. Originally served as a curiosity at banquets at the Burdick Hotel in 1856, the crunchy stalks soon won a place in the local diet. By the last quarter of the 19th century, celery, along with other salad vegetables, supplemented the traditional meals of meat, cooked vegetables, and bread. In 1890 Kalamazoo township,

with approximately 3,000 acres under cultivation, was the largest celery-growing region in the world. By the end of the decade 4,000 acres were under cultivation, and 400 farms employed a total of 3,500 persons in celery culture.

Local shippers sent huge quantities of celery to a widespread market, especially to tourist areas such as Mackinac Island, Washington, D.C., New Orleans, and the state of Florida. The volume shipped by train gave Kalamazoo a state ranking sec-

Kalamazoo's city scavengers—Bill Nye, Link Norman, and Hemmo Kroon—performed an unpleasant but necessary task in the 1890s. They hand-emptied the contents of privy vaults. Courtesy, Western Michigan University Archives.

Top
The letterhead of the short-lived Kalamazoo Cycle Company illustrated their bicycle basket, which was patented in 1891. M.E. Blood and Rush McNair headed the company. Courtesy, Western Michigan University Archives.

Middle
The Hinga & Morris' blacksmith shop of North Rose Street provided essential services such as shoeing horses and repairing wagons and other wheeled vehicles. Courtesy, Western Michigan University Archives.

Bottom
Milkmen such as F.S. Nichols of Kalamazoo sold their product by the pitcher in the 1890s. Good horses learned the route and stopped by themselves before each customer's residence. Courtesy, Kalamazoo Public Library.

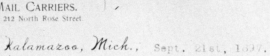

The Kalamazoo Cycle Co.,
Sole Owners and Mfrs. of
THE KALAMAZOO

Jobbers of all Kinds of
BICYCLE SUNDRIES

RUSH McNAIR, President.
EVERARD, Treasurer.
BLOOD, Sec and Gen'l Mg'r.

Dealers in
BICYCLES.

PARCEL CARRIERS,
CHILD'S SEATS,
BABY CARRIERS AND
MAIL CARRIERS.

FOR
BICYCLES.

208, 210 and 212 North Rose Street.

Kalamazoo, Mich., Sept. 21st, 1897.

Mr. C. C. Cutting,

"Noon-time in June time"
Idlewild

Above left
This turn-of-the-century pamphlet promoted the development of Gull Lake. A bicycle ride out to Idlewild was a favorite Sunday diversion. From the author's collection.

Above
The first Kodak camera introduced in 1888 produced round photographs such as this one of South Burdick Street looking north, circa 1890. The camera contained a strip of film allowing 100 exposures, and photographers shipped the entire unit back to the company for developing. Courtesy, Western Michigan University Archives.

Left
Small boys were among the employees of the Kalamazoo Wheel Works when this photograph was taken circa 1890. Courtesy, Kalamazoo Public Library.

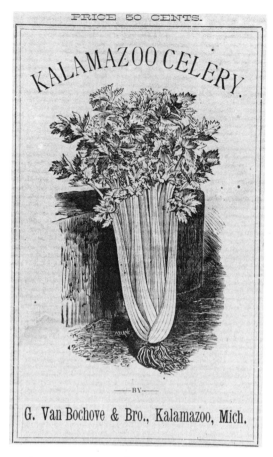

PRICE 50 CENTS.

KALAMAZOO CELERY.

—BY—

G. Van Bochove & Bro., Kalamazoo, Mich.

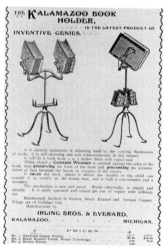

ond only to Detroit in total freight shipments throughout most of the decade. Celery growing, packing, and shipping assumed such a major role in the local economy that in 1897, following a bad growing season, the Kalamazoo Township Superintendent of the Poor reported spending twice the usual amount allotted for relief.

A number of factors contributed to this intense localization of celery culture. Land described by pioneers as "an impassable marsh and tamarack swamp covered with water the year around" constituted an ideal environment for the highly selective plant. Celery, which had originally been grown in Europe in salt marshes, needed muck, salt, and plenty of water. Geologically Kalamazoo was almost perfect. A layer of three to six feet of fertile, nonacidic muck—or decayed vegetable humus—had been deposited in a basin consisting of a sandy drift, surcharged with water, sandwiched between two layers of water-impervious clay. As a result water would rise at artesian wells sunk on the periphery of the basin, but when applied to the muck would not percolate below the underlying clay. Growers added salt to the soil as the final necessary ingredient.

In addition to a specific environment, celery culture demanded constant, patient

attention. Because of the specialized technology involved, growing was most efficiently managed in small plots. Poor immigrants from Holland, where agriculture traditionally consisted of intense cultivation of small holdings, flocked to an area where they could buy 5-to-10-acre plots of the swampland avoided by earlier arrivals. Some ditching proved necessary but ideal conditions required standing water about two feet below the surface. By dedicating themselves to learning celery culture and enlisting the help of their large families, the "Celery Dutch," as they came to be called, soon developed a monopoly in this extremely labor-intensive industry.

Celery growing, because of the plant's tenderness, was almost completely performed by hand. Seed sown in hotbeds around the beginning of March, after eight weeks of careful nurturing, produced delicate seedlings, ready for planting in the open fields. These fields were well fertilized with stable manure from the city's hotels, then plowed, leveled, and salted (a barrel an acre per year).

In plowing—one of the few tasks not completely done by hand—horses wore special hardwood shoes, six or seven inches across, to keep them from sinking into the muck. Farmers marked off rows about six feet apart to allow for an early and late planting. Then wearing the traditional wooden shoes, or "Klompen," they tramped down the muck. Wooden shoes were ideal for working in the muck because mud did not adhere to them as easily and, although continually wet, they did not rot like leather.

The entire family had to work hard to make a success of celery growing. Transferring the tender seedlings to the muck fields and carrying water for irrigation demanded long hours of patient backbreaking labor. Since the plants were too delicate for the strong pesticides then available, the little Dutch children continually faced the unpleasant task of picking off cutworms. After about eight weeks of growing, a two-week bleaching period produced the tender, white qualities preferred by contemporary taste. In the summer, wooden planks shielded plants from the sun, while during the fall, farmers using hand hoes patiently mounded earth over the rows to guard against frost. The exact time for harvesting was critical, since ripe celery had to be pulled within a day or two. This, too, was done by hand, preferably in the early morning

Cornelius De Bruin pioneered in commercial celery growing circa 1870. About two decades later Kalamazoo Township was the world's largest celery-growing region. Courtesy, Kalamazoo Public Museum.

Portage celery farmers harvest their crop circa 1900. If the plants were not pulled within two days after ripening, the crop would be ruined. Courtesy, Portage Public Library.

dew which, local tradition decreed, produced a crisper product. Finally the plants were wheelbarrowed out of the fields to be washed, trimmed, and tied up into lots of a dozen for shipment to the nation's tables, "fresh as the dew from Kalamazoo." Growers stored celery through the cold Michigan winter in trenches covered with muck, digging it up as needed.

Kalamazooans, proud of their success in celery, promoted the concept of the Celery City. As early as the 1870s celery had been hawked at the Michigan Central Railroad Station. By the 1890s, vendors boarded stopped trains and offered stalks of celery to puzzled travelers. People who remembered nothing else about Kalamazoo remembered celery. In 1896 William Jennings Bryan, campaigning for the presidency, delivered his famous "Free Silver" speech across the nation and recorded: "At Kalamazoo we received a large quantity of celery, sufficient to supply our table for several days, with the compliments of the Hollanders." Others wrote about the Kalamazoo-celery connection in a humorous vein. Fred Yaple, from nearby Mendon, wrote a poem about a Kalamazoo farmer's encounter with big-city bustle: "Farmer Dew! Farmer Dew! Took a trip up to the Soo - There was celery in his whiskers, for he hailed from Kalamazoo. . . ."

The 1899 *Kalamazoo City Directory* lists more than 350 individual celery growers and shippers. Each company sought a distinctive brand name. A sampling of

these brand names reveals both ingenuity and banality: Acme Celery Company, Big 4, Champion, Columbia, Crystal, Dutch, Empire, Enterprise, Eureka, German, Giant Selected, Gold Medal, Great White, IXL, Little Joe, Manila, Nine Point, One Price, Silver Medal, Silver Plume, Snow Flake, White Plume, Wolverine, and World's Fair. Some of the celery entrepreneurs, such as Samuel J. Dunkley of the Dunkley Celery & Preserving Company, maintained straightforward though unimaginative business names and turned their ingenuity to producing innovative celery products. Dunkley attempted with more or less limited success to market canned celery, celery salad, celery mustard, celery pickles, celery pepper, and celeryade drops. This last product was considered "medicinal."

Celery had long been suspected of having medicinal properties chiefly as a remedy for that vague but troubling category of "nervous disorders." During the 1890s patent-medicine manufacturers offered a wide range of celery medicines, including: Celery Bitters, Celery Vesce, Celery Crackers, Celerena, Celery-Cola, Paine's Celery Compound, and Sears Roebuck's Celery Malt Compound. Most of these products apparently relied on the "nerve-quieting" effects of celery oil. Most producers, however, took the added precaution of incorporating as much as 21 percent alcohol into the compound. It went down easier.

Kalamazoo itself boasted several such manufacturers. The Celery Medicine Company, in an 1895 advertisement, offered "Celery Tonic Bitters: the only true nerve tonic and appetizer." The P.L. Abbey Company produced a "celery preparation"; and the Quality Drug Stores mar-

keted "Kalamazoo Celery and Sarsaparilla Compound," claiming that it was a cure for "fever and ague, all forms of nervousness, headache and neuralgia," and a "positive cure for female complaints." Though the federal government later fined the Quality Drug Stores for fraudulent advertising, few consumers complained. A belt of celery compound laced with 21 percent alcohol certainly seemed to improve, or at least cheer up, a "nervous" disposition.

While the nervous gulped celery tinctures, women in need of similar bolstering sipped Kalamazoo's most famous medicinal cure, Zoa-Phora. In 1885 three prominent Kalamazooans ventured into the profitable realm of patent medicines and founded the Zoa-Phora Medicine Company. Latham Hull, president of the First National Bank also served as president of Zoa-Phora; Samuel A. Gibson, highly respected superintendent of the Kalamazoo Paper Company became vice-president; and Howard G. Colman, suc-

IF YOU have the least idea of purchasing a Buggy or Surrey call on us and we will convince you that our styles are attractive and that the

CONE COUPLER

Is a positive Anti-Rattler of real merit and of great durability. We are making a general line of Fine Vehicles, which have simplicity of construction and elegant appearance. Should you call you will receive courteous attention.

cessful druggist, doubled as secretary and treasurer. By the 1880s the firm's members identified themselves as "manufacturing chemists," while ironically the publisher of the 1893 *Kalamazoo City Directory* inadvertently printed in bold type below Zoa-Phora's listing: "Caution. Beware of swindling operations. . . ."

Huge display advertisements in newspapers labeled Zoa-Phora "Women's Friend," offering deliverance from "the slough of despondence and a sickness worse than death." Effective for women of any age because it was a remedy that went "at once to the seat of the problem," the nostrum proffered "a steady hand to guide the frail and sickly girl to and through the trying period that opened to her the untraveled paths of womanhood." Where other remedies failed during times of pregnancy, Zoa-Phora "buoyed up and strengthened and built up" and, as a woman passed "from the period of motherhood to the last period of life," it was still "her friend and main-

stay." Doubters could scan an appended list containing names of hundreds of "enthusiastic" Michigan women more than happy to testify that "Zoa-Phora never fails." The nostrum sold for a dollar in bottles curiously resembling pint whiskey flasks, and until the company folded in 1910, Victorian sufferers across the country found their lives "buoyed up" by Zoa-Phora, "Women's Friend."

The refining of another substance widely used in medicines of the period, peppermint oil, developed into an important local industry during the 1890s. Albert M. Todd began distilling and refining mint oil in 1868 at Nottawa in St. Joseph County, which was then the major Michigan mint-growing area. In the summer of 1891 he moved his operations to Kalamazoo and built the Todd Block at the corner of Kalamazoo Avenue and Rose Street.

A.M. Todd, a dynamic man, involved himself in a wide variety of activities. He excelled as a book and art collector, searching European galleries and shops and displaying excellent taste in his selections. As a political reformer he advocated many of the liberal causes of the day such as Prohibition and public ownership of utilities, yet maintained a widespread popularity. Running as a Democrat in a district that had been solidly Republican since the Party's birth in 1854, he was elected to represent the Third Congressional District in 1896, the only Democrat elected to Congress from Michigan that year.

Though peppermint had been commercially grown in Michigan since 1835, the major producing area in the United States

Above
Albert M. Todd, book and art collector, political reformer, and Democratic congressman, was better known as the "Mint King." By 1900 his Campagnia Farm had become the largest peppermint farm in the world. Courtesy, Western Michigan University Archives.

Left
The Cone Coupler Carriage Company, located at 1520 North Pitcher Street, produced quiet, durable, elegant buggies and surreys. Courtesy, Western Michigan University Archives.

Below
The factory warehouse of the Kalamazoo Carriage Works was located at 119 West Kalamazoo Avenue. Courtesy, Western Michigan University Archives.

had remained Wayne County, New York. Albert M. Todd more than any other individual is credited with wresting this control from New York State. By the turn of the century, 90 percent of the world's supply of peppermint grew within 75 miles of Kalamazoo and the A.M. Todd Company refined most of it.

The major factors that brought about this dramatic localization can be traced to Todd. He pioneered in shifting mint cultivation from the traditional burr-oak plains to muck land. Todd's two major farms were in muck land—"Mentha" in Van Buren County and the "Campagnia Farm," which was located near Fennville in Allegan County. At the turn of the century, Campagnia was the world's largest peppermint farm. Todd imported from

ed as a brake on industrial development until an upswing occurred in 1897. Despite this slump, America went all out to prepare the grandest, most ornate, and best-remembered World's Fair ever, Chicago's Columbian Exposition. More than 12 million individuals—one out of every six persons in America—visited the majestic "White City." Since Chicago was less than 150 miles away, many of those in attendance were from Kalamazoo. Some boarded excursion runs of the Michigan Central Railroad and, within a few hours, found themselves gaping at the marvelous dream world created at Jackson Park. Their eyes were opened to the world's diversity and to the marvels of modern technology. Winding their way down the "Midway Plaisance," they could purchase a ride on the original Ferris Wheel. This monstrous wheel, invented as the American answer to the Eiffel Tower, sported gondolas the size of boxcars. They could visit Sitting Bull's log cabin, a replica of Ireland's Blarney Castle, and Chinese, German, Japanese, Dahomey, or Lapland villages. Many ladies from Kalamazoo certainly must have been in the audience at the Congress of Women, held in the Women's Building, to listen to their own Lucinda

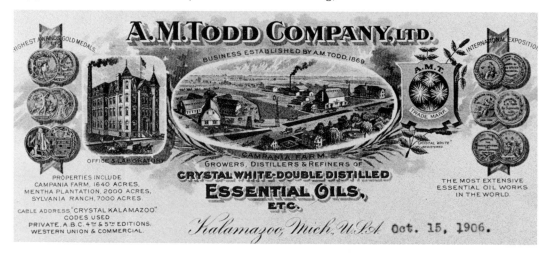

England a hardier, more productive variety of plant, the Black Mitcham, which soon replaced the traditional American variety. Most importantly, perhaps, Todd's relentless pursuit of quality control and his development of tests and standards drove the heavily adulterated American mint oils off the market, securing a worldwide reputation for Michigan mint as the finest quality available.

In 1893, two years after Todd began building his Kalamazoo peppermint empire, the nation experienced the beginning of a major economic depression. This act-

Hinsdale Stone speak on "Some of the Lessons of the World's Fair." While their wives were occupied with such uplifting pursuits, some of the men from Kalamazoo undoubtedly seized the opportunity to join the queue waiting for a glimpse of "Little Egypt," who shocked Victorian morality but still drew huge crowds with her native belly dance.

Nearly everyone visited the Manufacturers and Liberal Arts Building, an enormous structure containing more than 30 acres of ground-floor space. There they saw a variety of Kalamazoo products on display. The novel folding canvas boat manufactured by William A. King won an award of merit. Ihling Brothers & Everard received a top award for their display of duplicate whist trays, and their competitor, the Henderson-Ames Company, proudly proclaimed on their business letterhead that "Our exhibit at the World's Fair was awarded the medal and diploma for super-excellence of quality and design." Returning to what must have seemed a diminutive Kalamazoo after viewing these huge, gaudy displays, the excited travelers rearranged their parlors to make room for many souvenirs, allotted a place of importance to the huge pictorial volumes documenting this soon-to-vanish fairyland, and prepared to return to normal life—working for wages to earn a living.

Although 19th-century wages seem inadequate and the hours of work excessive by today's standards, Kalamazooans got by, took a vacation to a World's Fair now and again, and even improved their lot. The 10-hour day and six-day work week—for men and women, bosses and apprentices, in factories, stores, and offices—was established as the norm, and employers computed wages by the day rather than the hour. The state Bureau of Labor canvassed more than 5,000 male workers throughout Michigan just before the turn of the century. Superintendents averaged $3.87 for a 10-hour day; foremen, $2.79; millers, $1.79; molders, $2.55; mechanics, $2.01; factory workers, $1.75; teamsters, $1.33; day laborers, $1.27; and apprentices, 75 cents. In Kalamazoo, union cigarmakers earned $12 per week, barbers $8 to $12 per week, and police officers $1.75 a day. Of those canvassed 60 percent were married, 27 percent owned their homes, 55 percent reported that they could save something from their earnings over and above the cost of living, and 80 percent registered satisfaction "that times were growing better." Everyone received in his pay envelope exactly what he earned. Federal and state income taxes and social-security deductions were yet to come.

A similar poll of over 2,100 women revealed a wide variance in their wages compared to men's. Foreladies made an average of $1.11 for a 10-hour day; bookkeepers, $1.23; office clerks, $1.05; stenographers, $1.18; store clerks, 84 cents; teachers, $1.25 for nine months of 6.8-hour days; telephone operators, 58 cents; nurses, 70 cents; general factory workers, 83 cents; domestics, 49 cents; and apprentices, 40 cents or four cents an hour. In Kalamazoo women corset-factory workers got 80 cents for a 10-hour day; card-factory workers, 70 cents; and women sorting rags in the paper mills earned 67 cents a day. Few of those canvassed were married, only 13 percent. Less than six percent owned their own homes and 83 percent boarded. Only a third of Kalamazoo's working women reported being able to save anything from their earnings. Many children worked in the 1890s in Kalamazoo, as they did in most of the nation. Children under 16 took home only an average of $2.04 for a full week's work. The Bureau of Labor did not ask women and children if they thought times were getting better.

The Kalamazoo-produced Scientific Washer, which "sterilized" and washed clothes, ran on boy power. The company was located on Water Street. Courtesy, Western Michigan University Archives.

THE SCIENTIFIC Washer,

SCIENTIFIC WASHER MF'G BY WASHER CO KALAMAZOO. MICH. PAT' APPLIED FOR

THIS Machine is constructed on the most scientific princip'es.

Steam under pressure will sterilize and purify. In this machine the revolving cylinder is tightly closed by means of packed joints, holding a pressure that causes the warm suds and steam to penetrate the clothes and loosen the dirt.

As the cylinder rotates the clothes fall and strike on slats at the ends, thereby forcing the water through the clothes, carrying the dirt away leaving them sweet and clean.

By first sterilizing and then washing, the work is so perfectly done that by actual test an ordinary washing is done in one-half the usual time (without rubbing).

Let us put a machine in your house and it will prove this statement for itself and you.

DIRECTIONS:—To do washing easy, soak the clothes over night and use hot water. Load the machine light until you get used to running it and don't use too much soap. Turn awhile one way, then reverse turning both ways.

You can wash anything from a lace curtain to a heavy bed quilt. This machine can be built any size for family use or laundry work.

The Scientific Washer Co.,

Herbert S. Humphrey's hot water heater, pictured in this 1897 advertisement, was lit when hot water was needed. Courtesy, Western Michigan University Archives.

Herbert S. Humphrey's brother Alfred H. invented the "Humphrey Arc" gaslight. This revolutionized gas lighting and launched the General Gas Light Company which continues as Humphrey Products Inc. Courtesy, Western Michigan University Archives.

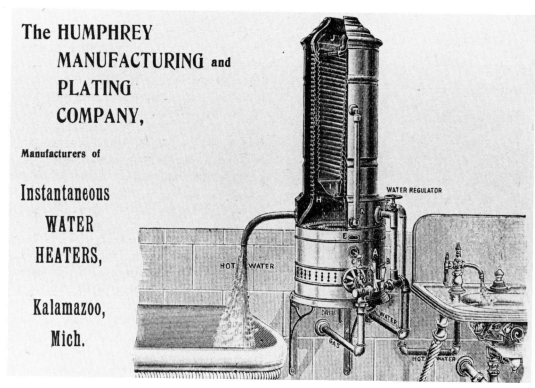

The HUMPHREY MANUFACTURING and PLATING COMPANY,

Manufacturers of

Instantaneous WATER HEATERS,

Kalamazoo, Mich.

Low wages and long hours remained the lot of factory workers during this period, and many of them labored their entire lives without making appreciable progress. Through a combination of hard work, ingenuity, and good timing, however, it was possible to leave the factory life behind. The final third of the 19th century was the "golden age of invention" in America and Europe. The study of science had grown increasingly popular. Americans eagerly gathered for public lectures on scientific topics, subscribed to journals such as *Scientific American,* and read of the newest technological discoveries in their local newspapers. Before the Civil War many school systems adopted courses in chemistry and physics, or "natural philosophy," as it was then called. Students stimulated by high-school physics demonstrations later applied scientific principles to the practical problems they encountered.

Across America, in cities, sleepy little hamlets, and on the farm, thousands of largely self-taught inventors tinkered and experimented. When their inventions filled a need at the right time, they often launched successful careers. Thomas Alva Edison, Alexander Graham Bell, and George Eastman won international fame and fortune, and many others achieved more modest successes. In southwestern Michigan, during the last quarter of the 19th century, inventors and factories to produce their inventions gravitated to Kalamazoo because of its encouragement of industry, central location between Detroit and Chicago, splendid transportation facilities, and ready supply of labor.

George Sheffield, for example, was a young mechanic who worked in nearby Three Rivers in the late 1870s. He lived on his parents' farm about seven miles to the east, but the Michigan Central's schedule did not permit him to ride the train to work. Rather than walk, Sheffield designed and constructed an ingenious contraption, which resembled a bicycle but had an additional support wheel that allowed it to fit the train tracks. He pedaled his invention, which he called a "railroad velocipede" back and forth, without authorization from the railroad company. On his way home one winter night he discovered a broken track, certain to cause a train wreck. Securing a lantern from a nearby farm, he flagged the train down and assisted in repairing the track. When the railroad authorities found out what Sheffield had done, they gratefully gave him authorization to operate his velocipede over that stretch of track. Furthermore, after viewing his invention, they asked him to build more velocipedes for their tie inspectors to use. Thus the Sheffield Velocipede Car Company came into existence in Three Rivers. Within a few years Kalamazoo also boasted a small manufacturer of this novelty, the Kalamazoo Railroad Velocipede and Car Company. Originally they only manufactured railroad velocipedes, but by 1896, when the company was incorpo-

Kalamazoo R. R. Velocipede AND Car Co.

KALAMAZOO, MICH. U. S. A.

...The Tire of our 1894 Steel Wheel is made without a weld

The SUREST and SAFEST Stock-Turner IN THE MARKET.

THE BEST IS ALWAYS THE CHEAPEST

MANUFACTURERS OF

Many Styles Steel Velocipede Cars,
Hand and Steam Inspection Cars,
Steel Wheeled Hand Cars,
Tracklaying Cars,
Iron and Steel Wheeled Push Cars,
Sugar Cane Cars, Mining Cars,
Canopy Top Cars, Dump Cars,
Metal Surface Cattle Guards.

rated, more than 50 employees turned out a wide range of railroad-connected equipment. Its turn-of-the-century letterhead lists an impressive number of specialties: section-hand and push cars, ratchet and friction jacks, cattle guards, rail benders, automatic stand pipes, express wagons, and many others. Soon the company erected a larger factory on Reed Street, and from this point shipped Kalamazoo-made railroad supplies all over the globe. In Australia, "Kalamazoos" became slang for self-propelled section cars, and as late as the 1970s, motorized versions of the Kalamazoo Manufacturing Company's velocipedes still traveled Alaskan railways.

George Sheffield and the Kalamazoo Railroad Supply Company enjoyed considerable success by designing and producing equipment for the specialized needs of railroad transportation. Local transportation needs also provided opportunities for inventors and manufacturers. Horse-drawn streetcars had provided Kalamazoo with cheap urban transportation since 1884. These streetcars, while convenient, did little to change Kalamazoo life, however, because they were constrained—both in size and speed—by the limitations of the horse. But the introduction of the electric trolley in 1893 effected a minor revolution in urban transportation and radically altered the city map.

The electric trolleys allowed for larger,

faster cars and much longer routes. Heretofore workers had usually lived within easy walking distance of their place of employment. Now, since they could live outside the central city and ride a fast trolley to work, suburban developments sprang up. As trolley lines radiated out from the city center, they brought a geographical redistribution of the population and created a crucial need for housing and neighborhood development. Real-estate development and construction companies prospered during this period. The South Side Improvement Company, for example, constructed hundreds of homes for industrial workers between 1896 and 1899. As the heavy electric trolley cars ran faster, however, they also became more dangerous to pedestrians.

Fred N. Root, a local ice dealer and part-time inventor, developed an amazing gadget in 1891 to lessen the danger of collision. It was a kind of specialized cowcatcher designed to save the lives of pedestrians paralyzed by the sight of an onrushing trolley. A trip rod extending in front of the trolley caused a large basket to spring from under the car and safely catch the victim. In theory Root's invention was ingenious, but in practice it had its problems. Pedestrians were not caught unless squarely centered in the tracks. Nevertheless many trolley companies adopted the "people catchers" in the 1890s and Root continued to produce them into the 1920s. Fred Root later developed a more feasible product, the "Root spring scraper," when he mounted heavy coil springs on scraper blades to

This 1894 advertisement pictures products manufactured by the Kalamazoo Railroad Velocipede and Car Company. From the author's collection.

Below
These workers were laying trolley-car tracks alongside the Kalamazoo County Courthouse. With its introduction in 1893, the electric trolley provided faster transportation to those who formerly walked or took horsedrawn streetcars long distances. Courtesy, First National Bank of Kalamazoo.

Professional photographers with the International Scenic Photograph Co. travel through Kalamazoo with their portable darkroom. Courtesy, Western Michigan University Archives.

prevent them from breaking when they hit an obstruction. This revolutionized road-scraping procedures and remains the operating principle behind modern snowplows.

While Sheffield, Root, and others were busy with their transportation innovations, Kalamazooans were responding to technological advances in other fields, such as photography. Two manufacturers of camera shutters operated in Kalamazoo in the 1890s. Cullen C. Packard, who had been one of the city's leading commercial photographers since the Civil War, invented a simple and particularly durable "behind the lens" shutter. In 1895 he established a company to produce and market this invention. Packard's company continued after his death, in 1898, as the Michigan

Photo Shutter Company and his invention—called the Packard Shutter—remained a popular and high-quality product. The other firm, the Kalamazoo Shutter Company, began as a partnership between Garrett W. Low and William Shakespeare, Jr. After Low died in the late 1890s, the company continued on for a few years but eventually folded.

William Shakespeare, Jr., also an inventor, applied the precision skills he had learned as a shuttermaker to his hobby, fishing. At that time fishing with a rod and reel was a complicated procedure that could be successfully learned only through periods of dedicated practice. Rewinding the primitive reels required a nimble thumb, and many a cursing fisherman lost his trout to a tangled mess of line. Solutions to perplexing problems often come to men while performing such mundane activities as shaving and William Shakespeare, as a youth, had a similar brainstorm. As Shakespeare later recalled, he "was seated on the edge of his bed engaged in pulling off a sock when he visualized the principle of this reel." In the 1890s, using a jeweler's lathe, he worked out his youthful idea to produce the first practical level wind reel. A few years later he developed a sophisticated, lightly applied brake that prevented backlash. Securing a patent on his invention, the "wondereel," in 1896, he began to market first the reel, then other fishing equipment. He was also an early advocate of the shorter fishing rod, now almost universally used. The availability of his "built like a watch" reel and shorter rods enabled the novice to learn casting in a relatively short time, and probably did more than anything else to popularize the sport. Business boomed as his product caught public attention. He maintained high quality standards, developed such products as "Kazoo Bass Lures," hired more employees, and Shakespeare fishing tackle from Kalamazoo became known and respected by fishermen the world over.

The last decade of the 19th century also witnessed the birth of several Kalamazoo industries that catered to the demands fashion made on women of the "Gay Nineties." Fashion forbade women of the time, whether wives of rich manufacturers or lowly apprentices earning four cents an hour, to appear in public unless securely bound in tightly laced corsets. The "Gibson Girl" ideal of the hourglass figure owed as much to corsets ribbed with whalebone stays as to natural endowment. Corseting, however, led to various health complaints and other problems. Corset stays made of whalebone—which was actually the horny substance called baleen through which whales sieved plankton, their main food source—grew brittle and broke with age. Baleen also produced a rather unpleasant fishy odor on warm days and, as whales were hunted to near extinction, it grew more and more expensive.

In 1883 Edward K. Warren of Three Oaks, a sleepy little hamlet in southern Berrien County, secured a patent on an invention that solved this problem. He aptly named his brainstorm "Featherbone," which consisted of cut-up splints of turkey feathers bound in thread. Several strips were sewn together to form a cord, which was strong yet flexible, making it ideal for corset stays and whip cores. Shortly after he launched into production, the little town of Three Oaks boomed. Warren himself developed a whip-core factory in 1885, and in 1891 a former partner, J.H. Hatfield, started the Featherbone Corset Company.

By 1893 Hatfield had moved his rapidly expanding enterprise to Kalamazoo. In 1895 the company offered 20 different styles of corsets and its advertising proclaimed "all stores sell them." The Featherbone Corset Company soon thereafter became known as the Kalamazoo Corset Company and had a massive factory building on the northeast corner of Eleanor and Church streets. A rival manufacturer, the Puritan Corset Company, started up in the city but never proved competitive. The Kalamazoo Corset Company in time became the largest corset factory in the world and eventually employed more than 800 workers, predominantly women. Under the harsh glare of naked bulbs, engulfed by the Gatling-gun chatter of sewing machines, and surrounded by mounds of glistening material, hundreds of Kalamazoo women stitched out their 10-hour days producing the corsets that molded the figures of the nation's women.

Petticoats were another essential part of contemporary feminine apparel. But prior to 1895, when a woman wanted a new petticoat she had to order it from a dressmaker. No one had thought of offering ready-made petticoats to consumers. In 1895, when Nellie McLarty told her husband John how much she paid for a new petticoat, he thundered that it was exorbi-

$500 in Cash
and
Diamond Prizes
For Record Bait-Casting.

You can enter the great Shakespeare Bait-casting Tournament without expense, make all your trials at your own home and win some of the magnificent prizes offered each month this season, for the longest bait-cast. Many beginners can equal professionals the first month and win prizes and break the world's records.

$100 in Prizes for Largest Fish
Write me to-day. The New Shakespeare Reel meets the wants of the critical fisherman whose purse is limited. It is the highest grade reel on the market and none sold at twice the price can touch it. Shakespeare Reels and Baits are sent free on trial, express charges prepaid, to any angler who sends name and address. The Shakespeare Revolution Bait makes the biggest black bass strike when no other bait—live minnows or frogs—can tempt him. They catch big strings of fish for people who never caught fish before. In the water they struggle as if alive and attract game fish from many yards away. Write to-day and try them free of all expense to you.

WM. SHAKESPEARE, JR.,
108 Shakespeare Bldg., Kalamazoo, Mich.
My reels and baits are for sale by all first-class dealers.

tant and one could be made of much better material for 50 percent less. Out of this commonplace domestic argument grew the idea for a new business venture and John McLarty, a blacksmith at the Kalamazoo Wagon Company, decided to leave the forge and try his hand at petticoatmaking.

Since it was the Victorian era, and McLarty had chosen to manufacture a product usually referred to as "unmentionables," he selected a high-class but euphemistic business name, the French Skirt Company. The blacksmith began cautiously. He rented two cheap rooms downtown, bought a couple of foot-powered sewing machines and a bolt of heavyweight black sateen, and hired two experienced dressmakers. Orders solicited from the wholesale trade almost immediately brought a heavy response. In three months McLarty required larger quarters and more machines and employees. In six months another move proved necessary. Mail orders from merchants all over the country poured in at a rate of $2,000 to $3,000 a day. With McLarty's low overhead, profits for the first two years ran to 100 percent. Within three years, 30 to 50 women employees produced an average of two dozen petticoats each in a nine-hour day. At a piece rate of eight cents, they made $1.92

William Shakespeare, Jr.'s fishing tackle helped popularize fly casting. This turn-of-the-century advertisement was circulated nationally. Courtesy, Western Michigan University Archives.

a day, a high wage for garment workers at that time. The French Skirt Factory produced one style, used one grade of material, and made one color available to consumers—black.

As might be expected, petticoat factories began springing up all over the country. With competition came price cutting and consumers were soon beguiled by a wide variety of styles, grades, and colors. When his salespeople began clamoring for new styles and different colors, shades, and materials, John McLarty, the pioneer petticoatmaker, decided it was time to take his profits and leave the business to those who had more of a head for fashion. He sold out to Walter Wormly and Fred Wickes who continued in this highly competitive endeavor until it folded in 1910. McLarty turned from skirts to

Above
These corsetmakers are hard at work at the Kalamazoo Corset Company, formerly the Featherbone Corset Company. When the company became the world's largest corset manufacturer, the majority of its more than 800 employees consisted of women. Courtesy, Western Michigan University Archives.

Right
Countless turkeys contributed feathers to mold American figures thanks to J.H. Hatfield's Featherbone Corset Company. Hatfield's former partner Edward K. Warren patented the idea for turkey-feather corset stays in 1883 as a replacement for whalebone. Courtesy, Western Michigan University Archives.

Facing page
Top
Dashing Orville Gibson handcrafted beautiful wooden mandolins from his workshop on East Michigan. Each instrument took him six weeks to complete. Courtesy, Gibson Company.

Bottom
Orville Gibson's unique stringed instruments filled his workshop in the 1890s. Courtesy, Gibson Company.

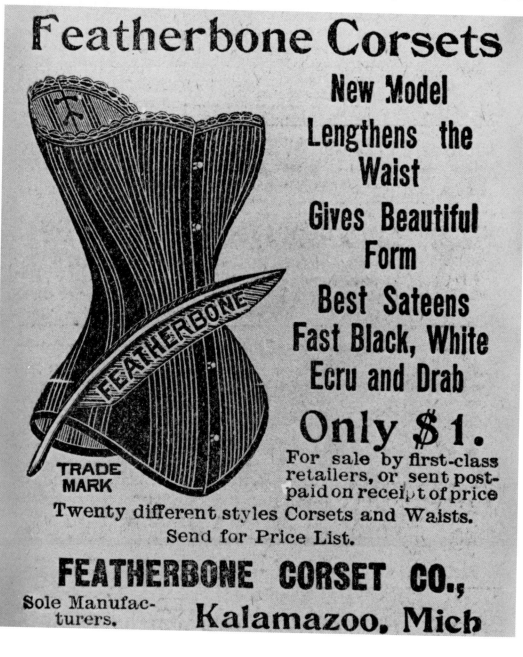

Featherbone Corsets

New Model
Lengthens the Waist
Gives Beautiful Form
Best Sateens
Fast Black, White Ecru and Drab

Only $1.

For sale by first-class retailers, or sent post-paid on receipt of price

Twenty different styles Corsets and Waists.
Send for Price List.

TRADE MARK

FEATHERBONE CORSET CO.,
Sole Manufacturers.
Kalamazoo, Mich

shirts and established the Traders Manufacturing Company in Kalamazoo.

While the ex-blacksmith was making a fortune in petticoats, young Orville Gibson achieved his particular dream. But money was not Gibson's goal: he wanted to make a better mandolin. He took a variety of jobs to support himself, including as a clerk in "Butters Restaurant" and a shoe salesman, but he spent every free moment whittling out mandolins. During the 1890s, when mandolin bands toured the country, mandolins took the spotlight away from other stringed musical instruments, although banjos and guitars stood ready in the wings, waiting a chance to upstage their rival. But Gibson did not like the looks of the traditional gourd-shaped mandolins. Potato bugs, he called them. So he crossed the mandolin with the violin to produce a streamlined offspring that not only looked but sounded better.

Orville Gibson, an old-fashioned craftsman and perfectionist, believed in doing everything by hand. He chose well-seasoned wood, preferring old furniture and black-walnut woodwork, from which he carved his beautiful instruments. No two mandolins turned out exactly alike and each took about six weeks to complete. This craftsmanship soon resulted in a fine reputation and Gibson mandolins were in great demand, particularly by professional musicians. By 1896 Gibson was able to quit his job clerking at the restaurant and manufacture musical instruments full-time. From his small second-story workshop on East Michigan, which became a hangout for local musicians, flowed a steady stream of custom-made instruments. Mandolins remained his specialty and in 1897 he advertised: "The Gibson mandolin was not on exhibition at the World's Fair but it is a world beater nevertheless."

The master craftsman could not conceive of mass-producing a quality product: it took time to make beautiful mandolins. But as his reputation grew, orders poured in at such a rate that Gibson was unable to fill them all. One firm requested the cost and delivery date of 500 mandolins. Gibson replied that "it would cost them $100.00 an instrument and take 500 years for delivery." Orville Gibson was an expert craftsman of remarkable talent, perhaps even genius, but obviously not a businessman. Nevertheless he revolutionized the design of the mandolin and other stringed instruments and was happy in

what he did.

Other Kalamazoo firms demonstrated a form of progressive adaptation in the 1890s. The Williams Manufacturing Company first made wooden windmills in 1867. In the 1880s they switched to steel windmills, and diversified in the 1890s to pioneer another agricultural commodity, the silo. Although it would soon become the ubiquitous complement to the barn, before the early 1890s the silo was totally absent from the rural landscape. American farmers first learned of silos around 1880, and in 1891 Professor F.H. King of the Wisconsin Agricultural Experiment Station launched a campaign to promote the use of ensilage as fodder. Ensilage, the entire chopped-up corn plant, provided a 40 percent increase in food value. Silos were necessary for the storage of this ensilage. The Williams Manufacturing Company produced America's first commercially made silos and also introduced a patented ensilage cutter. Originally constructed like a giant barrel with wooden staves held by steel hoops, silos were later made out of concrete blocks.

Another company that dated back to the 1870s, the Page Manufacturing Company, also went through a transition in the 1890s. The Page Company had been one of the first American manufacturers of machine-made croquet sets, but by the 1890s the faltering firm produced buggy parts. Soon after its reorganization as the Kalamazoo Sled Company in 1894, it absorbed another small plant, the Columbia Sled Company. The company's first big enterprise was wooden handles for feather dusters, but after a few years children's

sleds became the major product. In 1898 it began manufacturing lawn furniture and folding chairs to provide year-round employment. Sleds remained the major success, however, and they were produced in a variety of designs during this period: low, racing sleds for boys; higher, more ornate sleds for girls; and even baby sleds with stroller-type handles. The Kalamazoo Sled Company emphasized quality and, before long, more children coasted on their "Champion" sleds than any other brand.

In 1898 Kalamazoo employers and employees alike discovered a diversion from their normal activities—the Spanish-American War. American spread-eagle sentiment, stimulated by "yellow press" Cuban atrocity stories, the mysterious

sinking of the *Maine,* and a coterie of expansion-minded young Republicans, triggered a brief but "splendid little war." The tragically mismatched contest lasted less than six months and, while not a great war, it sufficed to create another generation of heroes. On April 23, 1898, President McKinley issued a call for volunteers and Kalamazoo responded in a burst of patriotic enthusiasm. Three days later the local militia unit, which became Company C, 32nd Michigan Volunteer Infantry, was mobilized. Like most other American units, it never made it to Cuba. However the men, while suited in wool uniforms at Florida embarkation camps, still suffered from disease, spoiled provisions, and semitropical heat.

Russell A. Alger, McKinley's Secretary of War who was originally from Detroit, appointed his friend, General William Rufus Shafter, a native of nearby Galesburg, to head the Cuban Expeditionary forces. Shafter, popularly known as "Pecos Bill," was a dashing infantry officer during the Civil War and Indian campaigns, but by 1898 his most noticeable characteristic was his 300-pound bulk. His gigantic frame was carted around Cuban battlefields in a buckboard. Despite Shafter's unmilitary appearance and unpopularity with the press, Kalamazooans were proud of their "hero of Santiago." After soundly whipping the Spaniards, he arrived back at the Michigan Central depot on October 6. He was greeted by a huge crowd, marching bands, a parade, and—probably most appealing to "Big Bill"—presented with a beribboned bunch of prime Kalamazoo celery.

Frank Henderson, president of one of the nation's leading military and fraternal uniform and regalia firms, would naturally have been interested in viewing such a grand pageant. He was probably not, however, a member of the vast crowd that honored General Shafter. Ill since 1896, Henderson was spending his last days in a recently completed "castle" in Henderson Park, his projected suburban development off West Main Street Hill. Henderson, who had started out in Kalamazoo in 1864 as a

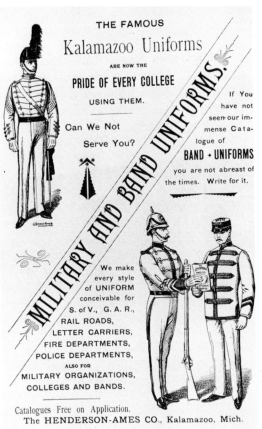

THE FAMOUS
Kalamazoo Uniforms
ARE NOW THE
PRIDE OF EVERY COLLEGE
USING THEM.

Can We Not
Serve You?

If You have not seen our immense Catalogue of
BAND + UNIFORMS
you are not abreast of the times. Write for it.

MILITARY AND BAND UNIFORMS.

We make every style of UNIFORM conceivable for
S. of V., G. A. R.,
RAIL ROADS,
LETTER CARRIERS,
FIRE DEPARTMENTS,
POLICE DEPARTMENTS,
ALSO FOR
MILITARY ORGANIZATIONS,
COLLEGES AND BANDS.

Catalogues Free on Application.
The HENDERSON-AMES CO., Kalamazoo, Mich.

trunkmaker, gradually specialized in producing Masonic regalia. He eventually manufactured a staggering variety of "uniforms, and supplies for all secret and military organizations, flags and banners, badges, furniture," and related costumes and paraphernalia. After an 1893 merger with the famous Ames Sword Company of Chicago, a contemporary account of the Henderson-Ames Company termed its output as "the most varied of any in the city of Kalamazoo, which is noted for its specialties." Henderson's death, in January of 1899, prevented him from witnessing a notorious scandal occasioned by the Spanish-American War, which brought disgrace to his beloved company as well as to Michigan's progressive governor, Hazen S. Pingree.

At the end of the war, someone on the governor's staff sanctioned a corrupt bargain in which the Henderson-Ames Company, through the dummy Illinois Supply Company of Chicago, purchased a large quantity of unused militia uniforms at a salvage price. After making a few minor alterations, the grafters sold them back to the state at full price and split about $35,-000—no small profit for those days. News of this corrupt deal shocked the entire state and rocked Pingree's administration. Five Henderson-Ames officials admitted their guilt, made restitution, and escaped prosecution. A number of state officials, however, were convicted and sentenced to prison for their involvement. Governor Pingree, though not personally

implicated in the scandal, was widely criticized when he pardoned the state officials as a matter of equal justice. The Henderson-Ames scandal thus contributed to an unfavorable public reaction to what was actually a progressive, well-intentioned administration.

A last look at the 1890s reveals a decade populated by inventors, entrepreneurs, promoters of all types, and laborers hungrily seeking their fortunes. Engaged in a dynamic struggle with economic forces and changing times and tastes, everyone sought his own niche. In an age when juveniles avidly read Horatio Alger novels, many local manufacturers demonstrated similar "rags-to-riches" success stories in such diverse endeavors as silos, sleds, patent medicine, and petticoats.

The time had not quite come for others. Take young Frank D. Fuller, for example. Throughout the 1890s he had tried a variety of pursuits with limited success. In 1890, in partnership with a brother, he had manufactured washboards and woodenware. Later he tried games, especially a billiard-type "carom board" he had designed. Eighteen ninety-five found him selling "standard dictionary and subscription books" through the Fuller Book Company. At the turn of the century, the *Kalamazoo City Directory* noted that he had "removed to Chicago." The "Windy City" beckoned, perhaps with more opportunity; but before long Frank Fuller would return to the "Celery City," and in the 20th century finally find his place.

L.W. WOODWORTH, Sec't'y & Treas.

The Henderson-Ames Company

MANUFACTURERS AND IMPORTERS OF

Military & Society Uniforms & Equipments, Regalia & Paraphernalia.

KALAMAZOO, MICH.

Dec 14 - 0

ADDRESS ALL CORRESPONDENCE
TO THE COMPANY

"Hello Bill" greeted out-of-towners attending the statewide Elks' convention in 1908. Kalamazoo's Puritan Corset Company offered a $10 first prize to the "best-appearing Elk" who laced himself into one of their products and marched in the grand parade down Main Street. Courtesy, Western Michigan University Archives.

Comstock inaugurated the first rural high school in Michigan. In the 1890s it featured avant-garde activities such as lawn tennis. Courtesy, Western Michigan University Archives.

This school bus carried students to the Comstock Public School. Courtesy, Western Michigan University Archives.

Pupils enjoy recess at the Comstock Public School circa 1900. Courtesy, Western Michigan University Archives.

CHAPTER VI
THE PAPER CITY: 1900–1917

Men and women worked together in the Kalamazoo Paper Company's rewind room (seen here circa 1910). Courtesy, Western Michigan University Archives.

The 20th century dawned on a dynamic Kalamazoo. Unparalleled prosperity and growth filled the first two decades of the new century. During the first 10 years, the increase in population was phenomenal: from 24,404 in 1900 to 39,437 in 1910, a 62 percent gain. New industries arrived to replace those that failed to adapt to changing needs and many already established plants expanded dramatically. Kalamazoo, with the world's largest concentration of paper mills, became known as the "Paper City."

The effects of change could be seen everywhere. As automobiles replaced horses and electric interurbans linked nearby cities, suburban developments crowded the city's periphery. One local contractor, John Burke, built more than 600 homes during this period. Kalamazoo was no longer an overgrown village but a vigorous young city, strong, prosperous, productive, and alluring. In 1906, as the older buildings along Michigan Avenue arched their Italianate brows in wonderment, the city's first skyscraper, the Kalamazoo Building, took shape.

Kalamazooans, eager to leave the pioneer era for a fresh epoch full of the promise of progress, rushed to join the 20th century, sometimes prematurely. The members of the Isabella Club were not willing to break up after the society had fulfilled its purpose of intellectually preparing Kalamazoo women for their part in the Columbian World's Fair. Thus, under the guidance of Lucinda Hinsdale Stone, the Twentieth Century Club was launched in 1893. The group's golden rule, "Do all the good you can," proclaimed their new function. In 1899 the clubwomen debated when the 20th century would begin: January 1, 1900 or January 1, 1901.

But Kalamazoo found itself securely launched into the 20th century—at least symbolically—in 1900 when George W. Taylor brought to town the first horseless carriage, a steam-powered Locomobile. Horses reared and dashed, crowds ogled and jeered, and Taylor soon sold his unlikely-looking contraption. But the seeds were sown for the development of an industry that would completely revolutionize American life. By 1905, 52 automobiles putted around the city, many of them driven by doctors. By 1918, according to the first records of the state license bureau, 5,892 cars and trucks were registered in Kalamazoo County.

The automobile, for better or worse, became an integral part of American life, influencing all subsequent developments. Through the leadership of men like Henry Ford, Michigan soon came to dominate the automotive industry. Kalamazoo, with its extensive carriage industry and excellent geographical location, might have developed into a major automobile center like Flint or Lansing. Hopes were high in the early years and several auspicious beginnings were made.

Kalamazoo's automotive possibilities brought Frank Fuller back from Chicago in 1902. In that year Fuller, his brother Charles, and Maurice and Charles Blood joined together to organize the Michigan Automobile Company. The company's first product, the Michigan, was developed by the Blood brothers, "highly ingenious and expert mechanics," who had manufactured and repaired bicycles since 1891. The Michigan, which looked more like a golf cart than a car, showed its bicycle heritage. It was powered by an air-cooled, single-cylinder engine, had a wheelbase of only 48 inches, seated two passengers, and weighed approximately 400 pounds. Priced at about $450, the

original Michigan was one of the cheapest cars in America at this time. By 1905 a modern four-story factory, located at the northeast corner of Prouty and North Pitcher streets, was capable of turning out 200 automobiles annually. The Michigan Automobile Company had produced $65,000 worth the previous year, and Kalamazoo consumers had bought half of them.

The little Michigan, like so many of the thousands of different automobiles manufactured in America, was not a lasting success. But the Michigan's exceptionally durable transmissions proved popular, and by 1909 the Michigan Automobile Company produced only components, espe-

Below
Kalamazoo County territorial pioneers, the last of a dying breed, gathered in Schoolcraft in 1905. Courtesy, Western Michigan University Archives.

Beautiful *Stream Line*   **Fast *as a Bullet***

Cornelian Light Car

$410   Top and Windshield $25 Extra   **$410**
Top and Windshield $25 Extra

The Easiest Rider of Them All

Not a large car whittled down, but a **designed light car.** The following high-grade mechanical features are **built** into this little car:

Full floating rear axle.

Independent spring seat suspension. (Patented and a great feature.)

Stream line body with beautiful and durable baked enamel finish.

Fifteen large set New Departure ball bearings.

Standard tread. 100" wheelbase.

Thirty-one Chrome Vanadium steel special drop forgings.

The most simple and the safest steering gear ever devised.

Sliding gear transmission with only three gears and no countershaft. (A real mechanical wonder.)

Sterling overhead valve motor: 2¼" x 4"; eighteen horsepower! a thousand pounds!

MECHANICALLY PERFECT

A speedy, easy riding light car, with the punch

BLOOD BROS. MACHINE COMPANY
ALLEGAN, MICHIGAN
Formerly of Kalamazoo

This 1914 Cornelian advertisement describing the automobile as "the easiest rider of them all" appeared shortly after the Blood Brothers Machine Company relocated to Allegan. Courtesy, Kalamazoo Public Library.

cially transmissions. These transmissions soon received national attention because of their quality and strength. Renamed Fuller & Sons Manufacturing Company in 1916, they further specialized during the 1920s in heavy-duty transmissions used by 85 different manufacturers of buses, trucks, and taxicabs. Frank Fuller had found his niche.

The Blood brothers, however, left the Michigan Automobile Company a year after its inception to establish their own factory. In 1904 the "Blood brothers side entrance tonneau touring car" hit the market. At 1700 pounds it was much larger than the Michigan and sold for about $1,500. It could carry six passengers, or the rear seat could be removed to convert it into what looked like a pickup truck. Though some of these "Bloods" were actually produced and sold, by 1906 the brothers had left the automobile business and were operating a machine shop. But their dreams of producing a commercially successful automobile did not end.

These dreams were renewed in 1909 when Howard Blood joined his father's firm as vice-president. In 1912 the Bloods produced the prototype of another automobile, the Cornelian. Lightweight, low to the ground, and powered by a four-cylinder engine, the Cornelian was a racer. After a good finish in a 100-mile race held in Kalamazoo in 1914, the Bloods decided to enter their speedster in the Indianapolis 500 the next year. That same year a *Kalamazoo Gazette* headline, predicting "Kalamazoo in Danger of Losing Big Industry," proved correct. The Bloods moved their factory to Allegan, lured there, perhaps, by Mayor Burrell Tripp's promise of an order of 1,000 Cornelians.

At Indianapolis the following May, famed driver, Louis Chevrolet, modified a Cornelian and qualified the little racer at 81.1 miles per hour. After 180 miles Chevrolet dropped out with engine trouble, ending the brief career of the Cornelian racecar. Though a few commercial models were sold, Mayor Tripp's 1,000-unit order never materialized. But the Bloods had also developed an exceptional component, the universal joint. Like the Fullers with their transmissions, the Bloods turned to manufacturing their strong point. While the Cornelian was soon forgotten, Blood Brothers universal joints became the standard on the market.

Another Kalamazoo-made automobile, the "Cannon Flyer" or "the Kalamazoo," met a similar end. In 1901 Frank Burtt left his job as superintendent of the Municipal Water Works to join Warren B. Cannon in establishing the Burtt Manufacturing Company. By 1903 the automobile Cannon invented was on the market. The Cannon was available in three styles ranging in price from $650 to $1,330. Although their factory had an annual capacity of only 40 units, it showed promise. In 1906 the state factory inspector remarked: "The Burtt Manufacturing Company, having grown out of its present quarters, is building a

By the turn of the century the number of Civil War veterans was diminishing quickly. In 1902 the 13th Michigan Infantry, pictured here, held their reunion in Kalamazoo. Courtesy, Western Michigan University Archives.

new plant . . . and developing a new automobile that is to have a full, ball-bearing crank shaft, which is something new in America. They contemplate going more extensively into the manufacture of commercial automobiles, having a forty horsepower engine, which means great propelling strength." These sanguine projections never panned out. By 1908 Burtt made only friction clutches and gasoline engines. His "Kalamazoo" engine remained a popular item. A 1914 advertisement reported more than 4,000 in operation throughout the world.

As increasing numbers of Americans purchased automobiles, Kalamazoo's once-prosperous carriage industry faltered. Each passing year saw fewer wagonmakers in business. By 1916 only Lull and the American Carriage Company still operated and they would soon fold. The Michigan Buggy Company attempted to meet this competition by expanding into automobile manufacturing. In 1909 they supplemented their "Tony Pony" line of buggies with another "Michigan" automobile. Their labor force rose from 348 in 1909 to 553 in 1913, and the old buggy factory hummed with new activity. A massive $350,000 promotional campaign was launched in 1913, advertising the "Mighty Michigan" in full-page spreads in the Saturday Evening Post and other widely circulated magazines. The ads proclaimed that more than 5,000 cars were already on the road and more than 300 improvements had been made in four years. The 1913 Michigan featured a 40-horsepower engine, a wide range of accessories, nickel mountings, upholstery "of the finest handbuffed leather, filled with the best curled hair," and a 22-coat finish of a unique shade of "Michigan, golden, auto brown," all for $1,585. That same year the more conservative-minded could purchase for $50.10 a specially designed buggy equipped with an "auto style top" and the distinctive golden brown paint. In spite of this extensive advertising campaign, before the year's end the Michigan Buggy Company suddenly went bankrupt. The huge factory on Reed Street lay idle.

The Limousine Top Company took over one of the buildings and began manufacturing demountable automobile tops. They later expanded into automobile body making and produced Auburn bodies. The Chamber of Commerce succeeded in attracting another automobile manufacturer, Albert C. Barley. In 1917

he moved his operations from Streator, Illinois, to the main Michigan Buggy plant. In Illinois Barley had produced the "Halladay." Once in Kalamazoo he developed the "Roamer," which was advertized as "America's smartest car." The Roamer was a less expensive imitation of the British Rolls Royce. Its rakish body with a Rolls Royce-type radiator, custom paint finish, powerful Deusenburg engine, wire wheels, electric clock, starter, and dash lights appealed to such movie stars as Mary Pickford and Buster Keaton. The Roamer Motor Car Company went on to produce a taxicab, the Pennant, and a cheaper model car equipped with a Continental engine that the proud manufacturer named the "Barley."

Other automobiles appeared briefly in Kalamazoo during this period. Around 1905 Charles B. Ford produced automobile bodies, as well as pianos, surrey bodies, fanning mills, and wood novelties.

Top
Despite a massive 1914 advertising campaign, the Michigan Motor Car Company failed within the year. Courtesy, Western Michigan University Archives.

Above
The 1904 letterhead of the Burtt Manufacturing Company pictured the Cannon automobile, the Kalamazoo gasoline engine, and their patented "tire setter." Courtesy, Western Michigan University Archives.

The "States" and the "Lane" truck were born and died around World War I. The Wolverine, an expensive speedster resembling the Stutz Bearcat and guaranteed to do 75 miles per hour, also appeared at about the same time. None of these pre-World War I automobiles made a lasting success. Not until the 1920s, with the arrival of the Checker Manufacturing Company, would Kalamazoo have a long-lived automobile firm.

This period brought failure to most Kalamazoo automobile manufacturers, but it saw the beginnings of an extremely successful industry, the production of wood burning stoves. Stoves were big business in Michigan at the turn of the century. Detroit led the nation in production and major factories were scattered throughout the state in smaller cities such as Dowagiac with its Round Oak Stove Company. A group of businessmen, previously involved in the industry in Detroit, were responsible for bringing stove-making to Kalamazoo. In 1901 Edwin Woodbury, W.S. Dewing, and William Thompson (who was elected mayor in 1906) organized the Kalamazoo Stove Company. Undoubtedly they were motivated by the recent inauguration of rural free delivery, which permitted cheap mass advertising to a previously untapped market, as well as by the success of such

firms as Sears, Roebuck and Montgomery Ward with their direct-to-the-consumer sales techniques. Why not manufacture stoves and market them the same way? Rural consumers, especially, were eager to cut out the middleman's profit.

By April 1902 "Kalamazoo" stoves were available in three styles: a steel range, a steel cookstove, and an "oak heater." Confident of their product from the very start, the promoters offered a 30-day trial test. Later they devised easy-payment terms, new to those times but familiar now: "We give you terms that will en-

In 1904 one of the worst floods in the city's history inundated the Kalamazoo Stove Company plant. Courtesy, Western Michigan University Archives.

Kalamazoo • The Paper City • Page 147

able you to use the stove while you are paying for it. We make it easy for you to buy." Kalamazoo Stoves were an immediate success. By the close of 1903 they had sold $200,000 worth of stoves. While massive sums were plowed back into advertising, the most important factor in this phenomenal success was the company's sales slogan. In 1902 the first attempt, "seeing is believing; trying makes believing doubly sure," had lacked punch. Then their advertising genius, Marco Morrow, came up with "From Kalamazoo Direct To You." That was a winner.

People all over the nation, who had never before heard of Kalamazoo, were soon chanting this catchy phrase and filling out order blanks. Kalamazoo Stoves were a good product, particularly the ranges. Ovens came equipped with a novel thermometer mounted on the door. Glass windows were later added, which first enabled cooks to view the inside of an oven without opening it. By 1914 the slogan was "A Kalamazoo Direct to You and Gas Stoves too," and by World War I the Kalamazoo Stove Company also produced furnaces, "kitchen kabinets," and tables. Thousands of housewives all over America popped bread into ovens proudly labeled "Kalamazoo" and the city had a thriving new industry.

While the chimneys at the Kalamazoo Stove Works and other local factories belched forth a steady stream of black smoke, proclaiming to all the world that times were good, the city's gentlemen did a little smoking of their own. They puffed cigars. Until Rudolf Valentino and increasing numbers of women smokers popularized cigarettes, the cigar was supreme. A turn-of-the-century advertisement testified that "the smoking population of Kalamazoo hardly knows what a poor cigar is, as those mostly smoked here are made by local firms."

Cigarmaking was a flourishing industry in Kalamazoo at that time. In 1904, 15 establishments produced 16 million cigars. Most were small concerns employing less than a dozen workers, but two firms, Verdon and Lilies, had large facto-

ries. The Lilies or Lilienfield Company, a branch of a Chicago firm, was reputedly the largest union cigar factory in the Midwest with 250 employees. The cigar industry was heavily unionized. As a result male cigarmakers worked an eight-hour day and received better than average pay. In 1904 the average wage was $2.45 a day for men, 90 cents for women, and 72 cents for children. Working conditions were good for the times and even included entertainment. Cigarmakers traditionally donated a portion of their income to make up the wages of a fellow laborer who read aloud while they worked.

Cigarmaking was a trade that demanded considerable training, and craftsmen performed specialized tasks. "Strippers," the least-skilled class, removed stems from the tobacco leaf. "Selectors" sorted leaves into piles of like size and color and tied them into bundles. "Bunchers" wrapped the proper quantity of filler in binder leaf and placed the embryonic cigars in wooden molds. "Rollers" cut the outside wrapper to an exact size, carefully fashioned the cigar into the correct shape, and bit off the end with nicotine-stained teeth as a final stamp of approval. Finally, highly paid "packers" selected similar-sized cigars, picked out the best for the top row, and carefully fit them into boxes.

Brightly colored wooden boxes, emblazoned with finely printed designs and distinctive brand names, provided an essential advertising technique. The Kalamazoo Cigar Company offered "Charles Darwin" cigars for a nickle each and "Charter Oak" for a dime. Charles Holt's "United States Senator" featured a portrait of Kalamazoo Senator Julius Ceasar Burrows. The Bell Cigar Company had "The Winner" and "La Cora"; Anthony J. Weaver produced "Little Duke's"; Verdon's made "La Verdo," "Wolverine Girl," and "Verdon's Twisters"; Sonfield & Gamble fashioned "Club Room" and "Sonnie Jim"; John Gemrich made his "Big Heart"; and Elias Goldberg his "Little Beauties." The Lilies Cigar Company employed reverse psychology in their advertising: "If you want a poor cigar don't

smoke the 'Kernel.' " F. Edward McGlannon widely promoted his "La Zoo," "Murphy," "Capitol," and "Game Trout" brands, and you could always tell a high-class smoker by the "Game Trout" in his mouth.

This major Kalamazoo industry suddenly collapsed in 1908. Following a union dispute, the Lilies Cigar Company moved to Detroit with its more manageable immigrant labor pool. The following year Verdon left also. Some former employees stayed in Kalamazoo and opened up their own small firms. By 1910, 24 different cigarmakers were operating. With the big factories gone, however, total production dropped dramatically and the industry dwindled away year by year. The last Kalamazoo cigarmaker, John Vander Weele, rolled his final stogie in 1968.

While cigar and buggy manufacturing dramatically declined during this period, the celery industry began a more gradual atrophy. Celery was still important in the local economy, but with a changing environment and the development of competing muck lands, Kalamazoo no longer held the monopoly it had enjoyed in the 1890s. But local producers still promoted the concept of the "Celery City" and developed new celery-related products. In 1910 the Kalamazoo Soap Company advertised "celery tar soap," and a new patent-medicine company began bottling "celerytone." Undoubtedly the strangest product connected with this celery craze came from nearby Yorkville on Gull Lake: Triabita, celery-flavored cereal.

Shortly after Dr. John Harvey Kellogg of Battle Creek introduced flaked breakfast cereals in the 1890s, competitors produced a host of strange-sounding imitations including Malta-Vita, Ce-re-o-la, Grain-o, and Eat-A-Biscuit. Dr. Price, a mysterious entrepreneur from Chicago, caught the cereal fever, came up with a novel twist, and in 1903 put Triabita on the market. The Price Cereal Foods Manufacturing Company purchased an old water-powered mill in Yorkville. There 50 employees soaked wheat kernels in a celery-flavored solution, then flattened, toasted, and packaged them. Boxes of Triabita carried the design of a little girl eating cereal, framed between wheat sheaves and celery stalks. But the company never quite mastered packaging. Consumers, overjoyed with finding one box jammed full were disgruntled with another box half-empty. This problem, combined with America's

rather understandable reluctance to try a bite of celery cereal, resulted in failure. The Price Cereal Food Company folded after a few years and the old mill was later torn down. But the dam, which still maintains the level of Gull Lake, is a surviving remnant of Dr. Price's celery-flavored dream.

While some still called Kalamazoo the "Celery City," it rapidly achieved the title of the "Paper City." The first two decades of the century saw a phenomenal growth in the paper industry. By World War I Kalamazoo had become the largest paper-producing area in the United States. Fully one-half of the city's labor force found employment in paper and allied industries.

The area's first paper mill, the Kalamazoo Paper Company, had begun operation

in 1867. This water-powered mill, located south of the city on Portage Creek, first produced a rough grade of paper made from bleached straw. It remained the major producer in the Kalamazoo Valley until Noah Bryant, John King, and Frank Milham organized the Bryant Paper Company in 1895. Their mill soon became the largest producer of book-grade paper in Michigan. Both these plants expanded their operations after the turn of the century and many new paper mills sprang up. Several of these new plants were constructed by a self-educated black contractor, Albert J. White, who had risen from utter poverty to become "one of the most highly respected citizens of Kalamazoo County."

Paper mills soon dotted the Kalamazoo River and its tributaries. John King left the

Above
Dr. Price manufactured his celery-flavored cereal Triabita in the mill at Yorkville. After a few years the firm failed and the mill was razed. Courtesy, Western Michigan University Archives.

Facing page
Top
These children and teenagers worked at Lilies Cigar Company at 318 North Church Street. The company produced La Azora and Kernel cigars. On the average, by 1904 children working in cigar factories earned 72 cents a day. Courtesy, Western Michigan University Archives.

Bottom
Male cigarmakers such as these men employed at F. Edward McGlannon's factory at 306 West Main Street earned, on the average, $2.45 a day by 1904. Courtesy, Western Michigan University Archives.

NOAH BRYANT, President.
A. P. KAUFFER, Vice Prest.

BRYANT PAPER CO.

FRANK H. MILHAM, Sec'y & Man
H. C. REED, Treas.

Manufacturers.

KALAMAZOO, MICH.

March 26, 1904.

Bryant mill to establish the King Paper Company in 1901 and, in 1915, the Rex Paper Company. George Bardeen, who in 1887 had opened the Bardeen Paper Company in Otsego, formed a partnership with M.B. McClellan and S.W. Simpson in 1906 to organize MacSimBar at the same location. George O. Comfort started the Monarch Paper Company in 1906, which later merged with the King and Bardeen Mills to form the Allied Paper Company. The Hawthorne Paper Company, created in 1911 by Austin H. Dwight, specialized in fine-quality rag paper. The Lee Paper Company in Vicksburg also developed into an important mill.

The majority of the men who founded and ran these new mills received their training at the old Kalamazoo Paper Company. There, under the guidance of Samuel Gibson, who developed that company, the men who would eventually run their own large mills learned the skilled art of papermaking. The presence of this training ground for papermakers was one reason for the amazing proliferation of paper mills throughout the Kalamazoo Valley. Another factor was the plentiful supply of water, an essential element in papermaking, provided by the Kalamazoo River. Unfortunately this stream also permitted the easy removal of the large quantity of waste materials associated with the industry, and later posed a serious pollution problem. The nearness of the Chicago market was also an important element. By 1912 Kalamazoo was linked to this and

other markets by a network of seven railroads: the Michigan Central main line and a South Haven Division; the Lake Shore & Michigan Southern; the Grand Rapids & Indiana; the Grand Trunk; the Chicago, Kalamazoo & Saginaw; and the Kalamazoo, Lake Shore & Chicago. Two million tons of freight were shipped annually from 11 freight terminals, and 75 passenger trains left five depots daily.

The presence of a large labor force provided the final requirement. This work force included many Hollanders. Some turned to paper-mill work for supplemental income as it became harder to earn a living in the celery business. Children from the large families necessary for celery cultivation grew up and also took jobs in the rapidly expanding mills. Work in the paper mills, hard, low-paying, but steady, appealed to the Calvinistic Dutch. Women and children found employment in "sorting rooms," where they separated specific grades of rags and paper. Men began at unskilled jobs, such as that of the "broke boy" who gathered up the waste paper that continued to flow when the machine went into "hay." With experience some worked their way up the hierarchy of mill jobs, occasionally all the way to the top.

Jacob Kindleberger's biography illustrates the possibilities of advancement. His early life reads like an Horatio Alger story. As a young child Kindleberger immigrated with his family from Alsace-Lorraine. At the age of 10, he went to work picking buttons from rags in a paper-mill sorting

Above
Soon after the Bryant Paper Company was organized, it became Michigan's largest manufacturer of book-grade paper. Courtesy, Western Michigan University Archives.

Facing page
Top
Scrap paper and rags were pulped in the beater room of the Kalamazoo Paper Company. Courtesy, Western Michigan University Archives.

Bottom
Kalamazoo Paper Company workers are seen in this circa 1890 photograph. Until the Bryant Paper Company began operating in 1895, the Kalamazoo Paper Company was the Kalamazoo Valley's major producer of paper. Courtesy, Western Michigan University Archives.

room, but he had to find them by touch because he was so nearsighted. Through the influence of a local minister, he acquired his first pair of glasses at 15, as well as his strong religious convictions. After gaining an education, the myopic young zealot became a crack salesman for an Ohio paper company. In 1909 Kindleberger and his brother-in-law, Harry Zimmerman, convinced a number of local investors including ex-blacksmith John McLarty, who still had capital left over from his petticoat venture, to back them in an attempt to manufacture waxed paper and vegetable parchment, a water-impervious paper product. They acquired the old Kalamazoo Beet Sugar plant located on the riverbank north of the city and went into production. Kindleberger's hard work and drive paid off: the company made rapid progress and soon expanded into the production of paper, printed bread wrappers, and waxed containers. The city of Parchment sprang up as a company town servicing the Kalamazoo Vegetable Parchment Company.

Local competition soon emerged. In 1914 George Irwin from Rockford, Illinois, founded the Saniwax Company, which specialized in waxed bread wrappers. The Sutherland Paper Company was founded in 1917 to manufacture waxed butter cartons and soon expanded into the production of lard containers, ice-cream pails, vegetable boxes, and an amazing array of other waxed products. It later merged with the Kalamazoo Vegetable Parchment Company.

These waxed-paper manufacturers developed their specialized products in response to genuine needs. Prior to this time the available packaging did not preserve the freshness of perishable goods. Bread, for example, whether it was "Mother's Bread" from the Witwer Baking Company on East Michigan Avenue or loaves of "Mamma's" or "Pan Dandy" from the Davison Baking Company on Portage Street, had a very short shelf life. The introduction of waxed bread wrappers during this period allowed greater efficiency at the bakery, cheaper prices, and fresher bread. America ate better because of Kalamazoo paper products.

The city was as proud of its success in paper as it had been of celery. "More paper is made in Kalamazoo than any other city in the world," citizens informed travel author, Julian Street, when he arrived in Kalamazoo on a transcontinental tour.

That evening Street took a walk and recorded what he saw in *Abroad at Home,* published in 1914:

I have never been in any town where so many people failed to draw their window shades, or owned green reading lamps, or sat by those green-shaded lamps and read. I looked into almost every house I passed, and in all but two, I think, I saw the selfsame picture of calm, literary domesticity.

One family, living in a large and rather new-looking house on Main Street, did not seem to be at home. The shades were up but no one was sitting by the lamp. And, more, the lamp itself was different. Instead of a plain green shade it had a shade with pictures in the glass, and red bead fringe. Later I found out where the people were. They were playing bridge across the street. They must have been the people from that house, because there were two in all the other houses, whereas there were four in the house where bridge was being played.

I stood and watched them. The woman from across the street—being the guest, she was in evening dress—was dummy. She was sitting back stiffly, her mouth pursed, her eyes staring at the cards her partner played. And she was saying to herself (and, unconsciously, to us, through the window): "If I had played that hand, I never should have done it that way!"

Chances are these Kalamazooans, so intent on their game, played with cards manufactured in their home city. The Kalamazoo Paper Box and Card Company, established in 1903, produced "Lily" brand cards. The American Playing Card Company, organized in 1890, by 1907 had established branches in New York and San Francisco. It employed 145 at the Kalamazoo factory alone. In 1904 some 18,000 decks of their "Golf," "Rover," and "Sportingman's" cards rolled out of this factory daily.

Probably the most famous cards from Kalamazoo were made for a game called "Flinch." In 1901 Authur J. Patterson, manager of Beecher and Kymer's Bookstore, patented the rules for this novel game, which was played with a deck of 150 cards. In partnership with his former employers at the bookstore, Patterson soon organized the Flinch Card Company. Widely advertised as "the acme of

parlor games; more simple than authors, more scientific than whist," Flinch remained a popular card game for a half-century.

While parlor games offered diversion to some Kalamazooans, other local inventors sought solutions to the problems of the age. Several addressed the embarrassing situation occasioned by falling trousers. For a brief time the Kazoo Suspender Company marketed a boys' suspender with an extra advantage, "called the Kazoo, it holds up the pants and stockings too." Walter Loveland patented a "fit-rite" belt in 1917, which was attached inside the trousers. Loveland guaranteed his "invisible belt" would "hold the trousers up and the shirt down."

Another inventor, Jay B. Rhodes, worked as a travel agent in 1909. He knew well the frustrations of travelers who contended with miserable roads and

a paucity of road signs. The "Rhodes Pathfinder" was his solution to the problem. The little gadget was mounted on the steering column of an automobile and hooked up like an odometer. Directions and distances to various points had been mapped out and recorded in the "pathfinder." The motorist merely selected his destination, adjusted the "pathfinder" to "O" when he reached the predetermined starting point, and set out in the right direction. When it came time to turn, a bell dinged and an arrow pointed to the right direction. It was an ingenious idea, but unequally sized tires and other factors created problems, and the "Rhodes Pathfinder" never replaced the road map.

Rhodes kept trying, however. He opened up a gas station on Douglas Avenue, where, presumably he gave directions to lost motorists with erratically dinging bells. Through his gas station experience, he saw other needs and developed other solutions. Eventually he hit on a successful one. By 1921 he was manufacturing service-station accessories and his patented "Rhodes self-ventilating oil funnel" continued to be the standard design as long as gas stations sold bulk motor oil.

If motorists had their problems, so did pedestrians. Crossing the street during the early 20th century presented hazards different from today's. While there was little danger of being struck by a speeding Michigan, Blood, or Cannon Flyer, a person still needed to remain vigilant, especially as to where he stepped. Horse-drawn traffic left more than tracks in the street. In the summertime, dust laden with germs from this form of pollution contributed greatly to the spread of disease.

Although the city's Committee on Streets and Sidewalks reported spending more money on cleaning streets than any other item, including paving, the work left much to be desired. As a result Caroline Bartlett Crane, former minister of the People's Church, led a campaign for clean streets in 1904. Under her guidance the Women's Civic Improvement League sponsored an experiment on six and a half blocks of Michigan Avenue. Squads of grumbling laborers, outfitted in new white uniforms and helmets, swept the brick street, stimulated "by the knowledge that hundreds of women's eyes were upon them." Though only partially successful, Kalamazoo's experiment in "municipal housekeeping" brought widespread publicity.

Caroline Bartlett Crane engaged in other crusades as well. In 1903, three years before Upton Sinclair's novel, *The Jungle,* focused nationwide attention on the horrors of the meat-packing industry, Mrs. Crane penned an expose of Kalamazoo slaughterhouses. Local conditions were abominable, although typical for slaughterhouses throughout most of the nation. After an unannounced inspection of the seven slaughterhouses that ringed the city, Mrs. Crane portrayed the conditions she found in prose sufficient to turn robust meat eaters into vegetarians. She described the buildings as "old, abandoned barns or sheds, unpainted, weather-beaten, warped, decaying and they are, without one exception, filthy to an unspeakable and unimaginable degree. Dense black cobwebs drape the open lofts and upper walls; but when one gets down

to within six or seven feet of the floor, nothing less than a hoe and plane long and conscientiously applied could remove from the walls, floors, posts and shelves the caked blood, grime, grease, hair, mould and quite unmentionable filth which covers every inch of every exposed surface." She found a burly individual skinning the carcasses, who "wiped the grease from his knife on the manure covered flanks of the cow, and when he was not using his knife held it by the blade in his mouth." One proprietor later sneered his justification to newsmen: "What did she expect to find, a parlor?"

Citizens and city officials, though thoroughly shocked, remained powerless to change conditions because the slaughterhouses were outside the city limits. Mrs. Crane soon remedied that situation. That same year the state legislature passed a model bill she had drafted, which enabled municipalities to pass inspection ordinances for meat sold within their boundaries. The reputation as a progressive reformer Mrs. Crane achieved through these and similar campaigns resulted in a new career. By 1909 she offered comprehensive "sanitary surveys" to other cities. Eventually more than 60 cities made use of her services and Caroline Bartlett Crane became "municipal housekeeper" to the nation.

While Mrs. Crane fought to reduce disease-breeding conditions, other Kalamazoo entrepreneurs offered "cures," seemingly for every ailment mankind was heir to. Those suffering from a bad complexion could visit Madame A.L. Hobbs on South Burdick Street for a treatment of her "skin bleacher," guaranteed to "cure and eradicate completely moth patches, brown spots, wrinkles, freckles, and pimples." Those who doubted the effectiveness of Madame Hobbs's treatment could observe several patients she kept on hand. Half of each patient's face had been cleared up by her remedy while the other half remained an untreated spectacle. The balding could drop by the Excelsior Medicine Company at Michigan and Portage to pick up a bottle of "Harrison's Hair Hastener (HHH)," which had been developed by a local barber.

Sufferers from rheumatism, neuralgia, kidney trouble, lame back, toothache, diarrhea, cramps, cuts, burns, and aches of all kinds could have their "faces brightened and hearts cheered" by laying down two-bits for a bottle of "Odell's Wonder-

ful Oil." The Ransom Street manufacturer, John A. Ver West, also noted that his nostrum was "a fine thing for horses in case of stomach ache or sprain." Those experiencing "a bearing down sensation, a sense of impending evil, pain in the back or back of head or bowels, creeping feelings up the spine, depressed spirits, dark rings under the eyes," and other troubles could stop in at the Alamo Avenue office of Mrs. Charles H. Stimpson for a package of "Opaline Suppositories" and soon be well on their way to "plumpness and health." Mothers could also purchase from Mrs. Stimpson a box of "Vanderhoff Bedwetting Cure" for a dollar.

Those who lived at a distance or were too ill to make it into town could send to the Physio-Medical Institute at the Kalamazoo National Bank Building for a special

Facing page
While minister of the People's Church, Caroline Bartlett Crane organized a manual training program (top) and the city's first kindergarten (bottom). Courtesy, Western Michigan University Archives.

PLEASE!

THE Women's Civic Improvement League has undertaken to keep Main Street clean. We ask YOU to help us. Please **do not throw anything**—paper, fruit skins, peanut shells or any other litter,—**in the street;** put it in **the waste-paper can** at the corner. And, **Gentlemen, please do not spit on the sidewalk,** or in the gratings, or anywhere but in the gutter.

Now, please don't throw **this** in the street!

Promotion was an important part of the 1904 "clean streets" campaign sponsored by the Women's Civic Improvement League. Courtesy, Western Michigan University Archives.

form that contained "all the questions pertaining to every disease known to medical science." Upon answering these questions, they would receive a reply from the ominously named J. Gore Galleher, who told them what to do to get well. Those feeling the need for a medicinal bath could visit Bowditch B. Frazee located in the basement of 305 East Michigan. There they could choose from a "steam, electrical, saline, medicated shower and needle, sulphur, tonic, friction, hydro-path, pack, sitz, herb, or antiseptic bath." How many complaints could be worse than the cure of an electrical bath and needle shower?

Kalamazoo's grandest medical scheme of this period, however, was perpetrated by the Yonkerman Consumption Remedy Company. It operated from somewhere in the huge old Mansard building located on the corner of Rose and Water streets. Originally the Lawrence & Chapin iron works, the structure then housed the

The street-cleaning campaign featured white-uniformed sweepers. Courtesy, Western Michigan University Archives.

Shakespeare Manufacturing Company. William Shakespeare, Jr., himself had patented the brand name of the remedy, "Tuberculozyne," in 1905, though he apparently remained a silent partner.

The front man, "Dr." Derk P. Yonkerman, who on investigation proved to be a registered veterinarian, operated this classic patent-medicine "scam." Nationally circulated advertisements proclaimed Tuberculozyne "the only known remedy for consumption." Bottles of the elixir, provided with labels displaying the honest-looking face and signature of Yonkerman, proved on analysis to be chiefly a mixture of glycerine, water, burnt sugar, and a dash of essential oil of almonds for flavor. Yonkerman charged $10 for a bottle containing five cents worth of ingredients.

After ordering the initial bottle, gullible sufferers were hounded to continue the treatment. They received a series of letters containing testimonials, such as "the case of the little Pierce boy for whom there seemed no chance of recovery; of J.A. Russell who was told that he had only 36 hours to live, and of Mr. Speet's little son in Holland, Michigan who was bedfast and his parents in dispair of his recovery yet after taking 'grand good tuberculozyne' these people all write us of their perfect health." They were then warned of "the sad results of stopping [treatment] too soon . . . a fatal mistake. Better to take a whole month's treatment

more than is needed than to stop a week or day too soon."

After the passage of the Pure Food and Drug Act in 1906, Yonkerman toned down his activities in America but shifted to a cosmopolitan market. Eventually the Australian government issued a proclamation · forbidding the importation of Tuberculozyne. In 1916 the Yonkerman Remedy Company finally ceased operations, leaving a forwarding address in care of the Shakespeare Company. Derk Yonkerman opened up a "veterinary surgeon" practice.

On the more ethical side of the medicine industry, the Upjohn Pill and Granule Company, after a good start with their "friable pills" in the 1880s, had experienced a business decline at the turn of the century. In the 1890s, competition developed compressed tablets that quickly became popular and business lagged for the Upjohns. Reorganized as the Upjohn Company in 1902, it produced a variety of other medicinal preparations, cold remedies, cough syrups, kidney pills, and especially laxative pills. The "good old days" of the friable pills, however, seemed a thing of the past.

But the introduction of a new, flavored laxative in 1908, Phenolax Wafers, ushered in a new period of prosperity for the Upjohn Company. Phenolphthalein, the chemical that gave these wafers their potency, had been discovered by accident to possess this property. The Hungarian gov-

ernment had added phenolphthalein, considered a harmless red dye, to certain untaxed cheap wines and consumers quickly noticed its laxative qualities. American consumers responded positively to a more controlled dosage of the chemical and, partially because of Upjohn's innovative promotional techniques, which included national contests for the best drugstore window display, orders literally flew in for Phenolax.

During this time of unparalleled pros-

perity, as more and more factories arrived to attract new workers and additional rail lines snaked their way to this mecca, a certain air of self-satisfaction descended upon elements of the "Paper City." Contemporary promotional literature reflected this attitude. *Greater Kalamazoo,* published in 1904 as an advertising giveaway, raised the question of "What Kalamazoo Wants." There the prospective citizen read: "Kalamazoo asks not the earthly praise or prayer of anyone. She has lots of bridges, railroads, paved streets, city lights, water, sewers, electric power and gas. She is handsomely lodged, well and neatly dressed. There is absolutely nothing she needs to insure her happiness or permanence."

Fortunately by 1912 condescension for those unfortunate enough not to live in this splendor was at least tempered by an invitation to come. *The Lure of Kalamazoo,* a promotional pamphlet published that year, contains: "Kalamazoo invites the world at large to come and see the city, to investigate its matchless opportunities for commerce and industry, its superior qualities as an abiding place. If you desire to share in the good things we have or care for the surroundings of convenience and culture, come to Kalamazoo."

The Lure of Kalamazoo was produced by the local Commercial Club, which in 1915 became the Chamber of Commerce. With the slogan "In Kalamazoo We Do," it energetically boosted the growth of the

Above left
Caroline Bartlett Crane advocated a savings system for the working class whereby collectors came to the door each week. Courtesy, Western Michigan University Archives.

Above
Kalamazoo slaughterhouses such as this one were the subject of Caroline Bartlett Crane's 1903 article in which she exposed the grossly unsanitary practices of the meat-packing industry. Courtesy, Western Michigan University Archives.

Left
Derk Yonkerman's 1908 treatise on consumption (tuberculosis) was filled largely with testimonials for Tuberculozyne. Courtesy, Mark McNee.

city throughout this era. Perhaps its greatest coup, in terms of long-lasting impact on the community, occurred at its birth in 1903 as the Press Club. That year, after spirited competition with other southwestern Michigan cities, Kalamazoo was designated as the site of the new State Normal School. This victory, coordinated by the Press Club, did not result merely because of the city's geographical location and previous educational traditions. Kalamazoo had pledged a number of considerations, including a cash gift of $40,000, a suitable site given free, and one half of the salaries of the teachers until a training school was erected. Prospect Hill, then a steep sandy ridge covered by tangled growth, was designated the site of the new Normal. Soon a majestic, classically columned structure crowned what Will Rogers later termed "the Acropolis of Kalamazoo."

Students rode up the east side of the steep hill in a specially constructed cable car. The ride was free except to green freshmen, who traditionally got bilked by upperclassmen into buying "trolley tickets."

Dwight Waldo, who had grown up in nearby Plainwell, served as first head of the school. President Waldo, strict yet fair, ran the fledgling institution with an iron hand, while providing excellent guidance during the tough formative years. Western Normal, created as a two-year teachers' college with a largely rural clientele soon developed a model training program in rural education that attained national prominence. As other structures dotted Prospect Hill, Western's student population grew from 107 in 1904 to more than a thousand by the end of World War I.

Students from the Normal and the other area schools, when seeking confectionary solace from their studies, could repair to a variety of local establishments catering to a sweet tooth. They might visit De-

Bolt's Confectionary on West Michigan Avenue, the Harvey Candy Company on South Burdick, operated by the fortunately named Bert L. Kitchen, or the grandest of them all, Miss Meadimber's Palace of Sweets. At the Palace, amidst a mahogany-decorated interior furnished with "handsome mirrors reflecting the beautiful soda fountain, the palms, cut glass, grill work, and various fancy bric-a-brac which go to make up this fairy like parlor," students might have sampled salted nuts, stuffed dates, "crystallized fruits," "perfection" bonbons, or an ice cream soda for five cents.

The making of confections was an important Kalamazoo industry at this time. The Hanselman Candy Company, founded in 1880, employed between 30 and 50 workers at the factory on East Michigan Avenue. They produced the Hanselman "Frozen Joy Bar," which they immodestly proclaimed was "No better than the best, but better than the rest" and ice cream, "the best thing sold that's icy cold."

Candy making was another specialized skill, learned only after months of experience. Machinery was used only for cheaper grades of candy; better varieties were exclusively handmade. Women were preferred in this highly competitive industry because they could be paid less. New "chocolate dippers" began by working chocolate on the slab; progressed to dipping nut clusters, where no uniformity of shape was demanded; and then on to single-nut dipping. More experience brought promotion to creme dipping, beginning with the cheaper varieties and on to better grades after mastery of the difficult art of twisting "strings" on top of each piece. The number and design of the strings designated the flavor of the creme center. An experienced dipper could produce 100 pounds of chocolate cremes in a 10-hour day. But a week's work would net these women

On December 9, 1909, fire destroyed the newly remodeled "old" Burdick Hotel, a Kalamazoo landmark for over half a century. Courtesy, Western Michigan University Archives.

Right
President William Howard Taft dedicated the New Burdick on September 22, 1911. It was the city's pride for the next half century. Courtesy, Western Michigan University Archives.

only from $4 to $12 in 1915 and, because of the seasonal demand for candy, they were periodically laid off.

Though the Kalamazoo labor force was not exactly "an army of well paid and contented workers," as one 1912 promotional piece boasted, conditions were relatively good for the times. Wages had edged slightly upward from the 1890s so that by 1908 men averaged $2.03 per day and women $1.16. The city remained remarkably free from the bitter labor strife that affected larger cities at this time. Some strikes did occur locally. In April of 1901 there were three. Truckers and loaders at the Michigan Central Railroad went on strike over wages, and 28 men struck at the Kalamazoo Spring and Axle Company because their workday had been increased to 11 hours. Forty women and girls went out at the Kalamazoo Pant and Overall Company because they were ordered to do a new type of work at the old piece rate. A reporter conveyed contemporary attitudes and his own lack of sympathy when he pointed out that the women already earned "$1.00 – $2.00 per day the year round" and that "nearly a score of men were thrown out of employment because of the strike."

When, in 1902, the 40 Kalamazoo labor unions were polled concerning what new state legislation they favored, they responded consistently with the common concerns of the day: a universal eight-hour workday, prohibition of competing prison labor, more stringent labor laws, and better laws governing sanitation in factories. A few unions, such as the Musicians Local 228, reflected the contemporary nativistic currents with a proposal to close "the country to all immigration for a number of years."

The state factory inspector during annual visits to Kalamazoo found violations comparable to those in other similar-sized cities. He ordered seats provided for ladies when not working, improved toilet facilities, and sworn statements by parents to verify the age of working children between 14 and 16. Most violations were of the new laws that had been created to protect working women and children.

While children grew less common in the factory, more women entered the job market. Most women laborers were single and usually dropped out of the labor force when they married. Women's wages remained substantially less than men's. In 1915 a State Commission of Inquiry into Wages and Conditions of Labor for Women published a detailed report of their findings gathered over a two-year period. They concluded that "a large percentage of the women wage-earners of

Walter J. Hodges
PRESIDENT AND GENERAL MANAGER

The New Burdick

FIRE PROOF CONSTRUCTION

Kalamazoo, Mich., _____ 191_

In 1912 the Kalamazoo Chamber of Commerce produced a promotional pamphlet celebrating the city's attractions. From the author's collection.

Welcome To Kalamazoo

On June 26, 1911, fire gutted the Hanselman Candy Company factory causing $150,000 damage. Courtesy, Western Michigan University Archives.

Facing page

Top
In 1907 women paper mill workers demonstrated the camaraderie of labor. Courtesy, Western Michigan University Archives.

Bottom
Prior to 1915, when the city went dry, scores of saloons like this one lined Kalamazoo's downtown district. Courtesy, Western Michigan University Archives.

Michigan are today receiving less than a living wage.''

Working women comprised two classes: those living at home and those "adrift." Employers felt that those living at home needed less to live on so they tended to pay them less. Part of the concept of the woman "adrift" was the issue of morality. The woman inspector who investigated the living conditions available to the approximately 5,000 female workers in Kalamazoo stated that where she lived could "mean either the redemption or the downfall of a girl." She found a variety of available rooms, ranging in price from one dollar to $3.50 per week. A second-floor room that rented for $2 a week was typical:

It was about 14 feet square, had two windows with shades and lace curtains, an iron bed, a commode, a mirror, a rocker and a straight back chair. The floor was painted, and had two small rugs. There was no clothes-press, but a corner of the room was curtained off for that purpose. It was a back room and seemed to be well ventilated. The paper was dark and cheerless. The room was heated with a drum on a stovepipe.

The bathroom was on the opposite side of the hall. It was furnished as all bathrooms are, but had no bowl. It was not very clean. There was no way of heating the water. There were four men boarders and roomers who had their rooms on the same floor and of course used the same bathroom.

The inspector encountered another problem, the lack of entertainment. Where, for instance, could a young factory worker entertain her boyfriend? His room was definitely out of bounds and even a short visit to hers suggested immorality. The parlor, with stereoscope viewing or perhaps a game of Flinch, was the traditional Victorian courting place, but usually not available in rooming houses. One landlady, when asked where a female tenant might entertain, replied, "I haven't any place. They can use the porch in the summer, but they can't set out there howling around all night, I tell ye!" Others would not rent to young ladies because of this nuisance. How could a girl marry and escape the factory with no place to entertain a boyfriend?

While a "decent" woman would not even consider entering the swinging doors of a tavern, men could, and there were plenty in the city to accommodate them. In 1903 the city contained nearly 50 saloons with half of that number crowded between the 200 block of West Michigan and the 400 block of East Michigan. A laborer might stop to quaff a few nickel beers while munching on a heavily salted "free lunch" or carry home his dinner pail filled with draft. John Frank at 215 East Michigan Avenue advertised "liquors by the gallon, free lunch every day." Tom Finn's Buffet at 124 West Michigan was "a popular resort for gentlemen" and "headquarters for sporting and theatrical people." While the Oxford Cafe on 115 East Michigan was "a rendezvous for gentlemen of congenial spirits" that supplied "wines, liquors, and cigars (suitable for medicinal purposes)."

Popular beers in Kalamazoo were "Berghoff's, a real German brew," which did not cause "biliousness" because it was properly aged; "Seipp's Extra Pale Beer," the "beer without a headache"; and the most popular of all, produced by the Kalamazoo Brewing Company, "the brew from Kalamazoo." This brewery was founded before the Civil War and operated under various names. In 1886 George Neumaier, an immigrant from the land that made beer famous, had acquired the brewery and shortly after moved it to the corner of Portage Avenue and Lake Street. Neumaier's son Alfred joined him in 1896 in brewing a high-grade lager beer with "bottled beer for family use a specialty."

In 1915, however, Kalamazoo voters, under a local option law, launched the city into the Prohibition era, four years before the rest of the nation attempted "the noble experiment." By 1916 Neumaier's brewery closed, the swinging doors of the scores of local taverns no longer swung, and "gentlemen of congenial spirits" sought other rendezvous. Some took advantage of the newly completed interurban that linked dry Kalamazoo with wet Grand Rapids. A 75-mile-per-hour non-stop ride on one of the special "Flyers" brought them to downtown Grand Rapids with its beckoning potations in an hour and 15 minutes. Some brought liquor for Kalamazoo consumption, hopping off before reaching the Rose Street depot where police vigilantly watched for such "bootleggers."

Other thirsty Kalamazooans either bought more of the alcohol-laden patent medicines that had survived the purge following the 1906 Pure Food and Drug

Crusade or merely sang the "Alcoholic Blues": "No more bourbon no more gin, goodbye whiskey, you used to make me frisky." Most took advantage of other sources of entertainment—the theater, vaudeville, or the novelty of the period, motion pictures.

In January 1906 Colonel William S. Butterfield opened a little theater on South Burdick Street, called the Bijou, which featured vaudeville acts and the "kinetoscope." Other motion-picture theaters soon followed. Butterfield began construction of the Majestic the next year which, when opened, featured nationally famous vaudeville performers. In 1909 the Fuller opened. A little later local audiences first saw Charlie Chaplin comedies at the Lyric and Orpheum. The Elite appeared in 1912 and by 1916 featured fare that included Theda Bara in "The Serpent," Vivian Martin in "Merely Mary Ann," and the darling of the movies, Mary Pickford, in her seven-reel "Poor Little Peppina."

Those who preferred vaudeville saw an increasing number of Gibson stringed instruments in the hands of the performers. As the fame of Orville Gibson's beautiful mandolins and guitars continued to spread, a group of five local entrepreneurs succeeded in convincing Gibson to organize a company to manufacture his products in 1902. They were to provide the capital and take care of production and marketing. Gibson agreed to work at the company for at least two years imparting his knowledge. But more importantly he consented to lend his name to the enterprise, the Gibson Mandolin-Guitar Manufacturing Company. The company's first catalog appeared the following year, illustrated with a beautiful young woman provocatively posed with a mandolin. It contained many testimonials, such as that of the Mexican Musical Monarchs who wrote that "Gibson's were the Creme de la Creme of string instruments." The instruments, though no longer exclusively handmade, remained high-quality and the business grew dramatically. Nationally circulated catalogs and aggressive selling techniques employed by Gibson salesmen soon produced an even greater reputation. Beginning in 1912 the company issued a trade journal for Gibson salesmen titled "The Sounding Board," which carried illustrations of famous bands using "Gibsons." The journal provided Gibson agents with effective new sales techniques and disarming slogans:

"Buy your second instrument first and save money"; "What you need you pay for whether you buy it or not"; "State nothing in the selling you would not put down in writing"; and "Pay as you play."

The Gibson success story was typical of the period from the turn of the century until World War I, an era of growth, adaptation and unparalleled prosperity. Kalamazooans seemed satisfied with their progress and looked expectantly to a future of continuing advancement. Promoters used innovative advertising techniques to reach out to previously untapped markets. The rest of the world was a market or a place to visit and compare to the good life at home. Victorian morals and attitudes as well as a sense of innocence prevailed. But this innocence would soon be tempered by exposure to the harsh realities of a modern World War.

Opposed to Weimer Hearing Case   Democrats Control Council   Drys Win Great Victory

THE WEATHER
WEDNESDAY
FAIR

KALAMAZOO TELEGRAPH-PRESS

HOME EDITION

VOL. 46. ESTABLISHED 1844.   KALAMAZOO, MICH., TUESDAY, APRIL 6, 1915.   PRICE TWO CENTS

One Brewery, 46 Saloons and 15 Clubs Go Out of Business in Kalamazoo May 1

New Council Will be Democratic

STATE MAKES GREAT
JUMP TO THE DRYS

HOW THEY VOTED

MAYOR AND
HENCHMEN
CONVICTED

Mayor Elect J. B. Balch and
Message of Appreciation

TRAFFIC HIT
DEATH BLOW

CHAPTER VII
The Debt-Free City: 1917–1939

In 1917 the Gibson Company's "daylight plant" on Parsons Street was the industrial showplace of the city, reputedly the most modern workplace in southwestern Michigan. The following year Orville Gibson died in New York City. While he had never been an officer of the company that proudly bore his name, that name and Gibson's reputation as an expert craftsman lived on. Kalamazooans were too preoccupied with world events to long lament Gibson's passing. The nations were at war and America had sent her young men to fight in Europe on an idealistic quest—"a war to end all wars."

Sons of laborers and factory owners alike rushed to join the colors when President Wilson announced a call to arms in April 1917. Kalamazoo County responded as it had in previous wars—with over-

THE **Sounding Board** SALESMAN

VOL. 6   AUGUST, 1917   NO. 2

New Home of the Gibson Mandolin-Guitar Company.
The new factory, is located at 219-225 Parsons Street, Kalamazoo, and is one of the most modern in the city.

Gibson Mandolin-Guitar Co.
Kalamazoo, Mich., U. S. A.

whelming enthusiasm. Cheering crowds and marching bands playing patriotic airs sent off early volunteers at the Michigan Central depot. One idealistic young recruit, eager for action, later recalled a typical concern: "Our principal worry at that time was not whether or when we would return to our homes, but whether or when we would be ordered to France." His worry was unwarranted because he and many other of Kalamazoo's young men fought in the major battles of the war. More than 2,200 from Kalamazoo County served in uniform and approximately one out of 20 never came back, victims of battle or disease.

Many local volunteers served with the 32nd "Red Arrow" Division, especially the 126th Infantry Regiment, which was commanded by Colonel Joseph Westnedge from Kalamazoo. The unit arrived in France in February 1918 and took part in such famous battles as Meuse-Argonne, Chateau-Thierry, and Soissons. Selected for occupation duty, the 126th did not return to Camp Custer for demobilization until May 1919. Colonel Westnedge, Kalamazoo's hero, died of illness shortly after the armistice. His brother Richard had given his life during the Philippine Insurrection, and in their joint honor West Street was later renamed Westnedge Avenue.

Another contingent of Kalamazoo men served with the 85th Division, known as the "Polar Bears." It was composed of men recruited from Midwestern states with heavy winters. Stationed in and around Archangel in northern Russia, they suffered severe cold while fighting the Bolsheviks, or "Bolos" as the troops called them. Eleven months after the armistice had supposedly ended hostilities, America remained involved in a civil war between the White and Red Russian

armies.

On the Kalamazoo home front, patriotism ran high in support of the war. Kalamazooans endured wheatless and meatless days, grew victory gardens, and bought more than $11 million worth of bonds during the five Liberty Loan drives. Propaganda became an important element of this first modern war, and the Kalamazoo County Patriotic League avidly encouraged "right" thinking by sponsoring "patriotic mass meetings," where celebrities like Clarence Darrow delivered orations and "Camp Custer's Crack Band" provided stirring martial music.

Name changes reflected anti-German sentiment, as: sauerkraut became "liberty cabbage," the nearby Ottawa County town of Berlin was renamed Marne, and Kalamazoo-manufactured Roamer radiators were now made of "liberty silver" rather than German silver. A few months before the war ended, a Student Army Training Corps was established at Western State Normal School, and 400 uniformed students lived in barracks, ate in mess halls, and marched to class. Firms such as Henderson-Ames and Ihling Brothers relegated fraternal needs to the back shelf and devoted full production to snappy military uniforms and accoutrements. Ihling Brothers operated a military store at Camp Custer where their specially tailored uniforms were in great demand.

Although the war dominated most daily activities, other important developments took place. Progressive factions had advocated a series of diverse measures for some time; as the "war to make the world safe for democracy" gave further impetus to the movement, a wave of reform swept the country. Prohibition had already come to Kalamazoo and soon the Volstead Act of 1919 would usher in a national "dry decade"; women finally won the right to vote; and provisions for the direct primary, initiative, referendum, and recall had recently modified Michigan's constitution. Other progressives concentrated on reforming corrupt and inefficient municipal governments.

Even though corruption had never been a problem in Kalamazoo's city government, a group of local businessmen led by Dr. W.E. Upjohn and the Chamber of Commerce had advocated, for more than a decade, a more efficient method of governing the city. Using as its models such cities as Galveston, Texas, Des Moines,

Iowa, and Dayton, Ohio, where experiments in municipal reform had already proven successful, a charter commission composed largely of businessmen developed a new system of government for Kalamazoo. It was designed to operate in a manner similar to a business organization. An elected city commission would serve as a counterpart to a board of directors. This policy-making body would appoint a city manager who, like a plant manager, would administer policy. A mayor, appointed by the commission from its elected membership, would preside at meetings but exercise only ceremonial administrative functions.

As the war raged in Europe, Kalamazoo voters adopted this charter on February 4, 1918. In April they elected the first city commission, composed primarily of local businessmen, including Dr. William E. Upjohn, William Shakespeare, Jr., and Albert J. Todd. They appointed as first city manager, Harry Freeman, secretary of the Chamber of Commerce. Newly established businesslike practices soon brought greater efficiency to City Hall. The commission viewed the heavy interest then being paid on bonded indebtedness with a practical businessman's aversion and inaugurated a "pay as you go" fiscal policy. This economic philosophy would prove very important in setting future trends.

Returning veterans were greeted by bands and familiar crowds, but they found a rapidly changing society. Disillusioned by the horrors and ultimate failure of the war to end all wars, America longed to return to prewar "normalcy" but never did. The war had destroyed the nation's innocence and the era of the 1920s would reflect the abandoned hopes and morals of a "lost generation." As expatriate American authors wrote novels of bitterness, American women emphasized their newly won equality by deemphasizing their femininity. When the boyish look with the unaccentuated figure and "bobbed hair" became fashionable, Kalamazoo's once-thriving corset industry faced hard times.

Despite increasing testimony concerning the harmful effects of the corset, American women continued to prefer tight lacing accompanied by a few gulps of Zoa-Phora. A British scientist in 1904 had shown that corset wearing could be fatal to monkeys, but it was changes in fashion brought about by the "flapper" era that struck the death blow to the corset. The

The Kalamazoo Corset Company factory stood on the corner of Eleanor and North Church streets. Courtesy, Western Michigan University Archives.

THE KALAMAZOO GAZETTE

EIGHTY-SEVENTH YEAR—NO. 123. (News of the World) KALAMAZOO, MICH., U. S. A., :DAY, NOVEMBER , 1918. (By Associated Press) PRICE FIVE CENTS.

HUNS QUIT!

PEACE COMES AS GERMANS SIGN FOCH'S TERMS OF SURRENDER

WASHINGTON, D. C.—It is officially announced by the State Department here that the armistice conditions drawn up by the Allied governments and the government of the United States and placed in the hands of Marshal Foch and his military associates have been signed by the German plenipotentiaries who made their way through the French battle lines under the protection of a white flag. By signing these drastic conditions the German government makes complete surrender to the Allied nations, and the carrying out of those terms, which will begin immediately, strips Germany of further capacity for military effort and guarantees that whatever peace terms the Allied nations may dictate to Germany at the final conference will be carried out to the letter. To all intents and purposes the great struggle which has laid half of Europe in ruins and cost the lives of millions of human beings is now at an end, hostilities having been

industry had remained strong in Kalamazoo until this time. The Kalamazoo Corset Company had reorganized in 1914 to emerge as the largest corset factory in the world. Their new line of "Madame Grace" corsets was widely advertised in *Ladies' Home Journal, Vogue,* and, of course, the *Corset and Underwear Review.* As part of the reorganization, James H. Hatfield, who had brought the original Featherbone Corset Company to Kalamazoo, left the firm to form the National Corset Company (later abbreviated "Naco").

Following the war both firms attempted to adapt to the "corsetless era." Changing needs resulted in a product evolving from one that artificially created the physique that society demanded to one that provided help for those who needed it the most. The Naco Company began marketing a new line of girdles, corsets, brassieres, and rubber reducing garments. In 1922 the Kalamazoo Corset Company became the Grace Corset Company to emphasize its new image. Product trade names—"Graceful Stout," "Grace Girdle," "Madame Grace Gracefulette," and "Madame Grace Brassiere"—indicated the new direction. Naco had failed by 1929, but the Grace Corset Company successfully adapted and continued in a somewhat diminished capacity until it

Above
Despite the end of World War I, anti-German sentiment continued for years. Courtesy, Western Michigan University Archives.

Left
The "corsetless era" following World War I spelled doom for these Madame Grace corsets. From the author's collection.

eventually moved to New Jersey in the 1950s.

As the corset fell and women breathed easier, they found strength for other activities. After over two decades of frenetic social reform and peripatetic municipal crusading, Caroline Bartlett Crane had paused just prior to World War I to devote more time to her family. But the old spark for reform still smoldered. It had flickered briefly during the war when she headed the Michigan Women's Committee Council of National Defense, and, finding fuel in her domestic setting, blazed anew in 1924. That year, in response to a national contest sponsored by Secretary of Commerce Herbert Hoover's "Better Homes in America" organization, Mrs. Crane designed a house. Not just any house, her "Everyman's House" was to be the perfect home for the typical American family of the period with a wage-earning husband and a homemaking wife. It was a "space-saving, step-saving, time-saving, money-saving small house," and was the first home actually designed with the needs of the housewife in mind. The kitchen, "the hub of the house," was designed for convenience with items used most frequently in close proximity. The adjoining nursery saved a mother from having to trudge endlessly up stairs.

Securing the cooperation of local businessmen, who advanced labor, building materials, and furnishings against the potential sale of the structure, Mrs. Crane supervised the building of "Everyman's House." Within two months an unpretentious colonial-style home stood complete on its then-suburban lot halfway up Westnedge Avenue Hill (where it still stands). Not only was it finished in time to meet the contest deadline but "Everyman's House" received the first prize, selected over more than 1,500 entries submitted by other American cities. More than 20,000 visitors trooped through the house during the period it was on display, Caroline Crane penned a book describing her creation in 1925, and, even though replicas did not spring up across the country, architects and contractors at least began to think along similar lines.

In the area south of the city, near Everyman's House, celery was still extensively cultivated. Although celery continued to diminish in economic importance, it remained a popular symbol for the city—certainly more colorful than paper. When Kalamazoo turned out for its gala four-day centennial celebration in June of 1929, a historical pageant highlighted the festivities. The finale featured an attractive young lady allegorically posed as "Celery, queen product of Kalamazoo County, disporting herself in a modernistic mood."

Despite this popular image each passing year saw less acreage under celery cultivation. Several factors contributed to celery's demise: deep wells sunk by the paper mills lowered the water table and dried much of the swampy muck land; residential and industrial development brought an increase in property values; the spread of celery blight, probably resulting from a failure to rotate celery with other crops; and the popularity of other varieties grown elsewhere. As late as 1939, however, there were still 1,180 acres of celery fields within the vicinity of the city and the annual crop was worth $1.5 million dollars. Many large Dutch families continued to rely on celery as a major source of income, and travelers passing through the city would never have realized that celery was no longer "Queen."

In a 1938 promotional pamphlet, the "Old AAA Traveler" observed: "try to drive into or out of Kalamazoo without having great bunches of celery and bags of peanuts offered you every block or so." An out-of-state tourist stopped to ask one vendor if there was any special affinity between celery and peanuts. The "red cheeked Dutch youth" supplied a terse but masterful rationale: "If they don't want celery, maybe they want peanuts; if they stop to buy peanuts, maybe they'll buy a bunch of celery." Another "hawker" recalled that "Some city kids used to razz us about selling that celery every Saturday. We didn't care, we knew they weren't making as much as $100 clear on a good weekend."

By the 1920s pansy cultivation had become a rather important complement to celery growing. Pansies were introduced to Kalamazoo celery fields shortly after the turn of the century and grew best in the same type of soil that was ideal for celery. Because pansies bloomed before celery-planting time, a field could accommodate both crops. In 1927 approximately 30 growers on Kalamazoo's southside raised pansies on a large scale. The annual production of four million plants was trucked to Detroit, Chicago, and other large cities for distribution all over the country. While Kalamazoo had lost its celery distinction, it could now boast of raising more pansies than any other city in the world.

Another agriculturally based industry, mint-oil refining, was still heavily centralized at Kalamazoo's Todd Company. However, the mint industry went through a tumultuous period in the 1920s. American consumers' ready acceptance of mint-flavored chewing gum, toothpaste, and candy had resulted in a major increase in domestic mint-oil consumption. Following a bad growing year in 1924, a "great frost" in May 1925, and a Japanese earthquake that severely reduced that country's production, a worldwide shortage of mint oils occurred. Prices for peppermint oil shot dramatically upward from $4.50 a pound in 1924 to more than $30 a pound in 1925. Small-town bank vaults reeked with the smell of mint, as growers and distillers hoarded their supply against a further price increase. Brokers bought mint like stocks and bonds, and violence broke out when disgruntled growers dynamited peppermint stills. High prices spurred growers to plant more acreage and the farmer's traditional plight resulted—the more they grew, the lower their profits. Prophetic of the great crash that would soon hit the stock market, the mint bubble burst in 1929 and prices tumbled to less than production costs.

That same year the A.M. Todd Company moved to its modern new factory on Douglas Avenue. Albert M. Todd, mint king, public servant, and generous benefactor to the arts, died in 1931, and the presidency of the company passed to his son, Albert J. Todd. Despite bad times for growers, the Todd Company remained successful as a refiner and distributor. Although mint-flavored products were a luxury, consumers maintained a steady demand for gum and candy throughout the Great Depression. By 1934 the Todd Company had diversified into manufacturing other aromatic chemicals used in perfuming soaps, but still maintained its position as the "world's largest producer of peppermint and spearmint oils."

During the 1920s Kalamazoo still hoped to produce a commercially successful automobile, despite many earlier failures. The Roamer was quite popular in the early 1920s. When President Taft visited Kalamazoo in 1921 to speak on the League of Nations, he was proudly escorted around the city in a sporty Roamer. Although many celebrities liked the flashy car, not enough ordinary folks did, and in 1928 the last Roamer rolled out of the Reed Street factory.

Two other automobile factories began operating on Pitcher Street. Shortly after the war "Dort" automobile bodies were produced in a South Pitcher Street plant that had formerly been part of the Lull

Albert M. Todd's office at the southwest corner of North Rose Street and West Kalamazoo Avenue was a veritable museum of choice art and rare books in 1925. Courtesy, Kalamazoo Public Museum.

Carriage Works. In 1921 Handley Motors began manufacturing another Kalamazoo automobile on North Pitcher Street. Originally called the "Handley-Knight" because of its Knight engine, when the company began to equip the car with other engines in 1923, it became simply the "Handley." Unique little handle attachments on top of the headlights permitted easy recognition of this model and prompted the slogan, "If it carries handles, it's a Handley." This distinction was not enough to ensure success, however, and the firm folded in 1923.

That same year the Checker Cab Manufacturing Corporation moved to Kalamazoo from Chicago. Established there in 1920 by Morris Markin, Checker outgrew its facilities in three years and chose Kalamazoo for relocation because of the availability of the two vacant automobile factories, Dort and Handley. During the firm's early years, bodies were produced at the old Dort Plant and the cabs were assembled at the Handley site. By 1925 Checker produced 1,000 taxicabs a year and claimed to be the country's "largest exclusive cab makers." The taxicabs, affectionately known by drivers as "iron brutes," were furnished with heavy-duty clutches, differentials, and transmissions, and constructed specifically for hard city driving. As early as 1925 these vehicles were estimated to last 200,000 miles; that year company officials boasted "no Checker Cab has ever worn out." After 250,000 miles the first taxi produced was still in operation on Chicago streets. Checker made products to last and Kalamazoo finally acquired an automobile plant that would also.

Curiously enough, the taxi firms that operated locally at this time, Kalamazoo Hack & Bus, Red Top, Macomber, and Carey & Leach, used Yellow Cabs and Dodges rather than Checkers. But Kalamazooans were well served by public transportation anyway. They could ride electric interurbans to Grand Rapids or Battle Creek, or trains in almost every direction. A variety of bus lines, including Rapid Transportation, Southern Michigan Transportation, Lewis Rapid Transit, and Greyhound, provided almost hourly out-of-town service. The increasing number of buses and private automobiles soon nudged the faltering interurbans and streetcars out of the competition. The in-

Below
In 1921 this model F-28 Roamer chassis, equipped with a Rochester Deusenberg engine, traveled 105.1 mph at Daytona Beach to set a world's record. Courtesy, West Michigan University Archives.

Facing page
This 1922 Roamer advertisement made an appeal to individualists. Courtesy, Western Michigan University Archives.

The Goal:
Individualism

Roamer is essentially a made-to-order car. Only in certain mechanical units is the purchaser limited in his specifications.

An advertising writer recently asked one of our mechanics if he tried to picture in his mind, as he played his part in building a Roamer, just what type of man or woman his work must suit.

"Well," was the reply, "I think of an English Countess I saw once; of a dare-devil young college speed-maniac, and of an artist who uses beautiful combinations of lines and colors. I try to do my work so that all three of them would think, when they saw the car, that it had been built just for them."

It is scarcely an exaggeration to say that that mechanic spoke for the Barley Motor Car Company as a unified organization. We build for individuals—and for the most discriminating individuals.

terurban went under in 1929, and city buses replaced the last trolley in 1934.

Commercial air service was also available by the late 1920s. Kalamazoo developed Michigan's first municipal airport, Lindbergh Field, and in 1929 the city received Michigan Airport License Number 1. That final year of the Roaring Twenties, when the bill for a decade of fast living and easy spending came due, proved a memorable one for Kalamazoo as well as the nation as a whole. During the summer the city paused from its normally bustling business activity to celebrate its centennial. The editor of *Our Line,* an advertising journal put out by the Kalamazoo Laundry Company, noted the splendid steady growth that had taken place and observed "as a city our boots are greased and our clothes neatly pressed." In a promotional pamphlet the Chamber of Commerce emphasized the city's amazing industrial diversity and prophetically advanced a soon-to-be-tested hypothesis: "Should a depression hit one class of industry, the others may be in fine condition to absorb the surplus of labor, and the general prosperity of the city [will] continue."

While airplanes droned with greater frequency above the happy city, content in the knowledge of its certain future,

more citizens worried about the stability of these aircraft than the soundness of their economy. A 1926 plane crash at the Climax homecoming that had killed three people was still fresh in their memories. Little did they know that an even more serious crash would come not from the sky but from Wall Street. On "Black Thursday," October 24, 1929, as panic seized the stock market, the entire nation plunged into a massive economic disaster —the Great Depression.

The city was profoundly affected by what became an entire decade of industrial depression. In 1929 the city's roster of firms numbered 175, but had shrunk to 151 by 1937. Old established companies such as Henderson-Ames closed their doors forever, and city and county relief rolls swelled with the unemployed. In Kalamazoo the unemployed were not put on the "dole"; able-bodied men on relief constructed a variety of public works. Consequently city taxes went up and it looked as if "pay as you go" would have to be abandoned. But shortly thereafter the federal government came to the assistance of the nation's hard-pressed local governments by funding county relief agencies, and the CWA, PWA, WPA, CCC, and a host of other "alphabet programs" pro-

vided funds for public-service employment. Federal money funded a number of projects in Kalamazoo, including the construction of a new post office on Michigan Avenue, a new athletic stadium for Western State Teacher's College, a County Building, and Bronson Park's modernistic art-deco fountain, which commemorated the pioneer's westward movement.

The nadir of the Depression came in 1933. In February Governor William Comstock closed all of the state's banks for a week and people had to survive on what cash they had on hand. The previous year, wages of all city employees had been reduced; now the city was forced to meet its payroll in scrip. Western State Teacher's College President Dwight Waldo, fearing that his teachers would not be paid for months, immediately drove to Lansing and secured cash. Waldo faced a much bigger threat over the next two years, when the governor, hard pressed to reduce his budget, advocated closing the college. After a hard-fought campaign Dr. Waldo and his assistant (and soon-to-be-successor) Paul Sangren prevailed over the governor, however, and Western remained open.

Despite the unprecedented challenge to government and industry resulting from

On the occasion of the city's 100th birthday, a writer for the Kalamazoo Laundry Company's publication *Our Line* observed, "as a city our boots are greased and our clothes neatly pressed." Courtesy, Kalamazoo Public Library.

KALAMAZOO
A City of Industries

KALAMAZOO
CHAMBER OF
COMMERCE

This pamphlet published by the Chamber of Commerce on the eve of the Great Depression promoted the industrial diversity of Kalamazoo. Courtesy, Western Michigan University Archives.

the Depression, the city government retained its conservative attitude, lowered taxes thanks to federal relief assistance, and maintained its "pay as you go" fiscal policy. Throughout the 1920s and 1930s, Kalamazoo's government continued to be dominated by representatives of business. The majority of its mayors, commission members, and city managers were drawn from a pool of local business and industrial leaders.

In 1919 the city's bonded indebtedness stood at $760,896; by 1929 it had shrunk to $128,250; and in 1937 the tightfisted "pay as you go" policy was vindicated. By burning the last bond, Kalamazoo became the only city in America with a population of over 50,000 to be out of debt. In the midst of the Depression, Kalamazoo was the "Debt-Free City."

Although the Depression touched almost every aspect of the city's life, its effects were not as severe on Kalamazoo as on the rest of the nation. Local industry faltered during the early Depression but was back on its feet by 1934. This recovery was hastened by vast diversification which the Chamber of Commerce had noted in 1929, and by the willingness of manufacturers to further diversify into novel products. Perhaps the greatest benefit came not from diversity, however, but from the stability of the paper industry. Paper products remained in demand and this helped steady the rest of the local economy.

The 1920s had seen continued growth in the local paper industry. The King Paper Company, the Monarch Paper Company, and the Bardeen Company of Otsego merged in 1922 to form the Allied Paper Mills. The combined output of 10 paper machines and 34 coating machines placed Allied among the top producers of book paper in the nation. More than 1,500 employees produced 250 tons of paper daily by 1925. The Bryant Company continued strong and provided employment for 1,200. The Kalamazoo Paper Company merged with the Riverview Company in 1918 and became the nation's largest coating mill, with more than 1,000 employees in 1925.

In 1927 the workers at the Kalamazoo Paper Company, in cooperation with management, developed a welfare organization nearly unparalleled for the times. Employees contributed a small amount of their earnings each month to a general welfare fund and the company's stockholders provided matching funds. An

Left
As this 1934 *Gazette* advertisement for the Kalamazoo Market House indicates, grocery prices may have been the only bright spot during the Depression. Courtesy, Western Michigan University Archives.

Below
Employed by the Kalamazoo Paper Company, these women worked in the sorting room of Mill No. 1. This photograph was taken in 1923. Courtesy, Western Michigan University Archives.

elected committee of workers determined the use of these funds.

The Hawthorne Paper Company was not a major producer in terms of bulk, but it did gain a nationwide reputation as a manufacturer of high-quality paper. While most other Kalamazoo mills used wood pulp, Hawthorne continued to make rag paper, which was ideal for bond and ledger stock. Its paper machines were specially fitted with brass and copper water connections to eliminate iron contamination, which could stain the high-grade product. Hawthorne specialized in tough watermark jobs, employing skilled craftsmen to fashion the "dandy rolls" that impressed a watermark design into the wet paper.

By 1937 the mills in the Kalamazoo Valley had a combined daily capacity of five million pounds of paper and their "yearly output would fill a solid train of boxcars reaching from Kalamazoo to sixty miles west of the Mississippi River." The demand for book paper continued strong

during the Depression because the unemployed read more. Although most mills ran at a diminished capacity and employees worked shorter hours, few were laid off. Twenty-five percent of Kalamazoo's work force found employment in paper mills at this time, and most were happy to have such jobs and proud of their occupation. Frank Rusati, an employee at the Lee Mill, for example, received national publicity when he turned down a considerable inheritance left him by his father. To claim this legacy he had to maintain a permanent residence in Italy. Rusati stated: "I would rather be a papermaker in America than the King of Italy."

Demand for waxed-paper and vegetable-parchment products also remained fairly stable. By the early 1930s the Kalamazoo Vegetable Parchment Company was known as "the world's model paper mill." After a humble beginning in an old sugar-beet factory with only 15 employees, growth had been dramatic and consistent. Paper mills were con-

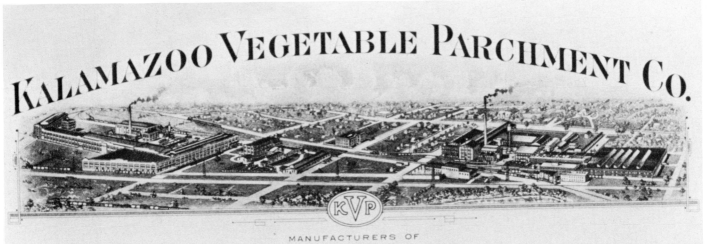

KALAMAZOO VEGETABLE PARCHMENT CO.

KVP

MANUFACTURERS OF
PARCHMENT, WAXED AND BOND PAPERS
PARCHMENT, MICHIGAN
(KALAMAZOO COUNTY)

OCT 6 - 1931

October 1, 1931

structed in 1918 and 1923, and by the early 1930s the company stretched for nearly a mile along the river and employed 1,300 people. A large measure of this growth can be credited to Jacob Kindleberger, the company's hard-working president. Kindleberger had himself performed many of the tasks he now oversaw, having gone to work at the age of 10 in a paper-mill sorting room. He paid close attention to details and ran the company like a benevolent despot, even to the point of making sure that his employees' personal morals and front lawns were in tune with his own high standards. "Uncle Jake," as he liked his subordinates to call him, firmly believed in the power of salesmanship and advertising. KVP advertised extensively at a time when few other paper companies did, and eagerly pursued even small orders. A 1924 advertisement for "Parchment Bond" suggests: "If your dealer can't supply you, just pin a dollar bill to your letter for 5 lb. pack to Dept. B."

Uncle Jake had determination and drive, and faith in the value of aggressive salesmanship. He also had a vision, which he revealed during a speech to company salesmen. Kindleberger's dream was that "the earth will be covered with KVP papers as the waters cover the sea." This was to be accomplished by aggressive, dedicated, persevering salesmen armed with Kindleberger's golden rule: "Your *company first,* your family second, yourself last." But on the day Jacob Kindleberger,

J. KINDLEBERGER

If you come to Kalamazoo, we will show you a new building, 70 ft. x 327 ft., with basement, erected to take care of the increased business that has come to us from our advertising in THE PHILISTINE. We have orders from every corner of the globe, and at the bottom of the orders you may read : " I got your address from reading Elbert Hubbard's article concerning your plant in the June PHILISTINE.,, (*Signed*)

J. KINDLEBERGER

care Kalamazoo Vegetable Parchment Co., Kalamazoo, Mich.

Manufacturers of Genuine Vegetable Parchment, Wax Paper and Household Specialties

This rig transported groceries to Kalamazoo and other western Michigan communities in the 1930s. Courtesy, George Massie.

master salesman, met "Yellow Kid" Weil, master con man, Uncle Jake met more than his match.

It was 1931, a gloomy period for Kalamazoo industry, and Uncle Jake had just returned from a well-deserved Mediterranean vacation. Ralph A. Hayward, his assistant, immediately informed him that two men had come to the office during his absence on what they described as a very important mission. They represented certain financiers from Germany, China, Russia, England, and America who were interested in acquiring high-quality paper mills suitable for manufacturing new and very profitable specialties. Hayward had told them they would have to wait until Kindleberger's return to discuss this important matter.

A few days later Hayward appeared at Uncle Jake's desk and announced that the same gentlemen had returned. The dignified executive took a moment to adjust his necktie and brush his hair, then after a quick glance in the mirror to reassure himself that he represented the proper appearance for such an important conference, he strode out to meet them. The men introduced themselves as Mr. W.J. Lakenan and Mr. Devereaux, the leader of the two, from Shanghai, China.

Kindleberger later described Lakenan as having an "honest face," giving him the appearance of a hard-working civil engineer. Uncle Jake thought Devereaux looked like an "English gentleman." He described him as "immaculately dressed, a very slender man about 5'5" tall, weighing about 125 pounds with a moustache curled up on the sides in true Kaiser fashion, horn-rimmed glasses with a large ribbon, dressed in a dark olive green suit of clothes with a bow tie and diamond stud." Devereaux's appearance made a favorable impression on Kindleberger but he had one peculiarity—yellow kid gloves, which he never took off, even when shaking hands. Little did Uncle Jake know but those gloves were the trademark of one of the most notorious con men in the business, Yellow Kid Weil, whose many exploits became legendary and later provided the inspiration for the motion picture, *The Sting*.

Devereaux established instant rapport by displaying an almost encyclopedic knowledge of the Mediterranean, a subject then dear to Kindleberger's heart. After an entertaining and relaxing conversation, Devereaux suddenly came to the point of the meeting. "We have come to see you," he said, "relative to the purchase of your company for the purpose of manufacturing specialties created by a Chinaman." Devereaux and Lakenan explained that they could not divulge either the nature of these specialties or the names of the principals, since there were other jealous financial interests eager to steal this amazing technology. But to prove their legitimate interest, they were willing to deposit one million dollars in a local bank and make available the remainder of the agreed purchase price within 30 days. Kindleberger, convinced of their sincerity, agreed to set up a meeting with the board of directors.

During this meeting the following week, Devereaux impressed everyone with his vast knowledge of philosophy and world history, rambling on for 45 minutes while the board members listened spellbound. Finally he stated the proposition, again in vague secretive terms, still not revealing the specialty. All the board had to do, he said, was to come up with a reasonable selling price and the agreement could be quickly consummated. After Devereaux left, Kindleberger and the other major stockholders wasted no time in coming up with a price. Allowing plenty of margin for "good will," they figured the company was worth $8.5 million, and each visualized the enormous profits he could make by investing the proceeds of the sale. Uncle Jake dreamed of a new automobile and another world cruise.

After more negotiations, during which Devereaux revealed a hint of the specialties they planned to produce on paper machines—a high grade of linen made from straw—Kindleberger learned that "the principals" would arrive to inspect the mill in a week. A half-century later employees remember that week as "the time we cleaned the mill." They scoured the plant until it gleamed.

Finally "the principals" drove up in a brand new Lincoln. The group consisted of Devereaux; Lakenan; Mr. Roseberry from England, "with all the earmarks of a true English gentleman"; Mr. Von Meuller from Berlin, "with all the earmarks of a Prussian"; and two "Chinamen," Mr. Woo and Mr. Chang, "principal stockholders of all the railroads and steel and paper mills in China." Kindleberger and Hayward proudly escorted the group on a

tour of the shining mill. All asked many knowledgeable questions. The Chinese asked repeatedly where they could obtain large quantities of straw to make the linen and seemed particularly impressed with the mill's cleanliness. This was only natural, for as Kindleberger later discovered, they were employees of a laundry and had been hired for $50 to play their part in the scheme.

A few days later Uncle Jake received a phone call urging him to come to Chicago, alone, to discuss important details concerning the future operations of the new company of which he was to remain president. Kindleberger arrived at the appointed time but Devereaux was tied up with other important deals. While waiting Lakenan showed him a book written by Devereaux and a magazine article that referred to him as the "great engineer and promoter." Both contained photographs of the Yellow Kid, which had been substituted for the originals. Lakenan said he had an errand to run and urged Kindleberger to accompany him. They drove all over the city, stopping at brokerage firms to transact what seemed to be extensive stock negotiations with huge bundles of dummy money. Kindleberger was made privy to a forthcoming deal in which Devereaux would buy mining stocks from an old man with a sick wife at a price far below their value. Devereaux stood to make millions. Finally, after meeting with Devereaux and Roseberry, an agreement was reached and Kindleberger cheerfully returned to Kalamazoo accompanied by Lakenan.

Later that week Von Meuller sent a telegram to Kindleberger informing him that the million-dollar security payment would soon be deposited. That same morning Devereaux phoned Kindleberger, saying he had "been caught with his pants down," and needed $40,000 or $50,000 immediately to complete his stock transaction with the old man. If he could not get the money, he would lose millions. Could Kindleberger let him have it for only a few hours? Kindleberger did not have the money, but Lakenan appealed to him, pointing out all that Devereaux was doing for him—now he needed help.

Uncle Jake paced his office but finally took the bait, hook, line, and sinker. He tried to borrow $40,000 from his bank, but could only get $15,000. Kindleberger jumped in Hayward's car and "passing everything on the road," they arrived in

Chicago just in time to deliver $15,000 cash to Devereaux by the deadline.

Kindleberger had vivid memories of the ride back to Kalamazoo. It was made in silence, but he did "a lot of secret thinking." The next morning he saw clearly what had happened. He'd been stung!

The local newspaper learned of the story, ran headlines, and poor Uncle Jake was the laughingstock of the Kalamazoo business community. Kindleberger wrote a detailed, 36-page account of the fiasco, desperately trying to explain how he, president of one of Kalamazoo's most prestigious companies, came to be duped. Kindleberger, in all fairness, took it like a man. Being himself "a master salesman," he drew a moral from the experience: "(If) men who are in the selling game will take a lesson from the methods used by these men in presenting their proposition with such ability, such dignity, such a courageous spirit, and stick until they win, they, too, would come out with orders instead of alibis."

Uncle Jake was not the first nor the last to be swindled by Yellow Kid Weil. Eventually, however, the master con man served a prison term after a conviction in another bunco scheme. In 1948, a year after Kindleberger's death, the reformed Weil published his autobiography, the colorful story of a lifetime of swindling.

As the publicity died down, the community forgot Uncle Jake's humiliation, encouraged perhaps by the benevolence he displayed during the worst days of the Depression. Determined that his employees would have sufficient income to take care of their families, he put them to work on community development projects when the plant slowed down. They converted a 38-acre tract of marginal land into a village park with sunken gardens, tennis courts, a baseball diamond, and a Community House; none of his employees went on welfare. Bleak Depression Christmases were brightened by Uncle Jake's annual party at which he presented all his employees with "a basket well filled with high-class foodstuffs."

Most Kalamazoo Vegetable Parchment Company employees resided in the "model village" of Parchment, the company town Kindleberger had planned in conjunction with a citizen's committee. In 1930 the village, having grown to a population of 500, received an official charter. Taxes remained low because the company provided water service, street mainte-

nance, and fire protection. Under the paternal guidance of Uncle Jake, Parchment continued to grow throughout the Depression; in 1939, with a population of 770, it became a city.

Kalamazoo's overwhelming success as the "Paper City" attracted a variety of allied industries. Some supplied raw materials and services needed by the mills in their daily operation, while others converted the output of paper into a variety of products. Other specialty manufacturers depended heavily on paper-mill business during their developmental years.

The paper industry used huge Fourdrinier machines to produce endless ribbons of paper up to a width of 156 inches. The first Fourdrinier paper machines, had been invented around the turn of the 18th century; modern machines are larger, refined versions of the original design. At the headbox, or wet end, of a Fourdrinier, pulp—cellulose fibers suspended in water—flows onto a moving belt of wire cloth. Water is drained out through this screen and squeezed out by cylinders at the press section, or couch roll. The wet paper is then transferred onto a layer of felt, which carries it through a battery of steam-heated cylinders until the paper is dry enough to support itself. Finally the dry paper is smoothed to the desired finish at the calender section, or coated with clay or some other pigment, then wound into huge rolls of beautiful clean paper.

Local firms manufactured components for the Fourdrinier machines. The American Wire Cloth Company, incorporated in 1927, produced the endless belts of fine screen used at the wet end. Skilled workers, using a huge loom, wove minute brass and bronze wires into a metallic fabric. The Riedel Brush Company, which had been founded around the turn of the century by Gus Riedel, a highly skilled craftsman from Germany, produced the specialized brushes that were used to apply an even coating to the paper. In 1940 Ward and Grant Wheeler, at the Wheeler Roll Company, began manufacturing the huge metal rolls needed for drying and burnishing the paper.

The Paper Makers Chemical Company had been founded in 1913 to supply local mills with the many chemicals necessary in the manufacture of paper. They specialized in refining rosin, the sizing agent needed to make paper less absorbent; satin white, widely used for coating paper; and a variety of cleaning chemicals. During the early 1930s the Hercules Powder Company of Delaware bought the plant. Another manufacturer of papermaking chemicals, the Kalbfeish Corporation, had been established in 1922. In 1929, as part of a general amalgamation of chemical producers that occurred during this period, Kalbfeish was taken over by American Cyanamid.

The large waxed-paper producers—KVP, Sutherland, and Saniwax—also had a history of attracting industries that catered to their specific needs. Mark Macomber, a salesman in the oil business, had developed a process for refining paraffine, a byproduct of petroleum, which eliminated its objectional oil-like odor. He had established the Crystal Wax Company in Joliet, Illinois, prior to World War I, and one of his first major customers was the newly established Sutherland Company. When the war produced a shortage of wax, however, the company folded and Macomber went back to the oil industry. But with the assistance of his old clients, the Sutherland Brothers, he established in 1925 the Kalamazoo Paraffine Company, which became a heavy supplier to local manufacturers.

Waxed-container manufacturers developed their own printing plants to produce brand-label products, especially bread wrappers. The Crescent Engraving Company, founded in 1906, had originally specialized in the production of plates used to print these labels and the local mills became major customers. The company later expanded into other phases of the graphic arts. Kelley Ink, established in 1929, produced the special inks used for printing on waxed paper.

Harry S. Baird and Homer Brundage, who had founded the Kalamazoo Blow Pipe and Sheet Metal Company in 1919, spent their initial years building the giant hoods and ventilating equipment required by local paper mills. During the early 1920s they had pioneered the development of a blower-driven heating delivery system, which replaced the less efficient gravity-flow system used in residential furnaces. After 1925, when they had further refined the blower to reduce noise, they found overwhelming acceptance by consumers. In later years, as the Brundage Company, they further specialized in large industrial fans and blowers.

Local paper mills were major customers

Durametallic employees pose circa 1934. Paul Jackson, second from the left, began working for the firm as a laborer and is now the corporation's president. Courtesy, Durametallic Corporation.

for a specialized product first produced in 1901 by the New Era Manufacturing Company. This firm fashioned strands of foil into flexible, metallic engine packings to provide an efficient seal around movable parts. Spurred on by local orders, the company experienced consistent growth and became the Durametallic Corporation in 1923. Continued success was assured in 1934, when Durametallic pioneered a revolutionary mechanical seal that replaced traditional packing. This "DuraSeal" became a major product during the 1930s.

The presence of the paper industry also assisted long-established firms to remain viable by adapting their production to changing needs. When the market for windmills diminished in the 1890s, the Williams Manufacturing Company had begun producing silos and ensilage cutters; it became the Kalamazoo Tank and Silo Company in 1904. When larger competitors edged the company out of this market, survival was again a question of diversification. The acquisition of a glazed-tile plant in Carbon, Indiana, led the firm into the production of vitreous tile tanks. It found a major customer in the paper industry, which used the tanks for storage of pulp and waste materials.

Similarly the Bird & Clarage Foundry, dating from 1872, had specialized in windmills. Its "Bird Wind Machine" was a favorite with consumers. After the demise of that industry, the foundry shifted to producing fans and blowers and became the Clarage Fan Company in 1915. When air conditioning became popular after World War I, Clarage installed huge fans and air-conditioning systems in paper mills, as well as in large hotels throughout the country.

Producers of paper products established local plants in order to be near their source of supply. Shortly after the turn of the century, the Kalamazoo Paper Box Company began producing a wide variety of colorful paper boxes; the Illinois Envelope Company, formerly in Centralia, relocated in Kalamazoo; and the Kalamazoo Stationery Company began operation. By the early 1930s the Kalamazoo Stationery Company had become the world's largest manufacturer of stationery supplies. In 1934, 400 employees turned out 300 million envelopes, three million boxes of stationery and 50 million tablets and packages of notebook paper. Schoolchildren throughout the nation scrawled their lessons on, or made airplanes out of, Kalamazoo-made products.

Several other firms specialized in paper labels. The earliest, the Bartlett Label Company, had been established in the 1890s. Shortly after the turn of the century, Louis Sutherland, formerly with the Bartlett Company, set up his own plant, the Kalamazoo Label Company Karl W. Lambooy, who had operated a successful printing firm in Albion, the Mirror Printing Company, moved to Kalamazoo just before World War I and also specialized in labels. The Lambooy Label Company grew steadily, bought out other local concerns, built its own plant on Portage Street in

1926, and by 1934 (when employees turned out five to 10 million labels daily) was one of the nation's largest producers.

The Merchants Publishing Company had moved from Chicago in 1903 and, by the 1920s, had developed into a major producer of paper advertising novelties. The firm specialized in promotional calendars featuring colorful illustrations derived from specially commissioned paintings. The designs chosen for calendars were an important aspect of merchandising. In 1925, when Charles W. Johnson, general manager of the company, outlined his rationale for selection he also revealed much about the popular taste of the period: "Experience has taught us the general public wants plenty of snap and pep in calendar design. There must be color at all times, vivid shades seem to take best. Figures are also popular, while strange as it may seem, moonlight scenes have quite a vogue. Those restful pastoral paintings suitable for the home do not make good calendars." Changing tastes, perhaps, contributed to the decline of the Merchants Publishing Company, but a branch specializing in large displays, Kalasign, developed into a successful enterprise.

Several local firms converted the high-quality rag paper produced by some Kalamazoo mills into printed office and legal forms, an industry that dates from 1869, when Otto Ihling moved from Milwaukee to Kalamazoo with $500 and the skills of a journeyman bookbinder. Originally engaged in general bookbinding and printing, he soon specialized in hand-bound blank books. By the 1890s Ihling's affiliation with the Masonic Order resulted in a further specialty, "blank books for all lodges and secret societies." In competition with Henderson-Ames, Ihling Brothers later offered a complete inventory of fraternal supplies, including costumes, "hoodwinks," furniture, and ballot boxes. The company became Ihling Brothers & Everard in 1887, and a steady stream of catalogs poured from the handsome Romanesque plant on the corner of East Michigan Avenue and Edwards Street. State printing contracts became increasingly important to them, and eventually the firm also specialized in printing and binding for local government units.

In 1903 Ihling Brothers & Everard purchased the patent rights for an ingenious loose-leaf binder designed by H.F. Bushong of Portland, Oregon. The binder

quickly became popular and production demands soon outgrew the available space. A separate organization developed, the Kalamazoo Loose Leaf Binder Company, and it, too, grew rapidly. After merging with the Remington-Rand Corporation in 1927, the plant moved to Benton Harbor. The former officers stayed in Kalamazoo to form the Loose Leaf Binder and Equipment Company. Later renamed Mastercraft, this firm also became a major producer of printed business forms.

The other major firm to specialize in form printing had been founded by Fred and Ward Doubleday in 1898 when they purchased the bindery of the old Kalamazoo Publishing Company. Doubleday Brothers soon expanded into printing the many forms needed by local governments and schools. They developed into the largest producer in the state of legal forms,

Fish and Fishermen

I have known

by Wm. Shakespeare Jr.

"A Kalamazoo Direct to You"

MALLEABLE KALAMAZOO STEEL RANGE

"By baking bread at home housewives should be able to reduce expenditure for food." —U. S. Department of Agriculture.

If you expect a woman to reduce home expenses by baking bread herself

GIVE HER A GOOD RANGE

Kalamazoo
Malleable Steel Range

The "Kalamazoo Malleable" is so designed that it bakes perfectly. And the best part about it is that it will bake just like that for years. Why not insure your future health and happiness by buying one NOW? The price has recently been reduced. You can buy for cash or on easy credit terms. AND

When you buy directly from the factory, YOU SAVE THE MIDDLEMAN'S PROFIT WESTERN STATE NORMAL SCHOOL USES A KALAMAZOO RANGE. It is a part of their high class equipment. We have thousands of other satisfied customers. It always pays to get the best.
Send for our new spring catalog showing our other reliable, money-saving lines. You can buy furniture, kitchen cabinets, sewing machines, washing machines, vacuum cleaners, aluminum and many other articles of household equipment, and have them sent "Direct to You" promptly.
WE ALSO MAKE HIGH GRADE FURNACES. A Furnace is the logical, economical way to heat a house. And Kalamazoo is the logical, economical place to buy it. Don't make the mistake of putting off the installation of your furnace until fall. Be ready when cold weather comes.
All you need to pay down on a range or a furnace is $25.00. You may pay the balance of the cash price October 1. Satisfaction guaranteed.
Ask for Catalog No. 22

KALAMAZOO STOVE COMPANY, Manufacturers, Kalamazoo, Michigan

Above
William Shakespeare, Jr., took the opportunity to tell some favorite "whoppers" in his 1924 fishing tackle catalogue. From the author's collection.

Above right
By 1922 Kalamazoo ranges manufactured by the Kalamazoo Stove Company came equipped with patented oven thermometers. Courtesy, Western Michigan University Archives.

Facing page
Top
Artisans employed in the rim bending department of the Gibson Guitar and Mandolin Company display some examples of their fine craftsmanship about 1917. Courtesy, Gibson Company.

Bottom
The imposing, brick Masonic Temple Building at the northwest corner of North Rose and Eleanor streets is shown in 1925. Courtesy, Kalamazoo County Chamber of Commerce.

their specialty. In 1911 Ward established his own firm, Doubleday Hunt and Dolan, and the two brothers engaged in spirited competition.

While the paper and allied industries provided a solid foundation for the local economy during the Depression, Kalamazoo's industrial diversity also proved a moderating influence. The Kalamazoo Stove Company remained remarkably strong and even expanded production during the 1930s. In the previous decade, when the Model T and better roads brought rural families into town more often, the company's mail-order business had declined, forcing a change of tactics. Largely through the influence of Arthur Blakeslee, who had worked his way up from clerk to become general manager in 1923 and president in 1925, the company introduced its own retail outlets in the early 1920s. By the late 1930s more than 300 factory branches located nationwide served as showrooms and retail outlets.

The Kalamazoo Stove factory, equipped with its own foundries, enamel plant and tinshop, sprawled over 20 acres in 1934.

More than 1,200 employees produced and marketed more than 200 styles of stoves, ranges, and furnaces. Two new models were a popular success that year. The "new moderne," a combination gas, coal, and wood range, was available in such popular color combinations as Nile green and ivory, pigeon blue and ivory, and pearl gray and white. The name of a new model furnace, the "Dictator," undoubtedly suggested by current world events, did not sound so appealing by the end of the decade, however. In 1935 the firm made large additions to its factory, added more than 800 new employees, and boasted an annual production of 100,000 units. By decade's end, families comprising a total of more than 12,000 people owed their livelihood to the Kalamazoo Stove Company.

The Shakespeare Company also diversified from its major line, fishing tackle, and prospered. During World War I practically the entire capacity of the plant had been devoted to production of trench mortar fuses under government contract. In 1921 the company further diversified, when a subsidiary, Shakespeare Products,

began manufacturing nonfishing products. By 1925 it had successfully marketed a novel, refillable "Kalamazoo Fibre
Broom." During the 1930s many leading
automobile manufacturers installed the
Shakespeare Company's new specialty,
carburetor controls; aircraft controls were
later produced. But fine-quality fishing
equipment remained the major product.
By the late 1920s more than 500 Shakespeare employees turned out thousands
of "built like a fine watch" reels, "honor
built from butt to tip" rods, baits "that
catch fish" and lines "that hold 'em."
The "Shakespeare mouse" and "Kazoo
Bass Bug" lures were also widely respected by America's fishermen.

The Kalamazoo Pant Company demonstrated ingenuity and also achieved success during the Depression. It had its origins in 1867, when Samuel Rosenbaum, a
dry-goods wholesaler from Three Rivers
Michigan, wheelbarrowed his entire stock
to Kalamazoo. He marketed his dry goods
and notions by horse and buggy through
the surrounding countryside and one item
sold exceptionally well—denim overalls.
Rosenbaum turned to manufacturing over-

Various types of stringed and fretted musical instruments lie in the racks of the Gibson Guitar and Mandolin Company's "daylight plant" circa 1917. Courtesy, Gibson Company.

alls himself and by the mid-1880s it was his sole occupation. Soon the Kalamazoo Overall Company branched into a related product and became the Kalamazoo Pant and Overall Company, producing a wide variety of Kazoo-brand trousers. In 1903 the company proudly advertised: "When you've seen Kazoo, you'll say they'll do." Around that time, too, it began utilizing bolt ends from men's trouser cuttings to produce boys' knickers. When the craze for golf knickers swept the country in the 1920s, the company drew on its experience in this area to turn out an exceptional and popular product.

The Kalamazoo Pant Company changed their emphasis during the 1920s from men's to boys' and students' trousers. In 1927, when a fad for corduroys spread

across the nation's campuses, returning Notre Dame students bought out every pair in South Bend. This prompted the Kalamazoo Pant Company to deliver America's first shipment of trousers by air as it quickly loaded a cargo of corduroys aboard a biplane, which landed on the only space available, a Notre Dame football practice field.

The company made a big success in 1931 with an innovation that changed America's pants forever: the "hip-zip knickers." This, apparently, was the first time anyone had put slide talon fasteners —zippers—on trousers and the company's advertising proclaimed "pull 'em on and zip 'em up—no belt to bother with." Close-fitting knickers equipped with back-buckle straps and a concealed zipper on the side finally solved the problem Walter Loveland with his invisible belt and the Kazoo Suspender Company had struggled with earlier. Hip-zip knickers would "always stay up without the use of belt or suspenders. You can't pull them off the hips." Business boomed and, by 1934, 300 employees turned out 500,000 pairs of trousers a year. The company later relocated its production operation to Mississippi, but Kalamazoo remained the center from which "Kazoo" trousers were distributed all over the nation.

The Gibson Company also prospered through adaptation and diversification. Following World War I, with its emphasis on martial marches and more strident music, the slower-paced mandolin declined in popularity. During the 1920s vaudeville entertainers in black face, and Dixieland and ragtime dance bands, had strummed countless banjos; the rage for Hawaiian music had popularized the ukelele; and western movie stars, when not chasing black-hatted "owlhoots" or kissing their horses, had sung lonesome ballads to the accompaniment of an ever-present guitar, ushering in the golden age of that instrument. The Gibson Guitar and Mandolin Company quickly responded to this changing market. In 1918 it produced its first banjos, and by 1925 Gibson craftsmen produced 47 styles and grades of fretted instruments, including mandolins, mandolas, mandecellos, mandobasses, guitars, Hawaiian guitars, harp guitars, mandolin-banjos, tenor banjos, cello banjos, guitar banjos, five-string banjos, plectrum banjos, ukelele banjos, and ukeleles. Widespread use in radio, stage, and dance orchestras, and by leading entertainers such as Rudy Vallee, resulted in a preponderance of higher-priced professional models.

Hundreds of agents and aggressive advertising widely promoted Gibson instruments while exploring and developing new markets. A half-page advertisement in the 1926 Kalamazoo Central High School *Delphian* featured Bill Haid of "Coon Sanders Original Night Hawks" strumming a Gibson banjo. The ad informed students that "Music is not only a pleasure. You can make it your vocation. Gibson players earn large incomes as professional orchestra musicians, teachers, concert and radio artists."

When the Depression hit and people had to make do with their old equipment, the demand for stringed instruments dropped sharply and Gibson was forced to lay off many employees. Through resourcefulness and diversification, however, the company soon called most of them back. Whereas Gibson had previously bought strings from other companies, it now recalled 35 employees in order to produce its own. For a brief period the company also tried manufacturing trombones. A subsidiary, the Kalamazoo Playthings Company, was formed to make use of the firm's excellent woodworking facilities, which had been partially idle because of the decreased output of stringed instruments. During the early 1930s this subsidiary produced nearly 100 varieties of high-quality wooden toys, including a model sailboat and a motorboat, the "Kalamazoo Rocket."

When the demand for stringed instruments increased in 1934 the company discontinued toy manufacturing and introduced a new line of "Kalamazoo" guitars, banjos, and mandolins. During that year approximately 250 workers produced 200 instruments daily, 75 percent of which were guitars. Gibson had become the "largest factory in the world devoted exclusively to making stringed musical instruments." By the end of the 1930s, the company was experimenting with another novelty, "electric guitars," later destined to become a major line.

Another business that flourished despite the Depression was the Peter Pan Bakery. It had been started as the J.B. Baking Company by Jay Brink in 1924. Business languished until Ennis L. (Jack) Schafer arrived in 1931. Schafer, a son of Dutch immigrants, stimulated growth through hard work and dedication. He modernized operations, built additions, and in 1933 became sole owner of the bakery. That same year his employees became the highest paid of any industry in the city when the Peter Pan Bakery became the first Kalamazoo firm to adopt the new NRA hours and wage scale.

Schafer's baked goods sold like the proverbial hot cakes. By 1934, 42 full-time employees baked thousands of loaves of bread that were trucked to retail outlets all over southwestern Michigan. Schafer continued to expand, buying a bakery in Battle Creek in 1934, one in Detroit in 1936, another in Lansing in 1938, until by the early 1940s he owned seven bakeries in six cities. But Kalamazoo remained the major location and by 1948 Peter Pan had become Schafer's Bakery.

Many a sweet tooth was satisfied at Adrian Zuidwig's Confectionary at 1602 South Burdick. This view of the candy shop was made in the mid-1920s. Courtesy, Western Michigan University Archives.

Credit for this remarkable success is due in part to Schafer's drive and determination, and in part to his cleverly selected brand name "Peter Pan," sure to appeal to children when sent to the store for bread. In addition Schafer had a flair for publicity and devoted a large budget in the 1930s to fund a series of unusual promotional ventures. Special excursions, write-in contests, brightly painted dirigibles, airplane skywriting, and full-page newspaper advertisements, all encouraged consumers to "Say Peter Pan to your grocer man."

One Peter Pan-sponsored excursion in September 1933 sent 300 southwestern Michigan grocers to the Chicago World's Fair. Forty years had passed; a world war had been fought; automobiles, airplanes, radios, and other inventions that were then "dreams" had become an integral part of everyday life; manners, morals, and dress seemed a century apart, but in the midst of another major industrial depression Chicago again sponsored a World's Fair. Despite the hard times, this "Century of Progress Exhibition," in honor of the centennial of Chicago's founding, attracted an amazing number of Americans just as the Columbian Exposition had two generations before.

The towering "Skyride," this fair's answer to the ferris wheel, thrilled the many visitors. Two gigantic towers supported lines of steel cable on which "rocket cars" hurtled more than 2.5 million passengers on a breathtaking ride across the lagoon. The Columbian Exposition had featured a classical motif, but the Century of Progress was modernistic. Examples of the international style and art deco were everywhere, including a 200-foot Havoline Thermometer, a 50-foot glass brick structure, and the trend-setting Chrysler Building. Thousands danced at the double-decked "dance ship" on the lakeshore, and everyone remembered the "Midget Village," where "sixty Lilliputians live in their tiny houses, conduct their diminutive activities, serve you with food, and entertain you with theatrical performances." Visitors from Kalamazoo were certain to tour the Agricultural Building where KVP maintained a display demonstrating the manufacture of vegetable parchment paper.

The Century of Progress World's Fair proved so successful that it was held again the following year, and Kalamazoo emulated Chicago on a smaller scale. In the summer of 1934 the Chamber of Commerce sponsored a "Kalamazoo Progress Festival" in celebration of the beautiful new asphalt paving on Michigan Avenue. The main attraction, however, was a "Made In Kalamazoo Exposition" at which all the paper mills and more than 40 other local manufacturers displayed their

Automobiles line South Burdick Street in 1927. This view was taken from Michigan Avenue. Courtesy, Kalamazoo Public Museum.

Kalamazoo • The Debt-Free City • Page 193

products and processes. The rest of the country may not have believed that the Depression was over but Kalamazoo could demonstrate, by its dazzling array of locally manufactured goods, that complete recovery was just around the corner. Kalamazoo industry stood strong and healthy.

Local industry grew even stronger as the decade wore on. The city jubilantly threw off the shackles of bonded indebtedness, and something that residents had long known became more widely publicized—Kalamazoo was a good place to live and work. Dr. Edward L. Thorndike, a highly respected sociologist, studied life in 310 American cities during the last years of the 1930s. He evaluated 37 factors, such as the infant mortality rate; per capita public expenditures for schools, libraries, and museums; public park acreage; rarity of extreme poverty; average wages; and number of homes owned. When he had tabulated his statistics, Thorndike found that Kalamazoo ranked among the top ten American cities in terms of general quality of life.

Life was good in Kalamazoo but the nation had been irrevocably affected by the events of the last two decades. As the 1930s drew to a close, Americans found themselves part of a new, faster-paced, ever-changing society, and some Kalamazooans looked back fondly to the less hectic "good old days." In a 1939 advertisement, the proprietor of the Perfection Bedding Company lamented:

Women no longer wear hoopskirts, petticoats, cotton stockings and button shoes. Back in the days when those sort of things were popular women did the cleaning, washing, ironing and raised families. Mothers were too busy to be sick. The men wore whiskers, plug hats, red underwear, and took a bath once a week. They drove buggies, rode bicycles, worked 12 hours a day and lived to a ripe old age. Now, women wear silk stockings, an ounce of underwear, bob their hair, paint their fingernails, smoke, paint, powder, and drink cocktails. The men have high blood-pressure, little hair, no whiskers. They play golf, bathe twice a day, never go to bed the same day they get up, ride in airplanes, work six hours a day and die young.

America could never return to those days, however, and future events would bring even more disruptive changes. On August 8, 1939, a violent tornado swept across Kalamazoo County, causing extensive damage on the southern side of the city, but it was merely a breeze compared to the storm that was unleashed less than a month later when Hitler's troops invaded Poland and hurled the world into another war.

CHAPTER VIII
THE MALL CITY: 1940–1980

In 1941 East Michigan Avenue took on a martial air. Courtesy, Kalamazoo Savings and Loan Association.

American industry finally began to shake off the deadening effects of the Great Depression as the 1930s drew to a close. Federal government and Allied spending for war materiel spurred increased industrial production, and Kalamazoo, as well as the nation as a whole, experienced boom years in 1940 and 1941. Employment reached heights unattained since the bright days of the 1920s. But as the unsolved problems inherited from the last generation's world war avalanched into another global conflict, fear of war replaced economic uncertainty. Although initially the American mood overwhelmingly reflected neutrality, as world events reverberated with the tramp of the goose step and the Banzai yell, echoes of preparedness mingled with the hum of industrial machinery. On December 7, 1941, Japan's attack on Pearl Harbor ended the uncertainty, and the United States faced its greatest challenge since the days of the Revolution.

Kalamazoo answered the call to arms with typical enthusiasm. Company C of the 126th Infantry, Kalamazoo's National Guard unit, was mobilized in 1940. By 1942 it was fighting in the South Pacific with the rest of the 32nd Division. Altogether more than 12,000 men and women from the county served in the armed forces during the long 44 months of America's involvement in the war. Nearly 9,000 saw overseas duty and approximately 400 paid the supreme sacrifice.

The home front received more emphasis than it had in any previous war. Families proudly displayed service flags with a star for every member in the service. Home guards drilled, factories and homes prac-

As suggested by this photograph, patriotism knew no age limit in Kalamazoo during World War II. Even children helped the war effort by collecting balls of tin foil. Courtesy, Kalamazoo Public Library.

ticed newly established blackout regulations, and air-raid wardens scanned the skies for bombers that fortunately never materialized. As price controls and rationing of food, tires, and gasoline became a way of life, men patched up their old cars, women their nylons, and war gardens grew on vacant lots. Civil War cannons and antique pewter fell victim to scrap drives; bond drives went over the top; and children bought war stamps and collected balls of tin foil.

War propaganda dominated literature, the movies, the news media, and even the comic strips, teaching Americans to hate the enemy as never before. As specific industries and agricultural products received priority ratings, and increasing numbers of women replaced men in factories to perform labor they had never been thought capable of, brightly colored war posters cautioned workers that "loose lips sink ships" and reminded them that their part in the war effort was essential to victory.

Army trainees from across the nation again thronged nearby Camp Custer and Kalamazoo established a USO in the fall of 1941 that provided snack bars, game rooms, and dances for more than 10,000 servicemen a month. Homesick GIs the world over listened to songwriters Mack Gordon and Harry Warren's peppy hit "I've Got a Gal in Kalamazoo." In 1942, when Glenn Miller's big band and others popularized the tune, students at Kalamazoo College voted Sara Woolley the real-life "gal in Kalamazoo," and she traveled across the nation appearing at bond drives and USO dances.

One out of every five people on the home front actively engaged in war work, and more than 17,000 Kalamazoo factory workers manufactured essential war materiel. The city's industries quickly geared up for defense work, converting plants to the production of the government's needs. Six companies received the prestigious Army-Navy "E" Award for production excellence: Atlas Press, Shakespeare, Balch, Gibson, Clarage Fan, and Upjohn. The war affected local industries more than anything else had before. Some firms experienced unparalleled prosperity and growth, which either ended after the war or was used to build even greater future success. Others languished due to shortages of materials or failed to withstand the conversion and reconversion of their facilities.

The Shakespeare Company dropped production of fishing tackle for the duration of the war and turned to the manufacturing of precision components for guns and military aircraft. Skilled craftsmen, experienced in producing delicate, "built like a fine watch" reels and existing precision machinery, proved easily adaptable to these new demands. Root Spring Scraper similarly converted its facilities and manufactured ramps for landing crafts. As a subcontractor for Chris Craft it produced more than 10,000 units by the war's end. Since spearmint and peppermint oil received designation as essential war crops because of the demand for gum and candy by servicemen, the Todd Company continued to process mint oils during the war.

The Upjohn Company devoted a good portion of its production facilities to government contracts. Many wounded in battle owe their lives to Upjohn products. The company grew hundreds of bottles of the new wonder drug penicillin, manufactured serum albumen, and packaged sulfa powder in the sterile containers carried by troops in their wound packets. Another contract called for compressing a secret powder into pills, which turned out to be the antiflash tablets added to artillery charges. In 1945 more than 1,300 employees produced an all-time high output of $40 million, double the 1941 level. However gross profits were lower because of essentially low-profit government contracts. Before the war the company had experienced consistent growth, but this tremendous wartime development stimulated the next three decades' explosive expansion. Shortly after the war's end the Upjohn Company purchased a 1,500-acre tract south of the city and began construction of a huge new facility.

Wartime production also stimulated the growth of the National Waterlift Company. It had been founded back in 1908 by Roland Fairchild to manufacture domestic water pumps, and in 1942 the little plant on Willard Street employed only eight workers. In 1943, after acquisition by Severens Balch, the company diversified into the manufacture of precision aircraft parts and tremendous growth followed. The company briefly returned to domestic water-pump production after the war, but by 1947 precision automobile and aircraft pumps had become the major output. As the missile industry boomed during the ensuing Cold War arms race, the company landed contracts for the production of components and business again skyrocketed.

The war gave an indirect boost to Kalamazoo's Kozy Coach Company. Clarence M. Lutes, an employee of the Grace Corset Company, had started Kozy Coach in 1930 when he built his first homemade travel trailer. By 1934, he had gone into full-time production of what was a novelty for the times. During the mid-1930s travel trailers became very popular and Michigan and northern Indiana emerged as the center of a burgeoning industry. But by the end of the 1930s, it seemed that the craze for trailers had run its course and business slumped for most manufacturers. Kozy Coach, because it emphasized quality, remained in business but with a diminished output. When wartime restrictions on construction created emergency housing needs, however, the trailer industry experienced another boom. Government contracts also contributed to Kozy Coach's prosperity. After the war, low-cost and temporary housing remained in strong demand, and to fill this need the travel trailer evolved into the now-familiar mobile home. Increasing numbers of manufacturers moved into trailer production, however, and strong competition gradually drove Kozy Coach out of business by 1960.

Military demands sparked business for the Bowers Lighter Company during the war. This enterprise grew out of a tool-and-die shop operated by Ernest Bowers in the old Verdon Cigar factory on Willard Street. Bowers branched into production of cigarette lighters during the slow days of the Depression. Business moderately expanded until 1942, when a shortage of

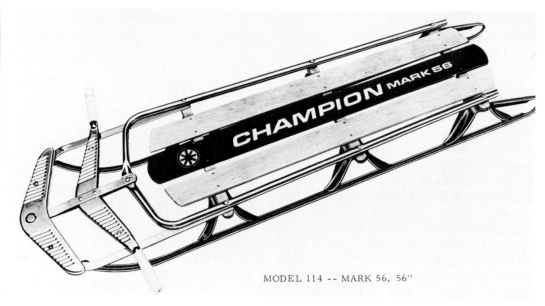

MODEL 114 -- MARK 56, 56"

brass caused the company to shut down. Six months later, however, Bowers received an enormous government contract to supply lighters for servicemen. The plant's 250 to 300 employees, mostly women, produced 12 million lighters during the remainder of the war, 55 percent of the total government lighter purchases. Business again shrank in the postwar period as many new competitors marketed lighters made from surplus metal, but Bowers Lighter Company continued production until the early 1970s, though at a diminished capacity.

The war had an opposite effect on the Grandbois Gum Company. Founded in the early 1920s by Urse G. Grandbois and Eugene W. Doty, the company gradually built up a nationwide business in chewing gum. However, sugar rationing during the war took a healthy bite out of this prospering industry. In addition, new competition emerged when veterans, discharged before the war's end, received priority rights to rationed products. Having access to sugar, they went into the chewing-gum business. The Grandbois Company tried to fight back through diversification. It manufactured novel medicinal gums, laxatives, sore-throat remedies, candy-coated licorice and raisins, all with limited success. When rationing ended, overproduction by the many new companies resulted in market prices below production costs. Even the bubble-gum craze that gripped the nation's youngsters could not provide enough business for Grandbois. Too much competition and a cutthroat market chewed up profits. The company was swallowed up by 1955.

The mighty Kalamazoo Stove Company, by the early 1940s one of the city's largest employers, experienced the most telling effects of the war. Shortly after mobilization the government ordered production halted in all stove factories, the annual volume of which exceeded $2 million. The huge plant shut down and the nearly 300 branch outlets, without anything to sell, closed their doors as well. Soon new machinery reequipped the factory and the Kalamazoo Stove Company turned exclusively to war production. From a tradition of warming the nation's families, the company turned to making it hot for the enemy as experienced stovemakers fashioned parachute flares, armor plate for tanks, and landing gear for warplanes.

Reconversion after the war posed a particularly tough problem because production facilities had been so drastically altered. The company installed modern new equipment at great expense and again produced stoves and furnaces. To recover some of this investment, it decided to abandon the traditional retail branch outlets. But when Kalamazoo Stove products were sold through ordinary retail dealers, they lost much of their mystique. Kalamazoo wood-burning stoves had been very successful before the war, but they became largely a thing of the past. The obstacle that eventually proved too great to overcome was the tremendous task of reconversion from war production. The war had banked the fire in Kalamazoo's magnificent stove works and the glowing embers, inadequately stoked, flickered out entirely by the end of the 1950s.

The famous Kalamazoo Sled Company

did not fare much better. When steel became unavailable during the war, the firm produced old-fashioned, all-wooden sleds. Some government contracts led to the manufacture of cargo toboggans used by arctic ski troops. After the war the company developed such novel sliding equipment as fiberglass disks, but production never reached prewar heights. The company coasted to a complete stop in 1969.

The once-robust celery industry, while not the giant it had been, remained important until the war, then declined at an increasing rate each year. The water table dropped, drying much of the muck land, and the property became more valuable as real estate than for agricultural use. In addition, Pascal celery, a green variety, became more popular with diners, replacing the local bleached type. Although Michigan continued to be a major producer, the industry moved from Kalamazoo to the muck lands around Decatur, Gun Swamp near Plainwell, and especially near Hudsonville to the north. This Hudsonville area, with its ideal muck land and heavy Dutch population, became the center of the Michigan celery industry by the 1960s.

Kalamazoo city directories graphically illustrate the rapid demise of this once-proud industry. From more than 350 celery growers listed at the turn of the century, the number shrank to 105 in 1939; 71 in 1942; 40 in 1943, 28 in 1945; 16 in 1948; 8 in 1952; 5 in 1955; 3 in 1959; and in 1961 only one commercial grower, Rufus Schuur & Sons, remained. The next year's directory listed no celery growers.

The paper industry, on the other hand, continued strong throughout the war. Government agencies needed tons of paper to document their many functions; as any GI could testify, forms seemed as essential to fighting the war as bullets. In 1945, 6,800 workers found employment in local paper mills, 20 percent of the county's total work force and 40 percent of those engaged in manufacturing. As late as 1948 the area's eight paper mills still boasted an output comprising the "largest tonnage of high grade papers of any city in the world."

During the 1960s, however, acquisition by merger or purchase by large corporations became the fate of the local paper

Though celery production declined after World War II, celery harvesting still continued in Comstock Township. These family members are harvesting their 1959 crop. Courtesy, Kalamazoo County Chamber of Commerce.

mills and this industry also seemed destined to diminish. KVP and Sutherland merged in 1960 and were acquired by the Brown Company in 1966. Allied bought Rex in 1967, and in 1968 the S.C.M. Corporation purchased Allied. In 1967 Georgia Pacific bought the area's pioneer mill, the Kalamazoo Paper Company. The new nonlocal owners failed to install new machinery, and as old paper machines wore out and shut down, the future did not look promising. The local paper industry continued as a major employer, but no longer was Kalamazoo the "Paper City," and each year saw a further deterioration in relative importance.

As Kalamazoo entered the second half of the 20th century, few foresaw the drop in economic importance of the paper industry or manufacturing in general that the next 30 years would bring. The 1950s witnessed another period of explosive population growth. The city's population had diminished slightly during the 1930s and had only grown by six percent in the 1940s, but it mushroomed during the next decade from 57,326 in 1950 to 82,089 in 1960. Some of the increase resulted from a burst of annexations that expanded the city's area, but there was a genuine increase in population. However, as in most Midwestern urban areas, population grew only slightly in the 1960s and apparently decreased somewhat during the 1970s as the surrounding townships gained.

Kalamazoo County's labor force grew even more drastically. In 1945, 33,650 persons found employment in nonagricultural jobs. This number climbed to 51,600 by 1952 and to 56,600 by 1957. Fully half of the labor force worked in factories producing manufactured goods. The number of manufacturers also grew, from 243 in 1948 to 320 in 1957. The wide diversity of these employers, coupled with the traditional stability of the paper industry resulted in steady employment. During the rather severe recession in 1958, Kalamazoo consistently led the state with the lowest unemployment rate. Wages also increased and, despite a high rate of inflation, workers enjoyed greater purchasing power. In 1957 the average wage paid in all manufacturing industries in Kalamazoo was $2.09 an hour, and papermakers earned an average of $92.55 for a 45-hour week.

Many working-class families utilized their increased purchasing power to buy an automobile. The 29,112 passenger cars registered in the county in 1940 had climbed to 42,141 in 1950 and zoomed to 56,455 by 1956. Many families also purchased homes after the war. Kalamazoo was traditionally a city of homeowners, and by 1950, 71 percent of all houses in the city were owner-occupied as compared to a national average of 55 percent. Home construction came to a virtual standstill during the war. Following it, construction materials were in short supply and a housing shortage posed a major domestic problem. But by the early 1950s, Kalamazoo experienced a tremendous building boom. By 1957 approximately 10,000 new homes with an average value of $15,000 graced the city and its suburbs.

That year, another Kalamazoo house won special honors for the city, when a nationally circulated magazine designated it a "Citation Home." Considerably different from "Everyman's House," this three-bedroom, ranch-style house with two bathrooms, a full basement, and a two-car garage featured "picture windows" across the front facade. Set on a suburban lot, Kalamazoo's Citation Home sold for around $24,000. As a "do it yourself" movement gripped the country following the war and smashed thumbnails became a badge of honor, many families purchased their ranch-style homes only partially completed and proudly finished the refinements.

A Kalamazoo manufacturer capitalized on this trend and enjoyed a prosperous business. Atlas Press, founded in 1911 to produce arbor presses, expanded during the 1920s into the field of hand tools and automobile service equipment. During the Depression the firm had developed a low-priced metal lathe, which appealed to many unemployed skilled craftsmen, and discovered a new market as a result. Throughout the war it devoted its facilities to producing government-contract, metal-working tools, but when "do it yourself" became America's slogan, the company greatly expanded into a variety of hand power tools. The quick response to this need brought phenomenal growth and by 1957 Atlas Press had become the country's "second largest manufacturer of machines of its size and class."

International events, meanwhile, continued to affect local manufacturers. America engaged in a "Cold War" with its former World War II allies, China and

Russia, while "Red scares" colored the nation's domestic life. In 1950 the Cold War heated up, boiling over into what became a three-year "police action" in Korea. As a result of these hostilities and the subsequent defense build-up, many local companies received lucrative government contracts. In 1953 Checker Cab won a mammoth 18-month contract that pushed its production value to an all-time high. This $22-million contract to produce more than 25,000 ton-and-a-half army trailers resulted in the hiring of hundreds of new employees.

Root Spring Scraper, specializing in heavy-duty snowplows, received an interesting government contract during this period. The Air Force and Army Corp of Engineers called on it to produce the largest snowplow ever built up to that time. The huge V-type plow, used to clear runways, measured 16 feet wide and 10 feet high. Too large even to fit on a railroad flatcar, it had to be shipped in sections.

Other honors besides government contracts flowed to Kalamazoo throughout the

1950s. In 1951 the National Municipal League designated it as one of that year's 11 "All American Cities." In 1957, the year Russia dealt a shocking blow to America's technological superiority with Sputnik's dramatic leap into space, the United States Information Service chose Kalamazoo over three other finalists—Topeka, Toledo, and Evanston—as the typical medium-sized American city. A traveling display, "Kalamazoo—Window of America," was developed to show the British what life in America was really like. The exhibit, which had the theme "Kalamazoo and How it Grew," opened in Manchester, England. The paper mills from Kalamazoo flew in paper plates, napkins, and table mats for the grand opening, a typical American breakfast. Thousands of Britons viewed exhibits featuring the diverse industrial output of the city, with more than 50 Kalamazoo-made products, ranging from hot-water heaters to cigarette lighters, on display. Each visitor received a special four-page souvenir edition of the *Kalamazoo Gazette*. It described the city

Automobiles and pedestrians on North Burdick Street were captured by the camera one late afternoon in the early 1950s. Courtesy, Western Michigan University Archives.

and included a note explaining that a normal daily issue "ran upwards of forty pages" and used paper that, if unrolled in a single stretch, "would reach from Kalamazoo to within less than ½ mile of London."

Kalamazoo Mayor Glenn Allen attended the festivities in Manchester. While there he received a special visit from Kalamazoo, Limited. This international firm of British office suppliers had grown out of the old Kalamazoo Loose Leaf Binder Company. As a result of this company's success, the name "Kalamazoo" was already very familiar to the British.

The "Kalamazoo—Window of America" exhibit traveled throughout Great Britain in 1957, and the following year Kalamazoo was again chosen for a similar display at the Berlin Industrial Fair. An estimated half-million Germans became familiar with "Kalamazoo—A Typical Midwestern City."

While Kalamazoo could be proud of its designation as a "typical Midwestern city," it could no longer boast "debt-free" status. Though the city government had stubbornly refused to relinquish the old "pay as you go" policy, it fought a losing battle. By the early 1950s miles of badly needed street paving, new parks, the construction of fire stations, and, most importantly, the decision to build a new sewage-disposal plant demanded a grudging sale of bonds. While no longer the "Debt Free City," events in the late 1950s soon produced a new nickname, the "Mall City."

As the rapidly expanding suburban areas funneled off most of the available public construction and maintenance monies, the downtown core physically deteriorated. Kalamazoo felt the same "creeping blight" that struck most other American cities in the mid-1950s. Increasing numbers of automobiles and trucks posed serious traffic problems for inner-city street networks. Competitive outlying shopping centers were developed to meet the needs of the growing suburban population. Long-established firms relocated to outlying areas, downtown retail sales fell sharply, and increasing numbers of stores and offices stood vacant or neglected. The situation became dramatically apparent to downtown property owners when a property-tax reassessment of the central business district in 1955 resulted in a decrease in valuation of more than a million dollars.

Concerned businessmen formed a

Downtown Kalamazoo Planning Committee in 1956, raised funds through membership fees, and in the spring of 1957 awarded the prestigious firm, Victor Gruen Associates, a $40,000 contract to prepare a long-range plan for the revitalization of the downtown. In March 1958 the imaginative plan, "Kalamazoo 1980," was presented for public reaction. The plan emphasized an auto-free central district with low-speed traffic arteries ringing the downtown core and a permanent pedestrian mall, a feature then under consideration by other American cities. That same year merchants organized the Downtown Kalamazoo Association, which assumed a leadership role in gaining acceptance for the plan.

After several months of intensive study, the City Commission decided to close two blocks of Burdick Street between Water and South streets, southwestern Michigan's busiest intersection, and construct the pedestrian mall. The $60,000 cost of the project was split between the city and property owners fronting the proposed mall. On June 1, 1959, workmen began ripping up the pavement on Burdick Street, and by August 19 the handsome two-block parklike strip stood complete. That day, as Tommy Dorsey's band played to more than 50,000 milling shoppers, Kalamazoo formally dedicated the nation's first, permanent, downtown pedestrian mall. The mall was extended another block to the south the following year. This daring first step provided the necessary impetus to reverse inner-city deterioration and revitalize the downtown area. As "urban renewal" became a common phrase across the nation, dozens of other cities with similar problems turned to the example set by the "Mall City," and Kalamazoo's citizens looked with renewed pride at the heart of their city.

The mall sparked a renaissance in the downtown area. Merchants remodeled their storefronts (unfortunately sometimes with contemporary facades incompatible with the original historic architecture), and the core of the city gained vitality. Planning continued and, in February of 1972, the city announced plans for a complement to the mall, the Kalamazoo Center. The Berkeley, California, architectural firm, Elbasani, Logan & Severin designed a "one of a kind development to keep the city's central core healthy." This joint venture between the Inland Steel Development Corporation and the

city, a unique mixture of free enterprise and government, proved to be another pioneering effort. The city provided more than $3 million, mostly through private contributions, and Inland Steel financed the remainder of the $17-million project.

The city held its breath in December 1973, as demolition experts leveled the 10-story Hanselman Building in a matter of seconds. By July 1975 the immense pile of rubble was gone and the proud new Kalamazoo Center stood open for inspection. Covering an entire city block adjacent to the mall, this 10-level, modernistic, steel and glass structure housed a 288-unit hotel, a conference and convention center able to accommodate thousands of visitors, and space for more than 40 retail shops, three restaurants, and a health club. It remains a "city within a city," where visitors can park in an adjacent structure and cross a connecting skywalk to find almost anything they need under one roof. In 1973 the mall was extended another block to the north. The city's core area quickened with renewed vigor and other revitalization projects, such as the Haymarket Historic District on East Michigan Avenue, promised further progress.

The birth of the Kalamazoo Center and an aggressive Convention and Visitor's Bureau, founded by the Chamber of Commerce, stimulated the dormant convention industry. In 1977, 195 conventions drew more than 56,000 visitors to Kalamazoo. By 1979 the industry had more than tripled its 1975 level as approximately 300 conventions that year each brought as many as 5,000 new faces to the city's downtown. All of the city, especially the downtown merchants, benefited from the millions of new dollars that poured in.

The convention industry, as well as the city's older industries and businesses, depended on an adequate transportation system for survival. Area transportation facilities experienced a dramatic evolution during the period following World War II. Streamlined diesel locomotives replaced steam engines, but train service continued to deteriorate. Just as automobiles and buses had spelled doom for interurbans and streetcars, cars and trucks seemed likely to do the same for railroads. Kalamazoo's once-magnificent passenger-train service dwindled to three unkempt trains a day by the late 1960s and freight service also suffered. During the late 1970s, however, the energy crisis and the city's determination to restore the historic Michigan Central Depot into a multifunctional transportation center affected the outcome. In 1975, when the first sleek, red, white, and blue Amtrak train purred into the city, it looked as though railroads might remain viable. In fact, as the Grand Trunk Western and Con-Rail freight systems continued to serve local industry and the energy crisis raised the cost of trucking, some plants such as Fisher Body turned to increased rail usage.

The construction of expressways, however, proved to be the dominant transportation development of the postwar era. Kalamazoo traditionally emphasized its splendid location almost exactly halfway between Detroit and Chicago. A major, two-lane highway, US 12, linked these markets, but because this route passed through the heart of the various urban areas in its path, a trip either way provided a frustrating four-hour experience, replete with bottlenecked traffic and scores of red lights.

In 1946 the State Highway Department had begun acquiring the right of way in Kalamazoo County for a projected solution to the problem. A limited-access, four-lane highway would bypass congested areas. Construction began in 1949, although most of it was completed between 1950 and 1960. Two parallel ribbons of concrete slashed their way across the green countryside, bowling over trees, leveling hills, and arching wide around curves. In September 1963 contractors completed the final segment in the county. Michigan's "Main Street," I-94, eventually linked Kalamazoo to the Midwest's major metropolises.

In 1961 construction began in Kalamazoo County on US 131, a north-south expressway intended to link the Mackinac Bridge with the Indiana Tollway. In September 1963, when the final 10-mile segment south of the city opened, Kalamazoo, bisected by these two great thoroughfares, became the "Expressway Crossroads of Southwestern Michigan." Motorists drove their huge, pre-energy-crisis automobiles at 75 miles per hour to the north, south, east, and west. The expressways, like great elongated mothers, nurtured the dozens of new motels, restaurants, service stations, and factories that nuzzled their interchanges. More than 30 common-carrier truck lines transported the city's products and raw materials. Kalamazoo stood closer to the nation's markets, and new companies looked with renewed interest on its potential.

In 1964 the General Motors Corporation, after a detailed inspection of 50 Midwestern cities, announced the location of its new Fisher Body Division Plant at Kalamazoo. Once again the city carried off a prize. In October 1966 the two-million-square-foot factory, largest of 10 such plants, stood ready at its 400-acre site at the intersection of Cork Street, I-94, and Sprinkle Road. Steel from Pittsburgh and Gary flowed to the Kalamazoo area to be fabricated into automobile body parts, then shipped to assembly plants throughout the United States. It was an operation beyond the wildest dreams of Frank Fuller, the Blood Brothers, or Albert J. Barley. Huge rolls of steel were—and still are—fed into one end of the huge plant, slit and

sheared to size, stamped into shape by more than 300 presses, and welded into subassemblies, to emerge from the other end of the factory as Chevrolet fenders, Pontiac roofs, Oldsmobile doors, Buick quarter panels, or Cadillac trunk lids. By 1967, 3,000 new jobs and an annual payroll of more than $27 million spurred the local economy. As a result labor grew scarce, the high UAW wages became the basis of comparison for other local industry, and Kalamazoo's labor force underwent transition.

Kalamazoo had never been much of a "union town." Unions flourished best amidst mistreated workers and sorry conditions, not in a prospering community. Some local unions had been around since the 1880s, but when an occasional strike flared up, public sentiment generally ran against the strikers. Besides, Kalamazoo workers had seen several examples of what strikes could do to their jobs. Shortly after the turn of the century, when a flurry of strikes hit the cigar industry, the larger cigar companies moved out of town. Union activity remained basically quiet throughout the 1920s but in 1932, when the management arbitrarily lowered wages, the city's streetcar workers struck. Some violence broke out but the strike ended before long. Two years later, however, the city's streetcars made their last runs.

During the Depression when the CIO sought to gain acceptance by the automobile industry and the streets ran red with strikers' blood in other Michigan cities, Kalamazoo remained calm. During the war years the CIO made substantial gains as United Steelworkers' charters went to Atlas Press, Dutton, Clarage Fan, Kalamazoo Tank and Silo, Gibson, Shakespeare, and others. Until the mid-1960s, however, militant union activity was the exception rather than the rule.

Union activity dominated local economic news in 1966. As the civil-rights movement and the Viet Nam War evoked demonstrations by America's youth, and placards, slogans, and marches became a familiar sight, similar militancy spread to the local work force. As the UAW became a strong force in the area, workers seemed particularly anxious to strike. With a tightened labor market due to Fisher Body's competition for 3,000 new employees, local unions realized that the advantage was theirs and the time opportune to push for delayed gains. Through-

General Motors Corporation's Fisher Body Division Plant, shown here while under construction in the fall of 1965, began production the following year. The factory, located on a 400-acre site, covered two million square feet. Courtesy, John Todd.

out the year stories of union organization among teachers and government workers filled the media. Communications workers at Michigan Bell turned down their contract. Allied Industrial Workers at Fuller, and United Steelworkers at Gibson, Atlas Press, Brundage, and Clarage Fan all went out on strike. Though strikes increasingly became a way of life in Kalamazoo, by 1980 only 25 percent of the county's total work force belonged to the 150 locals.

The Upjohn Company, the area's largest employer by the mid 1960s, had earned a reputation as a model workplace. It remained a nonunion bastion. In 1966, when the International Chemical Workers Union began preliminary organizational tactics, the company quickly counteracted them. Letters sent to Upjohn employees emphasized a long record of steady employment; management granted a four percent across-the-board raise and initiated improved grievance procedures, and the company effectively neutralized this unionization attempt. Upjohn stressed research and secured patents on new wonder drugs, and its growth continued at a phenomenal rate. By 1970 the company employed more than 13,000 workers worldwide with 4,800 in Kalamazoo. A mammoth plant and warehouse stretched over 27 acres under one roof. By 1978 annual sales were more than one billion dollars. In the first quarter of 1980, the company broke all previous sales records. That year approximately 6,400 local residents worked for Upjohn and the company predicted an increase to 10,000 by the century's end.

By the 1970s, changing circumstances altered Kalamazoo's traditional working environment. Although some firms such as the Upjohn Company, Durametallic, and KTS Industries, remained home-based, most other major employers had become part of larger nonlocal corporations. Problems of pollution abatement and energy conservation affected local industry as never before, and continuing high inflation relegated the one-income family to a luxury status. More women and minorities found their way into the county's work force and part-time employment became more common. The makeup of the labor force revealed a shift in emphasis as well. Traditionally at least half of the county's wage and salary earners worked in manufacturing industries. By 1977, out of a total county employ-

ment of 105,600, only one-third produced manufactured goods, approximately one-half worked in nonmanufacturing capacities in the private sector, and the remainder received their paychecks from burgeoning government units.

Just as the industrial revolution had spurred Kalamazoo's economy to move from agriculture to industry in the 19th century, the current technological revolution could result in a shift away from industry and research might well become the major product of the future. The Upjohn Company's overwhelming emphasis on research and the Eaton Corporation's major new research facility near Galesburg point in that direction.

Yet prognostications based on current knowledge, as Kalamazoo's history so readily illustrates, often prove wrong. Unforeseen events have periodically brought sudden change to the city's industries. The automobile developed from a toy to a necessity in less than 20 years, ruining a prosperous carriage industry while prompting the rise and fall of a dozen local automobile manufacturers. Labor unrest helped snuff out a vigorous cigar industry. Electricity destroyed a renowned windmill industry; legislated morality forced a prosperous brewery out of business; changing fashions throttled the corset factories; war blasted the mighty Kalamazoo Stove Company; and an unheralded depression closed the doors of other businesses. Changing times fostered industrial evolution, and the tears shed for the demise of some companies soon dried with the birth of others.

Through it all, the city grew, prospered,

The tornado of May 13, 1980, ripped through downtown Kalamazoo, killing five people and causing $50 million in property damage. Courtesy, Barbara Taflinger.

and remained vital. There is no reason to believe the future will be different. Industries will become outmoded, but others will take their place. The same factors that inspired past successes are sure to attract new developments. Kalamazoo County's ideal geographical location, excellent transportation system, four institutions of higher learning, vigorous Chamber of Commerce, diversified employment opportunities, and skilled work force will continue to attract new businesses and industry. And the almost legendary "good life" in Kalamazoo, the diverse cultural and recreational attractions, and the city's spirit, vitality, and pride will always make Kalamazoo a place where people want to live.

Not even the effects of nature in its most violent form—a killer tornado—could diminish the spirit of the proud city. On May 13, 1980, the sky turned sickeningly yellow as a cyclone sprang toward the unsuspecting city. Lifting up and touching down, it snapped trees and hurled barns skyward along M-43. After

ransacking the Westwood residential area, the giant whirlwind battered the heart of the city, blasting to the ground the St. Augustine Elementary School, which had been filled with hundreds of children only an hour before, mowing down century-old trees in Bronson Park, exploding the windows in the Industrial State Bank Building as glass shards and business papers rained everywhere. It tore out the rear wall of Gilmore's Department Store and splintered an entire block of businesses along Portage Street. The tornado killed five people, drove 1,200 from their homes, and caused $50 million in property damage. But the city shook off the shock of the worst disaster in its history, rolled up its sleeves, and within minutes began rebuilding its shattered visage. "Yes, there really is a Kalamazoo" had become a popular slogan. Now huge billboards and letters hand-taped to car windows answered the world's concern and emphasized the city's unconquerable spirit: "Yes, there still is a Kalamazoo."

Above
This view of tree-lined South Street looking west from Park Street dates from about 1907 Courtesy, Western Michigan University Archives.

Right
As this postcard shows, the Kalamazoo College campus consisted of two large buildings about 1911. Courtesy, Western Michigan University Archives.

Kalamazoo College, Kalamazoo, Mich.

From top
A postcard published about 1910 depicts Burdick Street, looking north from the South Street intersection. Courtesy, Western Michigan University Archives.

Various commercial establishments line Portage Street in this view looking toward Main Street about 1910. Courtesy, Western Michigan University Archives.

The courthouse figures prominently in this bird's-eye view from about 1910. Courtesy, Western Michigan University Archives.

Above
The Sisters of St. Joseph at
Nazareth Academy operated
Barbour Hall, a military school
for boys, beginning in 1902. This
photo was taken about 1912.
Courtesy, Western Michigan
University Archives.

Right
Students at South Burdick Street
School pose on the lawn circa
1910. Courtesy, Western Michigan
University Archives.

Above
A worker pauses from his labor in a Kalamazoo celery field, about 1915. Courtesy, Western Michigan University Archives.

Left
The city's Central Fire Station, pictured here circa 1910, stood at the northeast corner of Lovell and South Burdick. Courtesy, Western Michigan University Archives.

Right
F.E. McGlannon manufactured Miss Kazoo cigars at 306 West Main Street. This cigar box dates from the turn of the century. From the author's collection.

Below
In 1916 Kalamazoo's General Gas Light Company diversified into production of "radiantfire" gas heaters. Throughout the 1920s nationally circulated magazines carried full-page advertisements featuring heartwarming domestic activity centered around the glowing radiantfire heater. Courtesy, Humphrey Products, Inc.

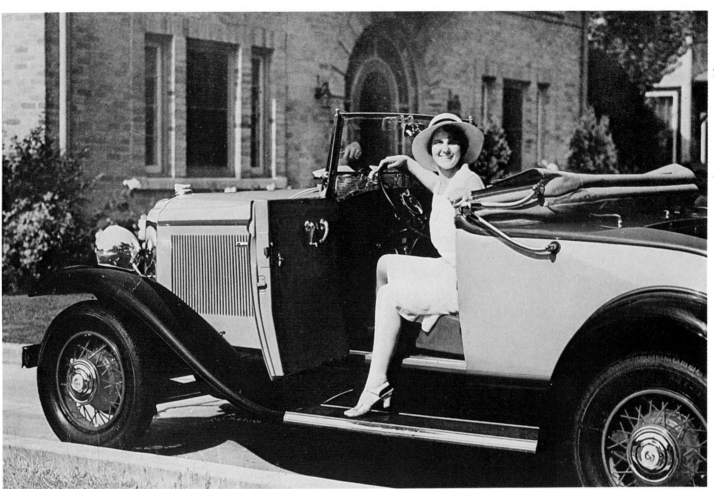

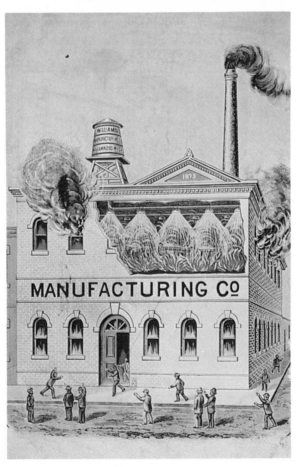

Above
Kalamazoo's Barnes Printing Company and Crescent Engraving Company developed a superior form of color printing in the early 1930s. This sample photograph demonstrating the printing was taken on Academy Street. Courtesy, Barnes Printing.

Far left
The Kalamazoo Corset Company's Madame Grace corsets were very popular in 1915. From the author's collection.

Left
The Williams Manufacturing Company first produced windmills and later made wooden tanks and silos. Their water storage tanks, common to 19th-century factory rooftops, made possible a gravity-flow sprinkler system. Courtesy, K.T.S. Industries.

Above
Elias Goldberg manufactured
Little Beauties cigars in a second
floor factory at 210 West Main
Street. This cigar box top is from
1915. From the author's
collection.

Right
La Zoos cigars were made by the
B & B Cigar Company at 306
West Ransom Street until 1924.
Pictured here is a La Zoos box
top from about 1921. From the
author's collection.

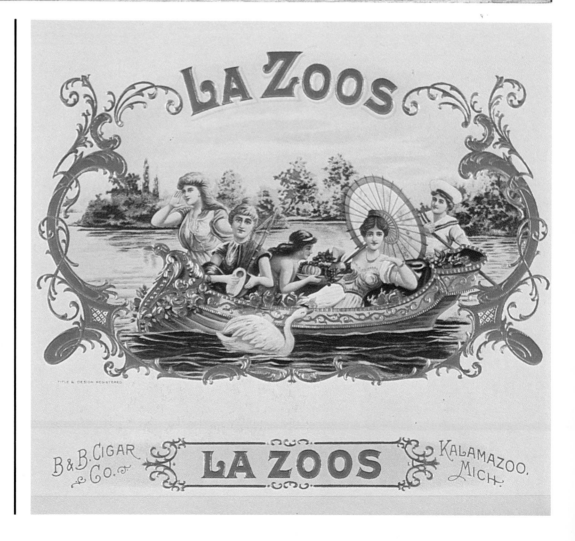

Above
The Michigan Central Depot looks almost deserted in this photographic view made about 1910. Courtesy, Western Michigan University Archives.

Left
The Kalamazoo Public Museum recreates a pioneer homestead using the logs of General William Shafter's birthplace near Galesburg. Photo by Kanti Sandhu.

Above
East Michigan Avenue
commercial buildings recall the
varied architectural styles in use
during the Gilded Age. The
second structure from the right
was designed by Louis Sullivan in
1886. Photo by Kanti Sandhu.

Right
The Ladies' Library Association
Building was the first structure in
the United States to be
specifically built as a women's
club. Photo by Kanti Sandhu.

Far left
The old Edwards and Chamberlain Building has a new lease on life as "The Haymarket." Photo by Kanti Sandhu.

Left
Built in 1895, the old Kalamazoo State Hospital water tower is a landmark for miles around. Photo by Kanti Sandhu.

Below
Until 1908 this structure on West Willard Street served as the Verdon Cigar factory. Later during World War II, the Bowers Lighter Company produced millions of cigarette lighters here. Photo by Kanti Sandhu.

Facing page
Top
The modern architecture of the Upjohn building blends in nicely with the natural landscape of the area. Photo by Kanti Sandhu.

Bottom
Children enjoy themselves at Milham Park in the summertime. Photo by Kanti Sandhu.

Above left
Kurt Newman's modern sculpture contrasts with the Art Deco lines of the County Building, constructed by the Works Progress Administration. Photo by Kanti Sandhu.

Left
Borgess Hospital combines classic architecture with modern technology. Photo by Kanti Sandhu.

Right
The falls in Comstock Park remind visitors of the importance of water power in Kalamazoo's history. Photo by Kanti Sandhu.

Below right
Pioneer meets Indian in the symbolic sculpture of the Bronson Park fountain. Photo by Kanti Sandhu.

Facing page
Parkview Hills, Kalamazoo's first "Planned Unit Development," combines open space with high-density housing. Photo by Kanti Sandhu.

Inset
The decade of the 1970s brought a new city slogan. Photo by Kanti Sandhu.

yes,
there
really is a
kalamazoo

Facing page
Clockwise from top left
In 1975 the Kalamazoo Center brought new life to the city's downtown. Photo by Kanti Sandhu.

The Fidelity Savings and Loan building mirrors activity on the Mall. Photo by Kanti Sandhu.

Pictured is the Art Deco entrance to the A.M. Todd Company's Douglas Avenue plant. Photo by Kanti Sandhu.

The new Kalamazoo County Building is located on Kalamazoo Avenue. Photo by Kanti Sandhu.

Candlewyck Apartments offers city living in a country atmosphere. Photo by Kanti Sandhu.

In 1929 the William Upjohn family donated the Civic Theater building to the community. Photo by Kanti Sandhu.

Left
Kalamazoo Iron Works, Kalamazoo, Michigan, circa 1884. Courtesy, Dover, 1971.

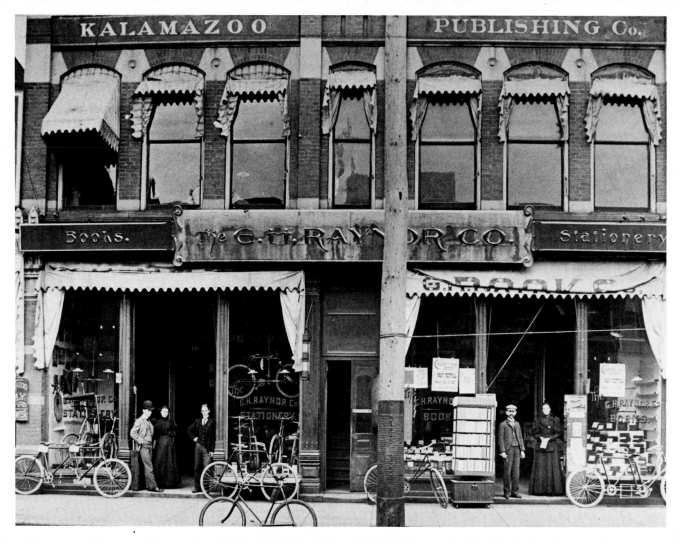

PARTNERS IN PROGRESS

By Larry Massie and Peter Schmitt

Today the community known as Kalamazoo contains many interrelated elements. Institutions of higher learning educate tomorrow's leaders and provide expertise for those of today. Rich cultural and recreational facilities bring nationwide fame. Financial institutions offer fiscal security and opportunity for success. Medical facilities guarantee comprehensive, modern health care. The local media both inform and set a high standard. Service industries fill needs ranging from housing to pension plans to legal advice. Retailers make available raw materials as well as technology's newest products. Local government provides other vital services while ensuring equal opportunity and fair play. At the center of the economic structure over 300 manufacturers employ thousands of area workers who produce an output ranging from pharmaceuticals to paper to peppermint.

But Kalamazoo is more than institutions, organizations, and firms. It is individuals. The people who inhabit Kalamazoo County provide a mix of ethnic types, political and philosophical persuasions, life-styles, ranges of income and educational levels, and all the other factors that result in America at its best. Kalamazoo, offering diversity, opportunity, goodness of life, and pride in a rich heritage, has well earned the

title, All-American City.

As Americans we learn of our nation's political, military, and social traditions in the classroom, but more elemental forces, which lie at the very heart of a great country, often escape our attention. When we pass factories, stores, and institutions, or are passed by trucks labeled with name brands and logos, when we read advertising and use products we may wonder but usually do not know the heritage behind these items so crucial to our way of life. Immigration, freedom, the frontier, and a continent filled with natural resources form the nation's heritage, and Kalamazoo's history flows from rich farmland, geographical and transportation assets, educational institutions, and diverse industries. Behind it all are people's dreams, inventiveness, pioneering, courage, dedication, and hard work. America's history is a panoramic portrait painted with daubs of color that are the stories of individual successes in places like Kalamazoo.

The picturesque history of local industrial and commercial successes, which provides a heritage and example for today's Kalamazoo, is a story worth telling. The following section, made up of many Kalamazoo industrial, business, and institutional biographies, constitute a source book of community pride.

Above
The D. Burrell & Son Carriage & Wagon Shop was located at 406 West Main Street. One of Kalamazoo's many manufacturers of wheeled vehicles, Burrell & Son manufactured carriages, wagons, and bobsleds. Courtesy, Kalamazoo Public Library.

Facing page
The bicycle craze prompted even bookstores to sell "wheels" in 1897. This building at 120 South Burdick Street was formerly Fireman's Hall. Courtesy, Kalamazoo Public Museum.

The American National Bank and Trust Company of Michigan

Kalamazoo, Michigan

Right
The American National
Bank in the 1940s.

Below
Demonstration house in
the bank lobby, 1934.

The American National Bank began during the Depression. Public confidence in banking was badly shaken in 1933. Five thousand banks had already shut down when President Franklin Roosevelt declared his Bank Holiday in March. Michigan's Governor W.A. Comstock declared his own moratorium on banking for eight days in February and 20 other states followed suit. Three of four Kalamazoo banks were struggling to meet their obligations. One, the Bank of Kalamazoo, occupied the 15-story skyscraper on East Michigan. A charter to organize a new bank was applied for and the application was approved on August 2, 1933.

Dorothy Delano, Grace Upjohn, Alfred Connable, Dwight Curtenius, J. Stanley Gilmore, William Lawrence, S.R. Light, Stephen Monroe, and Albert Todd became the directors of the new bank, The American National Bank of Kalamazoo. They chose Dunlap C. Clark of Chicago as their new president. Clark took quick action to restore local confidence. He planned to reopen in the same quarters and brought all former employees back to work. The new bank opened for business on November 1, 1933, and within a week it moved from zero to nearly one million dollars in deposits. American National acted as distributor for the Bank of Kalamazoo, and by 1941 had returned 87 percent on deposits.

President Clark and other bank officers spoke to many local organizations, making banking newsworthy. Clark felt home building might be a key to recovery and earmarked $200,000 of the bank's scarce resources for real estate development. In August the bank made the first FHA loan in Kalamazoo—$500 for two bedrooms and a bath. Clark also arranged to have a "demonstration house" built in the bank lobby. Townspeople crowded to see the latest in building techniques and home products made or distributed by local businesses.

The demonstration house proved so successful that the bank began using the lobby

to promote "Interesting Industries of Kalamazoo." More than 50 companies displayed and demonstrated their products over the next decade. Fuller Manufacturing, Atlas Press, Gibson Company, Clarage Fan, and other firms showed everything from baby carriages to frozen foods, fishing tackle, and electric signs. The displays generated their own traffic, underlining cooperation with the business community, and built goodwill.

Depositors' confidence returned. The bank reported over $3 million on deposit in 1934, and more than $6 million by 1938. During those first years, the bank installed a "Recordak" machine for filming checks, a proof machine, and in October 1937, a time lock for the vault. The Kalamazoo *Gazette* noted that the new system was gangster-proof, pointing out that "a holdup mob cannot afford to wait, since an alarm has been sent silently and automatically in case of a robbery." The bank paid its first dividend—2.5 percent—to stockholders in January 1941. Deposits stood at more than $10 million when America entered World War II in 1941.

President Clark supported the British War Relief Society in 1940. The bank assisted in the defense stamp and war bond program instituted in June that year. In August, American National was the first local bank to buy U.S. Treasury Bonds. "We consider it a patriotic duty," said Clark, setting up a special war bond center in the lobby. Clark left for active duty in May 1942, for two years with the Army Supply Headquarters in Washington, D.C. Dr. S. Rudolph Light acted as president while Clark was gone.

During the war, Kalamazoo residents worked long hours on a variety of defense projects. National income more than doubled while the consumer price index climbed only 30 percent. As a result, people put their money in savings accounts. American National's deposits tripled to $30,318,470 in 1945.

The postwar years brought many changes. Clark resigned in 1947 and Garret Van Haaften replaced him as president. Van Haaften had started in banking as a messenger for the old Kalamazoo National Bank, predecessor of the Bank of Kalamazoo. He rose through the ranks of American National, serving as cashier and first vice-president. Van Haaften continued American's involvement in community affairs, holding many positions in service organizations, including the Chamber of Commerce and the American Red Cross.

The American National Bank Building, built in 1929, continued to anchor the bank's activities—at 190 feet, the tallest building in Kalamazoo. The lobby with its metalwork of intricate art deco, imported stone, and woodwork, represented the good taste of an earlier era. Otto Stauffenberg, a native of Hamburg, Germany, worked 600 hours from a scaffold on the vaulted ceiling mural which he executed in

the Egyptian style so popular in the '20s.

People in the 1950s were on the move, and American followed them to the suburbs with branch banks. The first branch in Milwood opened in 1951 with conventional services and an important addition—a drive-up window. A Trust Department was established in 1952. The first trust account handled was the Kalamazoo YWCA. This time also marked a period of rapid growth for American National. Several new branches were opened in addition to the merger of the Plainwell Bank, The Home Savings Bank of Kalamazoo, The Home State Bank of Lawrence, The First State Bank of Mendon, and The Peoples Community Bank of Three Rivers.

Every now and then a very special person

works with an organization. Such a person was Hugh "Scotty" Smith, who retired in 1961 after 35 years with the bank. Scotty served as a special policeman and chief greeter of the bank. He once claimed that he knew more than 30,000 people in the city by name.

January 1964 ended yet another era for the bank. Van Haaften was named chairman of the board and Harold Jacobson was elected president. "Jake" started in the bank in 1935 as a file clerk, "to help out for a few days," while attending Western State Teacher's College. Under his leadership, the bank continued to grow. An early and outspoken advocate of the holding company concept, Jake testified in Lansing in support of the Holding Company Bill. In 1972 the American National Holding Company was formed. It now includes eight affiliate banks: The American National Bank and Trust Company of Michigan; The American Bank of Three Rivers, N.A.; The American Bank of Niles, N.A.; The American National Bank in Portage; The American National Bank in Battle Creek; The American National Bank-West, South Haven; The American National Bank in Western Michigan, Allegan; and Ludington Bank and Trust Company.

The following people have served as president of the bank since it was organized in 1933: Dunlap C. Clark, S. Rudolph Light, Garret Van Haaften, Harold Jacobson, Richard A. Kjoss, Harold H. Holland, Donald C. Smith, and its present president, Theodore F. McCarty. Harold Holland now serves as chairman of the board of directors of the bank and also chairman and president of American National Holding Company.

The American National Bank continues the dedication to the community started by Dunlap Clark almost 50 years ago.

Left
Harold Allen and S. Rudolph Light at the bank's war bond desk.

Below
The American National Bank Building under construction, 1928.

Right
The Arts Council of Greater Kalamazoo's sesquicentennial celebration, "The Gathering, A Time to Sing and Play."

Center Right
Kalamazoo Junior Symphony.

Below
Roger Askin, a member of the Kalamazoo Ballet Company.

Bottom Right
Poetry on Buses poems are displayed on the city's fleet of 54 GMC, R.T.S. buses.

The Arts Council of Greater Kalamazoo was formed in 1966 as a nonprofit community service agency to promote "cooperation and communication in the arts community" and to increase community awareness of the arts in general. Presently the Arts Council acts as the coordinating agency for 30 member organizations, which offer more than 1,000 art activities every year. The Council sponsors workshops, fund-raising events, the Poetry on Buses program, and Kalamazoo's annual summer arts festival. In addition, the Council helps members by serving as an advocate with local, state, and national government units as well as business and the community, coordinating events calendars, developing arts outreach programs, and providing management and technical assistance. The Council also promotes the arts in the local media and serves as a sounding board for new ideas. As many as 70,000 people will be served by current programs and projects.

Kalamazoo Junior Symphony

Recommended as a model for youth orchestras by the American Symphony Orchestra League, the Kalamazoo Junior Symphony is one of the oldest and finest such orchestras in the country. Organized in 1939 and financed entirely by memberships and ticket sales, the Youth Symphony attracts members from many communities in southwestern Michigan. The players, whose average age is 16, give three concerts a year in Kalamazoo. In recent years they have twice toured Europe and played to Canadian audiences as well. The board of directors sponsors a chamber music program and recently established a preparatory string orchestra for younger players. A most exciting innovation, the "Julius Stulberg Auditions," honors the man who conducted the orchestra from 1941 to 1974. Contestants from all over the country compete for cash awards and the opportunity to solo with the orchestra during the annual spring concert.

Kalamazoo Ballet Company

A former member of the Royal Winnipeg Ballet Company, Therese Bullard knew she could help provide professional experiences to young dancers in Kalamazoo while giving the public performances of artistic integrity. In 1969 she founded the Kalamazoo Ballet Company, a nonprofit organization that in 1971 became a member of the National Association of Regional Ballet. The Company has grown to 30 members who range in age from 10 to 30. Ms. Bullard continues as artistic director and has developed a varied repertoire that includes medieval and ethnic works, and modern and classical ballets. Along with its regularly scheduled Masqued Ball, Children's Concert, and Spring Concerts in Kalamazoo, the Company serves a growing Michigan audience with yearly community concerts and school lecture demonstrations.

Poetry on Buses

Martha Moffett saw a chance to give recognition and a wide audience to local poets in 1975. With city approval and arts council support, she organized the popular Poetry on Buses program in time for the bicentennial. Sixty-seven children and adults entered 142 poems in the first contest. The judges chose 22 for display on local buses. Since that time, Kalamazoo's bus riders have been treated to more than 200 poems chosen in competitions held twice each year. The Arts Council of Greater Kalamazoo sponsors each contest. The city commission prints display placards of the winning poems, one of which is presented to each successful entrant. Schoolchildren and adults have responded enthusiastically to the idea, and each competition now draws as many as 300 entries.

Barnes Printing Company

Charles H. Barnes won his first printing press selling subscriptions to *Youth's Companion* in 1886. The young high school student set up shop in his parents' attic on the corner of Oak and Axtell streets. He printed visiting cards for his friends on the tiny press and longed for more equipment. By 1889 he had enough to open C.H. Barnes and Company in a second-floor room at 121 South Burdick. The old Kalamazoo Publishing Company had its imposing offices just across the street. In those days, most printers depended on newspaper subscriptions and legal notices to supplement job printing orders. Nevertheless, most companies changed hands again and again as newcomers tried to make a name for themselves in the very competitive business.

Charles Barnes stuck to job printing and prospered. As time went on he moved into larger quarters—no easy job with heavy, cast-iron presses and lead type. The city directory for 1899 listed the company in its biggest and boldest type as "job printers and stationers," with offices in the Baumann Block at 317 South Burdick. An account book that year showed the printers working 10 hours a day, six days a week, at 15 cents an hour. They worked hard and steadily, for Barnes was a good employer and paid well. He helped to organize the Printers' Trade Association and served as its president.

Barnes specialized in business stationery, promotional flyers, and general job printing, advertising "Printing That *IS* Printing" in 1911. Ten years later, his son Harold joined him, and the firm moved to the northwest corner of Burdick and Water streets. Harold became a full partner in Barnes Printing Company in 1925 and president when his father retired in 1930. He helped the firm weather the Depression, World War II material shortages, and postwar inflation. Barnes Printing Company incorporated in 1950 with Harold as president and his son, Charles W. Barnes, as secretary-treasurer. In 1954 the firm built its present plant on Alcott Street. Air conditioning and humidity control now helped prevent expansion and contraction of paper during fine color-printing operations. It also lessened static electricity that interfered with automatic-feeding presses and folding machines.

When Charles W. Barnes took over as president in 1966, the company was nearly 80 years old. The printing industry had changed enormously in that period as offset and multilith machines replaced the earlier equipment his grandfather had known. Electricity and automated machinery now did the work of many a "printer's devil." Special sewing and trimming machines replaced much handwork as well. New color reproduction methods brought photographic clarity to advertising art. But some things didn't change in the first 80 years, or in the next 15 years for that matter. Barnes keeps his grandfather's first handpress on display in the front office as a reminder that the tradition of quality workmanship can still be passed from one generation to the next.

Left
Charles H. Barnes, founder.

Below Left
Harold E. Barnes.

Bottom
Charles W. Barnes.

Borgess Medical Center and the Sisters of St. Joseph

A young stranger stumbling through the streets, arrested as a drunk, and thrown into the city jail, provides a strange beginning for Kalamazoo's first hospital. After a few hours, the turnkey, realizing the youth was more than drunk, summoned a doctor who pronounced him deathly ill. In 1887 there was no hospital to move him to. A search for identification revealed only a rosary, and the police summoned a priest.

back to 1650, when it was established as a nonsequestered order in LePuy, France. The congregation was charged to follow the "three simple vows of poverty, chastity, and obedience" and to engage in "Christian education of the young and the direction of charitable works, such as hospitals, orphanages, and homes for the poor and the aged." Soon their black habits became a familiar sight throughout France wherever

Father Francis A. O'Brien, St. Augustine parish priest since 1883, responded to the call. In that jail cell crowded with drunks the young priest administered the last rites to the dying stranger. Later, Father O'Brien discovered that the youth came from a respectable family, who were shocked to learn that their promising son had died in jail. Father O'Brien was deeply moved and resolved to establish a hospital in Kalamazoo.

At first, he encountered little success in raising funds; after all, the city fathers reasoned, Kalamazoo had managed up to then without a hospital. Visited by Bishop Casper Borgess of Detroit, Father O'Brien related to his old friend his recent experience and desire to start a hospital. The following Christmas, Father O'Brien received a check for $5,000 and a note from the bishop explaining that the money was the last of his mother's legacy and that it was to be used for whatever the Father thought best. In 1889 Father O'Brien purchased an Italian Revival mansion situated on a block of land stretching from Portage to Lovell streets. He enlarged the home with an addition and Kalamazoo's first hospital opened on December 8, 1889, with 20 beds and a nursing staff of seven.

Eleven Sisters of St. Joseph arrived on July 5 of that year from Watertown, New York, in response to Father O'Brien's appeal for a religious order to operate the institution. The Watertown community had been established in 1880, but the origins of the congregation of the Sisters of St. Joseph go

they could assist the needy and afflicted. During the French Revolution, with the attempted annihilation of religion, several Sisters were martyred on Robespierre's guillotine.

The Sisters of St. Joseph first came to America via New Orleans to settle in St. Louis in 1836. Throughout the following decades other communities sprang up across the country. During the Civil War the Sisters of St. Joseph of Philadelphia, Pennsylvania, and Wheeling, West Virginia, won special commendation when they established military hospitals and administered to Blue and Gray alike.

Of the Sisters who answered Father O'Brien's appeal in 1889, four returned to Watertown. The original seven remaining, Mother M. Scholastica, Sisters M. Angela, M. Gertrude, M. Catherine, M. Frances, M. Philomena, and M. Elizabeth, took up residence in St. Augustine Parish until the hospital was ready. By August 15 they had taken charge of putting the hospital in readiness and appointed a medical staff of eight physicians. The hospital officially opened on December 8, 1889, and during that month admitted four patients.

From the beginning the Sisters and their new hospital faced opposition. Many considered it a "white elephant" and a public annoyance. Protestants did not like the Catholic management, Catholics feared an additional burden of expense, and even the local medical profession considered it a divisive force in their ranks. But the sick came to its doors in increasing numbers.

The 59 patients admitted in 1890 grew to 87 in 1894. By 1899 Borgess cared for 233 patients, 164 paid their own bills, city and county relief funded 29, and the hospital itself provided for 40 other "charity cases." That same year the Sisters took in $7,331.39 from hospital payments, donations, profits from a book store, and service fees for home nursing, while hospital expenses amounted to $3,711.83. They applied all but $3.56 of the surplus toward hospital indebtedness, which stood at $8,000 at the year's end.

Rates charged by Borgess Hospital at the turn of the century seem ridiculously low by modern standards. Private rooms, including board, nursing, and attendance, cost from $7 to $25 per week. Anesthetics and use of the operating room ran an extra $5. The Sisters offered private rooms with "the comforts and luxuries of home" and contemporary photographs reveal everything a Victorian would have desired, including a brass bed with tasseled bedspread, overstuffed chairs and wicker rockers, fireplace with a marble mantel covered with knickknacks, potted ferns, silk dressing screen, chandeliers, framed art prints, lacy curtains, and oriental rugs.

Despite this apparent splendor, the Sisters ran a tight ship. The Superioress might immediately discharge patients for breaking any of a list of 20 stringent regulations, such as "Patients are not allowed to talk to each other about their diseases. Patients must not throw anything whatever on the ground below their windows. Patients must not lie on the bed with their clothes on. No patient shall be allowed to have any book, pamphlet, newspaper print, or picture of an immoral or indecent character." Patients caught reading the latest issue of *The Police Gazette* or tossing bonbon wrappers out the windows were soon sent packing up Portage Street.

Apart from their work at Borgess Hospital the Sisters of St. Joseph displayed an amazing vigor during the early years. With Father O'Brien's assistance they opened Lefevre Institute, an elementary school adjacent to St. Augustine Church, in 1891. Largely through the influence of Sister M. Raphael, Father O'Brien's sister and a graduate of the University of Michigan Medical School and Johns Hopkins University, St. Camillus School of Nursing came into being in 1895. In 1897 the Sisters purchased a 200-acre farm on Gull Road and that fall opened Nazareth Academy, a secondary school for girls, and by 1902 they had added Barbour Hall, a military school for boys. The year 1899 saw the establishment of St. Anthony's School for the Feeble-Minded. In 1915 they converted another old mansion, the former Christian Weber residence at 325 Portage Avenue, into St. Agnes Foundling Asylum, an orphanage. In 1922 Nazareth Academy became Nazareth College, a 2-year junior college, and in 1924 a 4-year course was established and the first degree awarded in 1928. The Sisters even found energy to take on responsibilities away from Kalamazoo. In 1926 St. Joseph Hospital in Flint was transferred under their administration and in 1929 they established Mercy Hospital in Monroe.

On Easter Sunday, 1900, the Sisters revealed their dream for the future of Borgess Hospital. "We hope the day will come when we can secure a proper building, wherein ample room may be afforded to care for all who require our aid." Before the year had ended a new addition in the shape of a 4-story brick building covered the front grounds. Other additions followed in 1903 and 1907, until the original hospital building, reserved for an "Old People's Home," was scarcely visible.

Then a March 4, 1916, Kalamazoo *Gazette* article, headed "Award Contract For Big Hospital, H.L. VanderHorst to build $100,000 Catholic Institution," announced plans that would determine the future of Borgess Hospital. The intended site of the new structure was on Riverview Drive but a freezing March ride to the site by a group of doctors and Sisters caused them to reconsider. On March 19 another *Gazette* heading announced "New Hospital Site Purchased, 40 Acres of Land on Gull Road Taken Over by the Sisters of St. Joseph." On September 29, 1917, the first patient drove up the circular drive, beautifully landscaped with choice shrubs and bright flowers, to enter the majestic new Tudor Gothic Revival structure. The original hospital on Portage Avenue, referred to as Old Borgess, remained in use as an emergency hospital until 1928.

(continued)

Below
Monsignor Francis O'Brien.

Bottom
Rooms such as this one in Old Borgess made patients feel at home.

As World War I ended, an influenza pandemic spread from the Western Front, killing millions across the world and 500,000 in the United States alone. In Michigan hundreds died in military training camps and civilian homes. The Sisters responded with overwhelming courage, and 13 died administering to thousands of sufferers, fearless of contracting the extremely contagious disease. Hundreds of local influenza victims were treated at Borgess and the hospital suffered a loss of income from regular patients who feared contracting the disease months after the epidemic was over.

The whole city mourned on December 19, 1921, when Monsignor Francis A. O'Brien died. He had served the city's poor and ill for over 38 years. In 1922 a free bed was created in his honor at Borgess, a fitting memorial to his ideals. That same year, the hospital demonstrated pioneer concern for air pollution when a "smoke consumer" was installed in the huge smokestack.

When the 1930s brought the Great Depression, Borgess devoted more of its resources to charitable treatment of the economically dislocated. In March 1930, *Gazette* headlines announced that the Sisters were treating a baby found abandoned during a raging blizzard. The hospital allotted a small basement room to Dr. Homer Stryker during the late 1930s, where, tinkering in his spare time, he produced inventions that would revolutionize care of the injured, such as the Stryker frame and oscillatory, a cast-cutting saw. The hospital's modern Stryker Center honors his name.

World War II brought suffering to millions, but as in other conflicts it spurred tremendous medical advances. During and following the war high inflation became a way of life. However, surviving bills document that as late as 1945 patients were charged only $5.50 a day for a stay at

Borgess Hospital.

While the New Borgess Hospital seemed magnificent in 1917, the period following World War II brought so many additions, alterations, and innovations that the original structure is now scarcely visible. During the mid-1960s, Borgess evolved from a small community hospital to a regional medical center, offering a variety of specialized programs to the entire southwest Michigan community.

The 1968 construction of a cardiovascular laboratory for disease testing and diagnosis was the first step in the hospital's comprehensive cardiac programs. The ability to provide prompt and accurate diagnosis led to cardiac surgery programs

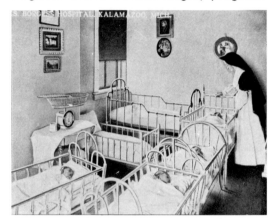

attracting top-level surgeons from around the world. As cardiology services expanded, the hospital added two more cardiovascular laboratories in 1976 and 1981. These increased services, important to the diagnosis of disease, were accompanied by an innovative cardiac rehabilitation program in 1971. That program was enhanced in 1976 by an inpatient Cardiac Rehabilitation Center where heart patients participated in monitored exercise to decrease their length of hospital stay and to increase their ability to return to normal activities. That program's success was crowned by the construction of a million-dollar Cardiac Rehabilitation Institute in 1980. The Institute is a freestanding exercise center for both post-hospital and heart-risk patients. It is the only one of its kind in the world today operating under the guidance of a community hospital.

A comprehensive neurology/neurosurgery program treating the spectrum of brain and nervous-system disorders began at Borgess in 1972. Today it features a 40-bed inpatient unit and 5-bed neuro-intensive care unit for specialized care following neurosurgery or illness. A computerized tomographical brain scanner is only one of the many special testing services available for the over 5,000 neuro-surgical tests provided at Borgess each year.

Area cancer patients who formerly sought needed treatment elsewhere now receive all the available cancer care modalities through the Borgess Midwest Oncology Center, which opened in 1968 with the construction of a cobalt therapy unit. Specialized cancer research enables Borgess physicians to determine appropriate treatment at the hospital's Oncology Research Laboratory, a service provided since 1971. The establishment of a holistic/biofeedback program in cooperation with Western Michigan University in 1977 led to the Institute for Holistic Medicine in 1978. Patients and professionals have a wide choice of resources for the most contemporary cancer treatments in southwest Michigan.

The year 1971 was the date for a comprehensive nephrology program at the Borgess Michigan Nephrology Center. Featuring facilities for the detection and prevention of kidney disease, the center also provides medical and surgical treatment as well as scientific research. The center offered the first kidney-transplant facilities in out-state Michigan, and is one of only a few Michigan hospitals with a perfusion team capable of preserving and transporting donor kidneys across the state for transplantation at Borgess or other hospitals. The period from 1975 to 1977 saw the installation of satellite hemodialysis units in Benton Harbor, Coldwater, and Battle Creek. The Borgess outpatient dialysis unit was expanded in 1978 to provide round-the-clock availability to its patients in the Borgess Professional Building North.

Borgess established the Midwest Alcoholism Center in 1968 as the first inpatient medical detoxification and outpatient alcoholism therapy site in southwest Michigan. The Midwest Alcoholism Center was noted in 1969 as the first hospital program in the state to train alcoholism therapists. Reaching into the community and specifically into the work place is the goal of the Occupational Health Program cosponsored by Borgess and the Greater Kalamazoo United Way since 1978. The program provides management and labor with a system to identify and assist employees whose personal problems interfere with job performance. The program's goal is to keep the qualified worker on the job and in touch with health resources.

The Borgess Mental Health Center touches all ways of life in Kalamazoo. Its 1971 opening of the William Upjohn DeLano Memorial Clinic expanded the existing inpatient mental health services of the Dorothy Dalton Pavilion. A pediatric mental health unit opened in 1980 at the request of Kalamazoo's legal and social ser-

vices as a helping site for those under the age of 17. And adults involved in continuing mental health treatment receive outpatient assistance through the group-living and therapy programs of St. Joseph Lodge.

Over 9,000 adults and 17,000 children visit outpatient and pediatric clinics in the hospital's Stryker Center, home of ambulatory care services. The Pediatric Preventive Medicine Program operates within Stryker, where it promotes child auto safety, poison prevention, dental hygiene, prenatal and postnatal care, infant development, and burn prevention programs which are demonstrated throughout Kalamazoo's elementary and secondary schools.

A $6-million Emergency, Trauma, and Surgi-Center opened on July 4, 1976, to provide comprehensive emergency and outpatient surgery services. It is the only emergency facility in the region equipped for cardiac operations and 24-hour emergency neurosurgical procedures. The medically equipped Critical Care Transport Unit is always ready to transport the critically ill or injured with complete medical care en route throughout southwest Michigan.

As Borgess Medical Center president Martin A. Verzi points out, today's hospitals are as concerned with the health of their communities as they are with caring for the ill. The annual Borgess "Run for the Health of It," which attracts 2,000 runners from throughout the Midwest, is one activity used by the hospital to emphasize Borgess Medical Center's role in disease prevention as well as treatment.

The dream conceived by Father Francis O'Brien nearly a century ago and nurtured over the years by the efforts of the Sisters of St. Joseph and thousands of dedicated health professionals is today's dynamic force in Kalamazoo health care. And as long as there are dreams, Borgess Medical Center will seek to fulfill them for the needs of its community, the people of southwest Michigan.

Bronson Methodist Hospital

Right
Bronson Methodist
Hospital, 1909.

Below
Bronson Methodist
Hospital's patient ward,
circa 1920.

Bronson Methodist Hospital is presently one of the largest employers in Kalamazoo County. Its ultramodern facilities provide inpatient and outpatient care for more than 100,000 people a year. The present hospital, with 478 beds and 48 bassinets, dominates the downtown Kalamazoo skyline. The hospital was little more than a dream in 1900 and the miracles of modern medicine were far in the future. On December 4, 1900, a handful of local doctors formed the Kalamazoo Hospital Association. With a gift of land from local business people and $500 each, the doctors began their hospital in a private home with 12 beds. Patients soon crowded the rooms; linens and other supplies were scarce. The hospital charged patients $1.50 a day, but not all could pay and funds were hard to come by.

The hospital was reorganized in 1903 and named after Titus Bronson, the town's first settler. Dr. W.E. Upjohn chaired the building committee that arranged for a new facility with 46 beds in 1905. In 1920 Bronson was affiliated with the Methodist Episcopal Church and changed to its current name.

Bronson Methodist Hospital's surgical and convalescent facilities were excellent, according to medical standards in the 1920s. The trustees approved an addition in 1928 which brought the total number of beds to 111. Despite the Depression, the hospital obtained a $100,000 grant from the Kresge Foundation on condition that $200,000 be raised locally. The community responded, and in 1938 a second addition was completed and equipped at a cost of $350,000. A growing town and revolutionary changes in medical care led the trustees to consider a master plan for hospital expansion in the 1940s. The Kalamazoo Foundation offered $200,000 if the community would rally again. Over 6,000 pledges rolled in and the hospital raised a total of $1,079,000. Bronson Medical Center opened in 1950 with both hospital facilities

and suites of doctors' offices. Improved medical practices cut the average patient's stay in half by 1950. As a result, Bronson Hospital had the capacity to care for some 20,000 inpatients a year.

Advances in treatment, equipment, and hospital services brought continued physical expansion. The hospital introduced its School of Nursing in 1905 and graduated its first three nurses two years later. In 1957 Truesdale Hall was built, providing residence accommodations for 200 students. The next decade saw the establishment of a Poison Control Center for the community, the first Hemodialysis Unit in western Michigan, and a 4-story addition to the main hospital.

Bronson Methodist Hospital added a wide variety of new and updated services during the 1970s. A new surgery department, a Trauma and Emergency Center, a Burn Center, and a Pediatric Intensive Care Unit were available by 1975. The hospital today provides general acute care in the major services of internal medicine, general surgery, obstetrics-gynecology, pediatrics, and family practice.

Developments in medicine and in the psychological aspects of illness have altered many facets of hospital care. Nowhere is this more evident than in Bronson Methodist Hospital's services for children. Newborn infants ordinarily move at once to the family-centered maternity care floor. While doctors formerly advocated strict isolation in special nurseries, Bronson now provides complete rooming-in facilities to allow infants to spend crucial first hours with their parents. Mothers may also take classes in child care before and during their hospital stay. Premature or distressed infants receive special care. Bronson's regional Neonatal Intensive Care Unit serves Kalamazoo and 28 southwest Michigan hospitals. It provides 45 beds, lifesaving equipment, and round-the-clock medical coverage. A special "baby bus" transports infants to the NICU from outly-

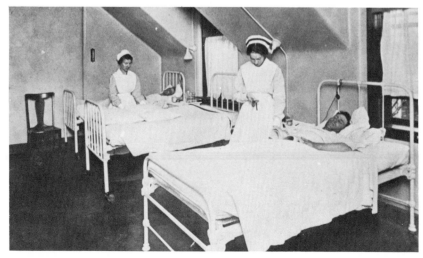

ing communities. This special-care unit provides family involvement as well, ranging from rocking chairs to support groups, a toll-free WATS line, and the services of a medical social worker.

Youngsters who come to the hospital find a homey Toddler Unit with child-sized equipment, playroom, television, and, most important, 24-hour visiting privileges for parents who may stay overnight to make the child feel at home. The Toddler Unit serves children under 10 who need surgery, diagnostic tests, or care for medical, neurological, or orthopedic problems. Older children find peer support in the Youth Center, where cheerful rooms, a piano, pool table, patio, and picnic area all help to make the patients' stay as non-threatening as possible. Play therapists, music therapists, and psychiatric counseling are available for patients with special needs.

Bronson added a special Pediatric Intensive Care Unit for critically ill children in 1974. Again family-centered care is stressed. Children need their parents most of all in times of crisis. Parents may at all times stay with the child and are encouraged to take part in routine patient care. Lifesaving monitoring equipment and specially trained staff members maintain

constant observation. This unit maintains a special ambulance to bring in children from outlying hospitals, a panel of consulting physicians, and a toll-free WATS line for out-of-town parents.

Bronson's regional Burn Center, added in 1973, offers intensive care and long-term follow-up for both children and adults. It provides a highly trained nursing staff, physical and occupational therapists, and a clinic for long-term reconstruction and therapy. The Burn Center is especially concerned with developmental and emotional problems in burned children.

Bronson offers a variety of workshops and teaching programs emphasizing the

medical problems of children. It also conducts an annual children's health fair and tours to introduce preventive medicine and help children overcome a fear of "the hospital."

Bronson has grown from a small 12-bed ward to a major regional medical center and teaching hospital with more than 2,800 employees. It operates not only a nursing school, but a training program for medical students and house officers as well. In addition, the hospital actively participates in paramedical education. Working in conjunction with several colleges, the staff conducts educational programs in hospital administration, radiologic technology, medical technology, pharmacy, physical therapy, social work, chaplaincy, and respiratory care.

Daniel Finch has been Bronson's president and chief executive officer since 1961. He replaced Dr. William Perdew, who served in that capacity from 1943 to 1960. The hospital is governed by 31 voting trustees, most of whom live in Kalamazoo. The president and executive vice-president, the chief of the medical staff, and his immediate predecessor are members by virtue of their positions. Bronson is a member of the American Hospital Association, the Michigan Hospital Association, and several

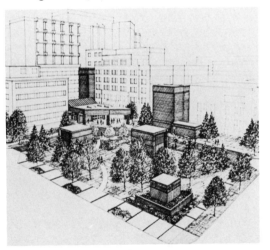

other professional organizations. It has been named the Great Lakes Regional Poison Control Center, the West Michigan Hemophilia Center, and the Regional Trauma Center for southwest Michigan. It houses the only Hyperbaric Unit in western Michigan.

Medical practice has changed more in the 81 years since Bronson Methodist Hospital's founding than in any other period of human history. The hospital has kept pace with the state of the art in medicine, expanding its facilities to meet community needs and continuing the tradition of high-quality personal care that goes back to 1900.

Left
Hospital nursery, 1942.

Right
Architect's rendering of the modern Bronson Methodist Hospital complex.

Kalamazoo • Partners in Progress • Page 237

Bennett, Lewis, LaParl, Hollander, Stephens & Milligan, P.C.

This firm has, for many years, been a top-rated law firm having a multipurpose practice with special emphasis on litigation, corporations, business, estate planning, probate, and real estate law, and represents many locally and nationally known corporations and insurance companies. The company is the successor of the firm of Farrell, Folz, Paulson, Bennett and Palmer, which was organized in the early 1950s.

Charles H. Farrell had practiced for many years in Kalamazoo, arriving in the city fresh from the University of Michigan Law School in 1904. Almost at once, the people of Kalamazoo sent Farrell to the state legislature, and in 1910 they elected him mayor on a reform platform.

Farrell tried hard to make Kalamazoo "a cleaner, better, and more prosperous place to live." During his two terms, he introduced "open" meetings and insisted that any citizen might be heard through oral petitions, which are still a part of each commission meeting. He proposed that Kalamazoo adopt the city manager form of government and unsuccessfully urged relocation of downtown rail crossings. Farrell also presided over the accession of Milham Park and Crane Park on Westnedge Hill; he created the city's first Parks Commission as well. Farrell was proudest of the housing and building inspection ordinances passed in 1910. Like other progressive reformers around the country, he wrestled with city accounting methods, franchise practices, and municipal sewer and lighting problems.

Other firm members continued to be involved in city and county government. Richard H. Paulson had been associated with Lucien F. Sweet, who later became circuit judge. He served as the Kalamazoo city attorney from 1945 to 1954 and was a mem-

ber of the County Board of Supervisors during the same period.

Thompson Bennett, prior to joining the organization, practiced with the firm of Howard and Howard, known for a short time as Howard, Howard and Bennett. He has served on the Kalamazoo City Commission, Kalamazoo County Board of Supervisors, and as associate municipal judge.

Dean S. Lewis joined the firm in 1959, and concentrates in corporations, business, estate planning, and probate matters.

John R. LaParl joined the firm in 1968. He has become established as a distinguished trial attorney, and in 1980 was elected a fellow of the International Society of Barristers.

Winfield J. Hollander was senior vice-president in the Trust Department of the First National Bank and Trust Company of Michigan, in Kalamazoo. He joined the firm upon retiring from the bank and currently limits his practice to estate planning and probate matters, in which he is recognized as an authority.

Ronald B. Stephens concentrates in real estate and business matters and has built a fine reputation in this field.

Richard A. Milligan, a former Kalamazoo chief assistant city attorney, has been active in litigation matters, as well as concentrating in municipal law and municipal bonds.

Past and present members of the firm have been extremely active in the local, state, and national bar associations. Charles H. Farrell, Richard H. Paulson, and Dean S. Lewis have all been state bar commissioners. Richard Paulson was the first attorney from Kalamazoo elected president of the State Bar of Michigan in 1953. In 1980 Dean S. Lewis became the second Kalamazoo attorney elected president of that association.

Clarage Fan, Division of Zurn Industries

Wind influenced the development of Clarage Fan from the very beginning. In 1878 Thomas Clarage left his job as foreman at Lawrence and Chapin's Iron Works to team up with another young foundryman, Charles A. Bird. Their Bird and Clarage Foundry manufactured steam engines and mill machinery but specialized in the "Bird Windmill." In 1885, after Bird withdrew and took his windmill with him, Clarage and his three strapping sons founded Thomas Clarage and Sons. By 1897 a business letterhead advertised shafting, hangers, pulleys, mill machinery, architectural iron work, and steam engines. The Clarage brothers noticed that many customers found these steam engines ideal for driving industrial fans, and in 1912 they diversified into the production of fans and blowers as a sideline. These fans soon became a major product and in 1915 the renamed Clarage Fan Company was back in the wind business.

This fan and blower business had grown from a gentle breeze into a strong wind by 1925, when the company boasted that "practically every school in Kalamazoo is properly ventilated by Clarage equipment." That same year the firm developed a new, more efficient fan soon installed in such famous hotels as the Palmer House in Chicago.

By the 1930s as the novelty, air conditioning, became increasingly popular in theaters, restaurants, and business offices, Clarage Fan further diversified from air handling to air conditioning. A feature of the 1934 "Made in Kalamazoo Exposition," held to demonstrate that the city's industries had successfully weathered the Depression, was a display of the new Clarage Duotherm air-conditioning unit that "heats and humidifies in winter; cools and dehumidifies in summer." Contemporary advertisements urged the city to "come in and get cooled off." By 1938 other Clarage advertisements proudly reported equipping the "world's largest hotel," the Stevens in Chicago, with 47 Clarage fans and eight Clarage "air washers."

Business increased from a strong wind to a gale during World War II, as the many large factories built without windows for blackout precautions required more air conditioning. As a result Clarage Fan won the prestigious Army/Navy "E" Award for production excellence in 1944. Continued growth during the decade following the war culminated in the acquisition of the huge plants formerly belonging to the Kalamazoo Stove Company in the late 1950s.

In 1967 Zurn Industries, "a total environment company specializing in air, land, water, and noise pollution control," acquired Clarage Fan. Continuing as part of Zurn's Air Systems Division, Clarage faced new challenges in the 1970s. The needs of that decade—industrial air-pollution control, fans for ventilation and air circulation, as well as protection backup systems for nuclear reactors—led to a repositioning in the market from light- to heavy-duty products. With energy conservation increasingly critical, greater efficiency rather than price became of utmost concern.

Then on May 13, 1980, Clarage Fan, after more than a century of experience with moving air, was itself moved by air when nature at her most violent, a tornado, struck. After smashing the downtown heart of Kalamazoo, the savage twister battered the huge factory, sending the roof skyward, imploding walls, and causing over $2 million in damage. Unbelievably, no one was injured. As company officials surveyed the damage, they naturally weighed the advantages of moving elsewhere rather than rebuilding, but the decision came quickly. Kalamazoo, close to sources of supply and markets, with its readily available pool of skilled labor, had been a good location for Clarage and there was a long tradition of mutual prosperity. Soon the old factory site bustled with new construction and more modern production machinery. Clarage Fan, an old hand at making wind, was not about to be blown away from Kalamazoo, even by a tornado.

Clarage Fan Company was forced to rebuild after its huge plant in the heart of Kalamazoo was destroyed by a tornado in 1980.

Right
Atlas Press employees at work, circa 1940.

Below
The Eames Mill, at the intersection of Oakland Avenue and Stadium Drive, was the first location of Atlas Press and later Western Michigan University's first theater building.

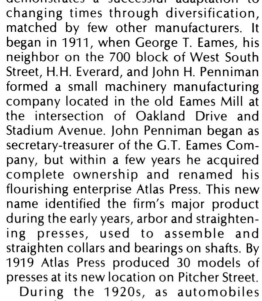

The history of the Clausing Corporation demonstrates a successful adaptation to changing times through diversification, matched by few other manufacturers. It began in 1911, when George T. Eames, his neighbor on the 700 block of West South Street, H.H. Everard, and John H. Penniman formed a small machinery manufacturing company located in the old Eames Mill at the intersection of Oakland Drive and Stadium Avenue. John Penniman began as secretary-treasurer of the G.T. Eames Company, but within a few years he acquired complete ownership and renamed his flourishing enterprise Atlas Press. This new name identified the firm's major product during the early years, arbor and straightening presses, used to assemble and straighten collars and bearings on shafts. By 1919 Atlas Press produced 30 models of presses at its new location on Pitcher Street.

During the 1920s, as automobiles emerged as a national necessity, Atlas Press capitalized on developing needs by diversifying into the production of a line of automotive garage service equipment and hand tools. In those pioneer days of the automobile, motorists often had recourse to the set of tools which came as standard equipment with each vehicle. Atlas Press manufactured kits containing basic tools such as a monkey wrench, hammer, and pliers for General Motors.

Business lagged during the Great Depression, and Atlas Press sought a salable new product. In 1933 the company introduced a 10-inch metal lathe that sold for half the price of competitive models. These lathes became popular, especially with unemployed mechanics trying to eke out a living at home. Atlas followed up on this success by developing other low-cost power tools, drill presses, milling machines, small shapers, and power saws, which became widely used for high school shop classes.

As the nation emerged from the Depression, a great demand developed for power tools used by woodworking hobbyists.

Atlas Press responded by purchasing the Power King Tool Company of Warsaw, Indiana, for manufacturing jigsaws, lathes, bench saws, band saws, sanders, routers, and other powered woodworking tools. Just as the plant began operation, America entered World War II, and production shifted to metalworking tools for industries on the government's priority list. As output of these tools vital to the war effort increased Atlas Press became the first local company to receive the prestigious Army/Navy "E" Award for efficiency in production.

Following the war, returning veterans anxious to continue working with their hands, a general shortage in the building trades, and more leisure time resulted in a nationwide "do-it-yourself" movement. Atlas Press responded with increased production of woodworking tools suitable for home workshops and enjoyed vigorous sales.

In the early 1950s Atlas Press purchased the Clausing Lathe Company of Ottumwa, Iowa, which produced industrial-type lathes. During the succeeding decades machine shops and factories across the nation installed thousands of Clausing lathes. By the mid-1950s, sales representatives in all major countries and over 2,000 retail outlets in America featured these products.

In 1956 Atlas Press joined forces with the Colchester Company of Great Britain and began marketing that firm's precision-quality industrial lathes in America. While Clausing lathes are no longer produced, Clausing/Colchester lathes maintain a similar enviable reputation. In the late 1960s Atlas Press became the Clausing Corporation.

By the 1970s it had become a tradition for the Clausing Corporation to respond to newly perceived needs through diversification. However, during the final years of the decade that diversification took on new

dimensions and resulted in a period of fantastic growth. In January 1978 Clausing acquired its first plastic moldmaking and manufacturing facility and others soon followed. Currently the corporation's Plastic Engineering Group consists of the following companies: Mol-Bee, Inc., P.E.I., and Pan-O-Grav, Inc., of Portage, Michigan; Moark Mold, Inc., of Poplar Bluff, Missouri; Los Angeles Die Mold of South El Monte, California; Janlin Plastics of Wisconsin, Inc., of Mont Hereb, Wisconsin; Janlin Plastics of Illinois, Inc., of Warren, Illinois; and Oxford Mold Die and Oxford Plastics of Oxford, North Carolina. Clausing's Plastic Engineering Group designs and produces plastic molds to customer specifications and manufactures plastic products for a wide variety of industries, including automotive, appliance, electrical/electronic, environmental control, and health care. Over 500 skilled personnel design, produce, and package items ranging from toy dominoes to automotive fuse panels.

Clausing's Industrial Distribution Group, the heart of the original organization, operates Clausing Machine Tools in Elgin, Illinois, which distributes throughout the United States the Clausing/Colchester lathes, radial arm drilling machines, Hydro CNC lathes, and the industrial drill presses still manufactured in Kalamazoo. A Pratt Burnerd American subsidiary in Springfield, Michigan, distributes manual and power chucks and collets imported from the F. Pratt Engineering Corporation of London, England. The Clausing line of drill presses is manufactured at the Kalamazoo plant on Pitcher Street, while the Clausing Service Center and Parts Manufacturing Facility located in Goshen, Indiana, provides nationwide repair and parts delivery and after-sales service for all machine tool products.

The advent of the 1980s brought even further diversification for the Clausing Corporation. On August 15, 1980, a merger with the Fife Corporation headquartered in Oklahoma City created a new division, Process Controls. In 1939 the Fife Corporation had pioneered in industrial automatic web-guiding systems which controlled materials processed in a continuous strip. By the time of the merger, Fife enjoyed the reputation as a leader in supplying systems not only for guiding but for gauging, inspecting, and spreading/expanding continuous flexible materials. Fife developed a unique "Scan-A-Web" system which utilizes a series of mirrors rotating in synchronization with a moving roll of printed materials to allow press operators, for example, to check the quality of printing without halting produc-

tion. Fife's Charlotte, North Carolina, plant produces properly applied, curved, rubber-coated rollers used to remove wrinkles and expand extensible materials. Four other wholly owned Fife subsidiaries, in West Germany, England, Japan, and Canada, each with its own manufacturing and/or assembly capabilities, give this group of the Clausing Corporation a multinational status.

In 1979 Clausing occupied its beautifully designed new corporate offices situated in a natural setting near Oshtemo, Michigan. From this headquarters in rural Kalamazoo County, policy decisions flow to Clausing Corporation's three groups, comprising 20 facilities and employing over 1,400 personnel worldwide.

Throughout 70 years of diversified growth the Clausing Corporation has enjoyed a beneficial relationship with Kalamazoo. The area's stable economy, reliable work force, and ideal geographical position have contributed to Clausing's success and in return the company has remained a strong supporter of the county. The future looks particularly bright for a continuation of this mutually successful partnership.

Below
Art deco entrance to the Atlas Press plant on North Pitcher Street, circa 1935. (Courtesy Kingscott Associates, Kalamazoo.)

Davenport College/Kalamazoo Branch, formerly Parsons Business School

Right
Parsons first occupied the upper floors of this building at the corner of Michigan Avenue and Burdick.

Below Right
Present location of Parsons Business School.

Times have changed since William Parsons and his brothers opened their chain of business colleges after the Civil War. Parsons taught penmanship and telegraphy when he came to Kalamazoo in 1869. Typewriters and telephones were still in the future. Young men made up 90 percent of his students in those years. They studied steamboating, railroading, and mining as well as bookkeeping and banking. Students obeyed strict rules, for Parsons believed moral character meant as much as technical skills. Students could not swear or chew tobacco in class, and those caught in "saloons, or any places of gaming or ill-repute" could face expulsion.

Parsons pioneered in what was later called learning by doing. His students telegraphed messages to other schools, handled banking transactions with special "college money," imported and exported merchandise, and tried as many real-life experiences as they could in the classroom. Enrollment grew steadily. Parsons first taught all courses himself in walk-up rooms on the corner of Burdick and Michigan Avenue. Then he moved to East Michigan and Portage, and to his own building at 135 North Westnedge in 1892.

Parsons continued as president for over 40 years. His son, William W. Parsons, succeeded him when he died in 1914. Each man modified the curriculum to keep pace with the business community. Both believed young men and women should "prepare for the active duties of life." In a time when many educators questioned whether women could master serious studies, Parsons Business School promised the same instruction to both men and women and made a special point of encouraging "business education for ladies." Each student progressed according to ability so that none would be held back by others "less inclined to hard study." Par-

sons wrote in one early brochure that his graduates finished their training like "a trained and muscle-hardened athlete," ready for the endurance race.

Edgar Stewart bought the college when William W. Parsons died in 1935. It was purchased by the Davenport Business Schools system in 1956, and Dexter Rohm took over as director 10 years later. With Rohm as president, Parsons Business School, Inc., purchased the Parsons Business School from Davenport Business Schools in 1977.

Parsons and his early students might still recognize accounting, sales, and secretarial programs, but they would be amazed at current offerings in computer programming, keypunch operating, medical administration, and travel and airline careers. On the other hand, Parsons would recognize today's standard for student conduct—that "cause for dismissal from a position in business" could be cause for dismissal from the school as well. But far more important, William Parsons would applaud the school's commitment to guidance, training, and placement.

Parsons Business School continues to help its 450 students define their goals and use their best resources. The new college campus, completed in 1980, offers the latest methods, equipment, and teaching techniques, just as Parsons did in 1869 when he put his students to work on a dozen telegraph lines running to his classroom. William Parsons said over 100 years ago, "we do not guarantee situations, but will use our influence in obtaining positions." Today the school offers continuing placement help so that "ambitions will not be limited by unsuitable employment."

William Parsons and his brothers saw a need in the 1860s for practical training as an alternative to the 4-year university; Parsons Business School carries on that same tradition more than a century later.

On July 1, 1981, Parsons merged with Davenport College, Grand Rapids.

De Nooyer Brothers Chevrolet

In 1926, when Calvin Coolidge sat in the White House and Americans first heard of talking pictures, Jerry DeNooyer and his brother Jacob rolled up their sleeves and started their first venture in the service department of the Cadillac and Richenbacher Garage in Battle Creek. The brothers soon saved enough to buy the parts inventory and new-car stock to go into business for themselves. They employed nine people in their first dealership and bought cars outright from the factory. As time went on, the brothers also acquired the Oldsmobile and Chevrolet franchises. Such franchises were not exclusive in the early days. If a dealership was to prosper, it would hold its customers with courtesy and service.

America's love affair with the automobile cooled a bit during the Depression, but the DeNooyers survived, even when fire destroyed their garage and everything in it the day before President Roosevelt ordered the Bank Holiday in 1933. The brothers rode out the Holiday and built again. They added new innovations suited to the times—car hoists for faster service, frame straighteners, a radio department, warranted service, even a "courtesy car" for customers. By 1941 DeNooyers had become the largest sales and service organization in Battle Creek, with 75 employees.

In 1943 the brothers looked to Kalamazoo, where they set out to buy "the biggest ground-floor garage in Michigan"— Frank Brophey's Chevrolet Agency on the corner of Portage and Lovell. Brophey had headed the agency for two decades, but now was willing to sell, and Jerry DeNooyer came in June as principal owner and operator of DeNooyer Brothers Chevrolet. Automakers suspended new-car production during the war, so the company built its reputation on used-car sales and customer service. The policies developed over the years in Battle Creek paid dividends in Kalamazoo. When the war ended, customers lined up to see the new generation of postwar Chevrolets.

Three of Jerry's sons, Bob, Gerald, and Lee, came home from the service and went to work learning the business from the ground up. They soon were joined by younger brother Jim. DeNooyer Brothers remodeled the agency and modernized the service department. The firm proved a training ground for several men who subsequently opened agencies of their own. Among them, Bob DeNooyer purchased the Chevrolet agency in Holland in 1953. Jim left to become a Chevrolet dealer in Albany, New York, in 1973, and Lee purchased a dealership in South Bend in 1977. Gerald, associated with his father and family in the agency since 1949, is now the principal dealer-operator in Kalamazoo, and is passing his father's training on to his own sons, Bill, Craig, Jeff, and Todd.

While many dealers fled to the suburbs in the '50s and '60s, DeNooyers remained downtown. Eleven thousand people work in the downtown area and find it convenient to leave their cars for servicing, whatever the make. DeNooyers provides a shuttle bus for their convenience. The agency has a staff of 100 employees and has enlarged its auto display and service facilities to cover 10 acres.

While its downtown location has benefited the company and its customers, in May 1980, that site was in the path of a tornado which struck downtown Kalamazoo. The buildings and inventories suffered extensive damage, but miraculously, no one at the dealership was injured. Hard work, cooperation, and even a spirit of optimism characterized the company's rebuilding following the storm. The agency's tornado damage totaled over half a million dollars.

Four generations ago, the first DeNooyers came to Kalamazoo as celery growers, strong in the conviction that they could make something of themselves. The family has kept that heritage and now looks forward to its second half-century in the automobile industry.

Left
A 1950 photograph of the main showroom on Portage Street, home of DeNooyer's "red carpet service."

Below Left
Jerry DeNooyer, founder; Gerald DeNooyer, president; Gerald's sons, Todd, Craig, Jeff, and Bill.

In 1898, America's "splendid little war" dominated local newspaper headlines with lurid Spanish atrocities, great naval victories, heroic charges, Teddy Roosevelt's Rough Riders, and Kalamazoo's own General Shafter. Amidst this excitement two young brothers quietly planted the seeds destined to grow into one of the city's most vigorous businesses. Ward F. and Fred U. Doubleday purchased the bindery of the old Kalamazoo Publishing Company and within the year moved their Doubleday Bros. & Co. to larger quarters on North Burdick Street. Originally the brothers conducted a wholesale business as they traveled throughout the state, specializing in county courthouse printing and binding needs, but soon branched into local government, bank, and insurance company business. Within a few years Doubleday Bros. became the state's largest publisher of standard legal forms, a distinction the company still holds.

Ward left and established a competitive firm, the Doubleday-Huber-Dolan Company in 1911, but business continued to increase for the original firm. In 1913, desperately in need of additional space, the enterprise moved to a larger facility at 241 East Michigan. This allowed a better retail counter and furniture showroom, by then an important segment of the business. A period photograph portrays a large display room packed with contents calculated to make an antique lover swoon. Banks of rolltop desks, aisles of leather and oak swivel chairs, clusters of wrought-iron tree and umbrella stands, rows of quartersawn-oak file cabinets, and sectional bookcases vie with displays featuring the novel "ball-pointed pens."

By the early 1930s looseleaf record books which allowed typewritten entries offered an alternative to the traditional expensive, leather-bound and handwritten county record books. Hand-binding record books remained an important business as did the printing of thousands of types of legal blanks, election supplies, indexes to vital statistics, and other forms.

World War II brought paper quotas, and gas rationing affected sales calls, but the company improvised and remained vital. Then on February 15, 1948, disaster struck. A Sunday morning fire in freezing weather

nearly gutted the plant, the ground floor fell through to the basement, and what did not burn was ruined by water. A hard blow and one that would have ended less vigorous concerns, but within a few months Doubleday Bros. had their presses running again.

Throughout the 1950s the installation of labor-saving equipment permitted increased efficiency and production. Again in need of additional space, the company built a modern one-story plant located on the south side of the city in 1958; succeeding years have seen large additions to this facility.

It was during this same period of time that Doubleday became the distributor for the Automatic Voting Machine. With this addition to their product line came a significant increase in their involvement in election printing. Supplying counties, cities, townships, and schools with precinct supplies, voting-machine strips, computer voting booklets, and absentee voting ballots makes Doubleday the largest election printing house in the state.

In 1966, a merger with Doubleday-Hunt-Dolan ended over 50 years of separation. The following year Standex International Corporation of Salem, New Hampshire, acquired the reunited Doubleday Bros. Company. Since then retail sales of office supplies and furniture have become increasingly important with the establishment of retail branches in Jackson and Lansing and the acquisition of other office furniture and supply companies in Benton Harbor and Flint.

Doubleday Bros. officers feel, "It's nice to have a tradition," and the current facilities demonstrate a healthy blend of old and new. Showrooms feature ultramodern modular office furniture and sophisticated "spectra-kode" color retrieval systems as well as traditional equipment. In the factory, modern offset printing presses hum next to chattering old-style letterpresses and linotype machines, fashioning type out of molten lead, still indispensable to custom printing. Meanwhile skilled hand-book-binders employing century-old techniques convert thread, gold leaf, and rich leather into beautifully bound volumes. That is tradition in action.

Fabri-Kal Corporation

Margarine tubs, cottage cheese and yogurt containers, cold-drink cups, and disposable plates have two things in common. They're part of the plastics revolution, and they're made in Kalamazoo by Fabri-Kal Corporation. In 1950 Robert Kittredge organized the only plastic-product firm in town when people still considered plastic an exotic material. Designers doubted that plastic could compete with paper, aluminum, or steel. Social critics talked about the throwaway society and sneered at "plastic" as a synonym for poor quality. Times have changed since 1950. Plastic has surpassed steel as a basic industrial material, and plastic packaging has come a long way toward replacing glass and paper. Under Kittredge's leadership, Fabri-Kal grew with this revolution into a company with annual sales of $40 million.

While plastic manufacturers produced nearly everything from raincoats to speedboats and water pipe to auto parts, Fabri-Kal specializes in thermoformed products for the food industry. The company's huge silos handle a half-million tons of pelletized resin in a year's time. In the plant, sheets of extruded plastic pass through thermoforming machines which press out containers of all shapes and sizes.

In the 1960s and 1970s, Americans came to expect plastic packaging. They appreciated soft-drink bottles that didn't break and cups that didn't leak. When they complained enough about hard-to-spread margarine, suppliers responded with a product so soft that it had to be merchan-

dised in plastic tubs. Over the years, Fabri-Kal became the country's largest margarine tub maker with production exceeding 100 million yearly in 1977. The firm also made yogurt and cottage cheese containers in incredible numbers. Hospitals, schools, and other institutions faced with rising labor costs and safety regulations found it less expensive to use "single-service ware," and many turned to products made by Fabri-Kal.

The firm moved to its present quarters on East Cork Street in 1962. With 285 employees, the plant operates around the clock, seven days a week, to achieve the most efficient use of energy and equipment. Rising energy and plastic costs necessitated more automated and faster machinery. One such machine now makes 113,000 coffee-cup lids per hour—a tenfold increase over equipment available in the 1950s. Special resins allow thinner but stronger walls, and all trimmings are recycled through extruding machines for reuse. Lightweight plastic requires less energy to make than steel or aluminum, less energy to transport during its useful life, and less energy to recycle. "When we make plastics," Kittredge feels, "we're borrowing energy," which can be returned in part when plastic "throwaways" are burned in waste-fueled generating plants.

Fabri-Kal has made its home in Kalamazoo for 30 years, and company officials actively participate in community affairs. Robert Kittredge is a trustee of Kalamazoo College and of Bronson Methodist Hospital, and a past president of the Kalamazoo Chamber of Commerce. The Fabri-Kal Foundation provides student aid, including 4-year, full-expense scholarships at Kalamazoo College and Western Michigan University; it also responds to other local needs. Plastics are part of America's future, and with a forecasted 10 percent annual growth rate, Fabri-Kal expects to remain in Kalamazoo for a long time to come.

Left
The company's pellet-storage silos.

Below
Fabri-Kal Corporation's plant is located at 3303 East Cork Street in Kalamazoo.

Opposite, Above Left
Durametallic's birthplace was 606 Cobb Avenue, Kalamazoo, in 1917.

Opposite, Above Right
The company's original plant at 2104 Factory Street.

Below
Durametallic's newly expanded facilities comprise one of the world's most modern manufacturing plants.

Pride—that best describes the impression received during a visit to the Durametallic Corporation located on the corner of Factory Street and Alcott Avenue. The company is understandably proud of its products, history, record of expansion and success, the employees who work there under safe and modern conditions, and the city it calls home. Furthermore, the American flag that has waved in front of the factory every single day since 1942 graphically demonstrates the way this company feels about its country.

The Durametallic Corporation, a child of the 20th century, began in 1901 when Henry P. White left his job as superintendent at the Advance Manufacturing Company and established a small factory on Cobb Avenue to manufacture some of the specialties he invented. His New Era Manufacturing Company produced and marketed a soap product, "Crystallo"; various products constructed of babbitt metal (an alloy usually consisting of tin, copper, and antimony commonly used for bearing linings); "metallic phosphoro," which, when added to certain metallic castings, promoted fusion and oxidation of the combining metals; and a novel metallic packing constructed of twisted strips of foil which, similar to a gasket, sealed moving machine parts from leakage of steam or fluid under pressure.

White's metallic phosphoro sold well during the early years, especially to railroads, and local paper mills proved good customers for the excellent foil packing. In 1911 White received a patent on this packing but as early as 1906 he installed lead foil packing in four valves on a huge Corliss steam engine in the Kalamazoo Paper Mill, an extremely important job for the future of the company. Unfortunately, Henry White, like many another able inventor, proved to be a poor businessman and by 1917 his firm stood on the verge of bankruptcy.

At that point, Charles C. Hall entered the picture. Hall had left a newspaper career in 1909 to establish the Kalamazoo News Company, an agency specializing in out-of-town newspapers, but by 1917, disillusioned by dealings with feisty newspaper circulation departments, the energetic entrepreneur sought another vocation. A chance meeting with Henry White who enthusiastically demonstrated his products sparked Hall's interest. An inspection of the valves on the Corliss steam engine, still operating with the same packing White had installed 11 years before, and sanguine testimony by the paper mill's engineer convinced Hall of the product's extraordinary merits. With a few other friends he bought into the New Era Company and that indeed began a new era for the ailing concern.

Kalamazoo's vigorous Chamber of Commerce caused another big break. During World War I, the Chamber hired a Washington agent, Phillip LaBree, to obtain government contracts for local firms. After visiting the Cobb Avenue plant, LaBree arranged for tests of metallic phosphoro by the Bureau of Standards. Those tests revealed that the product could reduce the amount of tin, a scarce wartime commodity, necessary to produce government-quality bronze. By 1918 Hall, now devoting his full attention to this new venture, armed with this Bureau of Standards report sold large quantities of metallic phosphoro to foundries producing brass and bronze.

New Era's metallic foil packings also caught LaBree's interest and he soon brought them to the attention of the Endura Manufacturing Company of Philadelphia, which handled fiber gaskets. Endura began marketing these metallic foil packings which they named "Durametallic" and also hired Hall to sell for them in the Midwest. Though this arrangement was short-lived, Hall, a novice to the art of salesmanship, received valuable advice and guidance from an experienced Endura salesman, George A. Denny, which helped him to develop the leadership abilities he used to build his company during the next two decades.

About this time, J.J. McQuillen, a salesman for the Pittsburgh Fiber Packing Company, affiliated with Endura, convinced the Pittsburgh and Lake Erie Railroad to try "Durametallic" packing on one of their steam locomotives. This successful test opened a new market for the amazing packing and during the 1920s, due particularly to railroad business, metallic foil packing became the company's major product. In 1923, attesting to the popularity of these packings, New Era became the Durametallic Corporation. In 1929 the

Top
Charles C. Hall bought into the New Era Company, predecessor of Durametallic Corporation, in 1917.

Center
Richard D. Hall, chairman emeritus, was president from 1950 to 1974.

Bottom
Paul Jackson became company president in 1974.

prospering corporation erected new facilities at its present location.

During the harsh days of the Great Depression, business naturally languished, but again C.C. Hall demonstrated imagination and vision. On a visit to an oil refinery he discovered a superior mechanical-type rotary seal in operation, manufactured by two men living in nearby Hammond, Indiana. Before nightfall that day he had secured a contract to manufacture and market their invention, and the "Dura Seal" helped spur Durametallic out of the Depression-caused doldrums. Given this impetus other successful products soon followed. In 1936 the company developed a unique, flexible-handled packing puller, "Dura Hooks." By 1937 business grew to over $100,000 a year and the firm again pioneered with the "Double Dura Seal," which first successfully sealed volatile materials such as propane and gasoline.

Durametallic produced seals essential to the war effort after the United States entered World War II. Synthetic rubber projects, 100-octane gasoline refineries, and the famous Manhattan Project utilized their products. During the war, business continued to grow, more employees joined the company, and extensive plant additions were constructed in 1942 and 1945.

Following the war, Durametallic became the "world's leading manufacturer of first-class flexible metallic and plastic packings and mechanical seals," as refineries and chemical plants throughout the world adopted the company's extensive line of seals. New needs stimulated an extensive research department to develop novel seals. By 1950 business had expanded to over one million dollars a year. Under the leadership of Richard D. Hall, son of the founder, this increased to over $12 million in 1973. Paul D. Jackson became president in 1974. Sales have continued to increase, exceeding $37 million by 1980.

The 1960s witnessed the opening of branches worldwide in Europe, Mexico, Brazil, and Australia. Wherever a need developed Durametallic established branches to provide or maintain its products. The 1970s saw tremendous growth and additional branch locations. As Americans became more concerned with pollution abatement, Durametallic's mechanical seals, more efficient than ordinary types, enjoyed increased popularity.

In 1978 a huge building expansion resulted in a block-long factory completely engulfing the original 1929 building. Employees helped design their own working areas for top efficiency and safety and the current facilities comprise one of the world's most modern manufacturing plants. The future looks even brighter as anything that flows, whether it's petroleum gas or steam in nuclear energy plants, needs to be sealed.

Durametallic's amazing success story owes much to initial excellent products, but the company continually developed better products to meet new needs and responded to increased competition by doing better itself. Perhaps even more important was Durametallic's attitude toward its employees and the community in which they live.

The career of Paul Jackson, who began working for Durametallic in 1933, illustrates this philosophy. Hired as a bookkeeper but really wanting to work with his hands, within a month he was out in the shop. Now Jackson is president of the corporation and can personally testify that since 1933 neither he nor any other employee ever lost an hour's wages through unemployment. What's more, a long string of safety awards demonstrate that Durametallic is the city's safest place to work. The firm hired and trained good employees and decided the best way to keep them was by fair treatment. If Durametallic was not in business to make a profit the company could not have survived, but as Paul Jackson says, "It's what you do with the bottom line that's important—profit for worthwhile causes."

Whether it's from the almost 400 local employees and their families who turn out for the traditional company picnic, the 40 needy families who receive Christmas boxes from the company's employees, or the country's institutions of higher learning which benefit from Durametallic generosity, it's not hard to find testimony concerning that "bottom line."

And that brings us back to pride.

Eaton Corporation Transmission Division

Over-the-road haulers shift gears made in Kalamazoo in seven out of 10 big rigs on American highways. Eaton Corporation's Transmission Division ships worldwide from four U.S. plants—to Europe, Africa, Australia, South America, and the Middle East. The division's main plant and North American headquarters is located in Kalamazoo.

It's a long way from transmissions to washboards and dictionary stands, but Kalamazoo's central location proved a deciding factor nearly a century ago when Fuller Brothers moved from Minneapolis. Then the company made washboards of Michigan basswood. Like its modern successor, the firm tapped markets on several continents, shipping 1.8 million washboards in its first five years of operation. Business declined, however, during the depression of the 1890s and the company closed its doors.

Frank and Charles Fuller pooled their skills in a new venture with machinists Maurice and Charles Blood, when they organized the Michigan Automobile Company, Ltd., on December 30, 1902. They were among the first three or four companies in Michigan to experiment with the horseless carriage. With Charles Fuller as chairman and Frank as general manager, the firm set out to make a wire-wheeled beach buggy to compete with the pedal-

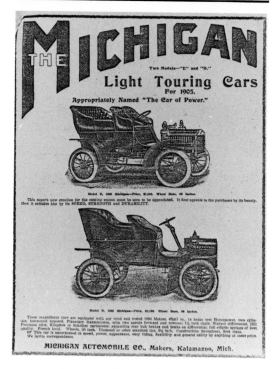

powered recreation vehicles popular in Florida. The company made about 100 of these lightweight runabouts, which came with a 3.5-horsepower engine, 2-inch by 28-inch tires, a tiller for steering, and two forward speeds. The "Little Michigan" sold for $450—nine months' wages for a factory worker.

The Blood brothers left in 1905 to form their own company, and W.E. Upjohn became treasurer. The firm's future looked bright. It was capitalized for $150,000 when *Motor World* carried a full-page advertisement for the 1905 "Michigan Light Touring Car." Fifty men now worked on two very substantial 4-passenger models selling for $1,100 and up. These cars came with 14-horsepower motors, two forward speeds, and reverse. They offered conventional steering and first-class construction. Even at this early date the company staked its claim on "Speed, Strength, and Durability."

By 1910, however, the firm turned its attention to making auto parts. It was reorganized as Fuller and Sons in 1913. Frank Fuller became chief executive, with Lawrence Fuller as secretary-treasurer and W.E. Upjohn as vice-president. The company now advertised "Automobile Transmissions, Dictionary Holders, Childs' Seats, and Parcel Carriers!" Many automakers began ordering their transmissions from Fuller and Sons. The company advertised transmissions exclusively in 1916, and employment jumped from 35 to 224. By 1919, 610 people worked at the 4-story plant at the corner of Pitcher and Prouty streets.

The auto industry changed drastically after World War I, and Fuller changed with

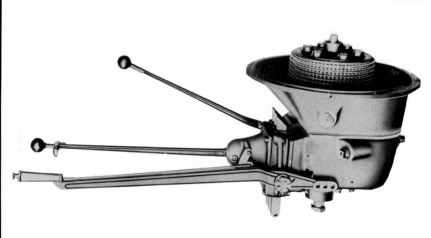

and Lee, as he rose within the organization to become president of Fetzer Broadcasting, contributed dedicated leadership.

As the war in Europe broke out and federal defense spending stimulated U.S. industry to emerge from the Depression, business in Kalamazoo boomed, and by 1940 WKZO had expanded its broadcasting time to 18 hours a day and joined the CBS Network. After the United States entered World War II, the city's industries converted to war production, and over 12,000 men and women from the county served in the armed forces. John Fetzer left his growing radio station to serve as National Radio Censor, heading the agency that kept vital security information off the air waves.

Returning after the war to a station with an increased power of 5,000 watts, Fetzer launched an expansion campaign. In 1945 he founded WJEF in Grand Rapids, and by 1949 the entire second floor of the Burdick Hotel had become Kalamazoo's "Radio City."

The following year saw another pioneering venture as "Radio City" also became "Television City." In 1950 television was still a novelty, which many thought would never amount to more than a toy, and again Fetzer faced local doomsayers predicting failure for this new venture. But as more and more people gathered in public places to watch those early tiny television tubes, and as huge consoles occupied a prominent place in many homes, Fetzer's vision was again vindicated. Television became an integral part of American life, generations were measured as pre- or post-TV, and it became the great American companion, while uplifting the quality of life especially for the elderly and the handicapped. What's more, Fetzer Television, Channel 3, in conjunction with WKZO Radio, developed Western Michigan into one of the nation's top advertising markets.

The 1950s brought continued expansion through formation and acquisition of other broadcasting stations—WJFM in Grand Rapids in 1951; KOLN-TV in Lincoln, Nebraska, in 1953; and WWTV in Cadillac in 1958. John Fetzer's lifelong interest in baseball blossomed into part-ownership of the Detroit Tigers in 1956 and complete ownership by 1962. The year 1958 saw the founding of the Fetzer Music Corporation. That same year Fetzer's rapidly growing organization moved to new facilities at Broadcast House, 590 West Maple Street.

The 1960s witnessed even greater growth as other stations joined the Fetzer roster—WWTV-FM (later WKJF) in Cadillac and KGIN, Grand Island, Nebraska, in 1961; WWUP-TV in Sault Ste. Marie in 1962; WWAM in Cadillac in 1968; and KMEG-TV

in Sioux City, Iowa, in 1969, the first UHF Fetzer station. And Fetzer pioneering produced a major media event of this decade. Cable television had been developed to bring television to valley "pockets" with poor reception. In Kalamazoo, however, viewers could receive two or three local stations by mounting an antenna on their rooftops. Consequently, when Fetzer Cable-Vision began operation in 1965, few saw the need and again came the familiar predictions of failure. But Fetzer's pioneering application of Cable TV, as a means to provide greater variety, soon produced widespread acceptance, an enriched life for the community, and brought silence to the critics.

Fetzer's familiar pattern of success continued during the 1970s, highlighted perhaps in 1977 when *Billboard* magazine named WKZO radio Station of the Year. The final year of the decade brought another pioneering venture with the installation of Kalamazoo's first "earth station" capable of receiving satellite transmissions.

In 1981, the national Broadcast Pioneers bestowed its prestigious "Mike Award" upon WKZO during the station's 50th anniversary celebration. After half a century of pioneering endeavors, founder John E. Fetzer remains strong, vigorous, and vital to the station's future. The little operation started by Mr. and Mrs. Fetzer in 1931 has grown to employ over 130 people in Kalamazoo alone and those ranks contained many 20-, 30-, and even 40-year veterans, happy to live in Kalamazoo and to work for Fetzer Broadcasting.

Left
Officers at Fetzer Broadcasting continue to look to the future.

Below
Today, Fetzer's broadcast facilities are located at 590 West Maple Street, Kalamazoo.

Fidelity Federal Savings and Loan

Below right
Fidelity Federal looked
like this in the 1960s.

Below
The association's
modern headquarters is
one of Kalamazoo's
architectural
showplaces.

"The cheerful climb of coins saved is a constant reminder to make every penny do its full duty, and that means prosperity," the Fidelity Building and Loan Association advised customers in a 1917 complimentary cookbook. Since then, generations of savers have counted on the firm to make their pennies do their full duty.

The association began in August 1897 when Willis J. Burdick left his position at the Kalamazoo County Building and Loan Association to become the first managing officer of the Fidelity Building and Loan Association. Prominent local citizens including John Pyle, Otto Ihling, Clarence D. Hayes, Howard Colman, and George F. Hopkins joined as charter members of the new association, created to assist families own their own homes.

Originally Fidelity's office was located on the second floor of a building at the southwest corner of Main and South Burdick streets, but by 1899 it was relocated to the second floor of the Humphrey Block over Sam Folz's Big Corner Store at Main and Portage streets. In 1912 the association moved to the Telegraph Press Building (later the Pythian Building) on West South

Street. Finally, in 1926, Fidelity permanently located itself on the ground floor of what was then the Elite Theatre Building.

The organization weathered the harsh financial climate of the Great Depression and none of its members lost a dime. In 1938 it became Fidelity Savings and Loan Association, and in 1945 its present designation, Fidelity Federal Savings and Loan Association, was adopted.

Willis J. Burdick guided the institution he had founded for nearly half a century, and upon his death in 1946 his twin sons assumed management responsibilities. Willis B. Burdick became president and Lorence B. Burdick was elected secretary-treasurer and later chairman of the board. Under their direction the association grew dramatically. The year 1956 saw the first branch office established in Milwood and in 1959 the West Main Branch opened (this later moved to the Maple Hill Mall). By 1962, when the Burdicks retired, assets had exceeded $30 million.

Growth continued at an even greater rate under Philip Hatfield, who succeeded the Burdick brothers. Hatfield joined Fidelity Federal in 1961, coming from Bedford, Indiana, where he had served since 1948 as managing officer of the Bedford Federal Savings and Loan Association, founded in 1927 by his father, Frank Hatfield. Under Philip Hatfield's leadership Fidelity opened the Allegan office in 1969, the association's first out-of-town branch, followed by the South Westnedge Branch in 1977, a Paw Paw location in 1979, and a Three Rivers facility in 1981.

While Fidelity's South Burdick Street headquarters had been extensively remodeled in 1950, the association demonstrated its commitment to the revitalization of the city's core in 1975 when the site underwent a major construction project. The skeleton of the old Elite Theatre Building remains hidden within a modernistic glass and brick structure designed by Diekema, Hamann Architects, which emerged as one of Kalamazoo's architectural showplaces. Fidelity further proved its commitment to Kalamazoo during the decade of the 1970s as it assumed a leadership role in financing and guiding community revitalization efforts.

By 1981, when Philip Hatfield retired, the association's assets had reached $160 million. Fidelity Federal enters the promising decade of the 1980s locally owned and under the direction of a third-generation savings and loan manager, David L. Hatfield. A bright future beckons as it develops more and more public-oriented financial services to become a "family finance center."

First Federal Savings and Loan Association of Kalamazoo

In 1893 a group of Kalamazoo businessmen gathered in the office of Civil War hero, then attorney, General William Shakespeare to form an association to assist local citizens achieve their goals through good habits of thrift. That year the Kalamazoo County Building-Loan Association began operation in a small office in the Shakespeare Block, 202 North Rose Street.

Howard S. Colman, president, and his board of directors—John McGoff, James H. Hatfield, William H. Langley, Charles H. Williams, Andres J. Shakespeare, Jr., Vernon T. Barker, Romine H. Buckhout, Edwin Martin, Frank B. Orcutt, and William Shakespeare—faced no easy task implementing their ideals. But they granted the first home loan, for $500, to Henry E. Randall, and the home he built, the first of thousands financed by First Federal Savings, stood on the corner of Portage and Phillips streets until 1980.

By 1924, with more and more people saving at the institution, the association moved to larger quarters at the present site of the main office and became The People's Savings Association. The year 1929 brought the stock market crash and a decade of hard times for financial institutions. Many banks unable to meet withdrawal requests closed their doors forever, but savings and loan associations, while affected by the panic, were able to pay withdrawals by rotation and hence weathered the crisis better. First Federal Savings of Kalamazoo even paid dividends during the Depression years.

During the 1920s and 1930s, the federal government acted to establish agencies to govern hard-pressed financial institutions. Congress passed the Federal Home Loan Bank Act in 1932, establishing the agency that supervises the activities of savings and loan associations. The Home Owners Loan Act of 1933 provided a system of federally chartered savings and loan associations and the National Housing Act of 1934 created the Federal Savings and Loan Insurance Corporation, which insures savings accounts in member associations. In 1937, after conversion to a federal charter, the

renamed First Federal Savings and Loan Association of Kalamazoo had membership in both the FHLB and FSLIC.

After the Depression, the advent of World War II brought other financial needs. U.S. government securities have always had a prominent place in this institution and First Federal helped the war effort by selling war bonds. When the veterans returned after the war, ready to move into their own homes, First Federal pioneered in southwestern Michigan with "GI" loans, making hundreds of thousands of dollars available. As the nation experienced a postwar housing boom First Federal's assets leaped from $5 million in 1944 to $10 million in 1951.

The "Fabulous '50s" saw an asset growth matched by physical development. The first branch office opened in 1955 in Paw Paw, another in Vicksburg in 1957, followed by three in 1959, in Milwood, Westwood, and Portage, and today 12 such branches serve southwestern Michigan. This physical expansion brought more and more First Federal savers, and the association grew in strength as assets reached $40 million in 1958, $60 million in 1961, and zoomed to over $300 million by 1981.

While the savings and loan industry nationwide has shown a similar increase in the period following the war, First Federal of Kalamazoo rates nationally in the top 10 percent of associations in total assets, and in Michigan is ranked 13th among associations belonging to the Michigan Savings and Loan League.

Right
The original location of First Federal Savings and Loan at 202 North Rose Street.

Below
The interior of First Federal in 1927 with president Robert C. Dexter in the foreground.

Kalamazoo • Partners in Progress • Page 253

Right
First National, behind the teller "cages," 1912.

Below Right
This turn-of-the-century photograph, looking south from Michigan Avenue and Burdick Street, shows First National on the east corner.

The oldest surviving national bank in Michigan, Kalamazoo's First National Bank and Trust Company, received its charter while America fought for survival during the Civil War. President Lincoln signed a National Banking Act in February 1863 to help finance the war and the following December 14, 20 Kalamazoo stockholders launched the First National Bank with Latham Hull as its president. The bank's seal featured a sheaf of wheat, symbolic of Kalamazoo's then predominantly agricultural economy, and service to the farm community became a cornerstone of its philosophy. While that economy shifted to industry with passing time, First National continued to be a national leader in agricultural lending.

During the early days banks served a local clientele with very basic functions, receiving deposits and making loans and investments, but First National's history has been one of expanding services, assets, and geographical coverage. In 1912 a merger with a neighboring bank, Michigan National, which began in 1856 as Woodbury, Potter and Wood's private bank, inaugurated a new period of growth for First National. In 1890 a man destined to become a great figure in the state's banking history, Charles S. Campbell, had joined Michigan National. The 1912 merger brought him the presidency of the combined banks which retained the name, First National. Campbell's vigorous leadership served the bank well during the following four decades until his death in 1953.

In 1916-1917 the bank erected a magnificent classical revival edifice on the southeast corner of Burdick Street and Michigan Avenue, the same site it had occupied since 1863. Renamed the First National Bank and Trust Company shortly after the addition of a trust department in 1920, the bank today maintains one of the state's largest personal trust operations. While the hard days of the Depression brought disaster to many banks, First National opened sound and solvent after the national Bank Holiday in 1934, and no depositor lost a penny of his savings. The first branch office opened in Vicksburg in 1936, and in 1979 the 34th such office was established near Battle Creek.

In 1940 the bank responded to a growing public need for personal credit by adding a Personal Loan Department, a service previously available only to businessmen. Then in 1952 First National pioneered a novel service, the credit card. From an initial experiment involving a few local merchants and handwritten records, the First National Charge Account service evolved into what is now a byword in the community and the oldest bank charge plan in the nation. Bank representatives traveled to Kalamazoo to study the charge system's workings and First National's success provided a model for other plans across the nation.

The three decades following this innovation witnessed a period of vigorous development for First National. In 1959 it led in offering in-plant banking services to local industry and business, and the bank's centennial year saw a conversion to computer processing of most accounts. The state legislature amended the law to permit corporations to own stock in commercial banks as bank holding companies in 1971, and the following year First National became the lead bank in what is now known as the First American Bank Corporation, the first multibank holding company in Michigan. From three affiliates with total assets of $330 million the corporation grew to 23 affiliates with assets of $2.4 billion by the end of 1980.

First National again pioneered in 1978 when it became the first bank in the state to introduce a photo-identification card, the Number One Card, which guaranteed customer checks. The following year saw installation of ATM machines, Ready Tellers, throughout the area, which again revolutionized banking.

In 1863 Latham Hull hand-signed every bank note. Now, customers insert plastic identification cards into computers and punch out financial transactions or open a drawer to receive cash. But the foundation of First National Bank still firmly rests on the same prudent philosophy that successfully guided it through those many years of growth.

Georgia Pacific

An ancient black tin box lettered in gold and bulging with carefully preserved manuscript business records, lists of first stockholders, original deeds, and colorful 19th-century stock certificates eloquently testifies to the heritage of the Kalamazoo Paper Company. This grandfather of all area paper mills began in 1866 when Benjamin F. Lyon, a successful Fitchbury, Massachusetts, paper manufacturer, arrived in Kalamazoo to interest local capital in starting a paper mill. Soon such prominent citizens as Silas Hubbard, John F. Gilkey, Allen Potter, and Henry Bishop jointly subscribed $50,000, and on October 1, 1866, the Kalamazoo Paper Company was organized with J.P. Woodbury as president.

By the following year at a 2-story wooden mill located south of the city on Portage Creek (the present site of the Monarch Mill), the company's one 72-inch machine converted straw from nearby wheat and rye fields into 10 to 15 tons of paper a week at a marginal profit. The year 1872 brought disaster to the young firm when fire destroyed the mill, but a promptly rebuilt brick structure demonstrated the stockholders' faith in their enterprise. Samuel Gibson, who had been brought by Lyon from Fitchburg as a bookkeeper in 1867, assumed command of the new operation and almost immediately the mill began to prosper.

What's more, Gibson attracted and trained a coterie of young papermakers who later established their own mills throughout the Kalamazoo River Valley. Among those who learned the art of papermaking under Gibson at the Kalamazoo Paper Company were George E. Bardeen of the Bardeen Paper Company and Mac Sim Bar, Noah Bryant, and Frank Milham of the Bryant Paper Company; John F. King of the King and Rex Paper Companies; Jerry Whitney of the Standard Paper Company; and W.S. Hodges of the Superior Paper Company. The presence of this training ground coupled with the area's geographical position, ample water facilities, and source of labor resulted in an amazing proliferation of paper mills. By the 1920s Kalamazoo was "The Paper City," with fully 50 percent of its industrial work force employed in producing more paper than any other city in the world.

Under Gibson's guidance the Kalamazoo Paper Company grew lustily while establishing a reputation for quality and craftsmanship. The output of the mill had doubled by 1879 and further increased through the installation of new equipment in 1885. In 1892 the Botsford Paper Company, later renamed the Wolverine Paper Company, erected a mill east of the city at the present site of the Kalamazoo Paper Company. In 1899 the Kalamazoo Paper Company acquired the Wolverine plant (Mill No. 2) and soon erected a new mill nearby (Mill No. 1), one of the most modern facilities in the country at that time. The firm sold the old mill on Portage Creek to the Gibson Paper Company.

Shortly after the turn of the century the Kalamazoo Paper Company, desiring a source for coated paper, encouraged the Riverview Coated Paper Company to move to Kalamazoo. In 1916 Riverview erected its own paper mill and the Kalamazoo Company built a coating mill; in 1918 the two firms merged. This gave the Kalamazoo Paper Company five mills manned by over 1,000 employees in 1925.

Following Samuel Gibson's death in 1899, his son-in-law, Fred M. Hodge, became president; his tenure resulted in a period of growth and expansion. Upon Hodge's death in 1932, A.E. Curtinius took over to lead the firm through the tough decade. The Kalamazoo Paper Company remained one of the few local mills that kept running throughout the worst of the Depression, and by the late 1940s the company's five mills produced 225 tons of high-grade book paper a day.

By the 1960s the Kalamazoo paper industry faced a period of diminished profits. However, as the Kalamazoo Paper Company celebrated the centennial of its founding in 1967, the Georgia Pacific Corporation eagerly acquired the company with its large capital and assets, well-seasoned work force, and enviable reputation for quality. Georgia Pacific invested in modern new facilities, a water purifications system, a de-inking plant built in 1976, and a recently completed $30-million paper machine rebuilding. A work force containing many 30-year veterans receives a stake in the future of the company through a stock option plan. Presently fewer machines operate at greater efficiency to produce approximately 400 tons of paper a day, paper whose quality is emphasized by the company's slogan "good paper since 1867."

A train wreck during the 1920s, with the Kalamazoo Paper Company's mill in the background.

Four Higher Educational Institutions Enrich Kalamazoo Community

Right
Nazareth College.

Below
Kalamazoo Valley
Community College.

Kalamazoo's diverse institutions of higher learning maintain a vital interrelationship with the community, stimulate economic and intellectual development, and provide a major cultural attraction. They make available sophisticated research facilities; faculty and staff are a source of expertise and provide a valuable educational resource. Their accomplishments attract residents and increase hometown pride, and as consumers of millions of dollars of products and services, they invigorate local business.

These institutions, including an independent liberal arts college, a human services college, a comprehensive public community college, and a multipurpose state university, through their diverse philosophies, strengths, and goals, have provided a rich educational asset for the area. During the 1970s, a period of diminishing resources and increased expectations, it became clear that more interinstitutional cooperation was necessary. On May 7, 1973, Kalamazoo College, Western Michigan University, Kalamazoo Valley Community College, and Nazareth College formally announced the creation of a local educational consortium. Its goals were to serve the community in complementary rather than competitive ways and through joint planning of programs and pooled resources raise the area's level of educational, social, and cultural opportunities.

A Presidents' Council, comprised of the presidents of the four institutions, facilitates and supports these goals. A coordinating committee, consisting of the chief academic officer and a nonacademic administrator from each institution, identifies, examines, and recommends likely areas of interinstitutional cooperation to the Presidents' Council. Various program committees serve as grass roots liaison groups to implement recommended cooperative efforts.

Projects that have already proved successful for the consortium include a student exchange program, that permits

students to take courses in member institutions at no added cost on a space-available basis; collaborative volunteer projects, concerts, social activities, workshops, and guest lecturers; cooperative grant proposals; faculty exchange and joint appointments; coordinated continuing education offerings; joint use of facilities such as computers, libraries, and athletic resources; and merging of duplicative programs. Perhaps the most important result has been the establishment and maintenance of communication, at all levels, among the four institutions.

This consortium has received national recognition as a model of cooperation and coordination for other institutions and governmental agencies concerned with higher learning.

The history of higher education in Michigan began in Kalamazoo's pioneer period. In 1833 the Michigan and Huron Institute received a charter from the territorial legislature as a private Baptist school. By 1836 the institution opened its doors in a 2-story frame structure in the newly renamed frontier town, Kalamazoo. In 1837 it became the Kalamazoo Literary Institute and in 1840 was renamed Kalamazoo College.

The 1892-1912 era marked the beginnings of the modern development of the college. As the sectarian academy evolved into a liberal arts college, endowment funds grew, new facilities sprang up, and its fame spread. From 1953 to 1971, the college experienced a vital period of growth including an enriched curriculum, the Kalamazoo Plan for year-round and worldwide education, and the attraction of an outstanding faculty. In 1972 George N. Rainsford became its 13th president, renewing the college's commitment to "sustaining the quality and discipline of its traditional liberal arts program while emphasizing leadership and value orientation to its students." In 1981 the college completed a 4-year capital campaign, rais-

ing more than $17 million, unprecedented in the history of the college and the history of greater Kalamazoo.

In 1903 the Press Club, forerunner of the Kalamazoo Chamber of Commerce, led a campaign that won the newly created Western State Normal School for Kalamazoo. The institution, created to train teachers for predominantly rural western Michigan, opened the new year with three faculty members and 117 students. The Normal School became Western State Teacher's College in 1927, and by the end of the 1920s enrollment exceeded 2,200. While the Depression brought hard times and decreased enrollment to the college, the year 1936 saw the first special 4-year nonteaching course offered, social work.

In 1941 the institution became Western Michigan College of Education, in 1955 Western Michigan College, and in 1957 Western Michigan University with five schools. As enrollment doubled to over 4,000 students following World War II, the campus expanded dramatically with the development of the west campus.

Western Michigan University, under the leadership of current president John T. Bernhard, now provides 155 major and eight coordinated major programs leading to bachelor's degrees, 62 programs leading to master's degrees, and nine programs each leading to specialist and doctoral degrees for over 20,000 students annually. A comprehensive continuing education division serves another 20,000 students each year with credit and noncredit courses.

Kalamazoo's college of human service professions traces its origins back to 1897, when the Sisters of St. Joseph established Nazareth Academy as a Catholic secondary school for young women. An outgrowth of the academy, the college initially offered junior-college level courses until 1924, when it received its charter from the state of Michigan. The first baccalaureate degrees were granted in 1928. During that year the college received accreditation and has retained that status in addition to having earned national accreditation for all its major programs. Today it boasts a 98 percent placement rate for its graduates.

The decades following the 1950s brought expanded and modernized facilities with a building program begun in 1959 on an entirely new campus located at Gull and Nazareth roads. Corporate ownership of the institution was transferred to a board of trustees in 1966; in 1971 the college became coeducational. Sisters of St. Joseph provided leadership until 1974 when the college installed its first male president.

From its beginnings as a Catholic institu-tion of higher education, Nazareth College has sought "to provide students with a person-centered education combining the liberal arts with preparation in careers dealing with the human services professions." In 1973 this philosophy was articulated in a new curriculum, which emphasized professional preparation in education, health fields, management, social services, and interdisciplinary studies backed by a sound complementary liberal arts program. Current president John Hopkins has continued to guide the college in achieving its mission and goals.

Kalamazoo's youngest institution of higher learning began on August 1, 1966, when the electors of the Kalamazoo Valley Intermediate School District voted overwhelmingly to create a community college. These citizens charged an elected board of trustees to develop a 2-year college offering a diversified range of vocational/technical, health, social service, general education, and liberal arts programs to fit the needs of a growing population in an increasingly complex society. In 1968, the 1,518 members of the "pioneer" class entered the Kalamazoo Valley Community College, seeking the opportunity to develop their educational goals through a variety of distinct programs and services.

By 1981 continued planning had created more than 55 different educational programs, most of them in vocational/technical areas designed for immediate employment upon completion. The college now serves more than 18,000 students annually in college-credit classes and provides a wide range of noncredit activities.

Under the leadership of its founding and current president, Dale B. Lake, Kalamazoo Valley Community College vigorously pursues its mission of providing high-quality comprehensive vocational and academic training for the residents of its service area, while continuing to respond to the expressed needs of the community.

Above
Western Michigan
University.

Below
Kalamazoo College.

Vintage stringed instruments, gleaming with the patina of ancient varnish, line the walls of the lobby entrance. Mandolins, guitars, banjos, a unique 37-string harp-zither, finely carved from rare woods, richly finished, inlaid with abalone, silver, and mother-of-pearl butterflies—this is the Gibson heritage.

This tradition of beautiful musical instruments began in 1890 when young Orville Gibson arrived in Kalamazoo with little more than a hobby and a dream. The hobby was carving mandolins, then the most popular stringed instrument, and the dream was to make them better. By 1896 the hobby became a vocation when he quit a job clerking in a restaurant to devote full time to his little workshop on South Burdick Street. The dream became reality when he redesigned the traditional gourd-shaped mandolin into a beautiful streamlined version that looked and sounded better. Each instrument, custom-made and completely hand-produced, took weeks to finish. As his superior products became popular with professional musicians, Gibson's fame spread, but the flood of orders went mostly unfilled.

Then in 1902, a group of local entrepreneurs organized a company to manufacture these instruments on a larger scale. Gibson agreed to impart his knowledge and, most important, lend his name to the enterprise, the Gibson Mandolin-Guitar Manufacturing Company. The following year a catalog appeared, more orders poured into the old bakery-turned-factory on East Exchange Place, and the original 13 employees, now using machinery, still could not keep up with the demand. Other catalogs followed, business continued to increase, and by 1911 the company moved to larger quarters on Harrison Court.

A large measure of this success resulted from the Gibson sales technique. Widely circulated advertisements appealed for more salesmen, and thousands of professional musicians and teachers across the country became "Gibson Agents," receiving *The Sounding Board*, a company journal jammed with current sales strategy and catchy slogans. In 1917 the expanding company constructed a modern plant filled with windows, a "daylight factory," on Parsons Street.

As other instruments replaced mandolins in popularity, Gibson responded with a diversified output. The company first produced banjos in 1918 and, as singing cowboys heightened interest in guitars, the company developed varied styles. In 1924, about 20 years ahead of the market, Gibson experimented with electric guitars. The Depression brought decreased sales and the company briefly diversified into wooden toys, but by the mid-1930s new models again boosted production.

During World War II, musical instruments gave way to vital war production, radar assemblies, glider skids, and precision machine-gun rods. Gibson won three Army/Navy "E" awards for production excellence, and its work force doubled as increasing numbers of women and older workers replaced employees called for service. In 1944 Chicago Musical Instrument Co. purchased Gibson, which later merged with E.C.L.—now part of Norlin Industries.

After the war Gibson entered a new era of even greater growth. During the 1950s Les Paul electric guitars came into their own and after Arthur Godfrey popularized ukuleles, Gibson produced thousands. Sparked by another large factory addition in 1950, the work force increased by 40 percent over the next five years. In 1957, mirroring contemporary automobiles with huge tail fins, Gibson introduced the "Flying V" electric guitar.

The popularity of folk songs, country western, and rock and roll during the 1960s resulted in an explosion of interest in fretted instruments and the factory that made the "frets heard round the world" experienced a 100 percent increase in production during the first three years of the decade.

Currently in Kalamazoo and a branch factory in Nashville, employees, utilizing custom-designed machinery as well as traditional handcraftsmanship, fashion American rock maple, black walnut, Sitka spruce, East Indian rosewood, South American mahogany, ebony from Ceylon, abalone and mother-of-pearl from the coast of Mexico, and nickle silver into instruments Orville Gibson would be proud to play—and they still can't make them fast enough for anxiously waiting customers around the world.

The Gibson name and heritage has been in the past, is today, and will be tomorrow, a most important segment of the history of fretted instruments.

Gilmore Brothers

John and James Gilmore learned storekeeping as apprentices in Belfast, Ireland. John received his coveted character reference in 1880, and one year later opened his own shop in Kalamazoo. Far from Belfast and married to a local girl, he struggled to build the business despite 18 competitors in the dry goods and "ladies' furnishings" trade. While others lined the 3-block business district on Main Street, John and his wife kept shop in a 25-foot storefront on South Burdick where rents were low—just $20.83 a month. Yearly sales increased steadily, and by 1883 James Gilmore joined his brother, John, in partnership. Sales were boosted by 33 percent and in 1884 the store was moved to larger quarters on the east side of Burdick Street.

Mary Gilmore died in 1891 and John four years later. James and his wife, Carrie, expanded the business, building their own store in 1899. Sales that year reached $154,614. When James Gilmore died in 1908, Carrie continued the family interest with her three sons, J. Stanley, Donald, and Irving. In 1910 she incorporated Gilmore Brothers with $400,000 capital. The next year she borrowed $125,000 through the Michigan Trust Company of Grand Rapids—no easy task at a time when bankers considered female executives poor risks. The firm then enlarged the store to the 6-story structure that came to be so familiar a part of downtown Kalamazoo. Carrie Gilmore married her next-door neighbor, W.E. Upjohn, in 1913, uniting the town's two prominent families. Upjohn joined Gilmore Brothers' board of directors in 1916. J. Stanley Gilmore and Ruth McNair were married in November that year, and Donald married Genevieve Upjohn a month later. Irving Gilmore, the youngest of the family, joined the firm in 1924, when he was 23.

It was during this period, 1924, that automobiles were making their presence known in Kalamazoo. Distance, once a deterrent for many a potential shopper, was no longer a problem with the arrival of the auto; however, sufficient parking in the downtown area was. Realizing this, Gilmore Brothers bought the old Farmers' Sheds property behind the store in 1925 and made available convenient parking for the many shoppers who had traded their bicycles and horse-drawn buggies for this newfangled mode of transportation.

Gilmore Brothers opened stores in Benton Harbor and Battle Creek in the late 1920s, but gave them up during the Depression, a period which brought many difficulties for local merchants. Sales for the entire store, during their lowest ebb, fell to just $900 a day, a far cry from the $20,000- to $40,000-range that was considered a good day's business back then. In order to save jobs and keep the store in business, salaries were cut from $12 to $10 a week.

Good times eventually returned along with the advent of synthetic fabrics, ready-to-wear, and "wash and wear" clothing. Kalamazoo County grew with expanding industry and the baby boom. Gilmore Brothers kept pace in its downtown store and, recognizing the trend toward suburban shopping malls, opened new stores at Maple Hill Mall in 1972 and Southland Mall in 1974.

Gilmore Brothers was to face a major natural disaster in the opening months of 1980. On May 13, a tornado of tremendous intensity struck the downtown store, toppling the rooftop water tank and sending the entire rear wall crashing down. Damage ran to $3 million, but Gilmore's opened again in just 10 days with a "Gone With the Wind" sale that brought the highest one-day receipts in the store's history.

Over the years, the Gilmore family has played a major role in civic affairs. Irving Gilmore was a key factor in making the downtown Kalamazoo Mall a reality. He was also instrumental in the implementing of the annual Gilmore's Christmas Parade, Downtown Sidewalk Days, and the Starlight Symphony Concerts that were held at the Gilmore Auto Ramp. "Gilmore's is Kalamazoo," he once said, adding, "we have been in the heart of downtown Kalamazoo for 100 years, and plan to be here at least another 100."

Below Right
Gilmore's first store, opened in 1881, was located on South Burdick.

Below
Gilmore's main floor at the turn of the century.

Right
Buffalo herd at the
Gilmore farm. (Courtesy
Jack Short.)

Below Right
Jim Gilmore Cadillac-
Pontiac Agency.

Harry Truman came to Islamorada in the Florida Keys when he wanted to get away from Washington, D.C. He used a 50-foot steel houseboat beached at the seaside as his "little White House" during the Korean Crisis. Hurricane Donna swept the houseboat far inland, where it came to rest at a highway junction, and there it sat as traffic crawled around it. Jim and Diana Gilmore found a special challenge in what everyone else called the battered hazard. They sought out the owner, bought the boat on the spot, and set about moving it on telephone pole rollers back to the beach. There they filled the hull with cement, refurbished the interior, and named their new vacation home Bay Bourne.

The Gilmores enjoyed challenges like this wherever they found them. Jim grew up in Kalamazoo and mastered the business world while working in his family's department store. There his father, J. Stanley Gilmore, was chairman of the board and Jim was vice-president, secretary, treasurer, and manager of the men's store. Jim Gilmore also found time to run for the city commission in 1959. With the highest vote total, he became mayor of Kalamazoo at a particularly exciting time. The USIA had chosen Kalamazoo as its representative American city. More than 20 million people viewed the agency's massive exhibit of Kalamazoo life and products when it toured English cities. Another 250,000 Germans saw a similar exhibit when "Leben und Arbeit in Kalamazoo, USA" was America's chief entry in the Berlin Free Fair that same year. Excitement continued in 1959. Anxious to revitalize the downtown area, the city followed the suggestion of Victor Gruen and Associates and turned its main downtown street into the country's first pedestrian mall.

The slogan W.E. Upjohn made famous— "Keep the Quality Up"—hangs on Jim Gilmore's office wall. As mayor he did everything he could in the next two years to

help Kalamazoo capitalize on the international attention generated by the exhibits and the mall. He also began to move away from the department store and into the varied opportunities now gathered under the heading of Jim Gilmore Enterprises.

Tired old buildings hurt the downtown in its competition with suburban shopping centers. Long before the vogue for historic preservation, Gilmore began buying and renovating older buildings. He owned and later sold the Grand Rapids and Indiana Line depot (now the Whistlestop Restaurant). He also gutted, renovated, and renamed the old Pratt Building at Michigan and Portage. As the Michigan Building, it became one of Kalamazoo's most prestigious office buildings and headquarters for Gilmore Enterprises. In 1960 he bought and refurbished the old Pythian Building on South Street near the mall. That same year he also purchased and held for some time the Peninsular Building at the northeast corner of Portage and Michigan.

Gilmore was devoting more and more time to his enterprises by 1961. In that year he acquired the McLain Agency to be his advertising division. At first he was his own biggest client, but most divisions were expected to pull their own weight. Within a short time, Gilmore Advertising numbered Gilmore Enterprises among its smaller accounts.

In 1961 Jim Gilmore bought the old

Paper City Motor Sales and renamed it Jim Gilmore Cadillac-Pontiac. He served as president and his father was assistant to the president. His management team included N.B. McLain, Robert McDonell, Neal Hycoop, John Schaberg, and Robert Fredrickson. The agency experimented with Mercedes-Benz and Peugeot and added Datsun cars and trucks in 1972.

For many years the Gilmore family spent time at Gull Lake. Interest in rural life and outdoor activities came naturally to both Jim and Diana, who grew increasingly concerned about the loss of farmland as suburban developers moved steadily out along the road to Richland. They acted on their concern in 1961, when they began the farming division of Jim Gilmore Enterprises. Presently the farming division controls 1,800 contiguous acres just south of Richland. In addition to corn production, the farming operation finishes several hundred head of cattle each year. It also produces 5,000 pigs a year on slatted floors in ultramodern farrowing, nursery, and finishing sheds. Not all the farmland goes to crops and livestock. The Gilmores set aside 26 acres in 1976 as a preserve for the area's largest buffalo herd. In December that year they purchased three buffalo cows and two bulls from Bill Cummings in Stanwood, Michigan. Natural increase brought the herd to 14, roaming freely over the brush and grassland of their new home.

The Gilmore Broadcasting Company came into existence in 1962 with the purchase of station KODE-TV, AM-FM, in Joplin, Missouri. Other stations under Gilmore ownership included KGUN-TV in Tucson, Arizona, WEHT-TV in Evansville, Indiana, WSVA-TV, AM-FM, in Harrisonburg, Virginia, and WREX-TV in Rockford, Illinois. Gilmore Broadcasting entered the cable-television field in 1978 when it acquired Cumberland Valley Cablevision, and a few months later the Western Ohio Cablevision system.

For several years Jim Gilmore joined forces with Charles Zeman to develop the three Holiday Inns of Kalamazoo as well as the Continental and Holiday Lanes bowling alleys. Gilmore Enterprises continues to take on new opportunities around the country. The firm now owns the Green Turtle Restaurant and Cannery in the Florida Keys and has just completed negotiating the purchase of one of the country's largest Chevrolet dealerships with 350 employees in Miami.

"Better Your Best!" says another of W.E. Upjohn's slogans in Gilmore's office. Perhaps that particular challenge is most evident in the success of the Gilmore Racing Team. The racing tradition goes far back

in the Gilmore family. J. Stanley Gilmore raced a Cadillac to South Haven as early as 1915. His son began to sponsor Barry County race-car driver Gordon Johncock in 1967. He backed a number of other drivers before he was approached by A.J. Foyt in 1973. Foyt drove a Gilmore car in 1977 for his fourth victory at the Indianapolis 500. A.J. has won at every racetrack in the driving circuit.

Jim Gilmore took social issues as seriously as business challenges. He served on the National Cancer Advisory Board and the Citizen's Committee on Environmental Quality. In Michigan he was chairman of the Water Resources Commission as well.

In 1960 Mayor Jim Gilmore had Victor Gruen prepare a master plan for "Kalamazoo—1980." Twenty-one years later Jim Gilmore keeps a model of that plan in his lobby. In many ways the city doesn't match the planner's expectations yet. The model underscores the issues that remain. The Gilmore family has witnessed many changes in Kalamazoo in the past 100 years. J. Stanley Gilmore, who participated in many of these changes, sits as chairman of the board of Jim Gilmore Enterprises. Over 90 years old, he still comes regularly to the office. Since 1977 Jim Gilmore III has been part of the team as well. Kalamazoo may never look like the model in the lobby, but Gilmore Enterprises will continue to play a part whatever its appearance may be.

Above
Gilmore Racing Team, 1967.

Below Left
The first Gilmore Broadcasting Company station, KODE-TV, in Joplin, Missouri.

Green Bay Packaging, Inc. — Kalamazoo Container Division

Kalamazoo Container Company's offices and plant at 2810 North Burdick Street.

The corrugated box, strong, inexpensive, and adaptable to hundreds of needs, is the workhorse of mass distribution. Were it not for these simple containers the American public could not enjoy the same high standard of living. The Kalamazoo Container Division of Green Bay Packaging, Inc., is one of the area's leading producers of this vital product.

Early in the 20th century Kalamazoo became the "Paper City," producing more paper than any other area in the nation, and many paper-converting operations were established near this source of supply. David A. Howard, who was well-established in the pulp and paper business, perceived the need for such an operation and, in May 1953 established Kalamazoo Container Company with Green Bay Packaging, Inc., of Green Bay, Wisconsin, holding a 50 percent equity.

Soon other local competition emerged, but Kalamazoo Container remained in the forefront by emphasizing service and quality. A major expansion occurred in 1960 with the addition of 70,000 square feet of plant and more flexible converting equipment. Growth continued strong throughout the 1960s, highlighted by the creation of a Fremont, Ohio, division in 1964 and further major additions to the Kalamazoo plant that year. In 1967 the Fremont Division was expanded sevenfold to 140,000 square feet with full corrugating and converting capability. In February 1964 David A. Howard sold his equity, and the company became a wholly owned subsidiary of Green Bay Packaging, Inc. Howard retired in 1969. The organization he developed to succeed him provided the necessary leadership for the challenges of the ensuing decades. Early in 1972, Kalamazoo Container became a division of Green Bay Packaging, Inc.

This vigorous organization, with corporate headquarters in Green Bay, Wisconsin, began in 1933 as the Green Bay Box Company. In 1962 that company and the Green Bay Paper and Pulp Company merged to form Green Bay Packaging, Inc. The period since that merger has witnessed a steady growth for the corporation. Paperboard mills in Green Bay and in Morrilton, Arkansas, nine corrugated container plants located in eight states, a plant producing folding cartons, a converting plant for diversified products, a sawmill operation, and extensive pulpwood farms make up a totally integrated, self-sufficient corporation considered one of the nation's leading producers of corrugated packaging. What's more, Green Bay's use of sophisticated techniques to increase efficiency and a corporate philosophy emphasizing environmental responsibility, have brought recognition as a world leader in the reduction of waste and pollution.

Unbleached kraft linerboard for facings made in the Arkansas mill and corrugation medium produced in the Green Bay mill are shipped to the Kalamazoo Container Division's 170,000-square-foot plant. There, 145 employees, many with 20 to 25 years' experience, utilize a full complement of specialized modern equipment to convert enormous rolls of paper into completely finished corrugated containers. Interestingly enough, corn starch, familiar to generations of youthful scrapbook pasters, provides the cementing agent. Color-printing operations render a wide variety of advertising designs for such major area customers as Peter Eckrich & Sons, the Kirsch Company, the Upjohn Company, Westinghouse Electric, and the James River Paper Company. Over 450 million square feet of corrugated board a year are shipped to customers located throughout the marketing area of western Michigan and northwestern Indiana.

The management feels that Kalamazoo has been an ideal location for the development of the company and is strongly committed to maintaining an equally successful future relationship. Thousands of consumers across the nation live better because of corrugated containers made in Kalamazoo.

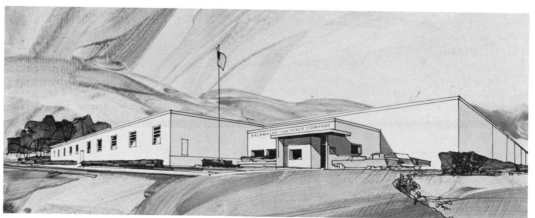

Hammond Machinery, Inc.

Left
Lee Hammond has been company president since 1941.

Above
Hammond Machinery, Inc., has been headquartered in a spacious rural setting at 1600 Douglas Avenue since 1928.

Winston Churchill once said "give us the tools and we will finish the job." For 100 years Hammond Machinery has been doing just that. Kalamazoo was a gaslight village with board sidewalks and dirt streets when William E. Hill came to town in 1881. He moved into a big empty foundry that covered the square block west of Rose from Eleanor to Kalamazoo Avenue. There the Kimball & Austin firm had made farm implements and steam engines for years. But times were changing, and machines changed with them.

Hill, a lumberman from Pennsylvania, ran one of Michigan's white-pine sawmills in Big Rapids. There he found ways to improve lumber production with steam-driven log turners and other advanced equipment. Kalamazoo provided Hill the rail connections for shipping to his markets. For the next 35 years, Hill sawmills followed the timber frontier. The company built a new foundry on Pitcher Street in 1906 and moved its entire operation there in 1912. However, the great logging era came to an end during World War I. After that, industrial America needed newer tools, this time for metalworking.

W.C. Hammond joined the firm as general manager in 1917. He developed entirely new markets in the next few years, including a line of machinery for printers. In 1921 the company purchased the grinding and polishing machine line of Webster and Perks, Springfield, Ohio, which brought the firm into the metalworking industry.

Hammond made arrangements to buy the company in 1926. Two years later he moved the plant out of a drab factory area to the spacious rural setting at 1600 Douglas Avenue. As Hammond Machinery Builders, the firm weathered the Depression, adding new machines to its product lines, chiefly for the auto and appliance industries. Lee Hammond became president in 1941, and a grandson, Robert Hammond, joined the business in 1973. As the years went by, the Hammonds added more and more working space to the Douglas Avenue plant, but left the tree-shaded grounds in front, where an old stone wall and wandering brook remind visitors of an earlier America. Hammond Machinery now has 167,000 square feet there and at a second plant in Otsego, which produces smaller machines and sheet metal fabrications.

Hammond has diversified to reduce the severity of recessions. Today the firm makes eight lines of grinding and polishing machinery for different markets, including 200 models. In the past 60 years, Hammond Machinery has shipped 127,000 metalworking machines ranging in price from a few hundred dollars to those costing in the hundreds of thousands. Those who worked with the firm and earlier developers of machinery have helped bring America from an age of hand tools, to steam and gasoline engines, to today's automated high-technology machines.

Kalamazoo has been proud of its toolmakers since the earliest engine builders and implement factories. Pioneer inventors, mechanics, and manufacturers would agree with Lee Hammond's belief that "modern man's material well-being is directly related to the creation of tools and machines." Hammond has spent more than 50 years of his own life making sure that industry had the tools to do the job.

Right
William G. Howard,
founder.

Below
John Howard, Richard
Howard, William
Howard (seated).

Long before the hurting stopped, William G. Howard and his parents knew he could never farm. Born in rural Cass County in 1846, he grew up helping his father. But now in one anguished moment he lost his arm in the newfangled McCormick reaper. Just 12 years old, he must go back to district school to fit himself for a new career. There he would be the only student studying beyond the eighth grade.

Neighbors pitched in to send him away to school. In 1867 he earned his sheepskin from Kalamazoo College. Then he read law in Nathaniel Balch's prestigious firm and gained the right to practice in 1869. He worked for a time at Niles and Dowagiac, serving a term as county prosecutor before returning as Balch's partner in 1873. As the years went by, he came to head his own office. He also took an active interest in many local firms, including the Kalamazoo Corset Company and the Lee Paper Company of Vicksburg. Townspeople elected him mayor in 1899, and his son Harry joined him in practice the same year.

Harry C. Howard graduated from the new University of Chicago in 1895 and passed his bar examination a year later. From 1902 to 1904 he served as city attorney. When William G. Howard died in 1906, Harry continued the practice without partners. He became the second tenant in the Kalamazoo Building when the city's first skyscraper went up in 1907, and the firm has remained in the building ever since.

Most early trial records have disappeared, but the cases Harry argued on appeal were printed for study by the higher court. Long-forgotten testimony comes back to life in these volumes, and Howard emerges as courtroom strategist and shrewd researcher. He is best remembered for carrying a patent infringement case to the U.S. Supreme Court on behalf of the Philo Beckwith estate. Beckwith, of the Round Oak Stove Company in Dowagiac, had developed a wood-range water reservoir with special heating properties. When competitors copied the idea too closely, Howard challenged the traditional remedy of justification and 6 cent damages and recovered actual damages and an injunction against future use unless royalties were paid to the inventor.

"Howard and Howard" appeared on the door when Harry Howard's two sons, William and John, joined the firm. William Howard studied at the University of Michigan and at Northwestern University where he received his doctor of laws degree in 1929. John earned his doctor of laws degree from the University of Chicago in 1935. William concentrated on trial practice and John focused on diversifying the firm by representing business clients such as Shakespeare Company, First National Bank, Kalamazoo Paper Company, Lee Paper Company, A.M. Todd Company, and Fetzer Broadcasting Company, among others.

Harry Howard died in 1946, but his sons continued as Howard and Howard. The firm now has 10 lawyers, including Bill's son Richard, the fourth generation in the firm, and has a diversified practice. Howard and Howard has been a partner in Kalamazoo's progress for over 100 years and plans to continue to be a partner in progress for years to come.

Illinois Envelope/Interpretive Education

During the early 20th century many paper-converting companies gravitated to Kalamazoo, "the Paper City." One such, the Illinois Envelope Company, after a 75-year career there, remains vigorously successful. It began in 1902 in Centralia, Illinois, then predominantly a coal-mining town, as an attempt to provide employment for the miners' wives and daughters. However, the company lacked a knowledgeable manager, failed to develop a successful marketing system, and within a few years faced bankruptcy.

Kalamazoo's Bryant Paper Company was the major creditor and so Noah Bryant interested a group of 200 local investors to subscribe to stock, and in 1906 the ailing business moved into a new building on Bryant Street. Conditions remained difficult for the Illinois Envelope Company during those early years but once in Kalamazoo, near its source of supply, with a capable manager and better marketing techniques, it survived. In 1914 a reorganization and the arrival of C.E. McKinstry as plant manager resulted in a stronger position. They were sorely tested in 1916 when the Bryant mill dam broke and flooded the entire first floor, destroying thousands of dollars of stock. In 1919, following the death of C.E. McKinstry, his son, M.S. McKinstry, succeeded him as general manager, remaining in that position until 1958.

The decade of the 1920s saw installation of modern equipment, glassine window machines, and automatic printing presses, and the company gained in strength by specializing in envelopes for commerce and industry. During this period workers received their wages in cash each week; consequently, payroll envelopes became a major product. During the harsh days of the Depression when many workers went without pay envelopes, the Illinois Envelope Company still managed to pay dividends to stockholders. By 1944 the company's annual report proudly announced dividends in excess of net profit, the sixth year in a row.

The year 1957 began a period of further development when John W. Lawrence and his family bought control. With Lawrence as president and general manager the following decades saw the installation of sophisticated new equipment, multiple color and offset printing presses, and automatic die-cutting machines that cut envelope blanks directly from the roll. Then, during the 1970s, the company realized the time had come for diversification.

In March 1973, Illinois Envelope purchased the Metro American Production Company which, renamed Interpretive Education, became a division with William G. Zirneklis as manager. The initial product line, 12 audiovisual programs designed for secondary-education students with learning disabilities, filled a vital need. During the following years this line expanded to over 125 different programs geared to secondary students and adult-education classes. With topics ranging from money handling to personal hygiene they provide an invaluable learning tool for teachers across the country.

In 1977 Illinois Envelope became I.E. Products, Inc., which in 1980 split into two companies. John W. Lawrence was named chairman of both firms, with Jerry G. Chew president of Illinois Envelope, Inc., and William G. Zirneklis president of Interpretive Education, Inc. In 1981 Interpretive Education launched an exciting new venture with the marketing of six initial microcomputer programs. This unique concept utilizes micro-computers programmed to provide a teaching tool that automatically individualizes content to the learner's own reading and comprehension levels.

Through imaginative application of sophisticated technology to satisfy old needs, these two companies are well-positioned for the challenges of the 1980s and beyond.

Below Left
Interpretive Education program's microcomputer teaches basic skills to students with learning disabilities.

Bottom
Current facility of Illinois Envelope Company, constructed in 1906.

Below
Humphrey arcs such as this lit America's streets at the turn of the century.

Below Right
This Humphrey ad appeared in *The Saturday Evening Post* on December 22, 1923.

In 1840 Edgar Allen Poe wrote, "Gas is totally inadmissable within doors." Poe died before gas became widely accepted; today natural and LP gas form an integral part of our civilization. A family of Kalamazoo inventors, the Humphreys, took a prominent role in bringing this about.

It started in 1886 when George Humphrey and two sons organized the Humphrey Manufacturing and Plating Company on North Burdick Street to manufacture scales. By the 1890s two other sons, Herbert S. and Alfred H., joined the company and they branched into the business of burnishing photographs using gas-heated rollers. These burnishers sparked Herbert S. to invent a pioneer water heater, and within a few years they specialized in this product. Humphrey gas water heaters achieved a worldwide popularity and the Humphrey Company flourished, but that is another story. For in 1901, Alfred H. left his job as manager and founded the General Gas Light Company to manufacture a novel product he invented, the Humphrey arc light.

By the 1890s, gas, usually manufactured by local companies, had become a popular method of lighting homes and urban streets. But the increasing adoption of electricity for street lighting threatened to consign hundreds of romantic "old lamp lighters" to the poor farm. Traditional gas lights were inefficient because the gas jets burned upward, like a bunsen burner, and despite reflectors they mostly lit the sky. Humphrey's ingenious product utilized a mantle composed of chemically treated fabric and could be placed in an inverted position, directing the light downward.

The Humphrey arc revolutionized gas lighting, made it competitive with the relatively expensive electricity, and provided another generation of songwriters with memories of "old lamp lighters." Business boomed for the General Gas Light Company. By 1906 a company plant filling an entire block on North Park Street was producing over 60,000 lamps a year. Branch offices in New York, San Francisco, Havana, London, and Bremen served a worldwide

market and eventually over 1.5 million Humphrey arcs lit homes and streets.

However, as electricity became cheaper and more available and the first primitive light bulbs gave way to more efficient types, gas lighting again waned in popularity. To survive, the company needed to develop a product to satisfy other needs. In 1916 it introduced another of Alfred Humphrey's inventions, the "radiantfire" gas heater, and a new period of prosperity followed.

Fireplaces, though inefficient and dirty, remained popular because of their romantic appeal as the traditional hearth of the home. Capitalizing on this appeal, Humphrey developed a little gas burner that fit within the fireplace, rendering it clean and odorless and freeing home owners from the chore of carrying wood in and ashes out. Increased efficiency as a form of supplemental heating was the radiantfire's major attraction. Gas flames heated "an incandescent mass of screen-like composition radiants," resembling "an interlaced mass of hot glowing twigs" which radiated heat throughout the room. Contemporary advertising proclaimed it the same type of heat that emanated from the sun and portrayed happy pipe-smoking gentlemen comfortably seated 12 feet from the radiantfire while other cold-footed specimens huddled a few feet from traditional gas logs and grates.

Throughout the 1920s, full-page advertisements in *The Saturday Evening Post* featured custom-painted, heart-warming domestic scenes, as collie dogs sprawled, half-clad children played, and grandmothers knitted before a glowing radiantfire heater. Business blazed anew and by 1925, with 700,000 units already in use, 300 employees were producing 150,000 heaters a year at the new plant on North Rose and Eleanor Street.

Radiantfire heaters were beautiful products. Surviving examples reveal a sturdy construction, gleaming brass, and elaborate designs transferred from wooden molds hand-carved by a Grand Rapids furniture craftsman. Over 30 models provided styles suitable as an "adjunct to a millionaire's mansion" as well as "within the reach of modest home owners." Decorators could choose Mission, Flemish, Old English, or Colonial styles finished in bronze, brass, silver, black, or "Verte Green Relief." By 1930 the company featured "aristocrats of the fireplace" available in period designs— Jacobean, Queen Anne, Louis XV, and models copied from a fire dog in historic Haddon Hall. They even developed a restaurant rotisserie that automatically turned meats before a bank of glowing "radiants."

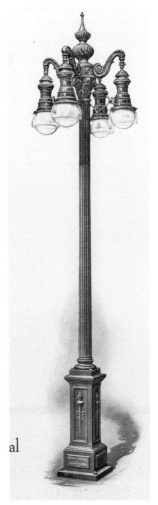

al

The HUMPHREY
Radiantfire

GOOD CHEER

The amazing success of radiantfire fireplace heaters promoted the development of a product that revolutionized commercial and industrial space heating. In the late '20s, General Gas Light Company introduced Humphrey gas-fired overhead heaters. Efficient, practical, and freeing valuable floor space, these heaters became tremendously popular in storage areas, showrooms, factories, and large office areas.

During the 1930s, the introduction of LP gas and the beginnings of the travel trailer industry led to a revival of the gas light business. Experienced in that area, the General Gas Light Company soon developed an exceptional product. By the '60s and '70s, when American enthusiasm for camping reached manic proportions, production of Humphrey indoor propane gas lights surged to more than 100,000 units a year. At that time, the company introduced another popular novelty, the "Cookit" outdoor gas grill-light combination, which allowed campers to see and cook at night from the same LP gas source.

World War II brought production of vital war materials. Commercial activities continued at a slower pace while the company devoted its facilities to manufacturing precision gun sights for aircraft, traversing mechanisms, and armored vehicle parts.

During the late '50s, when company executives saw the development of an unfavorable trend in the heater business, they decided the time was ripe for further diversification. Automation appeared to be the wave of the future and the firm tied its fortunes to this burgeoning field by venturing into the pneumatic branch of the fluid power industry. The General Gas Light Company sold the heater product line to another company and purchased a tract of land at the corner of Kilgore and Sprinkle Road for the location of a new facility.

In February 1960, the General Gas Light Company became Humphrey Products and moved to a modern new plant. There the firm manufactured pneumatic controls as well as gas lights. The new valve business flourished in response to the increasing productivity demands of American industry, and the gas light product line burgeoned with the camping industry.

Humphrey's experience in pneumatic controls increased and in 1976 the company acquired an Illinois company with closely related products. In 1979 they expanded again, acquiring Screw Machine Specialties, Inc., a Grand Haven, Michigan, manufacturer of special machined parts.

Today, pneumatic control components, used in a large variety of industries from agriculture to aerospace, comprise Humphrey's principal line. Meanwhile, Humphrey gas lights continue to shine throughout the countryside, in Amish farm houses and North Woods hunting cabins, providing a common thread in the company's 80-year history.

In 1909, three Kalamazoo companies manufactured gas lights. Two have long since vanished, but Humphrey Products, through imaginative adaptation to changing needs, remains a vigorous, home-owned employer of over 300 local residents.

Above
The General Gas Light Company factory was located on North Park Street in 1925.

Above Left
This photograph shows a service station illuminated by Humphrey gas arcs.

Below
On June 30, 1921, an entire trainload of Humphrey radiantfires left the company's factory.

Below
The original location of Johnson-Howard Lumber Company on East Water Street.

A heritage of skilled builders and artisans who learned their trade in the Netherlands, a stable diversified economy, an exceptional percentage of quality-conscious home owners, and perhaps most important, a massive civic pride, have made Kalamazoo one of the state's better markets for building materials. The Johnson-Howard Lumber Company, by providing quality materials and exceptional service, capitalized on that market, prospered, and through its success contributed to making the city a better place to live.

The company began in 1899 when William E. Mershon established a feed mill at 119-121 East Water Street. Within a few years the Mershon Company diversified into building materials. In 1910 it was the Mershon-Bartlett Company, but that year Floyd B. Johnson and C. Ray Howard purchased the business and promptly renamed it the Johnson-Howard Company. Howard did not stay as a partner for long but Johnson saw no reason to alter the company name. His company specialized in building supplies but also added a line of "coal and fuel." Around World War I a fire temporarily interrupted business and by 1921 the firm moved to the corner of North Edwards and the Michigan Central Railroad (where its headquarters is today).

Throughout the following several decades, business for Johnson-Howard ebbed and flowed with the good years and bad as the national economy stimulated or depressed the building industry. During the 1920s construction boomed and the company supplied brick for the new State Theatre and additions to Borgess Hospital. Through the 1930s, as the Depression smothered the building industries and people devoted their meager savings to survival

rather than additions to their homes, supplies were plentiful and cheap, but carpenters and contractors knew desperate times. When the early 1940s brought an end to the Depression the reverse occurred. Money grew more plentiful but World War II diverted building materials to military needs. As mills sold most of their output to the government, lumber became difficult to stock, and wartime regulations restricted all home building. When the war ended in 1945, the Johnson-Howard Company was one of five lumber suppliers in Kalamazoo's north side that had remained in business.

When the government lifted building restrictions the construction industry bounced back. The year 1945 brought a boost to Johnson-Howard, as well, when Robert Van Blarcom joined the firm as treasurer. He was born and raised in Kalamazoo, worked briefly at K.V.P., received a teaching degree from Western State Teacher's College in 1936, and after teaching in East Detroit for a few years moved back to his hometown and learned the lumber business. When he joined Johnson-Howard be brought a vitality, affability, and pride in his city that attracted and kept customers.

In 1950 Floyd Johnson died and Van Blarcom bought the company. He again saw no reason to change its name. "Do-it-yourself" became America's slogan during the 1950s, and a new breed of customers, amateur builders and returning veterans, who after building their homes sometimes turned their interest into a vocation, became an important source of trade. Bob Van Blarcom's friendly disposition attracted the novice and he became well acquainted with many citizens as they worked to complete their homes.

Continuous growth followed as Johnson-Howard diversified into a home center where today's customers, including increasing numbers of women, can choose from a broad spectrum of over 10,000 items. The work force grew from four in 1945 to 26 in 1981. While four of the five north-side lumber dealers are gone, Johnson-Howard is vigorously expanding. Bob Van Blarcom is committed to Kalamazoo's north side, and through adaptive reuse of historic structures and by creating a favorable image in his own business, he intends to encourage pride in others that will ultimately benefit the entire city.

KTS Industries

"You let a man have his own way and he will live longer," Bradley S. Williams liked to say back in the 19th century. The company he founded in 1867 followed his advice. It built things "its own way" while adapting new products to changing times and needs and as a result is still going strong. The B.S. Williams Manufacturing Company started out making wooden windmills, "The Manvel," named after Williams' partner and son-in-law, Homer Manvel. As several other Kalamazoo windmill manufacturers offered increasing competition, and wood gave way to steel, the company developed a more modern line, "The Kalamazoo," and diversified into making wooden tanks to hold the water pumped by their products.

Shortly after incorporation as the Williams Manufacturing Company in 1889, experience in constructing tanks led the company to pioneer with the country's first commercial silos. During the 1890s it also diversified into production of ensilage cutters needed to fill the silos. As more and more farmers adopted the use of ensilage and silos became a familiar sight in the rural landscape, business boomed. The first silos composed of wooden staves like giant barrels gave way to cement block and still later to glazed-tile construction but the firm remained in the forefront of each change.

In 1903, with two other local windmill companies, the firm started the Riverside Foundry to produce iron castings. The following year, to better describe its major products, Williams Manufacturing became the Kalamazoo Tank and Silo Company. The increased availability of rural electricity snuffed out Kalamazoo's once-mighty windmill industry, and in 1914 Kalamazoo Tank and Silo acquired complete control of the foundry. However, wooden construction remained popular and that same year the firm converted over five million feet of Michigan white pine, Louisiana cypress, and California redwood into thousands of tanks, troughs, and vats.

Edged out of the ensilage-cutter market by competition from larger manufacturers, the company in order to survive, again needed to diversify. In 1918 the presidency passed from Homer Manvel to his nephew and namesake Manvel Homer Coombs. He converted an old brick factory in Carbon, Indiana, the source of a particularly fine variety of clay, and produced the famous "Kalamazoo" vitrified tile blocks. As laborers using wheelbarrows loaded hundreds of boxcars for shipment across the country, silos, creameries, barns, garages, and even picturesque "California Bungalow" homes constructed of "Kalamazoo" tile became a common sight. Tile tanks proved ideal for the storage of pulp and chemicals, and local papermills became prime customers.

During the slow days of the Depression, not content with an idle machine shop, the company again diversified and became one of the three original manufacturers of horizontal band saws, used in cutting metals. Output of these saws increased dramatically during World War II, when they were declared an essential wartime industry. In 1949 Manvel Coombs's son Jack became president, and the following decades saw continued prosperity.

In 1967 Kalamazoo Tank and Silo became KTS Industries to create a clearer image of its varied products and services. Currently

this vigorous home-owned company comprises three divisions. The Saw Division produces "the world's broadest range of metal-sawing machinery" and also markets a variety of imported saws. The Tile Tank Division specializes in designing and constructing reinforced tile masonry tanks for the paper industry nationwide. The Foundry and Galvanizing Division produces nonferrous sand castings and maintains a hot-dip galvanizing operation.

Around the turn of the century, Homer Manvel offered his employees a bit of wisdom: "Jealousy and envyness is at the bottom of lots of trouble in this world and the busier you and I keep the less we will encounter, and here is a bunch busy the entire year building silos." While KTS Industries no longer builds silos, continued adaptation to meet changing needs and "Uncle" Homer's sound philosophy still ensure success.

Left
In 1904, to better describe its major products, Williams Manufacturing Company became the Kalamazoo Tank and Silo Company.

Below
KTS Industries is located at 508 Harrison Street, Kalamazoo.

Kalamazoo County Chamber of Commerce

For nearly eight decades, the Chamber of Commerce has been a common ground for representatives of all segments of the community to join together in seeking ways to improve Kalamazoo County's economy— and the prosperity and welfare of all its citizens.

Since its origin, the Chamber of Commerce has either spearheaded or actively supported nearly every major development in Kalamazoo County's history. A "co-ordinator for progress," the Chamber has played a key role in generating the variety of assets that combine to make the community's quality of life among the 10 best in the nation.

Today's Chamber of Commerce stems from the Press Club, organized in 1903 to secure the newly legislated normal school for the city of Kalamazoo. In 1904, the year the school that would become Western Michigan University held its first classes, the Press Club was reorganized as the Board of Trade, located in the Fuller Building at 141-143 South Burdick Street.

Renamed the Commercial Club in 1905, for the next 10 years it energetically pushed for improved fire and water departments, schools, and playgrounds. Under the leadership of John Burke, prominent land developer and active Chamber participant for nearly 40 years, the Club headed a drive to upgrade area hotel accommodations. That campaign reached its zenith on September 22, 1911, when more than 50,000 people lined the banner-draped streets of the Celery City as President William Howard Taft dedicated the opening of the new Burdick Hotel.

In 1915 the Commercial Club became the Kalamazoo Chamber of Commerce. First located in the Telegraph Press Building, in 1927 it moved to the newly con-structed Commerce Building at 111 North Rose Street. In its first years as a bona fide Chamber of Commerce, local business leaders like W.E. Upjohn, Frank Milham, Jacob Kindleberger, John E. Fetzer, and Paul Todd headed community improvements that still affect Kalamazoo County.

In 1917 the Chamber combined five relief agencies into "Associated Charities," then created the Kalamazoo Community Chest in 1925. The Chamber promoted the city charter revision that in 1918 resulted in adoption of a city-manager form of government. And spurred by a Chamber-initiated campaign, in 1927 Kalamazoo became the home of the first municipally owned commercial airport in Michigan.

In following decades, the Chamber sponsored projects that included a pioneer smoke-abatement program, construction of public buildings, and establishment of war services programs and industry-education conferences. From new South Street headquarters acquired in 1951, it actively supported creation of the downtown Kalamazoo Mall. Completed in 1959, the nation's first pedestrian shopping mall stimulated revitalization of Kalamazoo County's commercial hub, which remains a viable financial and shopping center today.

In 1961, recognizing the interdependence between the city of Kalamazoo and the communities surrounding it, the area's largest and strongest organization for progress became the Kalamazoo County Chamber of Commerce. Since then, the Chamber has continued to develop programs to assist the growth and prosperity of its burgeoning, countywide service area. After moving to new headquarters at 500 West Crosstown Parkway in 1973, the Chamber developed its Convention and Visitors Bureau and coordinated the unique cooperative effort between business, private industry, and government that produced the magnificent Kalamazoo Center in 1975. Cornerstone of the county's multimillion-dollar convention and tourist industry, it stands on the site of the former Burdick Hotel.

Recently the Chamber has played major roles in efforts as diverse as Central Business District revitalization, countywide economic expansion, and airport renovation. The Chamber is home of the county's Consumer/Business Bureau, and sponsors career and economic education programs at work sites and in all nine school districts in the county. For nearly eight decades, the Chamber of Commerce has been a powerful force in molding a better Kalamazoo County, serving the needs of a diverse business and industrial base and the general welfare of the community.

The Kalamazoo Foundation

More than 1,500 major donors and hundreds of gifts to memorial funds have made the Kalamazoo Foundation one of America's leading community foundations. Ranked 11th at more than $34 million, the Kalamazoo Foundation stands first in the nation in per capita assets. The foundation was established in 1925 to hold gifts and bequests in trust for the benefit of Kalamazoo County and its residents. For over half a century the organization upheld its original charge: "for assisting charitable and educational institutions; for promoting education; for scientific research; for care of the sick, aged, or helpless; for the care of children; for the betterment of living and working conditions; for recreation for all classes; and for such other public, educational, charitable, or benevolent purposes as will best make for the mental, moral, and physical improvement of the inhabitants of the county of Kalamazoo. . . ."

Early grants remained very modest. Established with an initial gift of $1,000, the foundation made its first grant five years later—$250 to help the public-school milk program in 1930. In fact, the trustees distributed only $3,750 in the first 10 years. Donald Gilmore became a trustee in 1928 and president of the board in 1934. He continued to serve until 1974. He did much along with his fellow trustees to establish the integrity of the foundation and to guide it toward its present role. After his retirement, William J. Lawrence, Jr., was appointed president and is currently serving in that capacity. Unlike private and corporate foundations, the community foundation provided a way for hundreds of local citizens to return something to the community and a way by which small efforts together could effect great ends.

New gifts and appreciating investments boosted the income as time went on. During World War II, the foundation awarded 34 grants totaling $92,741. After the war, the trustees granted three times as much money each year as they had in the first 15 years together. By 1975, grants reached nearly $2 million annually.

Following the mandate set in 1925, the Kalamazoo Foundation has continued to support innovative programs in the local schools. The trustees have also given repeatedly to Bronson Methodist and Borgess hospitals and to health-care programs ranging from the Constance Brown Society for Better Hearing to alcohol-abuse efforts. Human services grew increasingly important, accounting in 1979 for slightly over half of outlays. In the 1950s and 1960s, the foundation assisted a number of fine arts projects and continued to support the community's needs with grants for ball parks, tennis facilities, and swimming pools.

Government programs now provide "matching" grants for many projects, and the foundation has been able to assist local organizations in providing the necessary local funds. The directors have shown a particular willingness to provide seed money for new and experimental programs that might secure other funding with a successful beginning.

Community foundations play an important role in today's complex society. They provide a means by which individuals can see their gifts joined with others to fund local projects. Community groups, such as the Kalamazoo Chamber of Commerce, area banks, the probate court, and circuit court appoint trustees who bring a wide variety of interests to their task. The Kalamazoo Foundation also assures community involvement by limiting grants to nonprofit local organizations which must demonstrate that they have noted overall community needs and the services provided by other local groups. The record speaks for itself; as Howard Kalleward, executive secretary since 1966, has noted, it is a story of people working through the foundation "to make the community a better place in which to live, to work, and to raise a family."

The Kalamazoo Foundation has been serving the greater Kalamazoo area since 1925.

Left
Today the Kalamazoo *Gazette* is headquartered at 401 South Burdick Street.

Below
The original home of the Kalamazoo *Gazette*, circa 1837.

There's been a Kalamazoo *Gazette* almost as long as there's been the town itself. Henry Gilbert brought the *Michigan Statesman* to Kalamazoo County in 1835, changing its name to the Kalamazoo *Gazette* on January 23, 1837. He had 350 subscribers in 1846, when he sold the paper to his former apprentice, Volney Haskall.

County papers like the *Gazette* appeared weekly on a single folded sheet of four "sides." National news, government notices, and advertisements occupied at least three pages. Most local affairs appeared in one- or 2-line entries called jottings. Early settlers wrote letters to the editor, short stories, poetry, and occasional articles on local issues. Most editors aligned themselves with political parties, or with religious, immigrant, and fraternal interest groups. Occasionally a strong publisher appeared, like Volney Haskall or Andrew Shakespeare, but most papers passed through one owner after another.

Shakespeare printed the *Gazette* as a daily in 1872, charging subscribers eight dollars a year. Nearly 700 subscribers took the paper when F. Ford Rowe, a journalist from Rockford, Illinois, bought it in 1899. He added modern linotype machines and joined the Associated Press service, boosting circulation to 12,000 in his first seven years and to 21,000 in 1922, when he sold the paper to the Booth Publishing Company. The *Gazette* absorbed the Kalamazoo *Telegraph-Press* in 1916 to become the city's only daily. From 1912 until 1959 John K. Walsh served as editor, and Daniel M. Ryan replaced him when he retired. The paper has been owned by the Newhouse newspapers since 1977.

The *Gazette* serves well over 60,000 subscribers in seven counties of southwestern Michigan but remains a metropolitan daily with deep roots in downtown Kalamazoo. The paper moved to its present location in 1925 and enlarged its quarters in 1948 and again in 1968, more than tripling its working space. The first in

Michigan to use Wirephoto transmission, it was one of the first half-dozen papers in the nation to convert to electronic printing in 1959 and now receives news copy via satellite transmission.

But a daily newspaper is more than electronic printing and satellite communication. The *Gazette* puts together a news "package" designed to give people "what they need to live knowledgeably and productively." Demographic surveys test the market on every possible interest. The paper offers a regular "Viewpoint" column for reader comment and prints close to 2,000 letters a year. "My phone is listed," says editor Ryan, and readers feel free to tell him what they like and don't like. A single paper in a city has a responsibility for fairness. In times of social change, all sides may blame the press, but the newspaper has an obligation to present all sides of issues in its news columns, and its own views in its editorial columns.

In an age dominated by television, the *Gazette* circulation continues to grow. Dan Ryan believes that "people like to read about people." They want to know what others are doing, and they like to see them helping each other. They want to know about young people and older people and what's happening down the street. Newspapers give readers a chance to choose what they wish to read and to absorb it at their own speed. Advertisements and coupons help them cope with family budgets; want ads become a community information exchange. Papers provide background to world events along with coverage of state and local affairs. Reflecting the town's several colleges and cultural outlets, the *Gazette* gives more space to the arts and entertainment than most newspapers in the country.

The *Gazette* acts as a collective memory for the community as well. On occasions like the paper's 100th anniversary, or the nation's bicentennial, special historical editions give even newcomers a sense of community tradition. Yellowed clippings of bygone news fill many local scrapbooks along with old-fashioned snapshots and greeting cards. In a real sense, Kalamazoo's oldest business has fulfilled its longtime pledge to be "a member of the family."

Kalamazoo Radiology

As Caroline Bartlett Crane, Kalamazoo's ambitious, turn-of-the-century social reformer, attracted national attention through her clean streets, meat inspection, and prison improvement crusades, her husband, Augustus Warren Crane, carved out an equally spectacular career in the field of medicine. Dr. Crane established a general practice of medicine and surgery in Kalamazoo in 1894 and the following year he became the city bacteriologist, the first such position in Michigan. By 1906 he confined his practice to internal medicine and still later to diagnostic and consultive services. However, Dr. Crane's major accomplishments centered around his role as a pioneer in the field of radiology.

Wilhelm Konrad Roentgen first detected X-rays in 1895, and by March 1897 Dr. Crane had installed his first primitive and largely handmade X-ray machine. His earliest paper on the X-ray, first read before the Kalamazoo Academy of Medicine in 1898, "The Roentgen Ray in Disease of the Lungs," was later extensively reprinted and remains a pioneering classic in the field. Ultimately Crane's bibliography ran to over 40 items and his research and lectures in roentgenology led to adoption of improved methods. His work in application of the X-ray to gastrointestinal diagnosis, invention of the kymograph (the first X-ray instrument designed to study a single body organ, the heart), and other innovative applications resulted in numerous awards and international fame. In 1905 Drs. Crane and Pfahler were the first to recognize skin reactions to X-ray exposure. Crane's early concern with covering the X-ray tube with heavy shoe leather as a protective device, and his accidental use of high lead content plate glass for fluoroscopy probably saved him from the fate of most other pioneer radiologists, known as the "martyrs."

Dr. Crane's inventive genius manifested itself in other nonmedical applications as well, including a patented electric automobile starter in 1914, and an attempt to create a better golf ball by inserting aerobic bacilli into the ball's hollow core to maintain central pressure. In 1914 Dr. John B. Jackson from Rush Medical College joined Dr. Crane. Their practice, conducted from an office located in Crane's home at 420 South Rose Street, the present site of the Kalamazoo Police Department, thrived until Dr. Crane's death in 1937.

By that time patient volume had outgrown the X-ray office so Drs. Jackson, Volderauer, and Hildreth purchased land at 458 West South Street. There in 1939 a new building was completed which served the growing firm until 1976. However, the explosion of new knowledge, techniques, and equipment in the X-ray field those decades produced, and a staff that had grown to 11 doctors by 1973 necessitated frequent remodelings and additions. Then, in 1974, the old Third Christian Reformed Church at 524 South Park Street became available and the firm made the decision to construct a new building. The church was razed, and by July 1976 Kalamazoo Radiology occupied a modern structure designed by Haughey, Black and Associates, Inc. It contains over 25,000 feet of work space and many conveniences, including eight X-ray rooms, an ample film storage area, a computer, and a public waiting area seating 66.

The period since the 1950s, in particular, saw the X-ray field become increasingly more complex and sophisticated and as the area matured medically the number of doctors serving Kalamazoo rose from 150 in 1954 to 480 in 1981. Kalamazoo Radiology has responded by adopting new pro-

cedures and equipment as soon as they were clinically accepted and by adding staff to handle the increasing patient volume. Currently, the private clinic's 14 doctors, eight X-ray technicians, and 28 other support employees provide diagnostic X-ray services to the clinic practice, the expanded Borgess and Bronson hospitals, other smaller area hospitals, and also perform film reading for outside groups. Kalamazoo Radiology, the largest such group in western Michigan, has come a long way in the more than eight decades since Dr. Crane pioneered with his handmade X-ray equipment.

Right
In 1976 the Kalamazoo Nature Center restored an adjacent 1858 structure, the DeLano Homestead, as a Bicentennial project. There visitors experience pioneer craft demonstrations and learn the history of Michigan rural life.

Far Right
The Interpretive Center houses administrative offices, a laboratory, natural history shop, comprehensive environmental reference library, and live exhibits of animals and plants to interpret basic ecological principles.

It began with an insect collection and walks in the woods with a father who taught him to identify birds. Soon his curiosity as to why animals acted the way they did led young Lewis Batts, Jr., to serious study and the development of a lifelong respect for nature. In 1950 he began a 30-year career as a professor of biology at Kalamazoo College. As he studied the distribution patterns of birds and their relationship to humans, Batts became convinced that the behavior of certain species was an indicator of environmental conditions important to people. He became increasingly concerned about his observations of these birds in his own Kalamazoo environment.

As he surveyed his country he saw the results of burgeoning industrial and residential development based almost solely on economic factors—pollution of air, water, and soil; ugly buildings and roadways; fields paved with asphalt; plant life needlessly sacrificed; exhaustion of limited natural resources; and worst of all, increasing numbers of city-raised children who grew into adults without an understanding of their relationship with nature. As a biology professor he could teach his students, but Dr. Batts knew that if this trend was to be curbed a much broader effort to educate the general public in basic natural cause-and-effect relationships was needed.

Cooper's Glen, a secluded grove on the banks of the Kalamazoo River north of the city, long had been a favorite site for picnics, nature outings, and student field trips, but by the late 1950s dumping of solid wastes, asphalt manufacture, and gravel extraction threatened to end its natural beauty. This galvanized Dr. Batts to form a small organization of local citizens concerned with saving the glen and adjacent land. He took a year off from his teaching to raise the money to purchase the site and by 1961 the incipient Kalamazoo Nature Center began acquiring land.

By 1964 an Interpretive Center, a unique geodesic-domed structure, stood complete on a 500-acre preserve. It housed administrative offices, a laboratory, natural history shop, comprehensive environmental reference library, and live exhibits of animals and plants to interpret basic ecological principles. However, Nature herself provides the major attraction to the more than 100,000 annual visitors who see, feel, hear, smell, touch, and taste the changing seasons.

From the Interpretive Center five miles of pedestrian trails tunnel through forests of beech and maple carpeted with ferns and an ever-changing array of wild flowers; wind along the Kalamazoo River bank; traverse old farm fields reverting to natural meadows and thickets; and skirt marshes and cattail-bordered ponds alive with croaking frogs. Everywhere insects, amphibians, rare and common birds, muskrats, raccoons, chipmunks, and hundreds of varieties of plants lead unmolested lives.

Two hundred acres provide a demonstration farm where visitors see and touch farm animals and view Indian, pioneer, and organic gardens as well as cultivated fields, contrasting experiments in "natural" farming with artificial modern methods. The year 1972 saw the dedication of a 25-acre memorial arboretum which now contains hundreds of varieties of trees, shrubs, and flowers, providing an invaluable resource for species identification.

In 1976 the Nature Center restored an adjacent 1858 structure, the DeLano Homestead, as a Bicentennial project. There visitors experience pioneer craft demonstrations and learn the history of Michigan rural life. In 1977 the Living Systems Program began to test and demonstrate alternatives to using nonrenewable resources for the production of food, shelter, and energy.

The staff of the Nature Center, including many volunteers, conducts youth programs and guided interpretive tours, trains teachers in environmental education, offers research and consultation services, and produces a variety of natural history resources. A pioneering venture with no pattern to follow, the Kalamazoo Nature Center has served as a guide to other similar developments across the country. This nonprofit educational institution, unsubsidized by government funds, has made southwestern Michigan a better place to live.

Parkview Hills

While the Kalamazoo Nature Center serves as an ecologically oriented recreational facility and a tool for educating thousands of people, Dr. Lewis Batts knew that this alone would probably not reach those who made some of the greatest adverse changes in the natural environment—developers. An example was needed to change prevailing attitudes which placed overwhelming emphasis on economic factors at the expense of the environment. Dr. Batts determined to provide such an illustration through Parkview Hills, a planned unit development (PUD) calculated to demonstrate to contractors, planners, and engineers that ecological and aesthetic values need not be inconsistent with economics.

In 1970 Batts purchased a 288-acre tract of rolling submarginal farmland on Kalamazoo's south side and joined with Burton Upjohn to accomplish this demonstration. Upjohn, while directing the building and marketing, contributed the practical businessman's savvy necessary to blend environmental objectives with economic viability. Victor Gruen and Associates of New York, who had originated the idea of Kalamazoo's downtown pedestrian mall in the 1950s, provided the planning. The Kalamazoo City Commission soon passed a PUD ordinance, allowing for rezoning compromises, and on June 5, 1970, construction crews began work.

Construction workers soon discovered that this was no ordinary project. Roads snaked around the existing landscape as bulldozer operators veered around bushes, and engineers learned new techniques in running sewer lines around and under trees. The entire project reflected Dr. Batts's ecological ideal, "to produce a state of harmony between people and the land." Dwelling lots platted on the high areas permitted scenic views for all, while low spots containing the best vegetation remained largely untouched. Structures designed to be "looked out of and not at" were integrated into the natural environment, and garages and embankments kept parked automobiles out of sight.

The tract bordered on two small natural lakes, Lime Kiln and Hill 'N' Brook; and Little Portage Creek, a moribund stream, when dredged and dammed provided two other lakes, Cherry Creek and Willow. Traditionally, deep wells provided city water but acres of blacktop and storm sewers channeling rain water via the Kalamazoo River into Lake Michigan failed to replenish the aquifer. By maintaining a high level on these two man-made lakes, water percolated down through a sand layer while a runoff system conducting storm water to

catch basins allowed detention of 70 percent of the rainfall. These bodies of water remained clean through the development of a raft that cut algae (rather than killing it chemically), the use of sand on roads in winter, and a fescue (grass) not requiring chemical fertilizer as sod.

Over 100 acres remain permanent open space, including at least 20 feet around marshlands and waterways. Four miles of nature trails ramble through groves of wild cherry and oak, providing excellent hiking and cross-country skiing.

Following the basic ecological principal that the success of any community depends on diversity, Dr. Batts worked at achieving it in several ways. Structures include a mixture of condominium townhouses and apartments, rental apartments and townhouses, and single-family homes, as well as three small office buildings, a 10-shop convenience center, a 200-seat restaurant, and a community clubhouse. Architectural diversity was ensured by engaging a variety of architects. While traditional neighborhoods consist of residents of similar income levels, the wide variation in price levels at Parkview Hills guarantees a healthy mixture of residents' backgrounds. Bank presidents, doctors, and lawyers rub elbows with newlyweds, retired persons, and clerical workers, bound only by a common love of nature.

Through this amalgamation of sophistication and Arcadian ideals, Dr. Batts and Mr. Upjohn demonstrated to the world that it is cheaper to leave nature intact than to destroy, and a phenomenal rate of tenancy has provided final vindication for the experiment.

Parkview Hills, a 288-acre planned unit development (PUD) on Kalamazoo's south side, has successfully demonstrated that ecological and aesthetic values need not be inconsistent with economic concerns.

Kalamazoo Savings and Loan Association

The need for a system to assist working-class Kalamazooans to finance their homes gave rise to the city's first building and loan association. Such associations were popular in the East, and Judge William W. Peck first learned of them during a trip to his hometown in New York State. Intrigued with the idea, he convinced a number of brother Oddfellows to join him and on February 11, 1886, the Kalamazoo Building and Loan Association came into existence.

The original constitution specified, "Its object shall be to enable its members, through their savings of weekly dues or assessments, to build or buy a home or to establish or carry on some business." Members bought stock in the association, paid 25 cents a week per share, and each time the treasurer accumulated $125 this cash was auctioned off to the member willing to pay back the most interest. Twenty-five cents amounted to something in the 1880s, when skilled laborers earned $8 to $12 a week and members were fined for missing a weekly payment. Needless to say, the system encouraged thrift and as members transformed their savings into home ownership the young association prospered and grew.

From the first tiny office on the second floor of 107 East Michigan the association expanded to larger quarters in a corner basement at Rose Street and West Michigan. In 1907 it moved to E.M. Dingley's new Telegraph Building, later the Park Building, and in 1911 again relocated to the Majestic Building, later the Capitol Theatre Building. Finally, in 1930, the firmly established association moved to its present location at 215 East Michigan Avenue. Within a few years, to emphasize its other functions, it became the Kalamazoo Savings and Loan Association.

William Murray served as the first financial secretary in 1886. Judge Peck's son, William H., succeeded him and served until 1933. Edward M. Kennedy held the position until his death in 1935, when Karl Hepp assumed the position until 1946.

The Depression brought bank panics, and prior to the system of federally insured savings some banks were forced to default and close. Because savings and loans maintained a different corporate structure they made payments on a revolving system and weathered the hard financial times better. No depositor lost any of his savings at the Kalamazoo Savings and Loan Association.

By 1947 Kalamazoo was nationally known as a city with an unusually high percentage of home ownership and thousands of those homes had been financed at Kalamazoo Savings and Loan. That year assets stood at $1.55 million, and Fred Reynolds was elected secretary-treasurer. In 1957 he became president. Under Reynolds's vigorous leadership and fundamental principle, "We finance homes, not just houses," the association made tremendous gains. By 1959 assets surpassed $17 million.

That year the association took an active role in the early stages of what would become an exceptionally successful revitalization of the city's downtown when it tore down several old structures and erected new facilities. Architecturally modernistic and incorporating many avant-garde features, the building boasted a heated sidewalk and driveway, closed-circuit TV, computer service, and the city's first drive-through service with a drive-up window. A grand opening celebration attracted thousands and ushered in a 2-decade period of further development as the association offered more sophisticated savings and banking service to increasing numbers of members.

By 1981 assets had grown to $158 million and within the year a merger with First Federal Savings and Loan of Detroit brought combined assets of nearly $4 billion, sophisticated computer facilities, better services, and more money available for Kalamazoo's burgeoning needs. While the passing years have produced changed life-styles and apartment and condominium living, the association's goal remains to encourage thrift and to assist families in achieving the security and independence that come from home ownership.

Kingscott Associates, Inc., Architects & Engineers

Kingscott Associates, Inc., Architects & Engineers has left its mark in Kalamazoo for more than half a century. Yet the thousands who pass through the Industrial & Engineering Technology Building on WMU's campus, the Kalamazoo Public Library, Sangren Hall, or New Central High School may never realize that Louis C. Kingscott and his architects did so much to shape the community. Kingscott started his firm in 1929. "It was an age of giants then," says current president James Bentley, speaking of Frank Lloyd Wright, Mies van der Rohe, and other strong-willed individualists who dominated their fields. Louis Kingscott led his firm through the trying times of the Depression and wartime shortages. Always active in politics, he secured a variety of government projects during those years. Later, when the postwar baby boom began, he specialized in school designs.

The firm commanded wide respect throughout the Midwest. Kingscott kept 60 or more employees at work in Kalamazoo and at four regional offices as far away as Iowa and Washington, D.C. Times changed for many architectural firms in the 1960s, and Kingscott changed with them. In January of 1973, Jim Bentley came from the Iowa office to head Kingscott Associates. Ownership of the firm was broadened. The company was reorganized, bringing all operations under one roof in Kalamazoo and trimming the staff to between 30 and 40 people. By the 1970s architectural practice could no longer be "a launching pad for egos," as Bentley put it. The era of giants had ended in rising energy costs, government regulation, and tightened economy. Clients now wanted architectural firms with sound management practices. Employees wanted a sense of personal involvement in their company's projects.

The firm met both needs with a new way of practicing architecture—a team approach. People were organized into groups that could be assigned a project from start to finish. Now clients could deal with a single team leader on a one-to-one basis, and the leader could draw on the expertise of his team members as problems arose. No longer did each employee play only one small part in the design project. Now the team met again and again to review all stages. Independent "gatekeepers" watched over the process to maintain quality control, and all reported to the president.

Clients approved and the firm prospered in spite of recession, higher interest rates, and the end of the baby boom. Yet smooth management alone could not meet every need; the uneasy times at the end of the 1970s called for yet another response. Clients now wanted "management with heart." Understanding clients' needs seemed more important than ever before. Twenty-five years earlier, Louis Kingscott had advocated "optimum satisfaction for the owner," but now the firm would take positive steps to identify the components of that satisfaction with all the skill of practicing psychologists.

The '70s brought other changes as well. Bentley served for years on the Kalamazoo Historic District Commission and led the firm into exciting projects combining architectural heritage with present needs and technology. Kingscott Associates brought the old and new together in Michigan's first "intermodal transportation center" at the 1887 railroad station which is now on the National Register of Historic Sites. In 1979 the Michigan State Legislature acknowledged Kingscott's awareness by noting, "their implementation of energy-conservation programs and building recycling projects is an immense asset to us all."

As Kingscott Associates celebrated its 50th anniversary in 1979, the firm brought together "the traditions and standards established in 1929 with the knowledge and skill needed to prosper in the 1980s." As Bentley wrote then, "we now have the foundation to look ahead to our next 50 years."

Left
The award-winning Borgess Professional Building was designed by Kingscott Associates.

Below
WMU Printing Services Building, completed in 1940.

Above
Knappen Milling
Company's current
facility.

Right
Knappen Milling
Company, 1936.

When Kalamazoo County first opened to settlement in the 1830s, some men looked for land and others for water to turn the wheels of industry. Epaphroditus Ransom organized the Augusta Company in 1836 and laid out village lots where Augusta Creek fell to the Kalamazoo River. The company paid George Rigby $1,500 to dig a canal, build a dam and bridge, and lay the foundations for a sawmill. In the next 10 years this sawmill supplied timbers and ties to the men who built the Michigan Central Railroad. But once the railroad reached Kalamazoo in 1846, the mill was pushed aside for a flour mill shipping stone-ground local wheat to eastern markets.

Eugene Knappen was 13 when his family settled on farmland near Richland in 1833. When his father, Mason Knappen, died in 1857, Eugene and his brother continued to farm the land until 1892, when Knappen opened a country elevator in Richland. He was joined by his son, Charles.

Charles B. Knappen bought the Augusta Mill in 1929. The Depression brought problems, but he added on to the old mill in 1938, and again in 1941 and 1946. Charles B. Knappen, Jr., came to work when he returned from service after World War II. He headed the firm when his father died in 1962 and presently serves as chairman of the board. His son, C.B. Knappen III, is now president.

As late as 1963, water from the old canal still provided a third of the company's power. In that year, Knappen completed the modern 6-story mill which forms the heart of present operations. Machines in this new mill operate around the clock, turning two million bushels of Michigan "soft" white wheat into bran and flour. The wheat is "fluidized" with air and whisked along in tubes to keep it free from contamination. Modern machinery meets clean-air standards, and the entire mill is pressurized to prevent insects from entering through cracks around doors or windows. Half the mill machinery cleans foreign particles from the grain, and the other half grades, grinds, sifts, and packages bran and flour. Humidity and temperature are carefully monitored and care is taken that a uniform, dependable product is the end result.

Millers often considered bran a waste product to be fed to livestock, but the Knappen Company began producing bran for human use in 1930. Today all of this bran goes to cereal manufacturers and the flour to bakeries and flour blenders who appreciate the characteristics of Michigan's soft white wheat.

There has been a mill at the corner of Canal Street and Clinton for nearly 150 years. In pioneer times, settlers depended on water-powered mills for their local needs. All through the 19th century, flour and gristmills ranked third in Michigan's industries after sawmills and village blacksmiths. As late as 1900, more than 700 such mills dotted the state. But more and more flour came from "hard" western wheat ground in St. Louis, Minneapolis, or Buffalo. When the Knappens came to Augusta in 1929, there were 400 mills in Michigan. Now there are eight! Knappen remains competitive with special products

and modern equipment. Nevertheless, the firm opened a second endeavor in 1970—the Great Lakes Electronics Company which wholesales electronics parts around the Midwest. In addition, the Knappen Company provides local elevators with a full line of farm supplies.

The Knappens needed all of their pioneer spirit when a tornado struck the plant head-on in April 1977. The remains of a nearby house smashed into the top of the new mill; one warehouse was a total loss. All in all, the twister did a million dollars in damage in a few seconds. But the firm's 50 employees rallied to clear debris and make emergency repairs. The mill lost only 20 hours' running time in all. Knappen Milling Company celebrated its 50th anniversary in 1979.

Michigan Ice Service

In 1893 Kalamazoo suffered a particularly cold winter and by February the ice stood 14 inches thick on nearby lakes. While unpleasant for most, this inclement weather proved an auspicious beginning for George Steers's newly incorporated Kalamazoo Ice and Fuel Company.

George Steers had moved from New York State to Kalamazoo in the 1870s where he worked as a teamster. In the winter he hauled cordwood, then the only fuel used in Kalamazoo, and ice from storage houses in the summer. During this period most residences lacked refrigeration facilities and Steers's major customers were butchers and brewers, who cooled their cellars as beer slowly aged. The innovative Steers brought the first carload of coal to Kalamazoo in the early 1880s. He had difficulty at first convincing anyone to buy it, with wood so plentiful, but by the 1890s many had adopted coal burners.

However, ice remained his major interest. Before the age of mechanical refrigeration, ice was harvested from ponds and lakes in the winter and stored for summer consumption in huge icehouses. Gangs of men lived in bunkhouses while spending the winter practicing this specialized occupation. Burly laborers first scored the ice with horse-drawn ice plows, then used special crosscut saws to cut manageable cakes, which they hauled to thick-walled storage houses and packed between layers of sawdust. Huge icehouses often burned, so the Kalamazoo Ice and Fuel Company maintained numerous smaller facilities on Clark's Lake, Lime Kiln Lake, Oakwood Lake, Sand Lake near Nottawa in St. Joseph County, and in the city, where Arcadia Creek was dammed to form a pond where Western Michigan University's football stadium now stands. During warm winters the company harvested and stored ice farther north, hauling it to Kalamazoo via the railroad when needed.

The winter of 1907-08 proved particularly mild and as a result Steers became interested in producing artificial ice. In 1909 he installed a mechanical plant which oper-

ated like a huge refrigerator. Again many customers resisted this innovation and it took a few years to convince them that artificial ice was as cold as natural ice.

In 1916 George Steers, Jr., joined his father's thriving business and in 1922 they moved their operation to the lumber and planing mill on Kalamazoo Avenue, long operated by Dewing and Son. By 1925 they maintained 30 neighborhood ice stations, and another 30 ice wagons daily delivered blocks of ice to Kalamazoo consumers. As late as 1947, over 4,000 local families still relied on the company's ice delivery for home refrigeration.

George Steers, Jr., continued to operate the firm until his death in 1971 when Stuart Hargie, who had worked there for 25 years, and his son Michael bought the enterprise. During the following decade their energetic management caused business to increase fourfold. The renamed Michigan Ice Service markets wholesale ice throughout southern Michigan. Locally, old wooden ice boxes have found new life as eagerly sought antiques, but the company still supplies over 2,000 Amish families with block ice for home use.

New needs for ice have stimulated increased demand. Convenience dictates most ice sales now and 90 percent of the production is crushed ice. However, block ice added to wet cement keeps the temperature down, allowing it to cure stronger, and the company has furnished ice used in the construction of the Cook and Pallisades nuclear plants. As ice is predominantly a seasonal business, during the cold months the company reverses its role and markets coal and salt to melt icy sidewalks.

Sophisticated automated machinery installed in 1981 made the plant one of the most modern in the country, capable of producing 50 bags of crushed ice a minute. Michael Hargie is now president and he loves his business. It doesn't take high-pressure selling—a customer either wants ice or not—and most important, as Hargie says "there's no deceit in a bag of ice."

Left
Harvesting ice on Sand Lake near Nottawa.

Below Left
Kalamazoo Ice and Fuel Company office, 1914.

Right
Miller Lumber Company's original office, circa 1936.

Below
The firm's mill work department, mid-1930s.

Miller Lumber Company has been located at the corner of Lane Boulevard and Factory Street for more than half a century. Presently the largest retail building-material supplier in western Michigan, the company grew out of O.F. Miller's belief that "it might as well be carried on right." As an admiring reporter wrote in the *American Lumberman* in 1937, " 'right' it is with a capital R!" Orville Miller learned the lumber business from the other side of the counter. City directories listed him as a "contractor" as early as 1910. Over the years, friends and customers beat a path to his office asking for help locating building supplies. He saw "the demand grow and grow until the first thing I knew I was in a complete retail building-material business." Miller bought 13 acres of land near the old Roamer Motor Car plant on Factory Street and opened for business in 1928. His first office was no bigger than a toolshed, but in 1930 he had New York architect Aymar Embury II design a fine 2-story colonial headquarters at the front of the lot.

Many firms marked time during the Depression, but not Miller Lumber. Better to "get ready for a rush of business during the slack time" said Miller. He added storage sheds and a fireproof brick mill work building. Another 60-foot by 180-foot addition for offices and mill work came in 1937. That same year he started the Miller Sash and Door Company which serves lumberyards today in western Michigan, northern Indiana, and northwestern Ohio.

O.F. still headed the company when World War II broke out. His sons Fred and John were vice-president and treasurer, and William Klempp served as general manager. During the war the company made oak tread returns for army tanks, and bodies for military cargo trailers. The postwar upheaval hit the building industry hard. Lumber was scarce, other building materials hard to come by. Miller had to improvise its own rationing system to allocate dwindling supplies. When things eventually returned to normal, the company found itself facing a new development. "Do-it-yourselfers" arrived in growing numbers. They asked more questions and placed smaller orders, and they needed tools as well as building supplies. To meet their needs, Miller Lumber became Kalamazoo's foremost home-supply center.

The Miller lumberyard, which the *American Lumberman* described as "clean as a New England kitchen," has been a good place to work. Twenty-five of the firm's 95 employees have been there for a quarter-century or more. Ralph Gilbert came in 1965 as treasurer. He became president of Miller Lumber Company in 1969. Leonard Klok is presently executive vice-president and Henry Terlaak, treasurer.

California bungalows, redwood, and rock lath were all the fashion when Miller Lumber started. Now the styles are California ranch house, formica, and prefinished paneling, but some things at Miller are still the same—quality materials, dependable service, and the "big tree" log end in front of the office. Back in 1932, Miller Lumber ordered western redwood by the carload. The Redwood Sales Company sent along a bonus in one shipment—a log slice from a 600-year-old Sequoia. For nearly half a century, that log slice has stood as a reminder of O.F. Miller's faith in the lumber industry.

John B. Olheiser, Inc.

Realtors provide a vital function in the American way of life with its high degree of mobility and changing cultural patterns. A real estate company that has earned a reputation of honesty and sincerity is John B. Olheiser, Inc., of 3027 Portage Street.

John B. and Betty Olheiser launched the firm in June 1965 at its present location. John B. Olheiser had led a varied life, working in the Army Air Corps in the early 1930s, as a mill worker for U.S. Steel, and as an aluminum salesman. When John was transferred to Kalamazoo in 1956, his wife Betty started a career as a real estate salesperson with an established realtor. The following year John joined her. After eight years of learning and experience the Olheisers struck out for themselves, founding an organization oriented toward developing a staff of full-time dedicated professionals who would ultimately share in the firm's ownership.

John's solid philosophy, a dynamic mixture of innovation and fiscal soundness, and Betty's flair produced a vigorous growth record. Both assumed leadership roles in their profession as well, John as president of the Kalamazoo Board of Realtors and Betty as the only female member of Governor Milliken's Task Force on Land Use, created to make recommendations for preserving the state's environment. A well-trained staff, guided by Olheiser's philosophy of total dedication to serving the public and utmost attention to detail, and innovative marketing techniques featuring a creative advertising style resulted in an unbeatable system that came to be known as the "Olheiser Way." The firm developed a tradition as a training ground for young realtors, while hundreds of area homeowners benefited from the "Olheiser Way." In 1976 the firm was involved in the sale of nearly $20 million in property, 10 percent of the total volume of the Kalamazoo Board of Realtors.

In 1973 Woody King joined the Olheiser staff. Following graduation from Albion College with a degree in physics and mathematics in 1965, he had gone to work for

the IBM Corporation. Under IBM direction King evolved into an expert salesman with a territory covering southwestern Michigan; and he not only learned salesmanship but corporate discipline. Then, in 1973, on the verge of a transfer up the corporate ladder to Washington, King and his wife faced a difficult decision. They, like so many others, had fallen under the spell of Kalamazoo and were reluctant to leave. They chose Kalamazoo and a new career.

King adapted well to his new career as a realtor for Olheiser and within three years he was top salesman. He enjoyed particular success with the inception and marketing of two upper middle class developments, Sturbridge in Richland Township and Forest Hills in Portage. In 1978 Woody King experimented with his own enterprise, Selling Systems, Inc., a packaged series of presentations designed to increase the sales potential of any business. But the following year, when John and Betty Olheiser decided to retire and sell the business to their staff, they wanted King to head the new corporation. Consequently, in July 1979, Woody King became owner of John B. Olheiser, Inc.

King's innovative leadership, a blend of IBM-learned discipline and the heritage of common sense and decency from the Olheisers, sparked a new era in the company's development. King recognizes this as a critical period in the firm's history and his goal is to accomplish a shift away from a traditional entrepreneurial status, with success dependent on the charisma of the founder, to a corporation that will survive personnel changes. He utilizes sophisticated equipment including computer terminals and videotape training programs and has strengthened the loyalty of his sales force through an innovative stock option plan and a commission plan that encourages individual achievement. Despite the unparalleled challenges to realtors brought by the inflation-plagued and high-interest-ridden 1980s, the "Olheiser Way" continues as a well-respected asset to life in Kalamazoo.

John B. Olheiser, Inc., has been selling properties in Kalamazoo since 1965.

Pension & Group Services, Inc.

development is Pension & Group Services, Inc.

Established in 1965 by John M. Connors, Pension & Group Services, Inc., offers administrative, actuarial, and consulting services to employee-benefit clients. While a few large firms offered similar services for clientele in large metropolitan areas, the needs of smaller cities and rural areas went unanswered.

Kalamazoo's central location and progressive attitude proved conducive to the selection of the site of this new corporation. As the firm continued to acquire new clients, it became necessary to increase its staff. Exceptionally talented people experienced in the benefits field were encouraged to visit Kalamazoo and were asked to join P&G and make the city their home. Local residents joined the firm and were trained by a growing number of benefit specialists. From a meager beginning of two employees in April 1965, P&G now has 100 employees and operates in 50 states.

Much of the business history of Kalamazoo, as with many successful business communities, is the result of people having the foresight to develop widely needed products and services. A company that has been unusually successful in this

One of the nation's strongest management teams emerged, and with the support of dedicated, intelligent employees, a record 3,000 plans are now being serviced by P&G's staff. The corporation now operates nine divisions providing the following services on a fee-for-service basis: actuarial, administrative, computer, consulting, and health claim services; insured self-funded plans; ERISA reporting and disclosure; insured medical reimbursement plans; and health cost containment.

These employee benefit services are offered to many regional accounts including the First American Bank Corporation, Borgess Hospital, Jim Gilmore Enterprises, Industrial State Bank and Trust Company of Michigan, Checker Motors Corporation, Stryker Corporation, Clausing Corporation, several building trades, and the Michigan Educational Special Services Association (MESSA). The planned rate of growth in the future is as optimistic as the past growth rate. Pension & Group Services, Inc., forecasts employing 500 people within the 1980s.

Because of its growth and commitment to downtown Kalamazoo, Pension & Group Services, Inc., consolidated its headquarters into five floors of the Haymarket Building, a renovated office facility. Combining the beauty of 19th-century architecture with the modern refinements and technological advances of today, the Haymarket serves as an outstanding corporate headquarters. An ideal location, the offices are close to the city's economic center and major customers, and provide room for future expansion and an outstanding working environment for employees.

Pneumo Corporation, National Water Lift Company Division

A 1912 nonelectric water pump used to pump soft rainwater from residential cisterns to the point of use. This unique design used city water pressure in motor piston to drive pumping piston.

Even Jules Verne couldn't imagine guided missiles, jet transports, and aerospace technology when Roland Fairchild was born in 1876. Yet the company he founded, National Water Lift, is today one of the free world's largest producers of the flight-control equipment that makes jet travel possible. On the other hand, none of today's dictionaries tell us what a "water lift" might have been.

Roland grew up on Portage south of Washington Square. His father was a builder who taught by the old adage, "if you want it done right, do it yourself." Roland's brothers were builders, too. One sister took in sewing and another taught school. Young Fairchild studied drafting for a time and then went to work for his

petitors cut costs with cast iron.

Fairchild never really expanded, but he kept busy making better pumps all through the Depression. He patented a gear-driven deep-well pump in 1930 and a gearless pump a few years later. World War II found him still in the house where he was born and making his pumps next door. He had just taken on his first defense contract when he died suddenly in the summer of 1942.

Another local man, Severens Balch, bought National Water Lift from the estate two months later. Balch had been an engineer at the Watervliet Paper Company for years before going into business for himself in 1941. He decided to use his engineering background in producing the

brother-in-law, Fred Humphrey, as a machinist. Humphrey made pumps run by city water pressure and called them "water lifts." Fairchild was 33 and general manager of the Humphrey Company in 1904, but he thought he could build a better water lift and left to form his own company. He became president of National Water Lift that year. His vice-president, Fred Dewey, prudently kept his job as cashier in the Kalamazoo Savings Bank.

During the summer of 1909, the state factory inspector visited 196 manufacturers in Kalamazoo. He found Fairchild and two employees making water lifts in a small downtown plant. Over the next 10 years, the inspector never reported more than four people at work; yet Fairchild didn't intend to quit. He moved his operation to his side lot on Portage where his wife Charlene acted as secretary and later as vice-president. Fairchild patented his own water lift and branched into new fields as well. He invented the Kalamazoo Electric Pump in 1919 and soon after boosted his work force to seven. He kept his passion for quality parts and precision machining, using bronze bearings and cylinders to protect his pumps from freezing even when com-

increasingly complicated parts for modern airplanes. He made his wife Catherine vice-president and John Howard was named secretary. The company began making a gear housing for gun turrets on B-24 bombers with five machinists and four machines. Then came an order for landing-gear parts. Balch earned a reputation for precision work, but he hoped to gain several advantages when he bought National Water Lift. He would add additional equipment and skilled employees to his own operation. He would have an established domestic product when war production fell off. Finally, by assuming the name National Water Lift, he would gain the goodwill that Roland Fairchild had built so carefully over 33 years in business.

Balch consolidated the two operations on Willard Street and devoted all of their combined skills to the war effort. He took contracts calling for production runs machined to very close specifications. For orders requiring tolerances of "two-and-one-half-millionth" of an inch, Balch built special inspection devices capable of registering one inch on the gauge for each ten-thousandth of an inch on the product. The company soon became the sole sup-

plier for 40 different parts, yet never fell behind in its deliveries.

The government gave Balch a special award for his work. The citation noted his ability to redesign his old-fashioned equipment for precision work, saying "with this rebuilt equipment and superlatively trained workers, you have obtained tolerances and precisions heretofore thought impossible." Prime contractors sent Balch work when they had tried and failed to meet his accuracy. The award also noted that the company had improved its production record fourfold since the war began, yet never had asked for government financing.

Many firms had great difficulty retooling for peacetime production. National Water Lift returned to pump production, but "precision-obsessed engineers" around the country kept asking for specialized machine work. By 1948 the company made parts for automatic clothes dryers and the new automatic transmissions, as well as parts for brake systems and cylinder sleeves for Cummins truck engines. But the postwar years also saw the dawn of the jet age and the return of military preparedness. National Water Lift found more and more of its efforts going to fuel pumps for Lockheed Constellations and jet fighters, and carburetor parts for cargo planes. By 1949 this work made up the major portion of the business, and Balch moved to a new plant on Palmer Avenue. By 1954, when Balch built a major addition to the plant, Kalamazoo Pumps no longer figured in the company's expansion plans, and the pump line was sold to an Ohio firm the next year. Severens Balch retired in 1956 and sold the company to the Cleveland Pneumatic Tool Company. The corporate name was changed to Pneumo Dynamics in 1960. In 1974 it was changed to Pneumo Corporation. The next 20 years saw exciting ventures into space and renewed demand for

military aircraft, as well as increasingly complex designs for commercial air transport. National Water Lift grew with these challenges until 1,213 people worked at the company's four facilities. The 1970s brought several readjustments, consolidating the manufacturing operation in Kalamazoo and reducing the total number of employees.

Products became incredibly complex. An engineer might now work with computer help for nine months making the working drawings for one mechanism. Finished products might have 10,000 inspectable attributes. National Water Lift installed the first numerically controlled equipment in western Michigan to keep quality high. This new equipment could be programmed to start with a forging and create a finished product sometimes hours later. If the inch on a ruler had 20,000 divisions, these new machines could mill a piece of metal to the correct division time after time.

National Water Lift presently provides all the primary flight controls for the F-16 fighter plane and makes components for other fighters and helicopters, including the AV-8B Harrier scheduled for the U.S. Marines. In addition to making engine controls for General Electric, Pratt & Whitney, and Rolls Royce, NWL supplies flight controls for the Boeing 727 and 747, the Douglas DC-9 and DC-10, and the wide-bodied Lockheed L-1011.

Presently NWL has 958 local employees and 208 at a second plant in Beaufort, South Carolina. Many of these employees work in research. New aircraft require years of development and testing. NWL's proprietary designs may start some 10 years before an aircraft enters service, yet the company allows time for such planning to ensure that National Water Lift will retain its technical leadership as succeeding generations of aircraft become a reality.

Left
Highly sophisticated "Fly-by-Wire" flight control servoactuator used on one of the U.S. Air Force's latest jet fighter aircraft. Above the unit is a plastic model of the manifold portion of the servo-actuator. This manifold requires 45 machining operations and contains 140 separate passages and holes.

Below
Complex aircraft flight controls require precision machining to close tolerances. In order to attain such tolerances, NWL employs the use of modern tape-controlled machines.

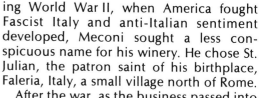

St. Julian Wine Co., Inc.

Right
Mariano Meconi,
founder of St. Julian
Wine Company.

Below Right
Exterior of the winery,
late 1930s.

The year 1921 found the country suffering that "noble experiment" in legislated morality, Prohibition, a good year for bootleggers but not for American wine. Nevertheless, that year saw the beginnings of what is now Michigan's oldest winery and largest producer of premium table wines when Mariano Meconi established the Italian Wine Company in Windsor, Ontario.

While the early 1930s brought the Great Depression and general hard times, at least after Prohibition was repealed in 1933 Americans could again legally enjoy alcoholic beverages. That year Meconi moved his operations across the river to Detroit. Three years later he relocated his

winery in Paw Paw, county seat of Van Buren County, the heart of Michigan's famous winegrowing district. There the area's hilly terrain and Lake Michigan's weather-tempering influence proved ideal for grape cultivation. Farmers grew varieties preferred by the large local juice producers and these Concord, Niagara, and Delaware grapes also produced a fine sweet wine.

Throughout the later 1930s, the Italian Wine Company flourished, bottling these sweet wines under a variety of labels. During World War II, when America fought Fascist Italy and anti-Italian sentiment developed, Meconi sought a less conspicuous name for his winery. He chose St. Julian, the patron saint of his birthplace, Faleria, Italy, a small village north of Rome.

After the war, as the business passed into the hands of Eugene and Robert Meconi, Meconi's sons, and Apollo Braganini, Meconi's son-in-law, business continued to expand and the winery grew in physical size and output. Americans developed a heightened interest in good wines during the 1970s and the company responded to this more sophisticated taste by producing drier types of table wines.

While it was not possible to produce such wines from the traditional varieties of sweet Michigan grapes, growers began planting French-American hybrid grapes developed to withstand the state's cold climate. Baco Noir, Chelois, Foch, Chancellor Noir, Seyval Blanc, and especially Vidal Blanc proved adaptable and the St. Julian Wine Company began buying increasing quantities of these superior wine grapes. From a small percentage in the mid-1970s hybrid wine grapes now comprise 80 percent of St. Julian total grape consumption. The company is Michigan's largest single buyer of such premium wine varieties.

Currently Apollo's son, David Braganini, is president of the company and under his leadership St. Julian is moving even more into the production of superior dry red, white, and sparkling wines. Chas Catherman, the company's expert wine maker, blends varietal juices for consistency, utilizing a mixture of ancient processes and sophisticated new techniques including centrifugal separation of impurities, multiple filterings, and huge stainless steel vats, to produce award-winning wines. In 1980 St. Julian wines won 23 awards, more than any other Michigan winery.

Each year over 300,000 gallons of St. Julian's fine wines flow from Paw Paw to a market throughout Michigan and nine other states. Thousands of visitors tour the winery, stopping in the hospitality room to taste wine and sample gourmet cheeses and related items. Braganini recently announced the opening of another winery in Frankenmuth, Michigan, where he will produce and age all of the company's prize-winning Solera Cream Sherry and begin producing champagne using the Old World *methode champaignoise.*

St. Julian is proud of its recently completed improvements, and Kalamazoo County citizens are extremely fortunate in having within easy driving distance a winery that is drawing national attention to Michigan's wine possibilities.

Stryker Corporation

Few local manufacturers within recent decades have demonstrated a more dramatic success story than the Stryker Corporation, whose products revolutionized care of the injured and spread Kalamazoo's fame to the world's medical profession.

Homer H. Stryker was born in Athens, Michigan, in 1894 and grew up on a nearby farm. He earned a degree from Western State Normal School and taught school briefly in Grand Ledge. He answered the call to the colors during World War I, serving in France as an army engineer. However, within a few years he was back in school, receiving a medical degree from the University of Michigan in 1925. During his internship and residency at the University Hospital in Ann Arbor, Stryker first demonstrated the inventive ingenuity and ability to develop practical solutions for medical problems destined to bring him worldwide fame. He put wheels on Bradford frames so patients could move about the wards and invented a double tube for drainage and irrigation, a principle still in use today.

Upon graduation Dr. Stryker set up a practice in Alma, Michigan, but soon returned to Kalamazoo where he served as county physician. In 1936 he returned to Ann Arbor to receive another three years of education in his real interest, orthopedic surgery. Returning to Kalamazoo in 1939, Dr. Stryker soon applied his ingenuity to two separate problems. He invented a practical rubber heel for walking casts and the famous Stryker frame for turning patients with spinal injuries. Other Stryker inventions soon followed: an over-the-bed frame to support limbs in traction, a grasping bar enabling patients to move themselves in bed, and a hip nailing board. In 1942 he patented the first oscillating saw, which cut casts without injuring underlying flesh.

Stryker Corporation came into being in 1946 as the successor to the business founded by Dr. Stryker in 1938. The company expanded with the introduction of

powered surgical instruments and customized, specialty stretcher-beds. Stryker's sales grew rapidly in the 1970s following the election of L. Lee Stryker, Dr. Stryker's son, as president and chief executive officer in 1969. Lee Stryker met an untimely death in an airplane crash in 1976. In 1977 John W. Brown became president and chief executive officer (and chairman in 1980). In 1979 Stryker became a public company.

Stryker Corporation now has over 500 employees and sales in excess of $40 million. The company develops, manufactures, and markets worldwide a broad line of powered surgical instruments; other operating-room devices and orthopedic implants; equipment for the handling, treatment, and care of patients; and cast cutters and cast-room equipment.

Homer Stryker, after 65 years of dedicated medical service, died in 1980, but the company he founded, the Stryker Corporation, continues to perpetuate the name of the person who did so much to ease mankind's suffering.

Left
Homer H. Stryker.

Below Left
Stryker Corporation's plant on Alcott Street before expansion of the facilities was begun.

Above
The company's office,
circa 1891.

Below Right
Albert May Todd.

The pungent aroma of peppermint emanating from the A.M. Todd Company offers passing motorists an olfactory treat ranking among Kalamazoo's most delightful attractions. The company has perfumed the air around its Douglas Avenue facilities since moving there in 1929, and its origins go back even further.

Albert M. Todd, while still a teenager, began experimenting with mint cultivation and distillation in 1868 at his home near Nottawa in St. Joseph County, then the leading Michigan mint growing area. During the last quarter of the 19th century, Todd revolutionized the American mint industry through development of steam power as a distillation process, introduction of hardier, more productive plants, and promotion of muck lands as growing areas. Most important, he drove the traditionally adulterated American oils off the market by bottling and selling his own quality product directly to worldwide consumers. In 1891 the Todd Company joined the rapidly swelling ranks of Kalamazoo industry when it moved to the newly constructed Todd Block at the corner of Rose Street and Kalamazoo Avenue. By the turn of the century, 90 percent of the world's peppermint crop grew within 75 miles of Kalamazoo and the Todd Company processed and distributed most of that supply to a world market.

Throughout the 19th century most mint oils went to foreign markets for medicinal uses. However, during the 20th century American consumers' demands for mint-flavored candy, chewing gum, and toothpaste produced a major domestic market, and this increased demand spurred the growth of the Todd Company. While the mint-growing industry experienced its ups and downs, and the Todd Company eventually dropped mint growing, as a processor and distributor it enjoyed continuous success. Even the Depression failed to affect the demand for mint-flavored products.

Few Kalamazoo manufacturers survived without diversifying their production but for over a century the Todd Company proved the exception to the rule. However, within the past decade the company expanded its range of flavors. Citrus oils, used primarily to flavor soft drinks, have developed into an important business, with the firm importing and distributing lime and lemon oil from Central and South America.

Following World War II the company engaged in extensive research, particularly concerning the verticillium wilt disease that had ruined Michigan mint growing. Continued research during the past decade by Dr. Merrit Murray of the Todd Company, who pioneered in producing genetic mutations of plants through controlled atomic radiation, has developed new, wilt-resistant varieties.

Albert M. Todd, a versatile and energetic man, practiced public service and philanthropy that succeeding generations have developed into a family tradition. He represented Michigan's Third Congressional District in 1896, Albert J. served on Kalamazoo's first city commission in 1918, Paul H. beginning in the early 1920s set a record for service on that commission, Paul Jr. in 1964 became the only Democrat elected to represent the Third Congressional District since his grandfather, and currently Charles is a Libertarian candidate for Congress.

The fourth generation of Todds now operates the company and remains a strong supporter of Kalamazoo through public leadership, generous donations, and support of a variety of civic projects. They feel that the future looks bright for a continuing, mutually beneficial relationship between Kalamazoo and their vigorous, home-owned company.

Unifab Corporation

War clouds darkened Europe when Kalamazoo Coaches, Inc., began making Pony Cruiser mini-buses in the summer of 1940. When the company was three weeks old, Fred N. Schroen joined the corporation as plant manager. In the next 10 years, Kalamazoo Coaches would make seven hundred 16- to 25-passenger buses for short-haul firms in many states, as well as in Canada, Cuba, Brazil, and Chile.

When America entered the war, the new firm found itself competing with tanks, planes, and guns for strategic materials. War Production Board administrators needed to be shown that defense plant workers would ride the Pony buses before they would approve construction. At one point, Kalamazoo Coaches, Inc., experimented with "catastrophe units" mounted on bus bodies. The city of Philadelphia bought one to be used in case of air raids. It came complete with special rescue equipment and mobile operating room.

Fred Schroen took over as president and general manager on December 30, 1942. Later he became sole stockholder and continues to head the company at the present time. Schroen guided Kalamazoo Coaches through the war years and the economic readjustment period in the late 1940s, seeing firsthand the problems of a company with a single product. He began taking orders for custom metal fabricating and changed the company name to the Unifab Corporation on September 20, 1951. Under Schroen's direction, Unifab Corporation became one of the best-equipped light-metal-fabricating plants in the area, with 60 employees and a 40,000-square-foot plant at 5260 Lovers Lane Road in Portage.

Unifab now serves industry, institutions,

and laboratories within a 200-mile radius of Kalamazoo with a diversified line of custom metal products. The firm introduced one such special product in 1960—its own line of animal-care equipment for research laboratories. The current Unifab Cage catalog lists 51 pages of cages, racks, and related equipment.

Over the years Unifab Corporation has become a "family business." Office manager Ruth Selbig came to work for the company in 1941, and treasurer Hazell Schroen in 1965. Son Steven Schroen joined Unifab full time in 1975. He learned the business in many capacities over the years and is now vice-president and finance manager. For more than 40 years, Fred Schroen brought gradual but steady growth to his company with quality products and a wide range of customer services.

Left
Steven F. Schroen (left), executive vice-president and son of Fred N. Schroen (right), president.

Below Left
A forerunner of today's motor homes, this 1950 modified Pony Cruiser was self-contained and custom designed.

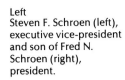

Right
U.K.C.'s home office is at 100 East Kilgore Road, Kalamazoo.

The United Kennel Club, the nation's second oldest and second largest all-breed dog registry, was founded in Kalamazoo in 1898. Except for a short stint in Chicago, U.K.C. has remained in Kalamazoo, the home of Chauncey Zaccariah Bennett.

Bennett wore many hats in Kalamazoo. He started in the 1890s as a clerk and traveling man for the Desenberg grocery firm, then made peanut-roasting machines at the Bennett Novelty Works. He put on a fireman's hat for the city of Kalamazoo during World War I and kept it for 10 years or more. But through it all Chauncey Bennett kept his passion for fine dogs. He became an expert on dog breeding in his spare time, and the more he learned, the more upset he became. Narrow-minded kennel clubs recognized only their favorite breeds, denying sanction to hundreds of legitimate dog raisers whose purebreds had no official standing at all. "Dog jockies," on the other hand, fleeced gullible buyers with false papers and substitution schemes.

Bennett took matters into his own hands in 1898, establishing an independent dog registry called the United Kennel Club. Working out of his basement, he wrote to breeders around the country, drew up standards, and extended his U.K.C. registration to purebred dogs. He took a much harsher view of inbreeding and mixed breeding than other clubs, stamping "inbred" on some certificates and threatening to drop kennel owners who bred closer than three generations. Bennett's integrity and high standards brought him increasing respect.

In 1905 he gave his ideas a wider audience in a U.K.C. journal which he named *Bloodlines*. From a small beginning, *Bloodlines* grew to be one of the largest dog magazines in the world by 1936. First and foremost Bennett preached registration, claiming in 1913, "90 percent of the public don't know what you mean when you speak of a dog as being registered, but they are learning mighty fast." He estimated that five million "cur dogs" roamed free while only a hundred thousand were registered with a kennel club. In down-to-earth prose rich with humor, Bennett swapped stories with other dog raisers and carried their advertisements, provided they met strict breeding standards.

By the late 1920s, dog breeding had become big business and Bennett could devote full time to his registry. He continued to hammer good breeding home with pithy sayings—observing in 1928 that "the wise man buys the Registration papers and pedigree and gets the pup thrown in FREE; the fool buys just the pups." Arguing that only registered pedigrees gave buyers

any assurance of careful breeding, he introduced a special Purple Ribbon ("PR") for dogs whose ancestors could be traced back six generations, while he required certification of three generations of ancestors to obtain U.K.C. registration. In due time a puppy could earn the coveted "PR" Registration Certificate and Pedigree showing U.K.C. numbers for seven generations—254 ancestors in all!

When Bennett died in 1936, U.K.C. registered 30,000 dogs a year and was considered the largest registration bureau "of its kind in the world." His daughter Frances carried on her father's work from an office in the old State Theater building. She married Dr. Edwin Fuhrman during the war, and he ultimately became president. By 1950 U.K.C. had offices in the Hanselman Building and a staff of 14. The Fuhrmans continued to operate U.K.C. until January 1973, when they sold the corporation to aerospace executive Fred T. Miller.

U.K.C. felt "working" dogs particularly suffered from the elitism of existing kennel clubs, which concentrated on the showing of dogs. Dogs bred for centuries to hunt, guard, and herd were being neglected and losing natural abilities and instincts. From its outset U.K.C. accentuated the need for maintaining working qualities and breed standards that complement those qualities.

Bennett moved at once to recognize one long-standing breed which he called the American (Pit) Bull Terrier. He gave his own dog, Bennett's Ring, U.K.C. number "one." U.K.C. adopted breeding standards and encouraged terrier fanciers to meet those standards. The American (Pit) Bull Terrier remains a popular breed with its own conformation shows and breeders' associations.

Coonhound owners also turned to U.K.C. "Cooning" was as ancient as Jamestown and as American as apple pie, but established clubs insisted that coon dogs be registered as foxhounds and virtually demanded that they be crossbred between bloodhound and fighting stock. Yet, as Bennett once put it, coonhounds hunted wily and pugnacious wild raccoons at night

Below
Chauncey Bennett founded the United Kennel Club in 1898.

in "the severest and most strenuous task ever assigned a sporting dog." U.K.C. published breeding requirements and physical specifications that led to recognition of six basic American coonhound breeds, the Black and Tan (1900), Redbone (1902), English (1905), Plott (1946), Bluetick (1946), and Treeing Walker (1945). Coonhounds now account for about 60 percent of U.K.C.'s registrations.

While working dogs like coonhounds remained perennially popular, other breeds caught the public fancy from time to time. In 1913, for instance, Bennett reported that purebred Airedales were hard to come by, and in 1928 Dachshunds were "scarcer than frog's hair." U.K.C. was the first to recognize one of the most popular breeds of the 1940s, the Toy Fox Terrier, and later on the American Water Spaniel and the English and Australian Shepherds. The club also responded to problems developing in the spitz classification originally intended for working sled dogs. In 1917 U.K.C. recognized the American Eskimo as a separate and distinct breed.

Frances and E.G. Fuhrman increased U.K.C. sponsorship of shows and field trials and began to license night hunts for wild raccoons in 1953. Fred Miller expanded this involvement even further. Presently, U.K.C. recognizes 900 clubs and licenses more than 3,800 purebred dog events each year in 44 states and Canada.

Coonhound owners look forward each year to two major events. One of those is Autumn Oaks, an event held each Labor Day weekend. At the Autumn Oaks in 1979, 6,000 people and 1,000 dogs took part in 3-day night hunts and two days of bench shows. The second major event is the U.K.C. World Coonhound Championship. In 1980, there were 184 entries for the 4-day finals from 21 states and Canada, having qualified out of 2,348 dogs entered in 44 regional qualifying events.

In addition to its work with coonhounds, U.K.C. sanctions championship conformation shows for the American Eskimo dogs, American (Pit) Bull Terriers, and Toy Fox Terriers. The club also initiated an obedience program for dogs in 1979.

U.K.C.'s registration has tripled since 1973, and Fred Miller designed a new building to meet its needs on the corner of Kilgore Road and Burdick. There U.K.C. registers a quarter of a million or more dogs each year. It is presently one of the Postal Service's largest daily customers in the Kalamazoo area, answering 1,000 or more letters a day. The Millers continue to publish *Bloodlines* regularly and have also added a second magazine, *Coonhound Bloodlines*. The two magazines follow the down-to-earth format initiated by Chauncey Bennett in 1905, carrying news of coming events, articles of general interest, and U.K.C. policies. Miller also continues Bennett's "Purple Ribbon Pedigree." The U.K.C. now actively registers 58 breeds. The club's new headquarters houses 40 employees and two IBM System-34 computers which provide 3- and 6-generation pedigree printouts and are the heart of U.K.C.'s sophisticated registration system.

As a local reporter summed up U.K.C.'s story years ago, "it began because a Kalamazoo man thought his dog the equal of any on earth and built a business to prove it." Thousands of dog owners in the United States and in 18 foreign countries now own purebred dogs because Chauncey Bennett, his family, and now Fred Miller and his family have kept those bloodlines recorded for more than 85 years.

Left
The club's new headquarters houses 40 employees and two IBM System-34 computers, which allow 3- and 6-generation pedigree printouts.

Below
Early Upjohn products.

Bottom
Dr. William E. Upjohn
on the ride to Vicksburg,
1900.

For six decades the Upjohn trademark featured history's most widely reproduced thumb in the act of crushing a pill to powder. The thumb belonged to an inventive young doctor from Hastings, Michigan, William E. Upjohn, M.D., and the "friable pill" process he patented in 1885 gave birth to one of America's most successful businesses. In 1883 when Upjohn first made his novel product, the contents of available pills were not precisely controlled and the often rock-hard pellets usually didn't dissolve inside the patient. Upjohn's "friable pills" answered both problems.

In 1885 the young entrepreneur moved his operations to Kalamazoo and with his brothers Henry, Frederick, and James founded the Upjohn Pill and Granule Company. The following year their first catalog, a list of 186 pill formulas, brought a booming business. A few years later William Upjohn purchased the company from his brothers.

Dr. Upjohn, a dynamic, multifaceted man, provided the vital force during the company's formative years and established attitudes and policies still in operation today. He posted signs throughout the plant, "Keep the Quality Up," and they did. Upjohn employees were among the first in the area to receive such unheard-of benefits as the 8-hour workday, one-half day off Saturday, and company-paid life insurance. Dr. Upjohn assumed a leadership role in the local political arena and Kalamazoo Chamber of Commerce, and he gave generously to the city and its educational institutions.

By the turn of the century, as medicinal tablets became generally available, business lagged. However, in 1908 the introduction of a popular new laxative in wafer form, Phenolax, ushered in a new period of prosperity. By the mid-1920s, as over 180 million of the little wafers tumbled off the production line each year, Upjohn employed more than 800 personnel and annually grossed over $4 million. Other popular products spurred continuing success. During the 1920s, Citrocarbonate enjoyed popularity as a gastric antacid. By the 1930s, Upjohn super vitamin D capsules offered an alternative to tablespoons of vile-tasting cod-liver oil, and by 1937 business had expanded to $12 million a year. In 1940 Upjohn first marketed Unicap multivitamin capsules, and in two years they accounted for 20 percent of the company's sales.

During World War II, Upjohn won an Army/Navy "E" Award for production of vital war-related products including sulfa drugs, penicillin, and serum albumen. In 1945 the company acquired a 1,500-acre site south of the city on Portage Road, and the next 35 years brought almost continuous construction of new facilities there.

Hormones, steroids, and cortisone became important products during the 1950s, and by the end of the decade the Upjohn labor force had expanded to 5,750. The year 1958 saw Upjohn stock first offered to the public; by 1959 shareholders increased from 500 to 29,000. The new "public company" entered two decades of fantastic growth marked by four major developments: diversification, heightened research, broadening of marketing activities, and increased activity in financial and public affairs.

During the 1960s Upjohn diversified into related areas, acquiring the Carwin Company, an industrial organic chemical manufacturer, in 1962, and CPR International Corporation, and T.P. Industries of Torrance, California, manufacturers of polyurethane products, in 1963. With the purchase of the Asgrow Seed Company in 1968, The Upjohn Company expanded into seed genetics. In the late 1960s, after acquisition of medical laboratories and a home health care operation, Upjohn entered the human health care sector.

Research had long been an important element of the company, and the past two decades witnessed a tremendous intensification and broadening of such activity. The research budget mushroomed from $13 million in 1958 to over $100 million 20 years later. That period saw the development and marketing of more than 35 new human-health-care products, more than 30 new animal- and plant-health products, new seed varieties, and other innovations. Sales increased during that period from $146 million to $1.3 billion. International operations grew from a half dozen countries in 1958 to a place among the leading U.S. multinational businesses in 1978. Recognizing that "disease has no political boundaries," Upjohn followed market penetration with construction of manufacturing facilities in 31 countries by 1978; today international operations comprise 40 percent of total sales. The corporation has responded to new marketing concerns, changing world situations, inflation, pollution, and government regulations through coordinated long-range planning activities, including a public affairs committee to analyze political impact on the business.

The Upjohn Company enters the 1980s as the Kalamazoo area's largest employer with 22,000 employees worldwide and 6,700 in the county. Through these jobs, millions of dollars in tax payments and generous charitable gifts, and as a major consumer of local products and services, The Upjohn Company stands as a major contributor to the good life in Kalamazoo.

Carl Walker & Associates, Inc.

During the past decade and a half, Carl Walker & Associates, Inc., a Kalamazoo-headquartered firm of consulting structural engineers, has made its mark on city landscapes from Maine to Montana and, as a local source for engineering expertise, has contributed to Kalamazoo's growth and revitalization. This mutually beneficial relationship between Carl Walker and Kalamazoo began in 1960 when the young engineer, fresh from the University of Michigan Graduate School and a 6-month tour of active duty in the army, landed a job with Precast Industries. A few years later, he succumbed briefly to the lure of the big city and took a job in Chicago. However, as a result of that experience, he came to realize how good life really was in Kalamazoo. By April 1965 Walker had returned to open a small office located at 428 West South Street.

At first, the firm provided engineering consulting services for a variety of clients with diverse problems; but, within a few years, a specialty developed—parking structures. The first such job was for Montgomery Ward in Albany, New York. Then, in 1968, Walker executed a 660-car structure for the Michigan National Bank in Detroit and since that time the firm has always had a parking structure design in progress. Over 160 completed parking facilities across the country carry the imprint of Carl Walker & Associates, Inc.

Much of this phenomenal success has resulted from the Walker philosophy that parking structures are supportive structures that should blend in with their surroundings and not exist as architectural statements in themselves. At the same time, their appearance should express their function so that they can be easily identified by motorists. Since parking structures are transportation interchange points at which people change their mode of travel, they should be arranged most efficiently to permit a maximum of driving and a minimum of walking.

Carl Walker & Associates, Inc., has always been in the forefront of parking structure development. The dominant trends in modern life are reflected in the evolution of parking structures from an experimental rarity in the 1960s to an integral part of urban American life. The energy crisis and resultant smaller automobiles and increased use of mass transportation have greatly affected that development. The availability of parking structures has strengthened formerly deteriorating central business districts and helped to decrease pollution since motorists can go directly to a parking place rather than cruising the streets looking for a vacant space. While traditional surface lots consume hundreds of acres of scarce green space, parking structures, elevated and concentrated, permit land use for other needs.

The past decade saw numerous local parking structure projects completed by the firm including those at Western Michigan University, Bronson Hospital, an addition to Gilmore's, the city structure at Jacobson's, and the city structure featuring a sky walkway to the Kalamazoo Center. Recent major projects elsewhere include a 1,233-car parking facility at the Renaissance Center and a 3,000-car facility at the Joe Louis Arena in Detroit; Parking Facility No. One for 3,000 cars at the Minneapolis-St. Paul International Airport; and a 10-story, 2,000-car facility in Houston, Texas.

Over 100 skilled employees in branch offices in Kalamazoo and Detroit, Michigan; Elgin and Chicago, Illinois; Minneapolis, Minnesota; Indianapolis, Indiana; Houston, Texas; and Denver, Colorado, receive direction from the corporate headquarters located in an impressive new building at 2121 Hudson Avenue. Comprehensive parking consultation services, now including parking structure restoration, remain a major area of expertise. Project management ranging from value engineering to sophisticated continuous budget control is also offered. In recent years the firm has diversified into agri-industrial engineering, providing service in designing storage and processing facilities for agri-industries.

Carl Walker & Associates, Inc., has blossomed into a vigorous enterprise during the years since 1965 and Kalamazoo's work environment, geographical setting, and living and recreational opportunities have been an important factor in that success.

Projects completed by Carl Walker & Associates, Inc., include the city parking structure addition and pedestrian skyway to the Kalamazoo Center (bottom) and the city parking structure at Jacobson's (below).

Wendy's Old Fashioned Hamburgers

The first Wendy's outlet in Kalamazoo, corner of East Michigan and Edwards.

R. David Thomas grew up in Kalamazoo. He stopped at "The Kewpee Restaurant" on East South Street near Burdick whenever he had an extra nickel. Proprietor Francis Blair advertised the Kewpee in the 1920s as "The Hamburg Sandwich Man: We Cater to All the Folks at Fairs, Lakes, Shows and Carnivals." Later Roy Wood managed the Kewpee until it closed in 1964. Thomas never forgot those hot and juicy "Hamburg Sandwiches."

As fast-food franchises blanketed America in the 1950s and 1960s, Thomas missed the old-fashioned taste of made-to-order meals. He opened a franchise of his own in Columbus, Ohio, in 1969, designed to bring the remembered goodness of the old "Kewpees" up-to-date. Named after his young daughter, "Wendy's" filled a real need in the food-service market and rapidly expanded until more than 2,000 outlets presently dot the countryside.

William Van Domelen came to Kalamazoo in 1960 to try the restaurant business himself. In 1974, when Thomas had just 60 outlets nationwide, Van Domelen purchased the Wendy's franchise for southwest Michigan, covering the territory from Muskegon to Battle Creek. Kewpee's was gone from downtown Kalamazoo, but on October 9, 1974, Wendy's took its place.

On the site of the old Harris Hotel at Edwards and East Michigan, Van Domelen's first location offered seating for 90 and, unlike other downtown restaurants, off-street parking for 70 cars. It also offered the first drive-through window in town and a salad bar for diet-conscious shoppers. Thomas's computer determined that Wendy's could supply hamburgers fixed in 256 different ways. But this was no ordinary fast-food outlet. The new restaurant stressed caned chairs, carpeted floors, and "tiffany-style" hanging lamps. Tables and counters offered laminated surfaces of turn-of-the-century advertisements. Even the wallpaper kept the historical theme. Tradition went beyond decor to the menu itself. While many chains moved to prepackaged frozen foods, Wendy's kept the "made-to-order" kitchen of the old-time "cafe." Not only freshly prepared hamburger patties, but steaming bowls of home-cooked chili underscored the old-fashioned food theme.

Van Domelen saw room for his kind of restaurant in the downtown area. He catered to noon-hour customers just as Kewpee's had and with the same success. Later in 1974, he opened a second Wendy's at Lovers' Lane and Cork Street, and by year's end had 80 employees. He presently operates five outlets in Kalamazoo County and 19 Wendy's in all, with some 600 workers. All are open seven days a week, 363 days out of the year.

Van Domelen's restaurants support a variety of community programs, sponsoring Little League teams, participating in college festivals, and helping sponsor the annual Junior Boys' National Tennis Tournament held at Kalamazoo College. In addition, Wendy's supplies coupons as prizes for contests run by many local organizations.

As a franchise holder, Van Domelen has the advantages of the parent company's research and marketing services and its management training institute. But Wendy's success in the Kalamazoo area owes a great deal to his skill as a restaurateur, and to the loyalty of the noon-hour customers, the college crowd, and the suburban families who appreciate his "small-meal" menus for their children. Not a little of his success can be traced back to R. David Thomas's childhood memories of "The Hamburg Sandwich Man" at Kalamazoo's own "Kewpee Restaurant."

ACKNOWLEDGMENTS

Without the enthusiastic support that came from local businesses, this book would not have been possible. We also found our work made easier by researchers who came before us. The late Willis Dunbar's exhaustive files and radio scripts on local industry were most helpful. John Houdek's index to newspaper articles on business developments in the 1870s and 1880s proved invaluable. Wayne Mann, Phyllis Burnham, and the staff of the Western Michigan University Archives and Regional History Collections patiently helped us find photographs, documents, and manuscript materials. We would also like to thank Ms. Catherine Senecal at the Kalamazoo Public Library and Ms. Mary Lou Stewart at the Kalamazoo Public Museum for their help as we looked for photographs. Kanti Sandhu assisted us with photographic work, and Ms. Opal Ellis and Ms. Judith Massie typed faithfully on the manuscript. Alexis Praus provided many helpful editorial suggestions, as did Randy Smoot of Windsor Publications. Beverly Schmitt, Mary Mitchell, and others read the manuscript, but we are responsible for errors that remain.

Windsor Publications would also like to thank the following members of its own staff, whose efforts helped make this book possible: Barbara Marinacci, supervisory editor; Kathy Cooper, project coordinator; Karen Story, business biography editorial director, and Phyllis Gray, business biography editorial assistant; Teri Davis Greenberg, picture and caption editor, and Anna R. Igra and Jana Wernor, assistant picture and caption editors; Hal Straus, copy editor; Roberta Goodwin, indexer; Doris Malkin, proofreading supervisor, and Andrew Christie, Diana Gibson, and Jeff Leckrone, proofreaders.

BIBLIOGRAPHY

Annual Reports of the City of Kalamazoo. Kalamazoo: various publishers, 1885–.

Annual Reports of the Village of Kalamazoo. Kalamazoo: various publishers, 1874–1884.

Atlas of Kalamazoo County Michigan Containing General Survey Maps of All Townships, Maps of Michigan, United States and the World. Chicago: H.C. Maley, [1913].

Balls, Ethel, and Lassfolk, Marie. *Living in Kalamazoo.* Kalamazoo: Ihling Brothers & Everard Company, 1958.

Beers, Frederick W., comp., *Atlas of Kalamazoo County, Michigan. From Recent and Actual Surveys and Records Under the Superintendence of F.W. Beers.* New York: F.W. Beers, 1873.

Bellson, Julius. *The Story of Gibson: the Man, the Instrument, the Heritage.* n.p., n.d.

Bennett, Samuel V. *Selected Population and Housing Characteristics by Tracts in Kalamazoo: 1950 and 1960.* Kalamazoo: W.E. Upjohn Institute for Employment Research, 1961.

Bigelow, H.F. "The Holland Dutch in Kalamazoo." Unpublished typescript, 1924. In Western Michigan University Archives and Regional History Collections.

Brannon, W.T. *"Yellow Kid" Weil.* Chicago: Ziff-Davis, [1948].

Brown, Alan S. "Caroline Bartlett Crane and Urban Reform." *Michigan History,* vol. LVI, no. 4 [Winter, 1972].

Buskirk, Phyllis R., and Ford, Kathrine H. *Selected Population, Housing, and Economic Characteristics in Kalamazoo County, by Tracts: 1960–1970.* [Kalamazoo]: W.E. Upjohn Institute for Employment Research, 1973.

Button, Harry J. "The Diary of Harry J. Button, 1893." Bound photocopy of manuscript. In Western Michigan University Archives and Regional History Collections.

The Celery City, n.p. [c. 1904].

The Centennial Celebration at Kalamazoo, Michigan, July 4th, 1876. Published by Order of the Executive Committee. Kalamazoo: 1876.

Central Business District Profile. Kalamazoo: n.p., [1963].

Commercial Club, Kalamazoo, Michigan. *The Lure of Kalamazoo: a Pictorial Presentation of Its Many Advantages for Industrial, Commercial and Residential Life in 1912.* Kalamazoo: n.p., 1912.

Cooper, James Fenimore. *The Oak Openings or the Bee-Hunter.* Leatherstocking Edition. New York: G.P. Putnam's Sons, n.d.

[Crane, Caroline Bartlett]. *Asylum Vs. Poorhouse or the Advantages of Being Insane.* Kalamazoo: Kalamazoo Publishing Company, 1918.

Crane, Caroline Bartlett, *Everyman's House.* With a foreword by Herbert Hoover. New York: Doubleday, Page & Company, 1925.

_____, *The Local Slaughter House and Meat Inspection.* n.p., [1903].

_____, *Report on Conditions Found at Our County Almshouse.* [Kalamazoo: Kalamazoo Publishing Company, 1908].

_____, *The Work For Clean Streets.* N.p., [1905].

Delano, George. "George Delano Diaries." Bound photocopies of manuscript diaries in 12 volumes, 1855–1895. In Western Michigan University Archives and Regional History Collections.

Dunbar, Willis. *Financial Progress in Kalamazoo County Since 1834.* Kalamazoo County Chamber of Commerce, [1966].

_____, *Kalamazoo and How It Grew.* Faculty Contributions, Western Michigan University, 1959.

_____, *Kalamazoo and How It Grew . . . and Grew . . . .* Faculty Contributions, Western Michigan University, 1969.

_____, "Those Were the Firms That Were," *Kalamazoo Magazine* [April, 1965].

_____, "Western Michigan at Work." A series of radio broadcasts on WKZO, 1946–1950. Transcripts at Western Michigan University Archives and Regional History Collections.

[Durant, Samuel W.]. *History of Kalamazoo County, Michigan. With Illustrations and Biographical Sketches of Its Prominent Men and Pioneers.* Philadelphia: Everts and Abbott, 1880.

Earl, Stephen Van Rensselaer. "Earl Diaries." Bound photocopies of manuscript diaries, 19 vols. 1860–1885. In Western Michigan University Archives and Regional History Collections.

Employment In Kalamazoo County. Kalamazoo: W.E. Upjohn Institute for Community Research, n.d.

Engel, Leonard. *Medicine Makers of Kalamazoo.* New York, Toronto, London: McGraw-Hill Book Company, Inc., 1961.

The Farm Journal Illustrated Rural Directory of Kalamazoo County Michigan. Philadelphia: Wilmer Atkinson Company, 1919.

Ferber, Edna. *A Peculiar Treasure.* New York: Doubleday, Doran, 1939.

Fisher, David, and Little, Frank, eds. *Compendium of History and Biography of Kalamazoo County, Michigan.* Chicago: A.W. Bowen and Company, [1906].

Flood Conditions In the Kalamazoo Area. Michigan Water Resources Commission, July 1957.

Foote, Mrs. George E. *History of the Twentieth Century Club.* N.p., [ca. 1953].

Gansser, Emil B. *History of the 126th Infantry In the War With Germany.* Grand Rapids: [Dean Hicks Company, 1920].

Goodsell, Charles True and Dunbar, Willis Frederick. *Centennial History of Kalamazoo College.* Kalamazoo: Kalamazoo College, 1933.

"Greater Kalamazoo." Supplement to *Kalamazoo Daily Gazette,* July 30, 1904.

Gull Lake Its History, Location and Advantages as a Place for a Delightful Outing, a Beautiful Place to Spend a Summer Vacation, a Haven of Rest from the Care and Worry of Home and Business, an Ideal Spot for a Summer Home. C.E. Cleveland, 1904.

Hager, David C. *Next Stop Kalamazoo! A History of Railroading in Kalamazoo County.* A Bicentennial Publication of the Kalamazoo Public Museum, [1976].

History of the Kalamazoo Fire Department Containing Historical Information Carefully Gleaned From all Available Sources and From Fire Department Records. Published by the Kalamazoo Fire Department Relief Fund Association. Kalamazoo: Ihling Brothers & Everard Company, 1900.

Hodgman, Francis, ed., "Surveyor's Original Field Notes, Kalamazoo County." Bound photocopy of manuscript, n.d. In Western Michigan University Archives and Regional History Collections.

Holland's Kalamazoo Directory for the Centennial Year 1876 Containing a Historical Sketch of the Village and a Complete List of all the Residents also a Classified Business Directory, With the Name and Address of the Merchants, Manufacturers and Professional Men, and Editorial Notices on Some of the Oldest and Most Prominent Business Houses, Manufactories, Organizations, Societies, Colleges, Churches, Schools, Village and County Officers, Etc., Etc. Chicago: Holland Publishing Company, 1876.

An Honor Roll Containing a Pictorial Record of the War Service of the Men and Women of Kalamazoo County 1917–1918–1919. Mrs. O.H. Clark, [1920].

Hubbard, Gurdon Saltonstall. *The Autobiography of Gurdon Saltonstall Hubbard Pa-Pa-Ma-Ta-Be "The Swift Walker."* With an introduction by Caroline M. McIlvaine, Librarian of the Chicago Historical Society. Chicago: The Lakeside Press, 1911.

Hudson, Mrs. Jacob. "Recollections of Kalamazoo Since 1834." Bound photocopy of newspaper articles appearing in 1880. In Western Michigan University Archives and Regional History Collections.

Illustrated Atlas of Kalamazoo County, Michigan. Containing General Maps of Kalamazoo County and City; Detail Maps of Townships, showing farmlands with areas and owners names, Railroads, Wagon Roads, Streams, Lakes, etc., etc.,; Detail Plats of Kalamazoo City and Interior Villages, Showing Dimensions of Lots, Location of Water Mains, Sewers, Buildings, etc. Also Maps of the Hemispheres, World, United States and Michigan, With Early and Present History of Kalamazoo County. Detroit: William C. Sauer, 1890.

"Interest": A Monthly Magazine . . . Vol. II, No. 8, October, 1928; Vol. II, No. 9, November, 1928; Vol. III, No. 4, June 1929, n.p.

Kalamazoo A City of Industries. Kalamazoo Chamber of Commerce. N.p., n.d.

Kalamazoo City Directory. Kalamazoo, 1860-1981. Title and publisher vary.

Kalamazoo County's Township Maps 1869.

Kalamazoo Fire Department Relief Fund Association. History of the Kalamazoo Fire Department: Containing Historical Information Carefully Gleaned From all Available Sources and from Fire Department Records. Kalamazoo: n.p., 1900.

Kalamazoo Gazette, 1837-. Weekly and daily newspaper, title varies.

"The Kalamazoo Gazette, Centennial Edition," Kalamazoo: January 24, 1937.

Kalamazoo Heart of Southwest Michigan. Chamber of Commerce, n.p., [c. 1940s].

Kalamazoo, Kalamazoo County Michigan 1853. Surveyed and Published by Henry Hart. Civil Engineer and Architect, 140 Pearl St. N.Y. Lithograph of Sarony & Major, New York. New York: Henry Hart, 1853.

Kalamazoo, Michigan. Automobile Club of Michigan. N.p., n.d.

Kalamazoo, Michigan, Centennial Committee. Kalamazoo Centennial Program and a Historical Review, 1829-1929. Kalamazoo, 1929.

Kalamazoo, Michigan 1894 Afro-American Journal and Directory Souvenir Edition. Kalamazoo: Kalamazoo Engineering Company, 1894.

Kalamazoo Telegraph, 1849-1916. Weekly and daily newspaper, title varies.

Kalamazoo and Van Buren County Rural Route Directory With Parts of Allegan, Barry, Calhoun and St. Joseph Counties. Battle Creek: DeRees & Bennett Publishing Company, 1926.

Kent County Circuit Court Records. Fifty thousand case files, 1837-1920s. In Western Michigan University Archives and Regional History Collections.

Kindleberger, Jacob. "How a Master Confidence Man and His Confederates Caught J. Kindleberger." Unpublished article in Western Michigan University Archives and Regional History Collections.

Knauss, James O. The First Fifty Years. A History of Western Michigan College of Education 1903-1953. Published by Western Michigan College of Education. Kalamazoo, Michigan. [Crawfordsville, Indiana: R.R. Donnelley and Sons Company,] 1953.

_____, History of Western State Teachers College 1904-1929. Published by Western State Teachers College Kalamazoo, Michigan. [Kalamazoo: Horton-Beimer Press, 1929].

Labadie's Souvenir of Picturesque Kalamazoo Containing Historical Sketches, Views of City and Public Buildings, School Houses, Churches, Private Residences, Business Streets, Factories and a few of the many Beauty Spots in and Around Kalamazoo, Michigan. Kalamazoo: E.E. Labadie, 1909.

Landing, James E. American Essence A History of the Peppermint and Spearmint Industry in the United States. Published as a contribution of the Kalamazoo Public Museum, [1969].

Life Is Good In Kalamazoo. Some Facts Concerning the Cultural and Business Center of Southwestern Michigan. N.p., n.d.

MacCarthy, Joseph P. A Tribute to Mr. and Mrs. Allen Potter. Kalamazoo: Ihling Brothers, Everard Company, 1910.

Map of Kalamazoo Co. Michigan From Special Surveys and Court Records under direction of Geil and Harley Topographical Engineers Engineered by Worley & Fraher. Surveys by I. Gross, C.E. Drawn by S.L. Jones, C.E. Philadelphia: Geil and Harley, 1861.

Massie, Larry B. A Preliminary Bibliography of the Published Material Relating to the History of Kalamazoo County, Michigan. Bound typescript, 1977. In Western Michigan University Archives and Regional History Collections.

McCracken, S.B. Michigan and the Centennial. Detroit: Detroit Free Press, 1876.

McNair, Dr. Rush. Medical Memoirs of 50 Years In Kalamazoo. N.p., [ca. 1938].

Meader, Robert Eugene, "Historical Directory of Kalamazoo, Michigan." Typescript. 36 vols. In Kalamazoo Public Library.

Michigan. Bureau of Labor and Industrial Statistics. Annual Reports. Lansing, 1884-1920. Title varies.

Michigan. Department of State. Census of the State of Michigan. Lansing, 1854-1904.

Michigan. Department of State. Manuscript Census of Kalamazoo County, 1884, 1894. In Western Michigan University Archives and Regional History Collections.

Michigan Federation of Labor Industrial History and Official Year Book 1908. Issued under the supervision of the Executive Board of the Michigan Federation of Labor. Detroit: American Printing Company, [1908].

Michigan Statesman, 1835-1836.

Michigan Telegraph, 1844-1849.

"Michigan Tradesman" 67th Anniversary Edition Number 3241, December 14, 1949.

Moore, Dr. Floyd W. Community Settlement, Development, and Progress. A Story of the City of Kalamazoo. Chapter One of a Thesis "The Evolution of a Modern City Free From General Fund Indebtedness," August 1, 1943. Bureau of Municipal Research Publication No. 10.

New Horizons at Ninety 1867-1957 Kalamazoo Paper Company. N.p., [1957].

Nostrums and Quackery. Chicago: American Medical Association, [1906].

Ogle, George A. & Company, comp., Standard Atlas of Kalamazoo County Michigan Including a Plat Book of the Villages, Cities and Townships of the County. Map of the State, United States and World. Patrons Directory, Reference Business Directory, and Departments devoted to General Information. Analysis of the System of U.S. Land Surveys, Digest of the System of Civil Government, Etc. Etc. Chicago: George A Ogle & Company, 1910.

Parchment the Paper City 1976. Parchment: Economy Printing Company, [1976].

Peters, Bernard C. Early American Impressions and Evaluations of the Landscape of Inner Michigan With Emphasis on Kalamazoo County. Thesis submitted to Michigan State University in partial fulfillment of the requirements for the degree of Doctor of Philosophy. Department of Geography, 1969.

Pictorial Souvenir of the Police Department and Kalamazoo, Michigan. Lansing: Wilkinson-Ryan-Haight Company, 1914.

Pioneer Collections. Report of the Pioneer Society of the State of Michigan Together With Reports of County, Town, and District Pioneer Societies. Lansing: W.S. George & Company, 1877-1929. 40 vols. Also 2 vol. index.

Polk, R.L. Michigan State Gazetteer and Business Directory. Detroit: R.L. Polk 1885; 1895-1896; 1911; 1917-1918; 1931-1932.

Portrait and Biographical Record of Kalamazoo, Allegan and Van Buren Counties, Michigan, Containing Biographical Sketches of Prominent and Representative Citizens, Together With Biographies of All the Governors of the State, and of the Presidents of the United States. Chicago: Chapman Brothers, 1892.

Potts, Grace J. Women With a Vision. Kalamazoo Ladies' Library Association, 1979.

Praus, Alexis A. Historical Markers and Memorials in Kalamazoo and Kalamazoo County. Kalamazoo: Kalamazoo Historical Commission, 1969.

Quarter Centennial Celebration of the Settlement of Kalamazoo, Michigan. Published by order of the Board of Directors of the Ladies' Library Association. Kalamazoo: Gazette Print, 1855.

Reminiscences and New Horizons. A Booklet to Commemorate the Fiftieth Anniversary of the Founding of Doubleday Bros. & Co. 241 E. Michigan Ave., Kalamazoo, Mich. Kalamazoo: Doubleday Brothers & Company, [1948].

Report of the Joint Committee of the Michigan Legislature of 1879, on Alleged Mismanagement, and Matters Connected Therewith, In the Michigan Asylum For the Insane At Kalamazoo; also a Supplemental Report of the Senate Committee Relating to the Same Subject,

Together With so Much of the Testimony Taken as Relates to the Abuse of Patients While in Said Asylum. By Authority. Lansing: W.S. George & Company, 1879.

Report of the Michigan State Commission of Inquiry Into Wages and the Conditions of Labor for Women . . . . Lansing: Wynkoop, Hallenbeck Crawford Company, 1915.

Ross, Mary Jane. *A History of Kalamazoo, Michigan.* Thesis presented to the faculty of the Department of History, the University of Southern California, in partial fulfillment of the requirements for the degree Master of Arts. N.p., 1942.

Rowe, Ford F. *Kalamazoo the Debt-Free City. The Reason Way.* [Kalamazoo: Ihling Bros. & Everard, 1939].

Sauer, William C. *Illustrated Atlas of Kalamazoo County, Michigan.* Detroit: W.C. Sauer, 1890.

Schmitt, Peter J. *South Street Historical District Papers.* [Kalamazoo: City Planning Department], 1973.

Schmitt, Peter, and Korab, Balthazar. *Kalamazoo: Nineteenth-Century Homes in a Midwestern Village.* [Battle Creek: E.P.I., 1976].

Seven Years Later, A Story of Progress in Downtown Kalamazoo. N.p., 1964.

75th Anniversary Ihling Bros. Everard Co. Kalamazoo, Michigan. Kalamazoo: [Ihling Brothers, 1944].

Sharpsteen, Harold. *The Life of John Henry Burke.* Kalamazoo: Ihling Brothers, Everard Company, [1948].

Special Committee on Fire and Water. *Concise History of the Fire and Water Department of the Village of Kalamazoo, Michigan From its Incorporation in 1843 to 1881 . . . .* Kalamazoo: n.p., 1881.

Starring, Charles R. "Hazen S. Pingree: Another Forgotten Eagle," *Michigan History,* Vol. 32, no. 2.

Stoddard, A.H. *Miscellaneous Poems.* Kalamazoo: [C.G. Townsend], 1880.

Swope, James. *Yorkville Michigan: The Age of the Mills,* Typescript, n.d. In Western Michigan University Archives and Regional History Collections.

The 32nd Division in the World War 1917–1919. Issued by the Joint War History Commissioners of Michigan and Wisconsin. [Milwaukee: Wisconsin Printing Company, 1920].

Thomas, James M., comp., *Kalamazoo County Directory With a History of the County. From Its Earliest Settlement. Containing Descriptions of Each Town and Village within the County. Also, the Names of All Persons Residing In the Several Villages in the County. With a New Census of Kalamazoo Village, and all the Villages in the County. 1869 and 1870.* Kalamazoo: Stone Brothers, 1869.

——————————, comp., *Thomas's Kalamazoo Directory and Business Advertiser For 1867 and 1868 Together With a History of Kalamazoo From its Earliest Settlement to the Present Time.* Kalamazoo: Stone Brothers, 1867.

Thomas, Nathan. *An Account of His Life Written by Himself.* Cassopolis: n.p., 1925.

25th Anniversary City of Parchment. May 14, 15 and 16, 1964. N.p., [1964].

United States Bureau of the Census. Manuscript Products of Agriculture and Products of Industry Special Schedules, Kalamazoo County, 1850–1870.

United States Bureau of the Census. Manuscript Federal Population Census, Kalamazoo County, 1840–1900.

United States Census, 1850; Kalamazoo County, Michigan. Typed and alphabetized by Historical Committee Lucinda Hinsdale Stone Chapter, Daughters of the American Revolution: Chairman, Mrs. Warren Allen. [Kalamazoo], 1942.

United States Department of the Treasury. Internal Revenue Assessment Lists, Michigan, 1862–1866.

United States Patent Office. Weekly Gazette, Specifications and Drawings. 1879 ff.

Van Bochove, Garrett, and Van Bochove, John. *Kalamazoo Celery: Its Cultivation and Secret of Success.* Kalamazoo: Kalamazoo Publishing Company, 1893.

Warren, Francis H., comp., *Michigan Manual of Freedmen's Progress.* Detroit: n.p., 1915.

Weissert, Charles A., ed., *An Account of Kalamazoo County.* Comprising volume III of *Historic Michigan Land of the Giant Lakes. Its Life, Resources, Industries, People, Politics, Government, Wars, Institutions, Achievements, the Press, Schools and Churches, Legendary and Prehistoric Lore,* edited by George N. Fuller. National Historical Association, Inc., [1926].

Welch, Richard W. *Sun Pictures In Kalamazoo. A History of Daguerreotype Photography in Kalamazoo County, Michigan 1839–1860.* An occasional publication of the Kalamazoo Public Museum. Kalamazoo, 1974.

Wood, Helen Everett, ed., *Delevan Arnold: A Kalamazoo Volunteer in the Civil War.* Kalamazoo: Kalamazoo Public Museum Publication, 1962.

Your City and Its Government. A Twenty Year Story of City Manager Government in Kalamazoo, Michigan 1918–1938. [Kalamazoo: Ihling Brothers, Everard Company], n.d.

Manuscript Sources.

Among the manuscript collections in the Western Michigan University Archives and in the Kalamazoo Public Library, the following proved very helpful: the Luke Whitcomb and Louisa McOmber Letters, for descriptions of Kalamazoo; the Milo Goss, Bradley Loomis, William Glover, and David Gilbert Letters, for descriptions of the California gold rush; the Public Library biographical clipping file and collection of Kalamazoo College seminar papers, for local business and industry. The John T. Houdek topical index to newspaper articles in the 1870s (in Western Michigan University Archives) proved particularly valuable. Ephemeral publications too numerous to cite individually provided a rich source for contemporary business advertisements. Such publications may be found in the Western Michigan University Archives and Regional History Collections.

INDEX

Published Books in Windsor Local History Series

St. Paul: Saga of an American City, by Virginia Brainard Kunz (1977)

The Heritage of Lancaster, by John Ward Willson Loose (1979)

A Panoramic History of Rochester and Monroe County, New York, by Blake McKelvey (1979)

Syracuse: From Salt to Satellite, by William Roseboom and Henry Schramm (1979)

Columbia, South Carolina, History of a City, by John A. Montgomery (1979)

Kitchener: Yesterday Revisited, by Bill Moyer (1979)

Erie: Chronicle of a Great Lakes City, by Edward Wellejus (1980)

Montgomery: An Illustrated History, by Wayne Flynt (1980)

Charleston: Crossroads of History, by Isabella Leland (1980)

Baltimore: An Illustrated History, by Suzanme E. Greene (1980)

Omaha and Douglas County, by Dorothy Deveneux Dustin (1980)

The Fort Wayne Story: A Pictorial History, by John Ankenbruck (1980)

City at the Pass: An Illustrated History of El Paso, by Leon Metz (1980)

Tucson: Portrait of a Desert Pueblo, by John Bret Harte (1980)

Salt Lake City: The Gathering Place, by John McCormickn(1980)

Saginaw: A History of the Land and the City, by Stuart D. Gross (1980)

Cedar Rapids: Tall Corn and High Technology, by Ernie Danek (1980)

Los Angeles: A City Apart, by David L. Clark (1981)

Heart of the Commonwealth: Worcester, by Margaret Erskine (1981)

Out of a Wilderness: An Illustrated History of Greater Lansing, by Justin Kestenbaum (1981)

The Valley and the Hills: An Illustrated History of Birmingham and Jefferson County, by Leah Rawls Atkins (1981)

River Capital: An Illustrated History of Baton Rouge, by Mark T. Carleton (1981)

Chattanooga: An Illustrated History, by James Livingood (1981)

New Haven: An Illustrated History, edited by Richard Hegel and Floyd M. Shumway (1981)

Mobile: The Life and Times of a Great Southern City, by Melton McLaurin (1981)

New Orleans, by John Kemp (1981)

Regina: From Pile O' Bones to Queen City of the Plains, by W.A. Riddell (1981)

King County and Its Queen City, Seattle: A Pictorial History, by James Warren (1981)

To the Setting of the Sun: The Story of York, by Georg Sheets (1981)

Buffalo: Lake City in Niagara Land, by Richard C. Brown and Bob Watson (1981)

Springfield of the Ozarks, by Harris and Phyllis Dark (1981)

Charleston and the Kanawha Valley, by Otis K. Rice (1981)

Albany: Capital City on the Hudson, by John J. McEneny (1981)

Selected Works-in-Progress

Dallas: Portrait in Pride, by Darwin Payne (1982)

Heart of the Promised Land: An Illustrated History of Oklahoma County, by Bob L. Blackburn (1982)

Winnipeg: Gateway to the New West, by Eric Wells (1982)

City of Lakes: An Illustrated History of Minneapolis, by Joseph Stipanovich (1982)

Rhode Island: The Independent State, by George H. Kellner and J. Stanley Lemons (1982)

Calgary: Canada's Frontier Metropolis, by Max Foran and Heather MacEwan Foran (1982)

Evanston: An Illustrated History, by Patrick Quinn (1982)

Norfolk's Waters: An Illustrated Maritime History of Hampton Roads, by William L. Tazewell (1982)

Hartford: An Illustrated History of Connecticut's Capital, by Glen Weaver (1982)

Pikes Peak Country: A Social History of Colorado Springs, by Nancy E. Loe (1982)

At the Bend in the River: A History of Evansville, by Kenneth P. McCutchan (1982)

Cape Fear Adventure: An Illustrated History of Wilmington, by Diane C. Cashman (1982)

Chicago: Commercial Center of the Continent, by Kenan Heise and Michael Edgerton (1982)

Windsor Publications, Inc.
History Books Division
21220 Erwin Street
Woodland Hills, California 91365
(213) 884-4050

THIS BOOK WAS SET IN
OPTIMA AND OPTIMA BOLD TYPES,
PRINTED ON
80 POUND MEAD OFFSET ENAMEL
AND BOUND BY
WALSWORTH PUBLISHING COMPANY.
COVER AND TEXT DESIGNED BY
JOHN FISH
LAYOUT BY
JOHN FISH
DEE COOPER
AND E. SHANNON STRULL
PARTNERS IN PROGRESS
LAYOUT BY
MELINDA WADE